CENTRAL ISSUES IN CONTEMPORARY ECONOMIC THEORY AND POLICY

General Editor: **Mario Baldassarri**, *Professor of Economics, University of Rome 'La Sapienza', Italy*

Published titles include:

Mario Baldassarri, Michele Bagella and Luigi Paganetto (*editors*)
FINANCIAL MARKETS: IMPERFECT INFORMATION AND RISK MANAGEMENT

Mario Baldassarri and Pierluigi Ciocca (*editors*)
ROOTS OF THE ITALIAN SCHOOL OF ECONOMICS AND FINANCE: FROM FERRARA (1857) TO EINAUDI (1944) (*three volumes*)

Mario Baldassarri and Massimo Di Matteo (*editors*)
INTERNATIONAL PROBLEMS OF ECONOMIC INTERDEPENDENCE

Mario Baldassarri, Cesare Imbriani and Dominick Salvatore (*editors*)
THE INTERNATIONAL SYSTEM BETWEEN NEW INTEGRATION AND NEO-PROTECTIONISM

Mario Baldassarri, Alfredo Macchiati and Diego Piacentino (*editors*)
THE PRIVATIZATION OF PUBLIC UTILITIES: THE CASE OF ITALY

Mario Baldassarri, Luigi Paganetto and Edmund S. Phelps (*editors*)
EQUITY, EFFICIENCY AND GROWTH: THE FUTURE OF THE WELFARE STATE

Mario Baldassarri, Luigi Paganetto and Edmund S. Phelps (*editors*)
THE 1990s SLUMP: CAUSES AND CURES

Mario Baldassarri, Luigi Paganetto and Edmund S. Phelps (*editors*)
WORLD SAVING, PROSPERITY AND GROWTH

Mario Baldassarri, Luigi Paganetto and Edmund S. Phelps (*editors*)
INTERNATIONAL DIFFERENCES IN GROWTH RATES: MARKET GLOBALIZATION AND ECONOMIC AREAS

Mario Baldassarri and Paolo Roberti (*editors*)
FISCAL PROBLEMS IN THE SINGLE-MARKET EUROPE

Mario Baldassarri and Franco Modigliani (*editors*)
THE ITALIAN ECONOMY: WHAT NEXT?

Mario Baldassarri (*editor*)
MAFFEO PANTALEONI: AT THE ORIGIN OF THE ITALIAN SCHOOL OF ECONOMICS AND FINANCE

Mario Baldassarri, Luigi Paganetto and Edmund S. Phelps (*editors*)
INSTITUTIONS AND ECONOMIC ORGANIZATION IN THE ADVANCED ECONOMIES: THE GOVERNANCE PERSPECTIVE

Central Issues in Contemporary Economic Theory and Policy
Series Standing Order ISBN 0–333–71464–4
(*outside North America only*)

You can receive future titles in this series as they are published by placing a standing order.
Please contact your bookseller or, in case of difficulty, write to us at the address below with
your name and address, the title of the series and the ISBN quoted above.

Customer Services Department, Macmillan Distribution Ltd, Houndmills, Basingstoke,
Hampshire RG21 6XS, England

Financial Markets

Imperfect Information and Risk Management

Edited by

Mario Baldassarri
Professor of Economics
University of Rome 'La Sapienza'
Italy

Michele Bagella
Professor of Monetary Economics
University of Rome 'Tor Vergata'
Italy

and

Luigi Paganetto
Professor of Economics
University of Rome 'Tor Vergata'
Italy

in association with
Rivista di Politica Economica, SIPI, Rome
and
CEIS, University of Rome 'Tor Vergata'

First published 2001 by
PALGRAVE
Houndmills, Basingstoke, Hampshire RG21 6XS and
175 Fifth Avenue, New York, N. Y. 10010
Companies and representatives throughout the world

PALGRAVE is the new global academic imprint of
St. Martin's Press LLC Scholarly and Reference Division and
Palgrave Publishers Ltd (formerly Macmillan Press Ltd).

ISBN 0–333–80204–7

This book is printed on paper suitable for recycling and made from fully managed and sustained forest sources.

A catalogue record for this book is available from the British Library.

Library of Congress Cataloging-in-Publication Data
Financial markets : imperfect information and risk management / edited by Mario Baldassarri, Michele Bagella, Luigi Paganetto.
    p. cm.
    ISBN 0–333–80204–7
    1. Finance. 2. Risk management. 3. Capital markets. 4. Banks and banking. 5. Finance—Italy. 6. Banks and banking—Italy. 7. Capital markets—Italy. I. Baldassarri, Mario, 1946– II. Bagella, Michele. III. Paganetto, Luigi.
    HG173 .F5144 2000
    332'.0945—dc21
                                                            00–066905

10   9   8   7   6   5   4   3   2   1
10   09 08 07 06 05 04 03 02 01

Printed and bound in Great Britain by
Antony Rowe Ltd, Chippenham, Wiltshire

Contents

Introduction*

Michele Bagella - Mario Baldassarri - Luigi Paganetto

Università «Tor Vergata»,   Università «La Sapienza»,   Università «Tor Vergata»,
Roma   Roma   Roma

1. - *The problem of information and risk management, which is the focus of the papers presented in this volume, is a central issue in current financial and monetary economic literature. Several recent theoretical and empirical contributions consider asymmetric information between investors and financiers as a major determinant of financial risk.*

In this framework, we may regard financial and banking innovation as, on one side, policy and individual agents' response to the problem of asymmetric information and risk management and, on the other side, as a self-generated innovation process posing new challenges to policymakers in terms of informational efficiency and risk control.

The innovation process in the financial markets generates new problems in terms of efficiency and risk control. In recent years new payment systems have emerged which increased the fragility of the banking system creating growing concern about the risk associated with these innovation processes. Furthermore the increasing degree of interdependence among payment systems of the different countries may lead to contagion effect of possible crises in a multicountry framework. Thus, it is necessary to characterise the equilibrium

---

* This monographic issue contains a selection of papers presented at the V Financial Conference, *Financial Markets, Imperfect Information and Risk Management*, held at the University of «Tor Vergata» CEIS - Rome, November 28-30, 1996.

in these systems and identify the implications in terms of safety and efficiency.

In this perspective financial and banking innovation may be regarded as, either a response to the trade-off (institutional changes in bank or stock market regulation) or as an exogenous transformation of the system (introduction of derivatives) posing new challenges in the information-risk puzzle.

On the first point, we may examine how innovation in bank's reserve management, in deposit insurance regulation and how diversification of bank activities and improvement in monitoring technology represent adequate responses to the challenge.

On the second point, we should assess whether the danger of derivative trading is that of increasing the underlying asset volatility or that of increasing the individual exposition to risk of derivative trading firms.

Recent literature results seem to support more this second hypothesis showing that there is no significant increase in underlying asset volatility after derivative introduction. It seems then that derivative trading indirectly increases the exposition to risk of more risk adverse savers when non transparency vis-à-vis managers, regulators and markets creates severe information problems and the financial situation of firms trading derivatives cannot be constantly monitored.

2. - The second viewpoint considers the banking innovation process as the policy and private agents response to asymmetric information problem and market imperfections.

The traditional approach of economics of information in financial economics starts from the critique of the Modigliani-Miller theorem which demonstrates the equivalence of internal and external firm financing sources. This theorem cannot be reconciled with some stylised facts of economic reality such as: (i) abnormal common stock returns at the announcement date of firms issuing equities, convertibles or bonds; (ii) changes in market value after changes in firms dividend policy; (iii) cost differentials between internal and external financing sources and bank credit rationing. The presence of market imperfections based on information asymmetries is the ba-

sis for the neo-keynesian theory of endogenous money. Recent theoretical analyses demonstrate how informational asymmetries between financiers and investors may generate financial rationing and positive cost differential between external (bank, stock market and venture capital financing) and internal financing. Models explaining bank financing inefficiency show that the investor informational advantage may cause equilibrium credit rationing.

Models explaining venture capital financing inefficiency show that when property right shares are bargained ex ante between an investor and a venture capital financier, an imbalance between relative bargaining strengths and relative contributions to the venture generates an inefficient division of property rights with a divergence between private and social optimum.

Models explaining stock market financing inefficiency show that, for example, in markets where firm managers possess an informational advantage, a new equity issue will be considered as a negative signal from stock market investors, explaining in this way the phenomenon of abnormal common stock returns at the announcement date of a new issue. Furthermore negative externalities into an economy may be generated by an efficiently functioning stock market, when the increase in efficiency is combined with other distortions in the real economy. An example of this may occur when increasing efficiency of financial stock markets may generate inefficiency in the real economy, in the form of pressure exerted by listed companies to maintain distorsions in the market for their inputs. Such companies, for example, may take advantage in the capital market and the input market, collecting rent from their suppliers and using this rent as a subsidy which improves the overall performance of listed companies. This can exert a pressure which pushes stock prices up; the more efficient the stock market the more rapidly this positive effect over the price will spread. The example is a typical second best phenomenon showing that, if informational asymmetries and other sources of extra costs (costs of coordination and risk of loss of control for small family owned firms) prevent small-medium firms from being listed in the stock exchange, increased stock market inefficiency may exacerbate distortions between large listed firms and small unlisted firms.

These and some other issues presented in the papers of the conference describe the potential inefficiences that may be generated by the informational problem.

Bank, stock market and venture capital financiers can reduce financing inefficiencies only by increasing their bankruptcy risk unless the informational asymmetry is directly solved. More informational efficiency could then shift the «financial inefficiency-financial intermediaries' risk» trade-off with positive effects on both risk management and investment financing.

This is, in our opinion the most important direction for research on banking and finance for the next years and this is the direction in which, we hope, the conference papers collected in this volume, have concentrated their effort with success.

3. - The selection of discussed papers which are included in this volume is divided into three sections. The first Imperfect Information, Financial Markets and Financial Intermediation: Empirical Analysis *deals with theoretical and empirical analyses on the functioning of the banking system and on bank-firm relationship in a framework of imperfect information. The second* Risk Management, Banking System and Financial Markets *deals with new approaches to management and evaluation of risk in its different facets: exposure to asset price and return variability of financial institutions' portfolios including derivatives, borrowers' insolvency risk and consequent evaluation of non performing loans in bank lending portfolios, exposure to currency risk for firms whose present and expected assets and liabilities are partly denominated in foreign currencies. The third part* Money, Finance and Macroeconomics *deals with various issues including measurement of banking system efficiency, reaction of financial markets to political and economic new and the relationship between financial and real sector in model of growth.*

I - IMPERFECT INFORMATION, FINANCIAL MARKETS AND FINANCIAL INTERMEDIATION: EMPIRICAL ANALYSIS

Portfolio Choice and Competition in the Banking System

Gabriella Chiesa*

Università di Brescia

1. - Introduction

This paper develops a model of imperfect competition for lending to study the links between firms' cost of capital, bank industrial structure and the overall availability of lending. Banking competition is imperfect in that a bank is constrained by its size. This results endogenously from bank's moral hazard vis-à-vis final investors, and it implies that the credit market equilibrium is non-Walrasian and it may entail credit rationing. The model predicts that firms' cost of capital, credit availability and banks' profit margins are linked to the cycle and to the bank industrial structure. Firms' cost of capital and banks' profit margins are higher the less capitalized and the more concentrated the banking sector, and are higher at the end of a recession when credit may be rationed.

The premise of the paper is that banks serve a special role as delegated monitors of borrowers (Diamond [5], Ramakrishnan - Thakor [8] and Boyd - Prescott [2]). Banks' intermediation activity is valuable in that it avoids the duplication of monitoring costs

* The author, Professor of Economics, is grateful to John Moore for most helpful advice and suggestions, and to Sudipto Bhattacharya, Mike Burkart, Vincenzo Denicolò, Mathias Dewatripont, Denis Gromb, Jorge Padilla, David Webb, Andrew Winton and Marie Odile Yanelle for discussions and comments. Financial support from CNR and MURST is gratefully acknowledged.

N.B. the numbers in square brackets refer to the Bibliography at the end of the paper.

that would be incurred with direct lending by final investors to firms, since in that case each investor would spend resources in *ex ante* monitoring (acquiring information about) the firm to lend to and eventually in *ex post* monitoring of (auditing) the firm's revenue to make sure that the loan is repaid whenever the firm has sufficient funds to do that.

However, by acting as an intermediary, i.e. by investing final investors' funds, a bank is subject to moral hazard problems vis-à-vis final investors, in that it may find profitable to underinvest in the monitoring of the firms to lend to betting on the lucky event that these firms succeed in repaying their loans.

If all risk were diversifiable, then banks' moral hazard problem would be solved at no cost. The outcome of a fully diversified credit portfolio is in fact certain and fully determined by a bank's choice of monitoring. Thus if a bank were underinvesting in monitoring it would be insolvent with probability one, and this is sufficient to make undermonitoring an unattractive option all together (Diamond [5]).

In a more realistic scenario not all risk can be diversified away, i.e. the returns of the projects that bank loans fund are not all independent[1]. One important reason that prevents fully diversified credit portfolios is systemic (macroeconomic) risk. Firms are more likely to succeed and repay their loans when the economy is booming than in a recession, since in a recession only the firms that are fit are likely to succeed and honor their debts. With systemic risk, a bank's *ex post* credit-porfolio return is then necessarily uncertain and state dependent, it is higher in a boom than in a recession. This makes undermonitoring, i.e. underinvesting in sorting out the firms that are fit, an attractive option, because there is scope for betting on the lucky event that firms, no matter their type, repay. Furthermore, this option is more attractive the larger is the amount of lending that a bank undertakes, since the profits it makes in the fortunate event that firms repay are increasing in the number of firms it has financed. This suggests that limitations to bank's lending reduc-

---

[1] This prevents delegation costs being eliminated through diversification and provides a scope for intermediaries putting at stake their own capital (HOLMSTROM B - TIROLE J. [7]).

es the profitability of undermonitoring, i.e. incentivate a bank to take good risk by investing sufficiently in information acquisition about the firms to lend to. We study the credit market equilibrium for this economy and find that in an equilibrium final investors, or under deposit insurance the Regulator, ration a bank's availability of funds so as to constrain the bank not to lend in excess of a (well defined endogenous) ceiling. A bank's lending ceiling is determined by the amount of capital a bank is endowed with and by (its choice of) the lending rate. The intuition for this result is that bank capital and bank's lending rate substitute and complement each other in defining the penalty that a bank suffers by underinvesting in monitoring, since by so doing it increases the likelihood of being insolvent and forgoing its capital and loans' revenue.

Banks compete in prices for loans to firms. Because banks are subject to lending constraints, this competion is imperfect and its outcome, i.e. banks' profit margins, firms' cost of capital and aggregate lending, is linked to the cycle and to the bank's industrial structure. The driving force for these results is that limitations to a bank's size provide banks with market power. Even in the event that a bank has set its lending rate above the ones set by its competitors, it still faces a (captive) market, i.e. it lends to the firms that by having been unable to obtain loans at better terms have no choice other than borrowing at the highest rate. This induces a bank to set its rate above the zero-profit level, and the more so the bigger is the size of its captive market, i.e. the higher is the overall demand for lending and the smaller is the amount of lending that a bank's competitors can undertake. The latter is ultimately determined by the number of competitors that a bank faces and the amount of capital they are endowed with. We find that the lower is banks' aggregate capital relative to the aggregate demand for lending and the more concentrated is the banking sector, the higher are the equilibrium values of firms' cost of capital and banks' profit margins. Banks' profit margins widen at the end of a recession, when banks have suffered loans' insolvencies (decumulated capital), and credit may be rationed.

The rest of the paper is organized as follows. Section 2 presents the model. Section 3 studies the game that is played when a bank raises financing to fund its lending. The solution defines the lending constraint that a bank faces when it competes in the lending market. Section 4 studies interbank-price competition for loans and characterizes the credit-game equilibrium as a function of the banks' aggregate capital, the aggregate demand for lending and the degree of concentration of the banking sector. Section 5 concludes.

2. - The Model

Imagine a credit market consisting of M entrepreneurs – firms –, I investors, n banks and lasting a single period. We shall name bank i, B_i $i = 1, 2,...n$. Everybody is risk neutral and maximizes the expected value of his wealth at the end of the period. Each entrepreneur can undertake one investment project that requires one unit of resources, but is endowed with zero wealth. Each investor is endowed with $1/m$, $m > 1$, units of resources that can be either stored at zero net return or deposited into a bank. Investors are in large number $(mI > M)$. A bank, B_i, lends to entrepreneurs and borrows from investors. Banks are endowed with an amount of aggregate capital, TA, that satisfies $TA > 0$, and is symmetrically distributed among banks, i.e. B_i is endowed with $A_i = A = TA/n$, $\forall i$. Additional capital is expensive (see Smith [9] for a survey of evidence on the cost of issuing equity), as a matter of simplicity it is prohibitively high.

2.1 *Project Technology*

Banks' lending consists of project financing. A project requires one unit at the beginning of the period and delivers a (random) return at the end of the period. The realization of this return depends on the macrostate realization at the end of the period, $s \in (s_u, s_d)$ where s_u, occurs with probability p, and the project type, $i \in (g, b)$. A type g project delivers an observable and verifiable return of x both in s_u, and in s_d, a type b project delivers an observable and verifiable return of x in s_u and of zero in s_d. The probability according to which a project funded by a bank is of type g depends upon the bank's choice of action $a \in (m, nm)$ where m indicates «monitoring», and nm «non-monitoring», i.e.:

$$\text{prob } (i = g \,|\, a = m) = \alpha$$
$$\text{prob } (i = g \,|\, a = nm) = l$$

Bank's monitoring costs $F > 0$. This cost is a non-pecuniary effort cost that bears on the bank.

An unmonitored project is negative in net present value, assumption $A1$:

(1) $px + (1 - p)lx < 1$

A monitored project is positive in net present value, assumption $A2$:

(2) $px + (1 - p)\alpha x > 1 + F$

Assumption $A3$: a bank's choice of action is unobservable.

The crucial ingredients of the model above are: *a*) the average loan return is uncertain (its realization depends on the macrostate realization); *b*) there is an action that a bank can take, which is unobservable and costly to a bank that positively affects loans' return realizations.

This action could be one of *ex-post* monitoring, like providing services tailored on the firm, or constraining the entrepreneur's choice of project by agreeing on the appropriate debt covenants with the entrepreneur and then monitor they are fulfilled[2]. Alternatively, it could be one of *ex-ante* monitoring, like costly testing the credit-worthiness of an entrepreneur in an (adverse-selection) environment where the percentage l of the population of entrepreneurs are endowed with type g projects, the remaining, $1 - l$, with type b projects, and the test result is either success or failure[3].

---

[2] This would be the case if an entrepreneur undertaking a type b project would enjoy private benefits, and these benefits were large enough to induce the entrepreneur, if unconstrained, to always choose the type b project.

[3] In which case, F is the cost of performing a test divided by the probability that the test result is success; $\alpha = \text{prob } (i = g \,|\, a = m)$ is the probability that the project type is g conditional upon the test result being success.

2.2 *The Credit Game*

Banks, entrepreneurs and investors play the following extensive-form game.

Stage 1: interbank-price competition for loans. 1*a*) B_i announces R_i, gross rate per unit of lending, $i = 1, 2...n$; 1*b*) firms choose which bank(s) to apply for loans, and contingent upon being accepted by more than one bank, which bank to borrow from. B_i, $\forall i$, chooses how many firms' applications to accept.

The outcome of the game at stage 1 determines B_i's lending rate, R_i, and volume of lending, L_i.

Stage 2: banks raise financing. B_i seeks deposit financing of amount $D_{di} = L_i$, and offers investors R_{di}, gross rate per unit of deposits, $i = 1, 2,...n$; investors observe R_i, L_i, R_{di}, A and choose whether to apply for a deposit contract with B_i[4].

Let D_{si} denote the aggregate quantity of funds that are offered to B_i at stage 2, and let D_i denote the aggregate quantity of funds that B_i effectively raises at stage 2. Then D_i = min (-D_{di}, D_{si}) and the total amont B_i's resources available for the execution of its lending contracts equals D_i. If $D_i < L_i$, then B_i defaults on its lending, B_i is bankrupt and the game for B_i ends. If $D_i \geq L_i$, then B_i has sufficient funds to meet its contractual obligations with firms and B_i reaches the following stage 3 of the game.

Stage 3: project monitoring. If $L_i > 0$, then B_i privately chooses how much to invest in project monitoring $\beta_i L_i F$, $0 \leq \beta_i \leq 1$, $i = 1, 2...N$[5].

Notice that B_i choosing β_i effectively chooses the riskiness of its lending portfolio. This is decreasing in β_i and socially optimal at $\beta_i = 1$.

---

[4] Alternatively, the bank could sell all or part of A in order to fund its lending and consequently reduce the amount borrowed from external sources. However it is easy to show that under this second alternative the bank's expected payoff would be exactly the same as in the case developed in the paper.

[5] Since B_i's action, i.e. B_i's choice of β_i, is unobservable, the timing of B_i's choice of monitoring is irrelevant, and a game form where B_i chooses β_i contingent on R_i, R_{di}, L_i at the outset, is by all means equivalent to the one defined in the paper.

3.- The Equilibrium of the Game at Stages 2-3

This section analyzes the game at stages 2-3, when a bank raises outside finance and chooses how much to invest in monitoring. Let $L^P(R_i, A)$ denote the maximum volume of lending that B_i finds incentive compatible to monitor efficiently, i.e. B_i's choice of monitoring is $\beta_i = 1$. $L^P(R_i, A)$ which is depicted in Graph 1, is derived below and is defined by:

$$(3) \quad L^P(R_i, A) = \begin{cases} g(R_i)A \equiv \left[\dfrac{1}{1 + F' - \alpha R_i} \right] A & \text{if } R_i < \left(\dfrac{1 + F'}{\alpha} \right) \\[2em] \infty, & \text{if } x \geq R_i \geq \dfrac{1 + F'}{\alpha}, \text{ where } F' \equiv \dfrac{F}{1 - p} \end{cases}$$

$L^P(R_i, A)$ is increasing in B_i's lending rate, R_i, and capital A and is unbounded if and only if $R_i \geq (1 + F')/\alpha$, which is feasible if $x \geq (1 + F')/\alpha$. In what follows we shall refer to $L^P(R_i, A)$ as the lending constraint of B_i.

GRAPH 1

BANK LENDING CONSTRAINT

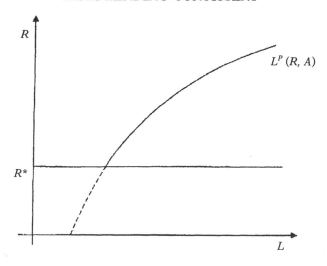

Let R^* denote the lending rate that allows to recoup in expected value the amount of resources invested in a monitored project:

(4)
$$R^* = \left(\frac{1+F}{s} \right) \qquad s \equiv p + (1-p)\alpha$$

Let $R_i \geq R^*$ – by elimination of $B_i's$ strictly dominated strategies at stage 1 –, and let $B_i's$ volume of lending be $L_i > 0$.

PROPOSITION 1: 1) if $L_i \leq L^P (R_i, A)$; then B_i, $i = 1, 2...N$,:

a) at stage 2 offers investors the deposit rate $R_{di} = 1$, which will be paid at the end of the period with probability one, and funds all its lending; b) at stage 3 sets $\beta_i = 1$ (monitors all its lending).

The expected value of $B_i's$ wealth at the end of the period, $\Pi (L_i \leq L^P (R_i, A))$, is:

$$\Pi (L_i \leq L^P (R_i, A)) = [R_i s - (1 + F)] L_i + A > A, \text{ for } R_i > R^*,$$

$$\Pi (L_i \leq L^P (R_i, A)) = [R_i s - (1 + F)] L_i + A = A, \text{ for } R_i = R^*;$$

2) if $L_i > L^P (R_i, A)$. Then the volume of deposits risen by B_i is $D_i = 0$. B_i cannot fund its lending and the expected value of $B_i's$ wealth at the end of the period is:

$$\Pi (L_i > L^P (R_i, A)) = A. \forall R_i$$

We now prove that proposition 1 is true.

The amount of resources investors are endowed with – the amount of loanable funds – exceeds the number of projects that can be undertaken and hence financed. Therefore, no matter how many banks seek outside financing, in the equilibrium of the game at stage 2, an investor will be kept at his reservation utility, the payoff he gets by storing his asset. We analyze below the game at stages 2-3 as if there was just one bank. The results we will derive then apply to any bank that seeks financing.

Recall that x is the maximum value of a project return, and R^*, given by *(4)*, is the lending rate that allows to recoup in expected value the resources invested in a monitored project. Since an unmonitored project is negative in net present value (by assumption $A1$), and all the agents in the economy are rational, the lending rate that a bank sets at stage 1, i.e. R, will satisfy:

(5)
$$R^* \leq R \leq x$$

In what follows we analyze the game at stages 2-3 with the restriction that R satisfies *(5)*.

Consider a bank whose volume of lending is $L > 0$. In order to fund its lending the bank at stage 2 seeks outside financing of amount L, i.e. it sets $D_d = L$, and uses its capital as collateral for its contractual obligations towards investors.

Let $V = (R, L, A, R_d)$, where R satisfies *(5)*. Let $\Pi (\beta, V)$ denote the expected value of the bank's end-of-the-period wealth, conditional upon the bank raising outside financing that amounts to L, i.e. $D = \min (D_{dI} = L, D_s) = L$, as a function of V and β, the banks' choice of monitoring. $\Pi (\beta, V)$ is given by:

(6) $$\Pi (\beta, V) = p \, \Pi (\beta, V \mid s_u) + (1 - p) \, \Pi (\beta, V \mid s_d) - \beta FL$$

where:

$$\Pi (\beta, V \mid s_u) = \max [RL - LR_d + A, 0]$$

$$\Pi (\beta, V \mid s_d) = \max \{[\beta\alpha + (1 - \beta) \, l] \, RL - LR_d + A, 0\}$$

Let the equilibrium of the game at stage 2 be one where the bank funds its lending, i.e. $D = \min (D_d = L, D_s) = L$, and let agents' beliefs be consistent. Then the bank: *(i)* at stage 3 sets $\beta = \beta^*$, the solution to:

(7) $$\beta = \beta^* (V) = \underset{0 \leq \beta \leq 1}{\arg \max} \, \Pi (\beta, V)$$

(ii) at stage 2 offers a deposit rate R_d such that the investor's expected payoff, conditional upon the bank's wealth-maximizing

choice of monitoring – i.e. β* defined by *(7)* – equals the investor's payoff by storing his asset:

(8) $$\pi_d \left(R_d \mid \beta^* (V) \right) = 1$$

where:

$$\pi_d \left(R_d \mid \beta^*(V) \right) = \left(\frac{1}{L} \right) \{ p \ \min \left(R_d L, RL + A \right) +$$

$$+ (1 - p) \ \min \left(R_d L, [\beta^* \alpha + (1 - \beta^*) l] RL + A \right) \}$$

LEMMA 1: 1) if $L \leq L^P (R, A)$ where $L^P (R, A)$ is defined by *(3)*. Then the solution to the bank's optimization problem *(7)*, and to the investor's participation constraint, *(8)*, is $\beta^* = 1$ (i.e. all lending is monitored), and $R_d = 1$; 2) if $L > L^P (R, A)$. Then a solution to *(7)-(8)* cannot exist: for any $R_d \geq 1$, the solution to *(7)* is $\beta^* = 0$ (no-monitoring), and the investor's participation constraint fails to hold, the left-hand side of equation *(8)* falls below 1.

Proofs of all results may be found in the Appendix. Lemma 1 is driven by the assumption that an unmonitored (monitored) project is negative (positive) in net present value (by assumptions A1-A2). Hence if a solution to *(7)-(8)* exists, then necessarily it is one where the bank's wealth maximizing choice of monitoring is $\beta^* = \beta^*(V) = 1$. For a given bank's lending rate, R, and capital, A, $L^P(R, A)$ defined by *(3)*, is the maximum volume of lending such that $\beta^* = 1$ and the investor's participation constraint is satisfied.

Bank's capital, A, defines the penalty that the bank incurs by not monitoring, in which case the bank defaults in the bad macrostate and loses its capital. The rate at which the bank lends, R, defines the bank's reward to monitoring, since in the bad macrostate an entrepreneur repays R with probability α if the bank has invested F – has monitored the project – and with probability $l < \alpha$ if it has not. As the bank's volume of lending increases, for any given amount of bank's capital, the stake that the bank takes per unit of lending decreases, and the bank's incentives to monitor are kept in check by an increase in the reward to monitoring, i.e. L^P (R, A) is increasing in R and A.

Investors are in large number, and are all the same, i.e. they all follow the same strategy. Therefore if the investor's participation constraint, *(8)*, is satisfied then the aggregate quantity of funds that are offered to the bank, D_s, satisfies $D_s > D_d = L$, and the amount of outside financing that the bank effectively raises equals its lending $(D = L)$. If the investor's participation constraint fails to hold – if the left-hand side of *(8)* falls below 1 –, then no investor is willing to lend to the bank, i.e. $D_s = 0$, and consequently the amount of outside financing effectively raised by the bank equals zero $(D = 0)$. The investor's participation constraint is satisfied if and only if $L \leq L^P (R, A)$ (by lemma 1), and $L^P (R, A) > A$ (by $R \geq R^*$, and assumptions *A1-A2*). Hence lemma 1 implies proposition 1.

4. - Interbank Competition for Loans and Credit Market Equilibrium

We solve for the equilibrium of the whole game. This amounts to solving the game at stage 1, the interbank-price competition for loans, whose crucial feature is in that banks face (endogenously) lending constraints and consequently have market power.

A bank's market power results from the fact that the amount of lending that its competitors can make is limited. Even in the event that B_i's lending rate is the highest, B_i's volume of lending and profits are not necessarily nought, since the set of firms that cannot be financed by B_i's competitors (B_i's captive market) is not necessarily empty. This provides B_i, $\forall i$, with the incentive to set its lending rate above the zero-profit value, and the more so the bigger is the size of B_i's captive market, i.e. the higher is the overall demand for lending, M, and the smaller is the amount of lending that B_i's competitors can undertake. The latter is ultimately determined by the number of competitors faced by B_i and the amount of capital they are endowed with. We will find that the lower banks' aggregate capital relative to M, and the lower n, i.e. the more concentrated is the banking sector, the higher are the equilibrium values of firms' cost of capital and banks' profit margins. Firms' cost of capital and credit availability are linked to the bank industrial structure and to the cycle. Banks' profit margins widen at the end of a recession when banks have suffered loans' insolvencies (decumulated capital) and the aggregate demand for lending is pushed up by the economy's recovery, and credit may be rationed.

4.1 *The Equilibrium of the Game at Stage 1*

The game of interbank-price competition is solved backwards, i.e. we start from stage 1b). At this stage, firms have observed banks' lending rate and B_i's lending constraint is $L^P(R_i, A)$, given that B_i, $\forall\ i$, sets $R_i \geq R^*$ and $R_{di} = 1$ (by proposition 1).

A firm's equilibrium strategy is to apply to all banks, so as to maximize its chances of borrowing at the best terms, and conditional upon being accepted (offered a loan) by more than one bank, choose the best offer. The equilibrium strategy of B_i, $\forall\ i$, is to accept loan applications (offer loans) up to its lending constraint $L^P(R_i, A)$ (by proposition 1).

Denote with L_{di} the demand for lending to B_i, L_{di} is given by the number of firms that conditional upon receiving B_i's offer accept the offer. Let R_{-i} be the vector of lending rates set by banks other than B_i; let $\boldsymbol{B}$ define the set of banks whose rates are all equal to R, and let n' be the number of banks that are in $\boldsymbol{B}$, where $0 \leq n' \leq n$. Given firms' and banks' optimal strategies above, in the outcome of the game at stage 1b), B_i's demand for lending, $L_{di} = L_{di}(R_i, R_{-i})$, volume of lending, $L_i = L_i(R_i, R_{-i})$, and expected profits, $\pi_i(R_i, R_{-i})$, are as follows:

1) if there are no ties at R_i, i.e. $R_j \neq R_i$, $\forall\ j \neq i$ ($B_i \notin \boldsymbol{B}$). Then:

$$(9) \qquad L_i(R_i, R_{-i}) = \min\ [L_{di}, L^P(R_i, A)]$$

$$(10) \quad L_{di} \equiv L_{di}(R_i, R_{-i}) = M \max \left[0,1 - \Sigma_{R_j < R_i} \frac{L^P(R_j, A)}{M} \right];$$

2) if there are ties at R_i, i.e. $B_i \in B$. Then:

$$(11) \quad L_i(R_i, R_{-i}) = L_{i\in B} = \left(\frac{1}{n'}\right) \min\{L_{dB}, n'L^P(R,A)\}$$

where:

$$(12) \qquad L_{dB} \equiv M \max\left[0, 1 - \sum_{Rj<R} \frac{L^P(R_j, A)}{M}\right]$$

L_{dB} is the overall demand for lending faced by the n' banks whose rates are all equal to R, i.e. the left over by banks whose rates fall below R; $n'L^P(R, A)$ is the overall lending capacity of the n' banks whose common rate equals R. Thus *(11)* satisfies the consistency requirement that B's aggregate lending cannot exceed B's overall lending capacity no B's overall demand for lending. More than that, *(11)* states that banks that set the same rate lend the same amount. The underlying assumption being that firms' indifference between loan offers of any two banks B_i, $B_j \in B$, $i \neq j$, results in equal treatment – equal lending – of B_i, and B_j (by $R_i = R_j$, $i \neq j$).

B_i's expected lending profits are:

$$(13) \qquad \pi_i(R_i, R_{-i}) = [R_i s, -(1+F)]L_i$$

where: $s \equiv p + (1-p)\alpha$, and $L_i \equiv L_i(R_i R_{-i})$ is given by *(10)-(11)*. The expression in squared brackets in *(13)* is B_i's expected profit per unit of lending, given that B_i rewards investors at the rate $R_{di} = 1$, paid with probability one, and monitors each of its loan (by $L_i \leq L^P(R_i, A)$, and $R_i \geq R^*$).

Notice that if $n'L^P(R_i, A) > L_{dB}$, i.e. the banks in set B are demand constrained, and if $L_{dB} > 0$, i.e. the set of firms that could not borrow at a rate below R is non empty. Then for $R > R^*$ and R_i that tends to R from below:

$$(14) \qquad \lim\inf \pi_i(R_i R_{-i}) > \pi_i(R_i = R, R_{-i})$$

$$R_i \to R^-$$

where: $R_{-i} = (R_1, R_2, ... R_j, R, R, R, R, R)$
                    $n' - 1$ times

B_i's lending rate R_i, being slightly lower than R is sufficient for B_i gaining strict priority with respect to all its $n' - 1$ competitors whose rates equal R, i.e. $L_{di} (R_i - \varepsilon, R_{-i}) = L_{dB}$. If at $R_i = R$, B_i is demand constrained, i.e. $n' L^P (R, A) > L_{dB}$, and $L_{dB} > 0$, then B_i's volume of lending and expected profits at $R_i = R - \varepsilon$, where ε is small, exceed the ones at $R_i = R$.

4.2 *Credit Market Equilibrium*

Define R^c as the lending rate at which banks' aggregate lending capacity equals the aggregate demand for lending, M, i.e.

(15) $nL^P (R^c, A) \equiv M$

where: $nL^P (R^c, A) = g (R^c) TA$ is banks' aggregate lending capacity at $R_i = R^c$, $\forall i$.

LEMMA 2: At $R_i = R^c$, B_i is capacity constrained no matter the rates charged by its competitors. if R^c if feasible, if $R^c \leq x$. Then B_i, $\forall i$, never sets R_i below R^c.

PROPOSITION 2: 1) if banks' aggregate capital is relatively scarce. If $R^c \geq x$, i.e.:

(16) $$\frac{TA}{M} \leq \frac{1}{g(x)}$$

Then all banks lend at the monopoly rate $R_i = x$, $\forall i$, and credit is rationed if inequality *(16)* is strict; 2) if banks' aggregate capital is relatively abundant. If:

(17) $(n-1) L^P (R*, A) \equiv (n-1) g(R*) \left(\dfrac{TA}{n} \right) \geq M$

Then $R_i = R*$, $\forall i$, and all firms borrow at the zero profit rate.

B_i's choice of its lending rate, R_i, affects both: *(i)* B_i's capacity, and; *(ii)* the priority of B_i's loan offers with respect to B_i's competitors' offers. Because of *(i)*, if B_i's lending constraint is binding, an increase in R_i raises B_i's profits, since B_i can lend more and at a higher rate – the direct profit effect. Because of *(ii)*, if B_i's lending constraint is not binding, i.e. B_i is demand constrained, and if $R_i > R^*$, then a decrease in R_i raises B_i's profits, since B_i attracts more borrowers as it undercuts its competitors – the undercutting effect. If banks use pure strategies, then B_i knows for sure whether is capacity constrained or demand constrained, and therefore it knows which of the two considerations above is relevant at a given R_i. A pure strategy equilibrium exists if, despite the fact that B_i is capacity constrained (demand constrained), B_i's upward deviation (downward deviation) is either unfeasible or unprofitable. This is the case if either, $B_i \forall i$, has a great deal of market power, i.e. the maximum amount of lending that B_i's competitors can undertake, $(n - 1) L^P (x, A)$, is such that the minimum residual demand for lending to B_i, i.e. $M - (n - 1) L^P (x, A)$, does not fall below B_i's maximal capacity, $L^P (x, A)$. In which case in the equilibrium all banks set their rates to the monopoly value, are capacity constrained but an upward deviation is unfeasible (part 1 of proposition 2). Or, at the other extreme, if B_i, $\forall i$, has no market power, i.e. the minimum amount of lending that B_i's competitors can undertake, $(n - 1) L^P (R^*, A)$, is sufficient to cover the whole market. In which case in an equilibrium all banks set their rates to the zero-profit value, R^*, are demand constrained but a downward deviation is unprofitable (part 2 of proposition 2).

A simple intuition for proposition 2 can be grasped from the following example. Imagine a situation where there are three borrowers and two banks B_i and B_j. Suppose that each bank can make no more than one loan. Then clearly there is no scope for banks competing for borrowers, since no matter the rate a bank sets it ends up making one loan, i.e. the maximum lending it can make. Both B_i and B_j will then rationally set their rates to maximum feasible value, i.e. $R_i = R_j = x$. This is what's happening when condition *(16)* is satisfied, i.e. $n L^P (x, A) \leq M$. Now, suppose instead that each of the two banks can cover the whole market, i.e. each bank can make at least three loans (serve all burrowers). Here competition is extremely intense, in fact if B_i's rate were above the one set by B_j it would lend nothing, the same reasoning applying to B_j. In this situation, no bank can do better than setting its rate to the zero profit level, R^*. This is what's happening when condition *(17)* is satisfied, i.e. $(n-1) \, L^P (R^*, A) \geq M$.

When neither *(16)* nor *(17)* is satisfied, matters are a bit more complicated and are dealt with in proposition 3 below. However, some intuition can be grasped from the following example. Imagine there are again three borrowers and two banks, and that each bank can make (no more than) two loans. Obviously, an equilibrium will entail one bank lending to one borrower and the other servicing two borrowers. The question is: what lending rates will be set? Given that all three borrowers will want to borrow from the «lowest rate» bank, one borrower will be rationed by the «lowest rate» bank and will thus be forced to borrow from the «highest rate» bank. So one bank's strategy is to set its rate high and make monopoly rent on the one borrower who is rationed from the «lowest rate» bank. Another strategy is to go for volume and try to serve two borrowers. Interestingly, this strategy would not entail setting one's lending rate at the zero-profit level since there is a probability that the competing bank will adopt the previously-detailed strategy. The strategy space of lending rates would (in equilibrium) include all rates that a bank is indifferent between and even the lowest rate would imply lending above the zero-profit rate.

PROPOSITION 3: if neither *(16)* nor *(17)* is satisfied, i.e. if:

$$(18) \qquad \frac{A}{L^P (x, A)} < \frac{TA}{M} < \left(\frac{n}{n-1} \right) \left(\frac{1}{g(R^*)} \right)$$

1) there exists a symmetric equilibrium in mixed strategy $(\mu^n, \ldots, \mu^n)$, where the common strategy profile μ^n is atomless in the interval $[R^n, x]$; 2) the expected profits to B_i, $\forall i$, are strictly positive: the lowest rate ever charged in an equilibrium with n banks, $\underline{R}^n$, satisfies:

(19) $\underline{R}^n > R^*$

(20) $\min (\underline{R}^o, x) > \underline{R}^n \geq R^c$

(21) $R^o: (n - 1) g (R^o) A \equiv M$

In inequality *(18)*, $A/L^P (x, A) \equiv 1/g (x)$ if $x < 1 + F'/\alpha$ (by *(3)*). If banks would use pure strategies, then B_i would know for sure whether it is capacity constrained or demand constrained at a given R_i. If capacity constrained (demand constrained), then an upward deviation (a downward deviation) would be both profitable and feasible (by *(18)*), i.e. if *(18)* holds then a pure strategy equilibrium cannot exist. However, if non-degenerate mixed strategies are used. Then B_i, $\forall i$, cannot predict beforehand whether is capacity constrained or how far it must lower its rate to undercut its nearest competitor. B_i's uncertainty about the rates charged by other banks induces a perfect balance between the desire to raise its rate so as to better exploit its captive market (the left-over by competitors whose rates fall below R_i) and the desire to lower its rate in order to gain priority over its competitors by undercutting them. In a mixed strategy equilibrium, the considerations that are relevant for B_i's choice of the rates to charge, i.e. the direct profit and the undercutting effects, just balance each other so that, for given strategies of the other banks, B_i is indifferent between all the rates over which it randomizes, each of them yields the same expected payoff. Notice that when condition *(18)* is satisfied, B_i, $\forall i$, has market power. The amount of lending that B_i's competitors can undertake at the zero profit rate, i.e. $(n - 1) L^P (R^*, A)$, is insufficient to cover the whole market. This implies that R^* cannot belong to the set of rates over which B_i, $\forall i$, randomizes, i.e. *(19)* is true and the equilibrium profits of B_i, $\forall i$, are strictly positive.

The higher banks' aggregate capital relative to the overall demand for lending, the higher the fraction of the market that B_i's competitors can cover. The size of B_i's captive market then shrinks as *TA/M* increases, and B_i, $\forall i$, setting its rate puts more weight on undercutting considerations. On comparing propositions 2 and 3, we see that as *TA/M* increases, the economy moves from an equilibrium where the firms that succeed in getting financing borrow at the maximum rate x (for TA/M that satisfies *(16)*), to one where firms' average cost of capital is lower than x but higher than the max (R^c, R^*) (for TA/M that satisfies *(18)*), and from this to an equilibrium where all firms borrow at R^* (for TA/M that satisfies *(17)*). The degree of fragmentation of the banking sector has a similar effect on a bank's market power. The higher n, the higher the fraction of banks' aggregate capital that is held by B_i's competitors. The larger then the share of the market that B_i's competitors can cover and the smaller the size of B_i's captive market. As n becomes large, the exploitation of the captive market becomes less and less important and more and more weight is put on undercutting considerations.

LEMMA 3: for n large: *(i)* if $R^* \geq R^c$. Then in an equilibrium all banks lend at the zero profit rate; *(ii)* if $x > R^c > R^*$. Then in an equilibrium the average lending rate is close to R^c.

5. - Concluding Remarks

This paper has incorporated incentive problems in the modelling of competition among banks. In particular we have shown that the unobservability of banks' choices of risk (banks' moral hazard) coupled with costly adjustment of bank capital provides banks with market power even in the absence of market frictions, e.g. product and spatial differentiation[6].

We have assumed that a bank acts on behalf of a coalition of shareholders (insiders) whose aggregate equity holding constitutes the bank (inside) capital, and taken bank capital as given, i.e. we have assumed that the costs of increasing the size of the coalition of insiders are prohibitively high. This is a simplifying modelling device of the more general idea that raising additional capital (increasing the size of the insiders' coalition) is costly. We have taken the investors' supply of funds as horizontal, i.e. banks do not

---

[6] Imperfect banking competition based on spatial differentiation has been analyzed by CHIAPPORI *et* AL. [3], BESANKO D. - THAKOR A. [1].

compete for investors' funds. Allowing for an upward sloping sup-ply function would bring about the issues of double side compe-tition examined by Stahl [10] and Yanelle [12]. Hovewer, to the extent that banks are subject to moral hazard and capital is cost-ly to adjust, the size of a bank, i.e. the amount of loans and de-posits that a bank can undertake, would still be constrained and consequently the banking system would retain an oligopolistic structure[7].

We have found that firms' cost of capital, credit availability and banks' profit margins are linked to the cycle and to the bank industrial structure. Firms' cost of capital and banks' profit mar-gins are higher the less capitalized and the more concentrated is the banking sector, and are higher at the end of a recession when credit may be rationed.

---

[7] This contrasts with the results of STAHL D.O. [10] and YANELLE M.O. [11] of one bank cornering the market, i.e. monopolizing deposits and thereby lending, and matches the results of WINTON A. [11] who analyzes delegated monitoring and bank structure in a finite economy, where bank capital is an alternative to diver-sification, and predicts that the banking sector will consist of several banks.

PROOF OF LEMMA 1. The solution to problem *(7)* is either $\beta^* = 1$, or $\beta^* = 0$ (because of assumptions *A1-A2*). Hence $\beta^* = 1$, if and only if:

(22) $\Pi\ (\beta = 1,\ V) \geq \Pi\ (\beta = 0,\ V)$

Using definition *(6)*, and noticing that the bank's expected pay-off conditional upon the good-macrostate realization, s_u, is the same irrespective of the bank's choice of monitoring, the bank's incentive constraint, *(22)*, can be written as:

(23) $\Pi\ (\beta = 1,\ V \mid s_d) \geq LF' + \Pi\ (\beta = 0,\ V \mid s_d),$

where: $F' = F/(1 - p)$,

$$\Pi\ (\beta = 1,\ V \mid s_d) = \max\ [\alpha\ RL - LR_d + A,\ 0],$$

$$\Pi\ (\beta = 0,\ V \mid s_d) = \max\ [lRL - LR_d + A,\ 0],$$

Clearly, if the bank's incentive constraint, *(23)*, holds, then necessarily $\Pi\ (\beta = 1,\ V \mid s_d) > 0$, and the bank choosing $\beta = 1$ is solvent in the bad macrostate, s_d, the state where the bank's monitoring choice affects the probability according to which loans perform. This in turn implies that a bank that chooses $\beta = 1$ is necessarily solvent with probability one, and therefore the investor's participation constraint, *(8)*, is satisfied at $R_d = 1$.

Let $R_d = 1$, and $\Pi\ (\beta = 1,\ V \mid s_d) > 0$. Then the bank's incentive constraint *(23)* can be written as:

(24) $\alpha\ RL - L + A \geq LF' + \max\ [lRL - L + A,\ 0]$

where: $\max\ [lRL - L + A,\ 0] = \Pi\ (\beta = 0,\ V \mid s_d)$ evaluated at $R_d = 1$.

Furthermore: $\Pi\,(\beta = 1,\ V\mid s_d) = p\,[RL - L + A] + (1 - p)\,[\alpha\,RL - L + A] - FL \geq A$, because $R \geq R^*$.

Suppose that the bank by choosing $\beta = 0$ repays investors with probability one, i.e. $RL - L + A \geq 0$. Then the bank by choosing $\beta = 0$ suffers all the consequences of financing negative-net-present-value projects, i.e. $\Pi\,(\beta = 0,\ V) < A$, and the bank's wealth maximizing choice of monitoring is necessarily $\beta = 1$ (by $\Pi\,(\beta = 1,\ V) \geq A > \Pi\,(\beta = 0,\ V)$). Sufficient condition for the bank's incentive constraint being satisfied, i.e. $\beta = 1$, is thus that L satisfies:

(25)
$$L \leq L^{P'}\,(R,A) \equiv \frac{A}{1 - lR}$$

(the bank choosing $\beta = 0$ is solvent in s_d).

Inequality *(25)* is satisfied on and above the $L^{P'}$ depicted in Graph 2.

GRAPH 2

BANK CHOICE OF MONITORING

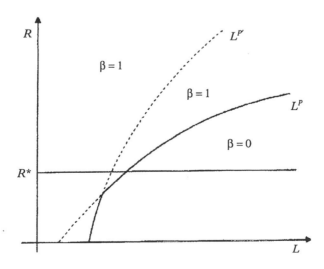

Now, let $L > L^{P'}(R, A)$, i.e. *(25)* fails to hold and therefore $lLR - L + A < 0$. Then, the bank's incentive constraint *(23)* reduces to:

$$\alpha\, RL - L + A \geq LF',$$

and holds if and only if L satisfies:

(26) $L \leq LP'(R, A)$

where: $LP'(R, A)$ is defined by *(3)*. Inequality *(26)* is satisfied on and above the LP' curve depicted in Graph 2.

Inequalities *(25)-(26)* imply that for $R_d = 1$, the bank's choice is $\beta^* = 1$ if and only if:

$$L \leq \max\, [L^{P'}(R, A),\, LP'(R, A)]$$

Let: $$l \leq \frac{\alpha(1 - p) - Fp}{(1 + F)(1 - p)}$$

where: $\alpha\,(1 - p) - Fp > 0$ (by assumptions A1-A2). Then at $R \geq R^*$:

$$\max\, [L^{P'}(R, A),\, LP'(R, A)] \equiv LP'(R, A)$$

This proves that if $L \leq L^{P'}(R, A)$, then the solution to *(7)-(8)* is $\beta^* = 1$ and $R_d = 1$, and therefore part 1 of the lemma is true.

Part 2 of the lemma is true if $L \leq LP'(R, A)$ implies that for any $R_d \geq 1$, the solution to problem *(7)* is $\beta = 0$. That this is true at $R_d > 1$ has been proved above. That $B^* = 0$ for $L > LP'(R, A)$, and $R_d > 1$ follows because the bank's incentive problem is more severe at $R_d > 1$ than at $R_d = 1$ (by $\Pi\,(\beta = 1, V \mid s_d)$ being decreasing in R_d).

PROOF OF LEMMA 2: at $R_i \leq R^c$, B_i is capacity constrained no matter the rates charged by its competitors, R_{-i}; $L_{di}\,(R_i \leq R^c, R_{-i})$ satisfies:

(27) $L_{di}\,(R_i \le R^c, R_{-i}) \ge M - (n-1)\,g\,(R^c)\,A =$
$$= g\,(R^c)\,nA - (n-1)\,g\,(R^c)\,A \qquad \text{(by (15))}$$
$$\equiv g\,(R^c)\,A \ge g\,(R_i)\,A \qquad \text{(by } R_i \le R^c)$$

where: $M - (n-1)\,g\,(R^c, A)$ is the minimum level of the demand for lending to B_i in the worst event that B_i is undercut by all its competitors. Because of *(27)*, B_i's volume of lending, $L_i\,(R_i \le R^c, R_{-i})$, satisfies:

$$L_i\,(R_i \le R^c, R_{-i}) \equiv g\,(R_i)\,A \equiv L_i\,(R_i = R^c, R_{-i})$$

Consequently B_i's expected profits at $R_i < R^c$ are strictly lower than at $R_i = R^c$, i.e. $R_i = R^c$ strictly dominates $R_i < R^c$, and if R^c is feasible, i.e. $R^c \le x$, then rates below R^c are never charged.

PROOF OF PROPOSITION 2: part 1 immediately follows by lemma 2. If condition *(16)* is satisfied, i.e. $x \le R^c$. Then at the maximum feasible rate, i.e. at $R_i = x$, B_i's capacity constraint is binding (by lemma 2). Part 2 is true because if condition *(17)* is satisfied, then at $R_i = R^*$, $\forall i$, B_i is demand constrained, i.e. $L_i\,(R_i = R^*, \forall i) = M/n$ $< L^{P'}\,(R^*, A)$ (by *(11)*, and *(17)*). However a downward deviation is strictly unprofitable, since R^* is the zero profit rate. Nor can B_i profit by upward deviating, since the set of firms that cannot be financed by B_i's competitors, whose rates are equal to R^*, is empty (by *(17)*).

PROOF OF PROPOSITION 3: part 1 i.e. the existence of an equilibrium in mixed strategy, follows by application of Dasgupta - Maskin [4] - summarized in Fudenberg - Tirole [6] pp. 487-89 -, as shown in Appendix *B* available upon request. Part 2 i.e. the conditions that the minimum rate occurring in a mixed strategy equilibrium, $\underline{R}^n$, satisfies, follows by elimination of dominated strategies and by the fact that all rates in the support of the equilibrium strategy yield the same (maximal) expected payoff. In particular, $\underline{R}^n > R^c$ follows by lemma 1; $\underline{R}^n > R^*$ because $M > (n-1)\,g$ $(R^*)\,A$ (by *(18)*), i.e. at $R^* + \varepsilon$, where ε is small and positive, lending is strictly positive. Hence $R^* + \varepsilon$ dominates R^* and a bank's expected profits are strictly positive $\underline{R}^n, < R^o$ is necessarily true for lending, and hence profits, to be strictly positive at the upper bound, x, since a bank whose rate realization is x is undercut by all its competitors (because μ^n is atomless). Finally, $\underline{R}^n < x$ follows by *(18)*, i.e. $M/n\ L^P\ (x, A)$. If by contraddiction, rates below x would never be charged, i.e. if $R^n = x$, then a bank would be better off by downward deviating (by *(14)*).

PROOF OF LEMMA 3: *(i)* follows because, for n large, $R^* \geq R^c$ satisfies condition *(17)* at proposition 2, in an equilibrium all firms borrow at R^*. The proof of *(ii)* is as follows. If $x > R^c > R^*$. Then condition *(18)* is satisfied, an equilibrium is in mixed strategy as defined at proposition 3. A bank whose rate realization is the lower bound of the support $\underline{R}^n$, is undercut with probability zero, because the equilibrium strategy profile, μ^n, is atomless, and is capacity constrained. This is necessarily true, since otherwise banks whose rate realizations exceed $\underline{R}^n$ would lend nothing and this would contraddict the fact that all rates in the support of μ^n yield the same (strictly positive) payoff (by proposition 3). Hence, given n banks and the equilibrium strategy profile, μ^n, the expected payoff to a bank whose rate is $\underline{R}^n$ is $E\ (\pi\ (\underline{R}^n)\ |\ n)$ given by:

$$E\ (\pi\ (\underline{R}^n)\ |\ n) \equiv E\ (\pi\ (\underline{R}^n, R_{-i})\ |\ \mu^n) = [\underline{R}^n\ s - (1 + F)]\ g\ (\underline{R}^n)\ A$$

Since $R^n \geq R^c$ (by proposition 3, and $R^c > R^*$), $E\ (\pi\ (\underline{R}^n)\ |\ n) > 0$. A bank that sets its rate to x, the upper bound of the support of the equilibrium strategy, is undercut by all its competitors (because μ^n is atomless). Hence, given n banks and the equilibrium strategy profile, μ^n, the espected payoff to a bank whose rate realization is x is $E\ (\pi\ (x)\ |\ n)$ given by:

$$E\ (\pi\ (x)\ |\ n) \equiv E\ (\pi\ (x, R_{-i})\ |\ \mu^n)$$

$$= [xs - (1 + F)]\ E\ \{\max\ [1 - \delta^n, 0]\ |\ \mu^n\}\ M$$

where δ^n is the fraction of the market that can be covered by banks $j \neq i$ whose rate realizations fall below x, i.e.:

$$\delta^n \equiv \left(\frac{1}{M}\right)\left[\sum_{j=1}^{n-1} L^P\ (R_j, A)\right]$$

For n large, δ^n is unlikely to deviate significantly from its expected value $E(\delta^n)$:

$$E(\delta^n) = \left(\frac{1}{M}\right)\sum_{j=1}^{n-1} E(L^P(R_j,A)|\mu^n) \equiv \left(\frac{1}{M}\right)(n-1)E(L^P(R,A)|\mu^n)$$

$$\equiv \left(\frac{1}{g(R^c)}\right)\left(\frac{n-1}{n}\right)g^n$$

where:

$$M \equiv g(R^c),nA \ (\text{by } (15)), \ E(L^P(R,A)|\mu^n) \equiv \int_{\underline{R}^n}^{x} L^P(R,A)d\mu^n(R)$$

$g^n \equiv E(L^P(R, A^n) | \mu^n)(1/A)$; i.e. g^n is the expected value of the lending capacity of B_i, $\forall i$, per unit of capital. Therefore for n large, i.e. for δ^n that does not deviate significantly from $E(\delta^n)$,

$$E(\pi(x)|n) \cong [xs - (1+F)] \ \max \ [1 - E(\delta^n),0]M$$

$$\equiv [xs - (1+F)] \ \max \left[1 - \left(\frac{g^n}{g(R^c)}\right)\left(\frac{n-1}{n}\right),0\right]M$$

Because all rates in the support of the equilibrium strategy profile, μ^n, yield the same payoff, $E(\pi(x) | n) \equiv E(\pi(x, \underline{R}^n) | \mu^n) > 0$ (by $R^n \geq R^c > R^*$). Hence for n large, $E(\delta^n) \equiv [(n-1/n)][g^n/g(R^c)]$ is not significantly greater than one. Since rates below R^c are never charged $g^n > g(R^c)$, and for $E(\delta^n)$ not to be significantly greater than one most banks must set rates close to R^c with probability close to one.

34   *Gabriella Chiesa*

BIBLIOGRAPHY

[1] BESANKO D. - THAKOR A., «Relationship Banking, Deposit Insurance and Bank Portfolio Choice», in MAYER C. - VIVES X. (eds.), *Capital Markets and Financial Intermediation*, Cambridge, Cambridge University Press, 1993.

[2] BOYD J. - PRESCOTT E., «Financial Intermediary Coalitions», *Journal of Economic Theory*, vol. 38, 1986, pp. 211-21.

[3] CHIAPPORI P. - PEREZ-CASTRILLO D. - VERDIER T., «Spatial Competition in the Banking System: Localization, Cross Subsidies and the Regulation of Deposit Rates», *European Economic Review*, vol. 39, 1995, pp. 889-918.

[4] DASGUPTA P. - MASKIN E., «The Existence of Equilibrium in Discontinuous Economic Games, 1: Theory», *Review of Economic Studies*, vol. 53, 1986, pp. 1-26.

[5] DIAMOND D., «Financial Intermediation and Delegated Monitoring», *Review of Economic Studies*, vol. 51, 1984, pp. 393-414.

[6] FUDENBERG D. - TIROLE J., *Game Theory*, Cambridge, MIT Press, 1991.

[7] HOLMSTROM B. - TIROLE J., «Financial Intermediation, Loanable Funds and the Real Sector», MIT, *Working Paper*, n. 95-1, 1994.

[8] RAMAKRISHNAN R. - THAKOR A., «Information Reliability and a Theory of Financial Intermediation», *Review of Economic Studies*, vol. 52, 1984, pp. 415-32.

[9] SMITH C., «Raising Capital: Theory and Evidence», *Journal of Applied Corporate Finance*, vol. 4, 1986, pp. 6-21.

[10] STAHL D.O., «Bertrand Competition for Inputs and Walrasian Outcomes», *American Economic Review*, vol. 71, 1988, pp. 393-410.

[11] WINTON A., «Delegated Monitoring and Bank Structure in a Finite Economy», *Journal of Financial Intermediation*, vol. 4, 1995, pp. 158-87.

[12] YANELLE M.O., «The Strategic Analysis of Intermediation», *European Economic Review*, vol. 33, 1989, pp. 294-301.

Financial Constraints on Investments: Evidence From Direct Revelation of Italian Firms

Michele Bagella - Leonardo Becchetti - Andrea Caggese*

Università «Tor Vergata», Roma

1. - Introduction

Several well established stylised facts in empirical literature such as abnormal changes in firm's market value after announcement of new issues or changes in dividend policies seem to contradict the irrelevance of financial factors in neoclassical models demonstrated at firm level, by the Modigliani-Miller theorem.

A microfoundation of the relevance of financial factors providing plausible explanations for these phenomena may be found in the asymmetric information literature which postulates the ex-

---

* Michele Bagella is Full Professor of Monetary Economics, Leonardo Becchetti is Researcher and Andrea Caggese is Voluntary Researcher.

Even though the paper is fruit of a common work, Section 2 can be attributed to M. Bagella, Section 3 to L. Becchetti and Section 4 to A. Caggese. The authors thank D. Archibugi, P. Ardeni, S. Bhattacharya, W. Brown, M. Ceccagnoli, G. Chiesa, G. Gros-Pietro, F. Guelpa, C.P. Himmelberg, M. Messori, G. Nicodamo, G. Orosel, G. Rotino, A. Santomero, G. Scanagatta, A. Pasetto, A. Riti and other participants to the Conference of the EAEPE (Rome, October 1995), to the IV Financial Conference of Tor Vergata (November 1995), to the Mediocredito Central Conference (March 1996), to the Financial Market Group Conference at LSE (June 1996) and to the 1996 Annual Conference of the Royal Economic Society in Swansea for their valuable comments and suggestions. Large part of the research for the paper has been developed with Servizio Studi of Mediocredito Centrale and grant from Mediocredito is acknowledged.

N.B. the numbers in square brackets refer to the Bibliography at the end of the paper.

istence of an informational advantage of managers on financiers. Asymmetric information models have been developed to explain inefficiencies in banking finance (Stiglitz-Weiss [32], Besanko-Thakor [10], Milde-Riley [27]), in stock market finance (Myers-Majluf [30] and Fazzari-Hubbard-Petersen [19]) and in venture capital finance (Admati-Pleiferer [1], Bagella-Becchetti [4] and Becchetti [7]).

Empirical tests of these models showed, in the last ten years, that methodological problems occurring when analysing stock market financing inefficiencies with daily stock market data may be overcome. More difficult, though, is the solution of problems occurring when firm financial contraints are analysed through the cash-flow-investment relationship with balance sheet data. The most important unsolved issues concern: *(i)* measurement errors in the Tobin's Q variable which generate biases in the measurement of the investment-cash flow relationship; *(ii)* problems in the estimation of the replacement cost of capital; *(iii)* distortions in panel data econometric techniques not based on mean group estimators; *(iv)* the ambiguous informational content of the cash flow variable which may proxy both financial constraints and future investment opportunities when firms and markets are still learning how to extract the latter from Tobin's Q (Gilchrist-Himmelberg [20]).

Given that the literature presents many contributions that nevertheless adopt the cash flow-investment empirical approach (in spite of the above mentioned methodological problems) we think that at the present state of art a direct test of firm financial constraints based on alternative approaches (logit analysis from qualitative datasets) would have a very high marginal value to complement the traditional analysis based on balance sheet data.

The «added value» of this paper consists of presenting such a direct test using survey data (the *Indagine sulle imprese manifatturiere* of Mediocredito Centrale, where firms are directly asked about their financial constraints). The consistency of information obtained with survey data is then carefully checked with several control variables and with descriptive and econometric evidence from balance sheet data for the same firms.

The paper is divided into three sections: the first surveys unsolved methodological problems on empirical analyses of firm financial constraints based on panel data. The second section explains the methodology adopted in the direct test of firm financial constraints and comments the results obtained. The third section presents descriptive and econometric analysis on balance sheet data that confirm the validity of information on financial constraints obtained from qualitative data.

2. - The Analysis of Financial Constraints on Firm Investments: Theoretical Microfoundations and Empirical Problems

Several theoretical contributions in the recent literature explain how financier's informational disadvantage may cause inefficiencies in bank, stock market and venture capital financing. Several attempts have been done to test empirically their conclusions at firm level using balance sheet data (Fazzari-Hubbard-Petersen [19] and Whited [32] for the US and Hoshi-Kashyap-Sharfstein [23] for Japan, Devereux-Schiantarelli [18], Becchetti [8], Schiantarelli-Georgoutsos [31] and Bond-Meghir [12] for the UK).

All of these papers, excepting Whited [32] and Bond-Meghir [12], assume the same «hierarchy of finance» theoretical approach. The approach, developed by Fazzari *et* Al. [19], starts from an intertemporal maximisation of firm present value subject to a capital depreciation constraint and to an additional source of fund constraint where the firm can fund investments by borrowing, by issuing new shares or by using after tax retained profits. While in the final specification of the full-information model the demand for investments is only function of the Tobin's Q, the «hierarchy of finance» approach originally introduces a lemon's problem between the firm and market financiers that significantly changes the picture.

The presence of «informational costs» of external finance generates in these models three groups of firms with three different regimes. In the first regime firms do not suffer from informational asymmetries and are therefore not financially constrained having access at equal price to internal and external financing source. In the second regime firms suffer from informational asymmetries and are financially constrained because the expected revenues from their project are lower than total (neoclassical plus informational) costs of external finance. This group of firms finance investments only if cash flow is available. In the third regime firms suffer from informational asymmetries but the expected revenues from their project are higher than total (neoclassical plus informational) costs of external finance. This group of firms invest even if it has no internal finance.

In order to discriminate among different regimes, the standard equation, tested in all these papers, is the following:

$$(1) \qquad (I \, / \, K)_t = \alpha_0 + \alpha_1 q_{t-1} + \alpha_2 (CF \, / \, K)_{t-1} + \sum_i \beta_i x_{it-1}$$

where $(I/K)_t$ is investment over capital stock evaluated at the replacement value, Q is average Tobin's Q as a proxy for future firm's investment perspectives, $(CF/K)_{t-1}$ is cash-flow over capital stock evaluated at replacement value and x_i is any additional variable used in the specification of the investment equation (the most commonly used are output, $(Y/K)_{t-1}$, which is significantly different from zero in case of imperfect competition and debt $(B/K)^2_{t-1}$, which is zero in case of Modigliani-Miller debt-equity irrelevance).

The hypothesis to be tested is the sensitivity of investments to cash-flow with both variables divided by the capital stock to avoid the influence of scale effects[1]. As it is well known, in a neoclassical framework with zero informational costs, we fall into the first regime in which firm investments depend on the ratio between firm value and the replacement cost of capital stock. If

---

[1] Some authors (DEVEREAUX M. - SCHIANTARELLI F. [18]) modify the standard specification adding asset and liability variables as regressors. The underlying assumptions are that: *(i)* total debt seniority or the debt/equity ratio increasing bankruptcy risks should increase agency costs of highly indebted «good firms» and that: *(ii)* an increase in total assets should reduce informational and external financing costs because more collateral may be provided as a guarantee for money lending.

informational problems arise and total costs are higher than expected returns we fall into the second regime. Investments are sensitive to other variables, access to external financing sources is rationed, or has additional costs, and investment plans are decisively influenced by yearly liquidity[2]. It is interesting to note that both firms being in second and third regime suffer from informational asymmetries and cost differential between external and internal finance but that the econometric approach may detect only firms being in the second regime.

This approach presents also several other problems. A first one is related to the evaluation of capital, for which replacement cost and not book value has to be considered. The procedure for the evaluation of the replacement cost of capital is standard (perpetual inventory method) and it requires only the initial book value of the capital stock, to which subsequent inflation-corrected yearly investments are added. This procedure, though, requires long time series to operate the iterating method and it implies the arbitrary choice of an average depreciation rate to apply to capital book values.

A more controversial issue is the evaluation of the Tobin's Q. An average Q is the usually adopted proxy for the shadow value of capital which should be correctly identified by marginal Q. The two variables coincide only under rather restrictive conditions (constant returns to scale, perfect competition and a single quasi-fixed factor). The estimated Q variable is then likely to be seriously biased (Chirinko [16])[3]. A solution for this problem, as observed

---

[2] CHIRINKO R.S. [16] affirms on the basis of theoretical results (CHIRINKO R.S. [15]) that measures of cash flow need not appear in the tested equations as Tobin's Q captures also liquidity constraint effects. Against this assumption there are the results of several published theoretical models, such as FAZZARI S.M. *et Al.* [19] and BOND S. - MEGHIR C. [12] and all the previously mentioned empirical results that show the theoretical and empirical relevance of cash flow when a lemon's problem exists.

[3] CHIRINKO R.S. [16] identifies three main sources of bias saying that: *(i)* the divergence between market sentiments and fundamentals creates distortions when marginal Q is influenced by excess volatility giving a biased measure of firm fundamentals which determine investments decisions; *(ii)* the generalization of applying fixed depreciation rates in the perpetual inventory method adopted for measuring capital stock may not be appropriate in times of rapid technological revolution with time changing rates of capital depreciation; *(iii)* tax and non tax components of the price of capital may also distort the evaluation of capital stock.

by Hoshi *et* Al. [23], is the division of the sample into subgroups. The differences in liquidity coefficients (and in sensitivity to cash flow) for firms belonging to different subgroups should be unbiased given that the Q bias is the same for the two groups of estimates[4]. Even for these solutions, though, an important caveat exists. The assumption that Q mismeasurement is equally severe in both subgroups is in fact debatable given that future profits of firms less tightly integrated in the financial system tend to be more misvalued by the market. Some authors' counterargument to this objection is that no empirical evidence of first order relevance of the three biases has so far been found (Blanchard-Ree and Summers [11], Hoshi and Kashyap [22]), and that a comparison of first and longer differences of investment equations often shows the irrelevance of the Q measurement error.

The simple advice of dividing in subsamples to solve the Q problem is implicitly followed by all other authors in previous contributions without additional control for the seriousness of the measurement error. Hoshi *et* Al. [23] opt for a «keiretsu»/«no keitetsu» division, trying to test if Japanese firms participating in a group which includes banks, may mitigate in this way agency costs. Fazzari *et* Al. [19] adopt a dividend payout and firm size plit criteria, while Devereaux-Schiantarelli [18] use firm size, firm age, investment perspectives (proxied with Tobin's Q) and firm industry. What is interesting in these results is the difference in the modifications of the basic model tested, in the criteria adopted to split samples, and in the interpretations of the findings obtained.

Another general problem in the interpretation of results from divisional criteria occurs if a «separating equilibrium» between bad and good firms exists. Investments of some firms may be more sensitive to internal liquidity just because these firms are those

---

[4] HOSHI T. - KASHYAP A. - SCHARFSTEIN D. [23] to support their approach affirm that: «the advantage of this approach is that, even though the individual estimate of the liquidity coefficients may be biased (say because Tobin's Q is mismeasured), provided that the bias is to be the same for two sets of firms, the estimated difference in the coefficients will be an unbiased estimate of the true difference» and again: «This approach is useful even if the estimated coefficients on liquidity are biased. This is because the difference in the estimated coefficients is an unbiased estimate of the true difference as long as the biases are the same for the two sets of firms».

with worse investment perspectives (bad firms) and are recognised as such by well informed financiers that increase their cost of external financing. It is then necessary to introduce some more control for firm investment perspectives and this can be done in several ways. First, the one followed by Fazzari *et* Al. [19] and by Becchetti ([7] and [8]), of carrying the estimate on an overall sample composed only of firms with positive net sales performance (good firms) for the time period considered in the analysis[5]. Second, the method of dividing a group by Q values, which should themselves be good proxies for future investment performance. If firms with higher Q are less sensitive to cash flow than those with lower Q this should be seen as an empirical validation of the «separating equilibrium» hypothesis.

Once all these methodological problems have been solved subgroup results may be seen as partial confirmation of imperfect information theoretical rationales. The results obtained on the size divisional criteria have this main interpretation: a higher sensitivity of small firms with respect to larger ones indicates a classical imperfect information result. Imperfectly informed financiers run larger risks with small firm financing than with large firm financing because in the first case the project risk coincides with (or is next to) firm risk, while, in the second case, there is less risk of firm insolvency due to a project failure[6].

Another divisional criterion of less debatable interpretation is the firm age. In this case, the fact that firms of more recent stock market listing are more sensitive to cash flow, should validate the Myers-Mayluf hypothesis that «debt dominates equity by minimising «lemons' problems» (Withed [32]), and that newer firms are

---

[5] This approach has been recently questioned by several authors to avoid serious sample selection bias SCHIANTARELLI F. - GEORGOUTSOS D. [31], GILCHRIST S. - HIMMELBERG C.P. [20].

[6] In a well-developed financial market with «fragmented ownership» the results may be completely different if the problem of «reverse causation» is not taken into account. In this case, an agency problem between managers and ownership is more likely to arise in large companies where the managers' stake is low relative to overall firm capital (HARRIS M. - RAVIV A. [21]). These managers may care more for firm growth than for firm profitability trying to increase investment quantity more than their quality. In this case overinvestment may occur and large firms may be more sensitive to cash flow than small ones.

more equity constrained than older ones because of lack of reputation.

3. - The Empirical Qualitative Analysis on the Mediocredito Survey on Italian Firms

The Mediocredito sample used for our analysis is composed of a set of 3852 firms for which both balance sheet and qualitative date are collected. Three selection criteria – an indicator of financial constraints and two filters – have been used to divide firms into subgroups.

The financial constraint indicator is used for a first subgroup division. We use the question which asks if constraints on investment financing (for the period 1989-1991) depend on: *(i)* «the scarcity of medium-long term financing»; *(ii)* «excessive cost of debt»; or *(iii)* «lack of guarantees» (Mediocredito [28], respectively questions 17.2, 17.3 and 17.4 in the questionnaire) to measure the extent of firm financial constraints. In these three questions firms are asked to indicate the existence of financial problems with a degree of intensity ranging from 1 to 3. The financial constraint indicator constructed as the sum of the three answers then ranges from a minimum of zero (no financial constraints) to a maximum of 9.

Questionnaire responses are often likely to be distorted because, for instance, the interviewer may have an interest to enhance or minimise problems in order to give a desired signal to the interviewer. We then use two filters to limit the effects of these distortions.

The first filter selects out, in the sample of financially constrained firms, only those with nonnegative nominal net sales rates of growth in the period 1989-1991. This is to avoid the inclusion of firms with a negative net sales performance whose financial constraints may depend not on asymmetric information, but on the low quality of their investments. 2496 firms with nonnegative net sales rate of growth have then been selected according to this criterion.

The second filter tries to control for answer distortions. We regard as «non credible» those firms declaring the problem of scarce medium-long term financing (Mediocredito [28], question 17.3) and, at the same time, the intense use of grants and soft loans to finance investments (Mediocredito [28], questions 16.4.2 and 16.5). The 69 firms selected with this method have been excluded from the sample of financially constrained firms[7].

The result of this preliminary selection leads to the definition of four groups of firms: firms with high financial constraints (*HFC*) with the complementary set of firms with non high financial constraints (*NHFC*); firms with medium financial constraints (*MFC*) with the complementary set of firms with non medium financial constraints (*NMFC*).

HFC firms are then those firms whose financial constraint indicator ranges from 3 to 9 (363) minus those firms excluded by applying the net sales rate of growth filter and the answer consistency filter (230 firms remaining). *MFC* firms are those firms whose financial constraint indicator ranges from 1 to 9 (848) minus those firms excluded by applying the net sales rate of growth filter and the answer consistency filter (564 firms remaining). The relative shares of the four groups in the overall sample are the following: *HFC* (6%); *NHFC* (94%), *MFC* (14.6%) and *NMFC* (85.4%).

The results from the geographical distribution of the four groups of firms show that, considering four large areas (North East, North West, South and Centre) the North East exhibits «ex-

---

[7] The internal consistency of the financial constraint indicator seems to be supported by at least four facts: *(i)* firms declaring difficulties in financing investments for excessive cost of debt have, on average, a significantly higher debt service of at least two points; *(ii)* firms declaring difficulties in financing investment for lack of guarantees have on average a significantly lower net asset/liability ratio; *(iii)* all subgroups of financially constrained firms according to answers given in other parts of the questionnaire find higher advantages in terms of financial solidity and easier access to credit from equity dilution and have a relatively higher preference for policy instruments directed at solving financial problems (Tables 7 and 8); *(iv)* among those declaring to be financially constrained when investing a significantly higher share of firms distributing zero dividend in the investment year is found relatively to the complementary set of non financially constrained firms.

cess financial constraints» with a share of *HFC* firms 1.34% higher and a share of *MFC* 2.25% higher than the respective overall sample shares (Table 1)[8].

TABLE 1

FIRMS' FINANCIAL CONSTRAINTS: GEOGRAPHICAL DISTRIBUTION

Region	N. of observations	% HFC	% NHFC	1	% MFC	% NMFC	2
Centre	551	86.39	13.61	−1.03	94.74	5.56	−0.71
North East	1.273	83.11	16.89	1.25	92.69	7.31	1.34
North West	1.679	86.10	13.40	−1.24	94.46	5.54	−0.43
South	349	85.96	14.04	−0.60	95.70	4.30	−1.67
Abruzzi	83	86.75	13.25	−1.39	97.59	2.41	−3.56
Calabria	8	81.82	18.18	3.54	137.50	0.00	−5.97
Campania	94	89.36	10.64	−4.00	93.62	6.38	0.41
Emilia Romagna	460	86.09	13.91	−0.73	92.17	7.83	1.86
Friuli V.G.	138	81.88	18.12	3.48	94.93	5.07	−0.90
Lazio	122	91.80	8.20	−6.44	95.08	4.92	−1.05
Liguria	90	81.11	18.89	4.25	92.22	7.78	1.81
Lombardy	1.159	86.71	13.29	−1.35	94.91	5.09	−0.88
Basilicata	6	66.67	33.33	18.69	83.33	16.67	10.70
Marche	144	82.64	17.36	2.72	95.83	4.17	−1.80
Molise	8	100.00	0.00	−14.64	100.00	0.00	−5.97
Piedmont	422	87.68	12.32	−2.32	94.08	5.92	−0.05
Puglia	75	88.00	12.00	−2.64	97.33	2.67	−3.30
Sardinia	28	82.14	17.86	3.22	96.43	3.57	−2.40
Sicily	44	77.27	22.73	8.09	93.18	6.82	0.85
Tuscany	240	86.67	13.33	−1.31	93.75	6.25	0.28
Trentino A.A.	41	87.80	12.20	−2.44	97.56	2.44	−3.53
Umbria	45	82.22	17.78	3.14	95.56	4.44	−1.53
Valle d'Aosta	8	75.00	25.00	10.36	75.00	25.00	19.03
Veneto	634	80.91	19.09	4.45	92.27	7.73	1.76

Variable legend:
HFC - firms with index of financial constraints > 2;
MFC - firms with index of financial constraints > 0;
[1] *HFC* - deviation from total sample average.
[2] *MFC* - deviation from total sample average.

---

[8] BAGELLA M. - BECCHETTI L. - CAGGESE A. [5] show that this result reflects a different behaviour of the banking system in the North and in the South toward small-medium firms with rationing prevailing in the North and higher cost of debt in the South. The authors find that the share of small-medium firms suffering from credit rationing is higher in the North, while the cost of credit size differential is nul in the North and near to three points in the South. This different behavior may have some role in explaining regional differences in the performance of the Italian banking system and in particular the much higher share of non performing loans in the South.

The results from sector distribution of financing inefficiencies provide more reliable evidence of sectoral financing inefficiencies given the larger number of observations considered (Table 2). In this case there is no coincidence in results from the two criteria adopted for group division as the pharmaceutical and electronic sectors have excess *HFC* firms and mechanical instruments, wood and tobacco sectors have excess *MFC* firms.

TABLE 2

FIRMS' FINANCIAL CONSTRAINTS: DISTRIBUTION
BY INDUSTRIAL SECTOR

Industrial sector	N. of observations	% HFC	% NHFC	1	% MFC	% NMFC	2
Non-metallic mineral products	215	6.05	93.95	0.08	15.42	84.58	0.78
Chemicals	146	5.48	94.52	−0.49	14.38	85.62	−0.26
Farmaceuticals	47	10.64	89.36	4.67	10.64	89.36	−4.01
Artifical fibers	8	0.00	100.00	−5.97	12.50	87.50	−2.15
Metal products	518	5.41	94.59	−0.56	14.29	85.71	−0.36
Mechanical Equipment	505	5.35	94.65	−0.62	13.47	86.53	−1.18
Office equipment and computers	20	0.00	100.00	−5.97	5.00	95.00	−9.65
Electronics and electrical equipment	323	9.91	90.09	3.94	16.10	83.90	1.45
Vehicles and vehicle components	65	4.62	95.38	−1.35	7.69	92.31	−6.95
Other means of transport	24	0.00	100.00	−5.97	0.00	100.00	−14.65
Precision instruments and apparels	54	3.70	96.30	−2.27	22.22	77.78	7.58
Food	133	6.77	93.23	0.80	16.54	83.46	1.90
Sugar, tobacco, etc.	70	7.14	92.86	1.17	20.00	80.00	5.35
Textile	341	6.74	93.26	0.77	15.54	84.46	0.90
Leather	56	5.36	94.64	−0.61	10.71	89.29	−3.93
Shoes and clothing	339	4.42	95.58	−1.55	12.68	87.32	−1.96
Wood and wooden furniture	164	4.88	95.12	−1.09	17.68	82.32	3.04
Paper and printing	307	5.54	94.46	−0.43	17.26	82.74	2.62
Rubber and plastics	202	4.95	95.05	−1.02	14.85	85.15	0.21
Other manufacturing	181	7.73	92.27	1.76	12.71	87.29	−1.94
Other non manufacturing	95	6.32	93.68	0.35	14.74	85.26	0.09
Electrical measuring equipment and telecommunications	28	7.14	92.86	1.17	14.29	85.71	−0.36
Aerospace	11	0.00	100.00	−5.97	9.09	90.91	−5.55

Variable legend:
HFC - firms with index of financial constraints > 2;
MFC - firms with index of financial constraints > 0;
[1] HFC deviation from total sample average.
[2] MFC deviation from total sample average.

An important result of almost all empirical analyses on firm financial constraints shows that small firms are likely to be more financially constrained, at least in Italy (Becchetti [7]), and in the US (Fazzari-Hubbard-Petersen [19]). This result is confirmed by our direct survey analysis (Table 3). *HFC* firms have in fact an average size of 148 employees, far lower than the average size of *NHFC* firms (304 employees). This result is confirmed by the other split criteria showing that *MFC* firms have an average size of 181 employees, far lower than the average size of *NMFC* firms (289 employees)[9].

TABLE 3

FIRMS' FINANCIAL CONSTRAINTS: THE ROLE OF FIRM SIZE, FIRM AGE, COLLATERAL, GROUP AFFILIATION AND R&D INVESTMENTS

	HFC	*NHFC*	*MFC*	*NMFC*
Average number of employees	148.3	343.5	180.9	288.6
ANOVA	110.5-249.64	252.9-323.2	116.2-179.6	265.2-343.1
Levene *T*-test	–6.15 (0.00)		–2.73 (0.007)	
Average foundation year	1972	1967	1972	1968
ANOVA	1970.1-1974.4	1967.68-1969	1970.6-1973.4	1967.2-1968-7
Levene *T*-test	5.13 (0.000)		3.50 (0.001)	
Ycarly average investment expenditure per employee	7.57	7.27	7.9	7.1
ANOVA	6.84-8.96	5.01-9.36	6.30-8.85	5.29-9.25
Levene *T*-test	25 (80)		–58 (54)	
% of firms investing in R&D	54.78	39.34	48.75	38.80
ANOVA	48.56-59.42	35.67-45_81	44.26-53.12	32.46-42.12
Group/no group affiliation				
No group	74.34	69.05	74.29	68.52
Stake: up to 10%	0	0.46	0.70	0.39
Stake: between 10% and 30%	0.43	0.46	0.35	0.48
Stake: between 30% and 50%	1.30	2.208	2.48	2.09
Stake: over 50%	23.914	27.80	22.16	28.49

Variable legend:
HFC - firms with index of financial constraints > 2;
MFC - firms with index of financial constraints > 0;
ANOVA: ANOVA 95% confidence intervals for sample meants; *Levene T-test*: test for the homogeneity of variances.

---

[9] Both differences are statistically significant. The Levene test for the significance of the difference in the two means for independent samples shows a much higher degree of significance for the *HFC/NHFC* case, while the contrary occurs if we use the *ANOVA test*.

Another important question often addressed in the literature is: does firm age matter in evaluating financial constraints? If it matters we have one of the most significant results supporting the imperfect information explanation of firm financing constraints, as young firms are expected to have a less established reputation with external financier. Previous empirical results showed that firm age matters in the US (Fazzari-Hubbard-Petersen [19]) and in the UK (Devereaux-Schiantarelli [18]; Becchetti [8]). Our results confirm this hypothesis showing that the average year of foundation for *HFC* firms is 1972, while that of *NHFC* firms is 1967. The difference between *MFC* and *NMFC* firms is slightly lower (respectively 1972 and 1968). Both Levene test and *ANOVA* test show how age means are significantly different for the respective two subsamples when both split criteria are used.

The qualitative part of Mediocredito survey consists of several dichotomous variables. Some of them are «yes-no» responses with a simple 1-0 code. Others present an affirmative response which varies according to an intensity scale. We give to these variables a «0-4 code» according to the high(4)-medium(3)-low(1) intensity of the affirmative response. An affirmative response with no indication for the intensity has been coded with the 2 digit.

The analysis of qualitative variables based on the above described data allows us to test several other assumptions of imperfect information models. One of these assumptions concludes that in Italy firms investing in R&D projects are likely either to experience higher cost differentials between external and internal finance or to be more severely rationed (Bagella-Becchetti [3]). In principle, in every country the informational gap should in fact be larger in these cases as its is more difficult for financiers to evaluate the expected profitability of R&D projects. This first factor, though, increases the marginal benefits for specialised financiers (equity financiers which become insiders of the firms such as venture capitalists) to provide financial support to the project. An inflow of these financiers that should eliminate the extra financial constraint for R&D projects is prevented, though in Italy, by the scarce development of a market of equity financiers for various reasons tax advantages of debt financing vis-à-vis equity financing, underdevelopment of the stock market and resistance to equity dilution of small firm owners). This hypothesis is supported by our statistical results on the Italian sample. Around 55% of *HFC* firms invested in R&D, while only 39% of *NHFC* did. The respective proportions in the case of *MFC* and *NMFC* firms amounts respectively to approximately 49% and 39%. The hypothesis of statistical association between R&D investment and financial constraints for *HFC/NHFC* firms is not rejected by chi-squared based tests, by tests based on pairs discordance and even, partially, by tests measuring the reduction in the prediction error (Lambda and Goodman and Kruskal tau). The degree of association between the two variables in the case of *MFC/NMFC* firms is lower, particularly if we consider tests measuring reduction in prediction error.

Results from previous analyses on Japanese (Hoshi-Kahyap-Scharfstein [23]) and Italian (Becchetti [7]) balance sheet data showed that intragroup participation (affiliation to keiretsus in the Japanese case) may reduce firm financial distress. This hypothesis is only partially supported by our results showing a 5% difference between *HFC* and *NHFC* «independent» firms (74% against 69%). This difference is almost entirely explained by a 4% difference in *HFC* and *NHFC* with more than 50% of capital participation. In this case, it is the difference between *MFC* and *NMFC* which is more significant (almost 6 percentage points) and also entirely explained by the difference in the more than 50% participation to the capital. The interesting implication of these results is that group affiliation seems to be a good remedy against financial constraints only if the majority stake is lost by the former owner.

Firms seem to be aware of this as only a minority of them, even in the group of the *HFC* (39%), is prepared to forgo part of its capital to solve financial constraints (Table 4). These results confirm the theoretical hypothesis of venture capital financing models on the risk of an asymmetry between relative contribution to investment performance and relative bargaining power

TABLE 4

FIRMS' WILLINGNESS TO EQUITY DILUTION

	NHFC	*HFC*	*NMFC*	*MFC*

*Is the firm prepared to accept financing in
the form of soft loans plus equity participation?*

	NHFC	*HFC*	*NMFC*	*MFC*
No answer	78.04	67.37	77.41	61.73
Yes	14.81	23.75	15.10	32.17
No	7.14	8.86	7.48	6.08

*Is the firm prepared to accept equity financing in
the form of acquisition of minority stakes
by merchant banks or venture capitalists?*

	NHFC	*HFC*	*NMFC*	*MFC*
No answer	78.13	67.73	77.49	62.60
Yes	12.01	21.80	12.72	24.78
No	9.85	10.46	9.77	12.60

*Is the firm prepared to accept equity financing in
the form of acquisition of minority stakes
by closed end investment funds?*

	NHFC	*HFC*	*NMFC*	*MFC*
No answer	78.16	67.73	77.52	62.60
Yes	5.56	8.15	5.71	9.56
No	16.27	24.11	16.75	27.82
Willingness to «equity dilution»				
No «equity dilution»	85.94	73.91	86.55	77.48
Dilution up to 10%	4.11	3.47	4 16	3.54
Dilution between 10% and 30%	6.79	16.08	6.23	13.82
Dilution between 30% and 49%	2.42	6.08	2.34	4.43
Dilution beyond 50%	0.71	0.43	0.69	0.70

Advantages in term of higher financial «solidity» from equity dilution

	NHFC	*HFC*	*NMFC*	*MFC*
No advantages	61.01	39.56	62.25	45.03
Relative advantages	4.74	9.13	4.10	10.28
Advantages (no indication of intensity	12.20	13.04	10.97	19.68
High advantages	10.13	12.60	10.21	10.63
Very high advantages	11.89	25.65	12.43	14.36

TABLE 4 *continued*

	NHFC	HFC	NMFC	MFC
Advantages in terms of easier access to credit from equity dilution				
No advantages	77.00	60.43	77.70	66.13
Relative advantages	3.89	60.86	3.58	6.56
Advantages (no indication of intensity)	4.66	6.08	4.10	8.51
High advantages	8.64	13.47	8.30	12.58
Very high advantages	5.79	13.91	6.29	6.20
Risk of loss of control from equity dilution				
No risk	46.32	37.39	47.90	33.51
Relative risk	16.15	22.17	16.24	18.08
Risk (no indication of intensity)	27.36	26.08	25.97	34.92
High risk	3.83	4.34	3.64	5.14
Very high risk	6.32	10	6.23	8.33
Risk of management coordination problems from equity dilution				
No risk	69.46	62.17	69.79	64.53
Relative risk	10.57	18.69	10.67	13.29
Risk (no indication of intensity)	10.38	7.39	10.18	10.28
High risk	6.26	7.82	5.86	9.21
Very high risk	3.31	3.91	3.46	2.65

between investors and financiers. Given that financiers usually have higher bargaining strength, it seems that, if financially constrained investors want to overcome their difficulties finding a financing partner, they have to forgo the majority stake of their equity and, for this reason, they do not see equity participation as the best solution to their problem. This hypothesis is confirmed if we consider that 73% of *HFC* firms declare to be not available for equity dilution.

The fact that venture capital financing or equity participation is not perceived as the optimal solution to firm financial constraints is confirmed when firms are asked about the usefulness of different policy measures in reducing financial problems (Table 5).

TABLE 5

USEFULNESS OF DIFFERENT POLICY INSTRUMENTS
FOR FIRMS WITH AND WITHOUT FINANCIAL CONSTRAINTS

	NHFC	*HFC*	*NMFC*	*MFC*
Are soft loans useful for small medium firm development?				
Useless	34.29	18.26	35.37	21.45
Quite useful	5.65	11.3	5.2	10.63
Useful (with no indication of intensity)	15.04	16.52	14.78	17.19
Very useful	26.06	42.17	26.82	28.19
Extremely useful	18.93	11.73	17.82	3.86
Are grants useful for small medium firm development?				
Useless	46.63	30.86	46.62	40.24
Quite useful	6.12	8.69	5.93	8.33
Useful (with no indication of intensity)	11.34	13.47	11.43	11.7
Very useful	21.83	37.39	22.32	25.35
Extremely useful	14.05	9.56	13.68	14.36
Are tax incentives useful for small medium firm development?				
Useless 23.40	34.29	36.53	22.61	37.80
Quite useful	5.72	9.57	5.38	9.22
Useful (with no indication of intensity)	18.25	9.57	17.15	21.10
Very useful	15.32	22.17	15.09	19.50
Extremely useful	24.19	36.09	24.57	26.77
Are accelerated depreciation schemes useful for small medium firm development?				
Useless	72.61	62.61	37.80	23.40
Quite useful	4.64	7.83	5.38	9.22
Useful (with no indication of intensity)	4.83	3.48	17.15	21.10
Very useful	8.83	12.61	15.09	19.50
Extremely useful	9.08	13.48	24.57	26.77

TABLE 5 *continued*

	NHFC	HFC	NMFC	MFC

Are tax credits useful for small medium frim development?

	NHFC	HFC	NMFC	MFC
Useless	71.78	59.57	72.17	64.54
Quite useful	4.28	8.26	3.92	7.98
Useful (with no indication of intensity)	6.16	6.09	5.81	8.16
Very useful	8.48	12.61	8.55	9.75
Extremely useful	9.30	13.48	9.55	9.57

Are tax incentives on profits useful for small medium firm development?

	NHFC	HFC	NMFC	MFC
Useless	53.51	39.13	54.35	42.73
Quite useful	4.25	3.91	3.95	5.85
Useful (with no indication of intensity)	13.56	12.17	12.65	18.26
Very useful	10.05	12.61	9.85	12.23
Extremely useful	18.64	32.17	19.19	20.92

Is merchant bank or closed end funds equity participation useful for small medium firms development?

	NHFC	HFC	NMFC	MFC
Useless	87.22	70.00	87.44	78.90
Quite useful	3.78	8.70	3.86	5.32
Useful (with no indication of intensity)	2.10	0.43	1.64	4.08
Very useful	3.84	11.30	3.89	6.56
Extremely useful	3.06	9.57	3.16	5.14

Are fondi di garanzia useful for the development of small and medium firms?

	NHFC	HFC	NMFC	MFC
Useless	91.99	77.83	91.85	87.06
Quite useful	3.23	10.00	3.32	5.50
Useful (with no indication of intensity)	0.77	0.87	0.67	1.42
Very useful	2.82	6.52	2.98	3.37
Extremely useful	1.19	4.78	1.19	2.66

Equity participation by merchant banks, closed-end funds, etc. is considered as a useful measure only by 30% of *HFC* and 21% of *MFC* firms. Equity participation is regarded as useful by a lower number of *FC* firms than almost any other measure such as: *(i)* tax allowances on reinvested profits (61% of *HFC* and 57% of *MFC*); *(ii)* tax allowances through tax credit (41% of *HFC* and 36% of *MFC*); *(iii)* accelerated depreciation allowances (38% of HFC and 76% of *MFC*); *(iv)* tax allowances not specified (78% of *HFC* and 77% of *MFC*); *(v)* grants (70% of *HFC* and 60% of *MFC*) and *(vi)* soft loans (82% of *HFC* and 79% of *MFC*).

All tests measuring financial association between the financial constraint variable and the variables reporting the declared usefulness of different policy measures in easing financial constraints, show that *HFC* firms attach greater importance to these measures than *NHFC* firms, with a difference usually ranging from 10 to 16 percentage points. The same difference is also found for *MFC* and *NMFC* firms. With these differences, almost all measures of variable association reject the null hypothesis of independence among financial constraints and usefulness of the different policy measures.

Another question that directly addresses the «equity dilution syndrome» of Italian firms is the required description of pros and cons of equity participation. 60% of *HFC* firms and 55% of *MFC* find no advantage in terms of higher financial stability from increased equity participation. Only 40% of *HFC* firms and 30% of *MFC* firms assume that equity participation may ease their access to credit, while 63% of *HFC* firms and 67% of *NFC* fear that equity participation might cause loss of control or coordination problems in firm management (38% of *HFC* firms and 36% of *MFC* firms).

Summing up the descriptive statistics results, four factors seem to discriminate between financially constrained and non financially constrained firms (age, size, R&D participation, and participation to group). When we pass, however, from descriptive statistics to a bivariate multinomial logit analysis we find that only two net effects matter (size and R&D participation). This result is robust through different logit specifications with and without the filter excluding poorly performing firms (Table 6). The reduced significance of firm age may be partially explained by collinearity among regressors. While in fact firm size and R&D participation

TABLE 6

MULTIVARIATE LOGIT RESULTS WITH AND WITHOUT
FAZZARI-HUBBARD-PETERSEN [19] FILTER*

	Low performers included		Low performers excluded	
	MFC	*HFC*	*MFC*	*HFC*
Intercept	-2.530	-2.91	-2.15	-2.53
	(2.32)	(0.30)	(0.23)	(0.30)
Small firms	1.29	0.65	1.29	0.58
	(0.23)	(0.29)	(0.23)	(0.29)
Medium firms	0.84	0.21	0.90	0.22
	(0.21)	(0.27)	(0.22)	(0.27)
Firm's age	0.33	0.12	0.14	0.004
	(0.12)	(0.19)	(0.13)	(0.003)
Collateral	-0.03	-0.07	-0.03	-0.08
	(0.10)	(0.02)	(0.01)	(0.02)
R&D participation	0.36	0.53	0.39	0.55
	(0.10)	(0.15)	(0.11)	(0.15)
R&D intensity	7.89	5.09	8.73	5.30
	(5.53)	(7.62)	(6.09)	8.00
Loss of	-0.16	-0.25	-0.17	-0.08
Control	(0.12)	(0.18)	(0.12)	(0.02)
Log likelihood	2491.59	1400.76	2166.10	1275.32
Chi square	84.41	40.37	74.40	38.13

Variable legend:
HFC - firms with index of financial constraints > 2;
MFC - firms with index of financial constraints > 0;
Small firms: 1 if firms with less than 50 employees;
Medium firms: 1 if firms from 50 to 500 employees;
Firm age: year of foundation;
R&D participation: firms with nonzero R&D expenditures;
R&D intensity: R&D expenditures/total assets;
Collateral: net assets/liabilities;
Loss of control: firms participated for more than 50%.
* The table reports multivariate logit coefficients with standard errors in parenthesis;

are positively correlated with each other[10] so that their net effects on financial constraints do not disturb each other, the negative correlation of size with age and participation to group makes it difficult for all of these regressors to be significant in the estimate.

---

[10] According to an empirical work of COHEN W.M.-KLEPPER S. [7] on US data R&D intensity is a random variable meaning that firm size is the only factor affecting positively and significantly R&D expenditure. As a consequence, also R&D participation is expected to be positively correlated with size.

4. - The Balance Sheet Analysis on Mediocredito Survey on Italian Firms

The balance sheet section of the paper presents descriptive and econometric analysis on several indicators and econometric estimates on the relationship between investments and internal and external financing sources. The indicators describe firm asset and liability structure for *NHFC*, *HFC* and for *NMFC* and *MFC* firms providing for each subgroup average value, standard deviation and tests for the significance of the difference among subgroup means.

Significant differences in the average of *NMFC/MFC* firms exist for the asset structure indicators, while only the relative amount of R&D expenditure is significantly higher on average for *HFC* firms with respect to *NHFC* firms (Table 7). Firms with higher financial constraints have more fixed capital stock mainly because of the higher incidence of R&D costs. The result is consistent with previously discussed findings on qualitative responses showing that R&D expenditure on total asset is almost twice as high for *HFC* and *MFC* as that for *NHFC* and *NMFC* firms.

Differences in the ratio between intragroup and bank financing do not appear to be significant among subgroups and they are also based on a restricted subset of firms with intragroup relationship (14-15% of total sample). Relevant differences occur in the net asset/liability ratio. Financially constrained firms have lower ratios (1.53 *HFC* and 2.06 *MFC* firms) than non financially constrained firms (higher than 3.30). This result confirms that investment financing, in absence of specific project valuation skills, penalises firms not disposing of enough real guarantees. This is consistent with models showing how, in presence of asymmetric information, the higher the ratio between investor and financier sources, the higher the investor costs in case of failure and the lower the risk of adverse selection (Bernanke-Gertler [9]). More financially constrained firms exhibit a slightly lower short term/-long term indebtedness ratio, a result which is apparently at odds with criteria for subgroup definition (*HFC* and *MFC* firms declared difficulties in medium long term financing). A deeper inspection

TABLE 7

BALANCE SHEET INDICATORS FOR FIRMS
WITH AND WITHOUT FINANCIAL CONSTRAINTS*

	HFC	NHFC	MFC	NMFC
1 Tangible and intangible fixed capital stock/total assets	41.55% (18.5%)	40.89% (18.1%)	*42.93% (17.5%)*	*40.58% (18.2%)*
2 R&D intangible capital stock/total assets	*0.21% (0,8%)*	*0.13% (0.8%)*	*0.20% (0.9%)*	*0.12% (0.8%)*
3 Debts vs. group/total liabilities	1.66% (6%)	1.22% (5%)	1.27% (5%)	1.24% (5%)
4 Long-medium term debts with banks/Long-medium terms debts with group	5 (12)	3.8 (9)	6.4 (13)	3.2 (8)
5 Short term debts with banks/ short term debts with group	10.7 (25)	17.0 (40)	*11.9 (23)*	*17.4 (41)*
6 Total debts with banks/total debts with group	16.15 (22)	35 (52)	18.05 (32)	23.08 (54)
7 Bonds/long-medium term debts	-99% (186%)	139% (274%)	134% (260%)	137% (271%)
8 Short term debts/long-medium term debts	8.89 (12.1)	9.97 (13.7)	*8.74 (13.2)*	*10.12 (13.7)*
9 Leverage (net asset/liabilities)	*1.53 (3.6)*	*3.31 (8.4)*	*2.06 (6.0)*	*3.41 (8.6)*
10 Long-medium term assets/ long-medium term liabilities	197% (165%)	184% (194%)	*201% (197%)*	*182% (191%)*
11 Self-financing/fixed capital stock	13.94% (20%)	14.69% (26%)	13.93% (21%)	14.77% (27%)
12 Investment/fixed capital stock	0.89% (2%)	0.66% (2%)	*0.91% (2%)*	*0.63% (2%)*
13 Added value/total sales	36.5% (14.6%)	36.4% (16%)	*37.39% (14.5%)*	*36.30% (16.1%)*
14 ROE	11% (29%)	10% (45%)	10.8% (45%)	9.9% (44%)
15 Total costs of financing/ bonds plus liabilities	*7.41% (3.7%)*	*6.56% (3.7%)*	*7.07% (3.6%)*	*6.53% (3.8%)*

* All indicators are calculated on 1991 data, except nos. 14 and 15, calculated on average 1989-1991 values.
   In parenthesis is the standard deviation.
   Significative differences between *HFC/NHFC* and *MFC/NMFC* averages are in italics.
   This ratio, as ratios 4-6, are calculated including only firms that have debts with group.
Ratio 7 is calculated only for firms with bonds.

of this result shows nonetheless that *HFC* and *MFC* have a less stable long term financial equilibrium (higher ratio of fixed capital stock/long term indebtedness) with respect to *NHFC* and *NMFC* firms.

Other indicators confirm that *HFC* and *MFC* firms have more difficult access to external financing sources: the two subgroups have a significantly higher cost differential in external financing (1% spread between *HFC* and *NHFC* and 0.50% spread between *MFC* and *NMFC*). This occurs even though their performance indexes (ROE, internal financing/fixed capital stock and added value/total sales) are not significantly different on average from those of *NHFC* and *NMFC* firms and their investment levels are significantly higher.

The financing cost differential can be probably explained by the higher cost of financing charged by banks to the two subgroups of *HFC* and *MFC* firms to compensate their significantly lower leverage with respect to *NHFC* and *NMFC* subgroups.

The quantitative analysis on balance sheet aims at confirming that investments of more financially constrained firms are relatively more correlated to changes in internal financing sources according to the mainstream interpretation of theoretical and empirical literature (Sections 1 and 2). A related goal is to verify if methodological problems occurring in estimating this empirical relationship with balance sheet data are so serious to bias results for this empirical relationship. We therefore intend to estimate an investment function for more and less financially constrained subgroups to detect if qualitative evidence on differences in financial constraints (through direct firm revelation in the questionnaire) is confirmed by econometric analysis.

The estimated equation is the following:

$$INV_t = \alpha_{0i} + \alpha_1 CFL_{t-1} + \alpha_2 CFL_t + \alpha_3 \Delta DB_t +$$

$$+ \alpha_4 \Delta DML_t + \alpha_5 \Delta DG_t + \alpha_6 \Delta OBB_t + \alpha_7 \Delta SF_t$$

(2) t = years 1990-1991; t-1 = years 1989-1990

where: *INV* is total investment/total sales; *CFL* internal financing[11]/total sales; ΔSF is changes in equities plus changes in debts vs. stockholders/total sales; ΔDB is changes in short term debts vs. banks and ICS[12]/total sales; ΔDML is changes in medium-short term debts vs. banks and ICS/total sales; ΔDG is changes in debts vs. group/total sales; ΔOBB is change in bonds/total sales and α_{0i} are 23 industrial sector dummies. *CFL* represents internal financing while other regressors represent external financing. Total sales are used in the denominator as they represent the best available proxy for firm dimension.

Estimates results are presented in Table 8. In the overall sam-

TABLE 8

EQUATION ESTIMATES

$$INV_t = \alpha_{0i} + \alpha_1 CFL_{t-1} + \alpha_2 CFL_t + \alpha_3 \Delta DB_t + \alpha_4 \Delta DML_t + \alpha_5 \Delta DG_t + \alpha_6 \Delta OBB_t + \alpha_7 \Delta SF_t *$$

Indep. variable	Total sample	MFC	NMFC
CFL_{t-1}	0.021274 (2.9)	0.087488 (3.23)	0.015444 (2.0)
CFL_t	0.00386 (0.5)	–0.01305 (–0.5)	0.002436 (0.3)
ΔDB_t	0.018352 (4.7)	0.014851 (1.4)	0.018021 (4.3)
ΔDML_t	0.014129 (2.8)	0.011627 (0.9)	0.01383 (2.5)
ΔDG_t	0.004378 (0.9)	0.034352 (1.4)	0.002317 (0.5)
ΔOBB_t	–0.02076 (–0.8)	–0.02466 (–0.4)	–0.02773 (–1.0)
ΔSF_t	0.00832 (1.7)	–0.00602 (–0.3)	0.00966 (2)
R^2	0.10424	0.18875	0.1035
R^2 adj.	0.09648	0.14123	0.09441
F stat.	13.43	3.97	11.33
Signif. F.	0	0	0

* *T*-stat values are reported in parenthesis.
** Only firms with complete balance sheet data for the three years are included..

---

[11] Net income plus shares of material and immaterial depreciations.
[12] *ICS* are Italian financial institutions specialising mainly in medium-long term financing.

ple estimate internal financing sources (lagged *CFL*) and some external financing sources (short term and long term banks and *ICS* financing, *ΔSF*) significantly affect investments. Subgroup results for *NHFC* and *HFC* firms are not significant because of the scarcity of observations for *HFC* firms with nonzero investments and are therefore omitted.

The relevant estimates are those for *MFC* and NMFC subgroups. Lagged internal financing CFL_{t-1} is four times higher for *MFC* firms than in the overall sample (while external financing sources are not). The situation is reversed for *NMFC* firms where external financing regressors (bank and stock market financing) are relatively more significant than in *MFC* and overall sample investment equations. The empirical results on balance sheet data are consistent with direct revelation of financial constraints by firms with questionnaire response. These findings seem to confirm that, in spite of methodological difficulties in panel data estimation, a more significant and stronger relationship between cash flow and investment reflects higher financial constraints more than just a proxy for future profitable investment opportunities.

5. - Conclusions

One of the main theoretical predictions of information economics on the issue of finance and investments is that informational asymmetries between financier and investors generate a market failure under the form of inefficient volume of aggregate investments. The cost differential between external and internal finance generated by this asymmetry may constrain investment opportunities to the availability of external finance for some groups of firms. The empirical detection of these financial constraints is then quite relevant as it may suggest that some room exists for state intervention under the forms of subsidisation of those subgroups more suffering from these constraints.

«Indirect» attempts to verify financial constraints at firm level have been recently seriously questioned because of methodological problems concerning balance sheet panel data analysis. This paper provides a direct measure of firm financial constraints which circumvents these problems combining qualitative data and balance sheet data from a Mediocredito survey on Italian firms. The main qualitative results of the paper are: *(i)* the individuation of geographical areas with excess financial constraints; *(ii)* the association of financial constraints with small firm size and R&D participation; *(iii)* the identification of firm preference of tax allowances with respect to the development of venture capital financing as solutions to financial constraints. This seems to be determined by an «equity dilution syndrome» and by the fear that equity participation will lead to loss of control and coordination failure in firm management.

The main quantitative results of the paper are: *(i)* the identification of relatively more financially constrained firms as a subgroup with relatively higher leverage, equivalent economic performance, but higher level of investment over capital stock and higher cost of external financing; *(ii)* the confirmation in the econometric estimate on balance sheet data that investments of relatively more financially constrained firms are more sensitive to internal financing sources. This finding shows that, in spite of methodological difficulties in panel data estimation, a more significant and stronger relationship between cash flow and investment reflects higher financial constraints more than just a proxy for future profitable investment opportunities.

BIBLIOGRAPHY

[1] ADMATI A.R. - PFLEIDERER P., «Robust Financial Contracting and the Role for Venture Capital», *Journal of Finance*, n. 49, 1994, pp. 371-402.

[2] ARELLANO M. - BOND S., «Some Tests of Specifications for Panel Data: Monte Carlo Evidence and an Application to Employment Equations», *Review of Economic Studies*, n. 58, 1991, pp. 277-97.

[3] BAGELLA M. - BECCHETTI L., «Business Cycle and Growth in an Economy with Financial Market Imperfections», in PHELPS E. - BALDASSARRI M. - PAGANETTO L. (eds.), *Finance, Research, Education and Growth*, London, McMillan, forthcoming, 1997.

[4] — — — —, «The Buy-Out/Property Right Choice in Film Financing: Credit Rationing, Adverse Selection and the Bayesian Dilemma», *Journal of Cultural Economics*, n. 19, 1995.

[5] BAGELLA M. - BECCHETTI L. - CAGGESE A., «Finanza, investimenti ed Innovazione in Italia: il divario nord-sud», Bologna, il Mulino, forthcoming 1997.

[6] — —, «Struttura del capitale, finanziamenti agevolati e redditività delle imprese manifatturiere italiane», *Rassegna Economica*, n. 4, 1995, pp. 813-38.

[7] BECCHETTI L., «Finance, Investment and Innovation: a Theoretical and Empirical Comparative Analysis», *Empirica*, n. 3, 1995.

[8] — —, «Finance, Investment and Innovation: an Empirical Analysis of the Italian Case», *Sviluppo Economico*, n. 1, 1994.

[9] BERNANKE B.S. - GERTLER M., «Financial Fragility and Economic Performance», NBER, *Working Paper*, n. 2318, 1987.

[10] BESANKO D. - THAKOR A.V., «Collateral and Rationing: Sorting Equilibria in Monopolistic and Competitive Credit Markets», *International Economic Review*, n. 28, 1987, pp. 671-89.

[11] BLANCHARD O.J. - RHEE C. - SUMMERS L., «The Stock Market, Profit and Investment», *Quarterly Journal of Economics*, n. 108, 1993.

[12] BOND S. - MEGHIR C., «Dynamic Investment Models and the Firm's Financial Policy», *Review of Economic Studies*, n. 61, 1994, pp. 197-222.

[13] BYGRAVE D.W. - TIMMONS J.A., *Venture Capital at the Crossroads*, Boston, Harvard Business School Press, 1992.

[14] CHIRINKO R.S., «Tobin's Q and Financial Policy», *Journal of Monetary Economics*, n. 19, 1987.

[15] — —, *Financial Structure, Empirical Investment Equations and Q*, mimeo, Chicago, University of Chicago, 1992.

[16] — —, «Business Fixed Investment Spending», *Journal of Economic Literature*, n. 31, 1993.

[17] COHEN W.M. - KLEPPER S., «The Anatomy of Industry R&D Intensity Distributions», *American Economic Review*, September 1992.

[18] DEVEREAUX M. - SCHIANTARELLI F., «Investment, Financial Factors, and Cash Flow: Evidence from UK Panel Data», NBER, *Working Paper*, n. 116, 1989.

[19] FAZZARI S.M. - HUBBARD G.R. - PETERSEN B.C., «Financing Constraints and Corporate Investment», *Broking Papers on Economic Activity*, 1988, pp. 141-95.

[20] GILCHRIST S. - HIMMELBERG C.P., «Evidence on the Role of Cash Flow for Investment», *Journal of Monetary Economics*, n. 36, 1995, pp. 541-72.

[21] HARRIS M. RAVIV A., «The Theory of Capital Structure», *Journal of Finance*, n. 46, 1991, pp. 297-355.

[22] HOSHI T. - KASHYAP A., «Evidence on Q and Investment for Japanese Firms», *Journal of Japanese International Economies*, n. 4, 1990, pp. 371-400.

[23] HOSHI T. - KASHYAP A. - SCHARFSTEIN D., «Corporate Structure, Liquidity and Investment: Evidence from Japanese Industrial Groups», *Quarterly Journal of Economics*, n. 90, 1992, pp. 33-61.

[24] HUBBARD G.R. - KASHYAP A.K., «Internal Net-Worth and the Investment Process: an Application to US Agriculture», *Journal of Political Economy*, vol. 100, n. 3, 1992, pp. 506-34.

[25] JAFFE D. - RUSSEL T., «Imperfect Information, Uncertainty, and Credit Rationing», *Quarterly Journal of Economics*, vol. 90, n. 4, 1976, pp. 651-66.

[26] KING R.G. - LEVINE R., «Finance, Entrepreneurship and Growth: Theory and Evidence, paper presented to the World Bank Conference «How do National Policies Affect Long Run Growth», *Estoril*, January 1993.

[27] MILDE H. - RILEY J.G., «Signalling in Credit Markets», *Quarterly Journal of Economics*, n. 103, 1988, pp. 101-29.

[28] MINISTERO DELL'INDUSTRIA - MEDIOCREDITO CENTRALE (Osservatorio sulle Piccole e Medie Imprese), «Indagine sulle imprese manifatturiere», *Quinto Rapporto sull'Industria Italiana e sulla Politica Industriale*, Milano, il Sole 24 Ore Libri, 1994.

[29] MODIGLIANI F. - MILLER M., «The Cost of Capital, Corporation Finance and the Theory of Investment», *American Economic Review*, n. 48, 1958, pp. 261-97.

[30] MYERS S.C. - MAJLUF N.S., «Corporate Financing Decisions When Firms Have Investment Information That Investors Do Not», *Journal of Financial Economics*, n. 13, 1984, pp. 187-221.

[31] SCHIANTARELLI F. - GEORGOUTSOS D., «Monopolist Competition and the Q Theory of Investment», *European Economic Review*, n. 34, 1990, pp. 1061-78.

[32] STIGLITZ J. - WEISS A., «Credit Rationing in Markets with Imperfect Information», *American Economic Review*, n. 71, 1981, pp. 912-27.

[33] WILLIAMSON S.D., «Costly Monitoring, Financial Intermediation, and Equilibrium Credit Rationing», *Journal of Monetary Economics*, n. 18, 1986.

[34] WHITED T.M., «Debt, Liquidity Constraints, and Corporate Investment: Evidence from Panel Data», *Journal of Finance*, n. 47, 1992.

Risk, Return and Adverse Selection: a Study of Optimal Behaviour Under Asymmetric Information

Leighton Vaughan Williams - David Paton*

Nottingham Trent University

1. - Introduction

Betting markets have often been used as a useful proxy for financial markets because they possess all their usual attributes, notably a large number of investors (or bettors) with potential access to widely available information sets, but also the property that each asset (or bet) possesses a well-defined end point at which it has a value which is certain. Further, the possibility for the use of inside information to earn abnormal returns from horse race betting is somewhat analogous to the operation of conventional financial markets, but is in some respects easier to measure and assess. For these reasons the information provided by an examination of horserace betting markets is a convenient and useful perspective from which to consider the evidence and interpretations of consumer/investor behaviour observed in conventional financial markets, and also the operation of these markets.

A number of studies have shown that the expected return to a unit bet at higher odds tends to be less than that at lower odds.

* The authors are respectively Senior Lecturer and Lecturer at the Department of Economics and Polities.

N.B.: the numbers in square brackets refer to the Bibliography at the end of the paper.

This has come to be known in the literature as the 'favorite-long-shot bias' or simply the 'longshot bias', the existence of which has been reproduced by many authors in respect of the racetrack.

Most such studies are based on data derived from parimutuel betting markets, in which winning bets share the pool which is made up of all bets, net of deductions such as taxes and administrative charges. Theoretical explanations for the apparent market inefficiency implied by the bias range from the consumption and investment preferences of bettors to the likely response of such bettors to the existence of positive information and/or transactions costs.

This paper addresses the issue of betting markets characterized by odds setters who may influence the distribution of prices separately from bettors. An explanation is proposed for the longshot bias in these markets which has no need for demand-side explanations.

Instead the bias is explained in terms of the supply-side behaviour of bookmakers who believe there are some bettors who possess superior information.

New empirical tests are employed to distinguish between these explanations. The conclusions indicate that the conventional demand-side approaches are inadequate in explaining the longshot bias in all types of race track betting market.

In Section 2 of the paper we discuss some of the explanations of the longshot bias extant in the literature. In Section 3, we develop a simple model of horse race betting which allows us to investigate the influence of any such insider trading on this bias. In Section 4, we go on to subject this model to empirical tests. Some concluding remarks are made in Section 5.

2. - The Longshot Bias: Some Background

Thaler and Ziemba [17] assess the evidence from a wide range of previously published studies of US parimutuel betting markets. Their central conclusion is that expected returns tend to be negative at long odds, becoming gradually less so at shorter odds and eventually positive (before deductions) at a cutoff point of about 4.5 to 1. At odds of below 0.3 to 1, they report a positive expected return after deductions, i.e. an expected profit. This bias was also found in a later study of the US racetrack by Ziemba and Hausch [22], although Swidler and Shaw ([16], p. 305), notably failed to confirm its existence in their study of a US racetrack chosen for its low turnover and ostensibly «uninformed bettors».

The UK operates its own version of the parimutuel, i.e. the totalizator or «Tote», but the majority of the turnover takes place with bookmakers who offer a fixed return to winning bets or an agreement to pay such bets at the starting price[1]. The bookmaking system also coexists with the totalizator in Australia though not in Hong Kong, which operates a totalizator-only system.

The bias reported in most US studies has been tested and confirmed for UK bookmaking data, e.g. Henery [9], Dowie [8]; for Australian bookmaking data, e.g. Bird, McCrae and Beggs [3], Bird and McCrae [2]; but not for Hong Kong betting markets, e.g. Busche and Hall [5]; Busche [4].

Traditional explanations of the observed favorite-longshot bias involve assumptions about the preferences and behaviour of bettors as consumers and/or investors. Quandt [13], for example, offers a theoretical model to demonstrate that the observed bias is a natural and necessary consequence of equilibrium in a market characterized by bettors with homogeneous beliefs who are risk-loving in the context of a mean-variance framework. The bias can also be explained in terms of betting as a consumpion activity. Thaler and Ziemba [17], for example, suggest that bettors may derive utility just from holding a ticket on a longshot.

Hurley and McDonough [10] instead propose an explanation of the favorite-longshot bias in parimutuel markets based upon the existence of two types of risk-neutral bettor: informed bettors (who know the true probability of a favorite winning) and uninformed bettors (who cannot distinguish the expected value of bets). They demonstrate that a favorite-longshot bias can arise

---

[1] The starting price is the official, independently determined assessment of the odds at which a sizeable bet could be placed with course bookmakers at the start of the race.

in such a market as a direct consequence of rational behaviour in the context of positive information/transactions costs, although they fail to find empirical evidence in support of this explanation.

Common to all the above explanations is that they are couched in terms of bettor behaviour. An explanation which owes more to an examination of the behaviour of odds setters has been proposed by Shin [14]. Essentially, Shin interprets the fixed-odds bookmaking system as a case of adverse selection in which the bookmaker faces a number of bettors who possess superior information, the proportion and identity of whom are unknown to the bookmaker. In the simplest modelling of this situation, insiders are assumed to know with certainty the result of a race while the rest of the betting population, i.e. outsiders, are simply noise traders. He demonstrates that in this uncertain environment, the comparative rates of change of revenue and cost facing the bookmaker are such as to induce in them a tendency to avoid setting very long odds. The consequence of this price-setting behaviour is for the normalized betting odds to understate the winning chances of favourites and to overstate the winning chances of longshots. This is the traditional favorite-longshot bias, explained in terms of the rational behaviour of odds setters operating in the face of some bettors trading as insiders. Evidence in favour of this explanation is provided by Vaughan Williams and Paton [19].

3. - A Model of Horse Race Betting

We build a simple model of a horse race betting market based on similar assumptions about the nature and type of bettors to those of Hurley and McDonough [10]. For simplicity, we restrict our model to two horses, a favorite and a longshot. We propose two sets of winning probabilities for the two horses. Firstly there are the true probabilities of winning, $[s; (1 - s)]$ for the favorite and longshot respectively. Secondly there are the subjective probabilities, $[a, (1 - a)]$ of the bookmakers, all of whom are identical and have equal access to public information. When all information is available publicly, we assume that the subjective probabilities are equal to the true probabilities. In the presence of some inside information, we assume that the expected value of a is equal to the true winning probability, i.e. $E(a) = s$.

There is a distribution of risk-neutral bettors. Some of these may be informed about the true probabilities, while the rest are noise traders who cannot distinguish the value of a bet. Bookmakers are also risk-neutral and compete on price up to the point that they expect the subjective returns to the set of bettors on each horse to be zero. For simplicity, we assume bookmakers have zero costs. The set of odds for the favorite and longshot respectively are $[O_f, O_l]$. The expected return to a unit stake on the favorite is $[E(a). O_f - (1 - E(a))]$ and on the longshot, $[1 - E(a)]. O_l - E(a)]$. If all bettors are noise traders, an expected net payout of zero on each horse implies that the bookmaker sets odds of $[1 - a)/a; a/(1 - a)]$. Where there is no privately held information, the set of odds are $[1 - s)/s; s/(1 - s)]$.

We now use this framework to investigate the implications of potential insider trading. To do this, we assume that bookmakers believe that a proportion w, of bettors hold private information which is potentially superior to that publicly available. We further assume that in reality there is no private information and that all bettors are simply noise traders. This implies that the bookmakers' subjective probabilities are in fact equal to the true probabilities. Thus here we are concerned solely with the threat of inside information and not its reality.

We consider two possibilities: the bookmakers believe that they have either underestimated or overestimated the favorite's winning probability a positive amount, α, (i.e. they believe $s = a + \alpha$ or $s = a - \alpha$). They do not know which is the actual case and assign an equal probability to each alternative.

We model a market consisting of two stages, the first before trading has commenced and the second prior to the race being run.

Stage 1: At the start of the market, the bookmakers set odds on each horse to allow for the fact that they may have underestimated the winning probability. Their implied probabilities on the favorite (longshot) are increased by the positive amount $B_f (B_l)$. Lower odds are now set on each horse as follows:

$$\left[\frac{(1-a-B_f)}{(a+B_f)} ; \frac{(a-B_l)}{(1-a+B_l)} \right]$$

Stage 2: As the market progresses, the bookmakers have a chance to readjust their subjective probabilities in the light of information revealed by the market. If neither horse is more heavily backed than the other, then bookmakers assume that no insider trading is present and adjust their odds accordingly[2].

In Stage 1, bookmakers believe that insiders will bet with certainty on the favorite if $s = a + \alpha$ and with certainty on the longshot if $s = a - \alpha$. Other bettors, not knowing which horse is underpriced, bet with equal probability on either horse.

The bookmakers expect the return to an insider from a unit bet to be:

Bet of favourite with certainty:

$$\frac{(a+\alpha).(1-a-B_f)}{(a+B_f)} - (1-a-\alpha)$$

Bet on longshot with certainty:

$$\frac{(1-a+\alpha).(a-B_l)}{(1-a+B_l)} - (a-\alpha)$$

The bookmakers expect the return to other bettors to be: (derived in *Appendix*)

---

[2] If insider trading is actually present, one horse is more heavily backed. The bookmakers are thus informed of which horse they have underpriced and the same result follows.

Bet on favourite with $pr = 0.5$:

$$\frac{a.(1 - a - B_f)}{(a + B_f)} - (1 - a)$$

Bet on longshot with $pr = 0.5$:

$$\frac{(1 - a).(a - B_l)}{(1 - a + B_l)} - a$$

For equilibrium, the overall expected net payout to the set of all bettors must be zero. In the *Appendix* we show that, when the expected net payout to each horse is equal, the equilibrium values of both B_f and B_l are both equal to $w\alpha$. Thus it is optimal for bookmakers to add the same amount to the implied probabilities of both longshots and favourites in the presence of perceived insider trading. The greater is the amount of private information which bookmakers believe to be held and the greater the estimated proportion of insiders, the greater will be the implied probabilities of winning for both horses. The implied equilibrium odds at Stage 1 are:

$$\left[\frac{(1 - a - \alpha w)}{(a + \alpha w)} ; \frac{(a - \alpha w)}{(1 - a + \alpha w)} \right]$$

Since the odds of both the longshot and the favorite are adjusted by the same amount, we can derive the longshot bias from the objective expected return. For any horse with objective probability of winning, s.

Thus as long as bookmakers believe there are some insiders with non-trivial private information, there is a longshot bias. The more inside knowledge that bookmakers believe to exist, the greater will be this bias.

In Stage 2 the odds are adjusted to the true probabilities, and the longshot bias is reduced. More realistically, the longshot bias decreases as the market progresses, a conclusion consistent with Kyle's [11] modelling of insider trading as a process of information:

$$E(Ret) = s.(odds) - (1 - s)$$

$$E(Ret) = \frac{s.(1 - s - \alpha w)}{(s + \alpha w)} - (1 - s)$$

$$E(Ret) = \frac{s}{(s + \alpha w)} - s - 1 + s$$

$$E(Ret) = \frac{s - s(s + \alpha w) - (s + \alpha w) + s(s + \alpha w)}{(s + \alpha w)}$$

$$E(Ret) = -\frac{\alpha w}{(s + \alpha w)}$$

$$E(Ret) = -\alpha w \left(\frac{1}{s + \alpha w} - \frac{s + \alpha w}{s + \alpha w} \right) - \alpha w$$

$$E(Ret) = -\alpha w \left(\frac{1 - s - \alpha w}{s + \alpha w} \right) - \alpha w$$

$$E(Ret) = -\alpha w (odds + 1)$$

revealed over time[3].

We now proceed to subject our model to empirical tests.

4. - Data and Estimation Results

4.1 *Data*

Our data set consists of observations on 5903 horses running in 510 races in the 1992 UK flat racing season from March 19th to May 18th inclusive. We follow Dowie [8], Tuckwell [18] and

---

[3] In KYLE's [11] model, all private information is incorporated into prices by the end of trading.

Crafts ([6] [7]) in using the forecast prices provided about horses on the morning of the race day to proxy for earliest prices. These prices are particularly useful in this regard since they are not susceptible to any pre-market influences on prices[4].

Data on the forescast price (*FP*) and starting price (*SP*) for each horse was gathered from relevant issues of the racing daily *The Sporting Life* and includes all races (except all-weather races) on standard racedays, i.e. days on which six or seven races took place and in which no horse was withdrawn too late for a fresh book to be formed.

Two adjustments are made to the *FP*. Firstly, in comparing the *FPs* and *SPs* we deduct from each *FP*, where appropriate, an amount based on the implied probability in the forecast odds of any horse(s) quoted in the morning but withdrawn before the start of the race. This is a similar deduction to that made by bookmakers when horses withdraw after a market has been formed under Tattersall's Committee Rules on Betting 4 (*c*). Secondly, it is common for a unique forecast price not to be quoted for some longshots. In these cases a price, known as the Bar Price, is allotted to these longshots. We exclude all horses for which only a Bar Price is quoted. Crafts [6] excludes some horses where the *FP* is less than the *SP* on the grounds that *FPs* are sometimes innately conservative. Since this is one of the phenomena we are investigating, however, we do not feel such a procedure is justified here. We are left with a sample of 4689 horses running in 481 races.

In order to estimate the expected return from a bet on each horse, we follow Henery [9] in using odds categories. Specifically we divide *FP* and *SP* into 25 and 26 categories respectively. The ex-post probabilities of a horse in a category winning are calculated as the number of winners divided by the total number in each category. The expected return to a unit stake in a particular category are then calculated as:

$$E \text{ (return)} = pr \text{ (winning).odds} - [(1 - pr \text{ (winning)})]$$

---

[4] With the minor exception of the small number of races about which ante-post prices (odds offered before the day of the race) are offered.

Grouping the observations in this way means that both the returns and odds variables are subject to some measurement error. The consequences of this for the regression estimates are discussed in Section 3.2 below[5].

Table 1 summarizes the spread of odds and the expected return to a unit bet for both *FP* and *SP*. In both cases, the odds frequencies are skewed towards favourites, but there are far greater number of outsiders at *SP* than at *FP*. Returns are lower on average at *FP* and in no odds category can bettors expect a positive return. At both *FP* and *SP*, returns decrease fairly consistently as the odds increase.

TABLE 1

DISTRIBUTION OF PRICES AND EXPECTED RETURNS TO £1 STAKE

Odds range	Freq (FP)	Mean E (ret)	Freq (SP)	Mean E (ret)
≤1	51	−0.0637	84	−0.0982
≤5	1164	−0.1698	1045	−0.1459
≤10	1663	−0.3315	1431	−0.2073
≤15	1493	−0.4156	832	−0.3620
≤20	193	−0.1140	716	−0.3426
≤40	110	−0.4364	487	−0.6242
≤100	15	−1	94	−0.4294
All runners	4689	−0.3109	4689	−0.2875

4.2 *Estimation Results*

Our model predicts lower expected returns for higher priced horses under the threat of insider trading and, in particular, suggests a linear relationship between expected return and the odds plus 1. We estimate the following equation for horse *i*:

---

[5] For more discussion of grouped odds, see BUSCHE K. - HALL C.D. [5]; WOODLAND L.M. - WOODLAND B.M. [21].

$$E \, (\text{ret})_i = \beta_0 + \beta_1 \, (\text{odds}_i + 1) + u_i$$

The intercept term is included to take account of a premium which may be levied in practice by bookmakers to cover their costs and is expected to be negative. A longshot bias is present if β_1 is significantly negative. Our model predicts that any longshot bias will be lower at starting prices than forecast prices. Thus we would expect β_1 to be lower (i.e. more negative) for *FPs* than for *SPs*.

As the observations are clustered within the various odds categories, least squares is likely to underestimate the standard errors. We therefore use White standard errors (White [20]), generalized to allow for cluster sampling. In addition, the fact that each of the odds categories contains a different number of observations may lead to increased heteroscedasticity problems. Thus we present weighted least squares estimates, weighted by the odds frequency[6]. Results are estimated using STATA version 4.0.

We estimate the model for *FP* and *SP* and report results in Table 2, columns I and II respectively. β_1 is significantly negative in both cases: at *FP* it is −0.0200 and at *SP* it is −0.0149. The measurement error in the dependent variable, noted above, implies that these estimates are biased towards zero. The estimated bias on β_1 in the *FP* equation (calculated as the ratio of the error variance to the total variance [see Green 1993, p. 281]) is extremely small (1.3%) whilst that for the *SP* equation is somewhat larger (9.6%).

However, after adjustment, the longshot bias is still greater at *FP* than at *SP*.

We investigate this further by pooling the data and including a dummy interaction term for the odds at forecast prices. The significant negative coefficient on this variable in column III suggests rejection of the null hypothesis that β_1 is constant across both samples but only at the 10% level of significance[7]. A link test (Pre-

---

[6] In fact, White's method does not require that the error terms are homoscedastic.

[7] The straightforward *FP* dummy is not significant at any level and is not reported here. In other words, the hypothesis that β_0 is the same across the two models cannot be rejected.

gibon [12]) suggests the inclusion of a quadratic odds term and this is reported in column IV. The fit of the model is improved slightly and the coefficient on the linear interaction term is now significant at the 1% level, providing further evidence of the greater longshot bias at *FP* than at *SP*. The estimated bias from measurement error on the pooled odds is 8.4%. This does seem capable alone of explaining the observed difference between the longshot bias at *FP* and *SP*.

4.3 *Longshot Bias at Forecast Prices*

We now concentrate on the longshot bias at *FP*, incorporating some of the race information which is available for each horse[8]. Firstly, we hypothesize that bookmakers believe that there will be less insider trading in situations where more public information is available. In order to identify and distinguish such situations, Vaughan Williams and Paton [19] separate «handicap» races (where horses are allocated weights so as to equalize as far as possible their chances of winning) from non-handicaps. The idea behind this is that the past form of horses in handicaps is generally more established in the public forum than in non-handicaps. In the latter, therefore, bookmakers are likely to believe there to be greater possibilities for betting on the basis of privately held information.

It is possible that insiders may use public information to improve their private information. For this reason we suggest considering only higher grade handicaps as indicative of the absence of useful private information. The reason is that these race types (excluding both non-handicaps and handicaps rated below 100[9]) are subject to extensive media attention and might be expected by bookmakers to offer very little opportunity for non-disclosure of useful private information. In order to measure the change in the

---

[8] In view of the small estimated bias on *FP* noted above, we do not pursue that issue further here.

[9] Handicaps are normally rated between 0 to 60 for the lowest grade handicap races and 0 to 115 for the highest grade.

longshot bias for high grade handicap races compared to other races, we include the interaction term between this dummy variable and forecast prices plus one.

Secondly, the market may be able to provide, ex-post, information on which races bookmakers believe insider trading to be prevalent. Our theoretical model suggests that bookmakers' odds will reflect the true probabilities throughout the market when there is no perceived insider trading. In this case, there is more likely to be no movement in the odds from *FP* to *SP*. Hence, a dummy variable is included for horses whose odds do not move as well as an interaction term with forecast prices plus one.

Lastly, there is some evidence (Henery [9]; Shin [15]) that both the level of returns and the longshot bias may vary with the number of runners in a race. We therefore also include the number of runners and the interaction term between number of runners and odds as control variables.

Results of this specification are reported in Table 3, column I. The two previous interaction terms are indeed positive suggesting that the longshot bias is lower in higher grade handicap races and where the odds do not move. The straight dummy terms are both negative. This implies that the fixed premium levied by the bookmakers is greater in these cases.

A link test again suggests the inclusion of a quadratic term. This is done in column II. Once again our results are robust to the different specification. Indeed, the odds variable, as well as its interaction with the dummy, are now even more significant. Interaction terms with the quadratic variable are never significant and are not reported here.

The model is replicated on starting prices in column III. Although the longshot bias is again present, none of the variables which we use as proxies for perceived insider trading prove to be significant. This provides further evidence that the threat of insider trading has less of an effect on the odds as the market progresses[10].

---

[10] Of course, these coefficients may be somewhat biased due measurement error on the odds variable, as discussed above.

5. - Conclusions

The favorite-longshot bias, i.e. the tendency for the normalized prices available about short-odds events to understate the objective winning probabilities, has been demonstrated historically in a variety of racetrack betting markets. Traditional explanations have emphasized the psychological profile and risk preferences of bettors, while some recent explanations have characterized this bias as a rational response by bookmakers facing some bettors who may possess and trade upon superior information.

This paper has tested a large new data set for the existence of this bias and identifies several methods for isolating data likely to be characterized by above-average and below-average amounts of perceived insider activity.

We find a higher longshot bias at forecast prices than at starting prices and argue that this is consistent with information on insider trading being revealed to bookmakers as the market progresses. In addition, proxy variables for the extent of perceived in-

TABLE 2

WLS ESTIMATES OF EXPECTED RETURNS*

	(I) *FP*	(II) *SP*	(III) Pooled	(IV) Pooled
Odds+1	−0.0200***	−0.0149***	−0.0143****	−0.0188****
	(0.0087)	(0.0062)	(0.0043)	(0.0059)
(Odds+1)²				7.63 *e*–5
				9.94 *e*–5
FP dummy			−0.0093**	−0.0179****
x Odds+1			(0.0049)	(0.0076)
FP dummy				5.80 *e*–5
x (Odds+1)				(4.08 *e*–4)
Constant	−0.1501***	−0.09349***	−0.1034**	−0.0549
	(0.0779)	(0.0895)	(0.0550)	0.0568)
R^2 (*adj*)	0.2517	0.4164	0.3529	0.3735
n	4689	4689	9378	9378

* White standard errors are in brackets
** indicates significance at 10% level, *** at 5% and **** at 1%.

sider trading seem to be successful in explaining at least part of this bias. In particular, the bias at *FP* is lower both for high grade handicap races and where odds subsequently do not move. Thus our empirical work supports findings that the concept of insider trading can help to explain the longshot bias.

TABLE 3

WLS ESTIMATES OF EXPECTED RETURNS
AT FORECAST AND STARTING PRICES*

	(I) *FP*	(II) *SP*	(III) Pooled
Odds+1	−0.0144** (0.0079)	−0.0260*** (0.0128)	−0.0137**** (0.0047)
$(Odds+1)^2$		5.11 *e*–4 (3.79 *e*–4)	
Handicap dummy	−0.0819*** (0.0374)	−0.0609*** (0.0296)	−0.009 (0.0162)
Handicap *x* (Odds+1)	−0.0079*** (0.0036)	−0.0060*** (0.0029)	6.05 *e*–4 (9.42 *e*–4)
No. movement	−0.0593*** (0.0316)	−0.0222*** (0.0118)	0.0599*** (0.0297)
No. movement *x* (Odds+1)	−0.0055*** (0.0026)	−0.0023**** (8.61 *e*–4)	0.0023 (0.0047)
No. runners	−0.0040 (0.0056)	−0.0050 (0.0053)	−0.0023 (0.0047)
No. runners *x* (Odds+1)	−5.64 *e*–4 (3.93 *e*–4)	−5.79 *e*–4 (3.80 *e*–4)	1.51 *e*–4 2.35 *e*–4)
Constant	−0.1810*** (0.0784)	−0.1333 (0.0913)	−0.1078**** (0.0416)
R^2 (adj)	0.2667	0.2845	0.4018
n	4689	4689	4689

* See notes Table 2.

The bookmakers expect the return to a noise trader from a unit bet on the favorite in presence of suspected insider trading to be:

$$E(ret_f) = \frac{(1-a-B_f)}{(a+B_f)} . s - (1-s)$$

The bookmakers believe that $s = a + \alpha$ with pr (0.5) and $s = a + \alpha$ with pr (0.5):

$$E(ret_f) = 0.5 \left[\frac{(1-a-B_f).(a+\alpha)}{(a+B_f)} - (1-a-\alpha) \right]$$

$$+0.5. \left[\frac{(1-a-B_f).(a+\alpha)}{(a+B_f)} - (1-a+\alpha) \right]$$

$$E(ret_f) = 0.5. \left[\frac{2a.(1-a-B_f)}{(a+B_f)} - 2 + 2a) \right]$$

$$E(ret_f) = \frac{a(1-a-B_f)}{(a+B_f)} - (1-a)$$

Similarly, expected return on the longshot is:

$$E(ret_f) = \frac{(a-B_l).(1-s)}{(1-a+B_l)} - s$$

With $s = a + \alpha$ with *pr* (0.5) and $a-\alpha$ with *pr* (0.5), this reduces to:

$$E(ret_f) = \frac{(a - B_l).(1 - a)}{(1 - a + B_l)} - a$$

Total expected net payout (*TEP*) on each horse is given by:

TEP = *w.E* (ret to insider) + (1–*w*). *e* (ret to noise trader)

We require *TEP* to be zero for both horses:

TEP (favorite) = 0

$$w.\left[\frac{(a+\alpha).(1-a-B_f)}{(a+B_f)} - (1-a-\alpha)\right] + (1-w).\left[\frac{a(1-a-B_f)}{(a+B_f)} - (1-a)\right] = 0$$

which reduces to: $\alpha w - B_f = 0$
$$B_f = \alpha w$$

TEP (longshot) = 0

$$w.\left[\frac{(1-a+\alpha).(a-B_l)}{(1-a+B_l)} - (a-\alpha)\right] + (1-w)\left[\frac{(a-B_l).(1-a)}{(1-a+B_l)} - a)\right] = 0$$

which reduces to: $\alpha w - B_l = 0$
$$B_l = \alpha w$$

Thus under the threat of insider trading, bookmakers increase their implied probabilities by an equal amount for both the favorite and longshot.

BIBLIOGRAPHY

[1] BIRD R. - MCCRAE M., «Tests of the Efficiency of Racetrack Betting Using Bookmaker Odds», *Management Science*, vol. 33, 1987, pp. 1552-62.

[2] — — — —, «The Efficiency of Racetrack Betting Markets: Australian Evidence», in: HAUSCH D.B. - LO S.Y. - ZIEMBA W.T. (eds.), *Efficiency of Racetrack Betting Markets*, London, Academic Press, 1994, pp. 575-82.

[3] BIRD R. - MCCRAE M. - BEGGS J., «Are Gamblers Really Risk Takers?», *Australian Economic Papers*, December, 1987, pp. 237-53.

[4] BUSCHE K., «Efficient Market Results in an Asian Setting», in HAUSCH D.B. - LO S.Y. - ZIEMBA W.T. (eds.), *Efficiency of Racetrack Betting Markets*, London Academic Press, 1994, pp. 615-6.

[5] BUSCHE K. - HALL C.D., «An Exception to Risk Preference Anomaly», *Journal of Business*, 1988, vol. 61, pp. 337-46.

[6] CRAFTS N.F.R., «Some Evidence of Insider Knowledge in Horse Race Betting in Britain», *Economica*, vol. 52, 1985, pp. 295-304.

[7] — —, «Winning Systems? Some Further Evidence on Insiders and Outsiders in British Horse Race Betting», in HAUSCH D.B. - LO S.Y. - ZIEMBA W.T. (eds.), *Efficiency of Racetrack Betting Markets*, London, Academic Press, 1994.

[8] DOWIE J., «On the Efficiency and Equity of Betting Markets», *Economica*, 1976, vol. 43, pp. 139-50.

[9] HENERY R.J., «On the Average Probability of Losing Bets on Horses With Given Starting Price Odds», *Journal of the Royal Statistical Society*, vol. 4, n. 148, 1985, pp. 342-49.

[10] HURLEY W. - MCDONOUGH L., «A Note on the Hayek Hypothesis and the Favorite-Longshot Bias in Parimutuel Betting», *American Economic Review*, vol. 85, 1995, pp. 949-55.

[11] KYLE A., «Continuous Auctions and Insider Trading», *Econometrica*, vol. 53, 1985, pp. 1315-35.

[12] PREGIBON D., «Goodness of Link Tests for Generalized Linear Models», *Applied Statistics*, vol. 29, 1980, pp. 15-24.

[13] QUANDT R., «Betting and Equilibrium», *Quarterly Journal of Economics*, vol. 93, 1986, pp. 66-83.

[14] SHIN H.S., «Optimal Betting Odds Against Insider Traders», *The Economic Journal*, vol. 101, 1991, pp. 1179-85.

[15] — —, «Measuring the Incidence of Insider Trading in a Market for State-Contingent Claims», *The Economic Journal*, vol. 103, 1993, pp. 1141-53.

[16] SWIDLER S. - SHAW R., «Racetrack Wagering and the "Uninformed Bettor": A Study of Market Efficiency», *Quarterly Review of Economics and Finance*, vol. 35, n. 3, 1995, pp. 305-14.

[17] THALER R. - ZIEMBA W., «Parimutuel Betting Markets: Racetracks and Lotteries», *Journal of Economic Perspectives*, vol. 2, 1988, pp. 161-74.

[18] TUCKWELL R., «The Thoroughbred Gambling Market: Efficiency, Equity and Related Issues», *Australian Economic Papers*, vol. 22, June, 1983, pp. 106-8.

[19] VAUGHAN WILLIAMS L. - PATON D., «Why is there a Favourite-Longshot Bias in British Racetrack Betting Markets?», *The Economic Journal*, forthcoming, vol. 107, n. 1, 1997.

[20] WHITE H., «A Heteroscedastricity-Consistent Covariance Matrix Estimator and a Direct Test for Heteroscedasticity», *Econometrica*, vol. 48, 1980, pp. 817-30.

[21] WOODLAND L.M. - WOODLAND B.M., «Market Efficiency and the Favorite-Longshot Bias: The Baseball Betting Market», *Journal of Finance*, vol. 49, n. 1, 1994, pp. 269-79.

[22] ZIEMBA W.T. - HAUSCH D.B., «Arbitrage Strategies for Cross-Track Betting on Major Horse Races», *Journal Business*, vol. 33, 1990, pp. 61-78.

Investment and Economic Instability

Giorgio Calcagnini - Enrico Saltari*

Università di Urbino

1. - Introduction

This paper aims at analyzing the role of uncertainty on investment and, consequently, on macroeconomic fluctuations. We focus on two types of uncertainty: demand and interest rate uncertainty.

From a theoretical point of view, we will follow recent economic literature concerning stochastic models of irreversible investment decisions, while empirically we will restrict our attention to the Italian economy.

The following discussion will mainly start from results presented in two previous papers (Calcagnini - Saltari [9]; Saltari - Calcagnini [17]), and will try to integrate them within an unified framework but without building a general equilibrium model.

We start by analyzing the influence of interest rates on investment demand. It is well known that, with the traditional neoclassical framework (r_t) a higher interest rate level will depress investment demand. It is perhaps less well known that with reversibility a higher interest rate volatility σ_r^2, will stimulate investment

---

* The authors are respectively Assistant Professor and Professor of Economics, Faculty of Economics.

N.B.: the numbers in square brackets refer to the Bibliography at the end of the paper.

demand. With irreversibility, the effect of higher interest rate volatility depends upon the assumed stochastic process that drives r_t. Indeed, the exact way σ_r^2 affects investment is the result of two opposite effects: a positive one due to the convexity of the firm's present value (and to Jensen's inequality) and a negative one due to the increase in the option value of waiting. In this paper we show that under the assumed stochastic process for r_t, an increase in interest rate volatility will make it profitable for a firm to postpone its investment decisions (Saltari - Calcagnini [17]).

As for demand, its role in determining investment spending seems clearer. While the expected demand growth rate has always a positive influence on the demand for fixed capital, both in the reversible and irreversible case, the effect of demand volatility (σ_Y^2) depends upon the nature of investment projects. When they are irreversible, an increase in demand uncertainty reduces firms' investment spending, while in the case of reversibility the exact relationship between uncertainty and investment relies on other assumptions like, for instance, the type of returns to scale (Calcagnini - Saltari [9]).

The negative role of demand uncertainty is reinforced when firms' financial and real decions are looked at simultaneously. Under uncertainty, a higher demand volatility is likely associated with higher probability of financial distress which firms tackle by reshaping their asset composition: increasing their liquid assets and postponing or giving up profitable investment opportunities (Hendel [15]). In other words, under given assumptions, both interest rate uncertainty and demand uncertainty show the same kind of relationship to investment decisions and are also (positively) correlated. In a single equation model estimation setting this correlation could give rise to multicollinearity problems, that is, only one volatility measure may result statistically significant.

Our results provide empirical evidence mainly in favor of demand uncertainty variables: an increase in the expected demand growth rate is generally associated with higher investment, while an increase in its volatility always depresses the accumulation rate. Moreover, increases in σ_r^2 seem to positively affect investment, while results for the level of the real interest rate are mixed: only during the period 1979-1995 r_t is significantly and negatively correlated with I_t.

Notwithstanding these results, we still do believe that interest rates play a significant role in explaining fluctuations on investment. However, our study, like many others, partially fails to pinpoint a reliable impact of interest rates on investment spending (Fazzari [13]). One possible explanation of this apparent paradox is that interest rates seem to affect investment decisions through the financial accelerator (see above) and the more traditional (real) accelerator: sales may change because shocks to r_t influence consumers' decisions[1]. As long as cash-flows are positively associated with sales, a higher interest rate level or volatility means both lower sales and an increase in the likelihood of financial distress, and consequently lower investment spending.

The preceding discussion provides a useful framework according to which investment fluctuates, mainly as a consequence of shocks to r_t. Indeed, our data seem to support this interpretation, at least when the two measures of volatility (demand and interest rates) are taken into account: in a simple Granger causality analysis σ_r^2 significantly causes σ_Y^2, while the opposite (i.e. $\sigma_Y^2 \rightarrow \sigma_r^2$) is not supported by empirical evidence.

Our paper is organized as follows: Section 2 briefly examines two stochastic models of investment decisions with interest rates and demand as sources of uncertainty, respectively; Section 3 describes the way we constructed our uncertainty variables and discusses the results of the estimation process. Finally, Section 4 is a summary and conclusion.

2. - Investment Under Uncertainty

In this Section we will analyze the firm's problem of determining its investment when interest rates and demand are uncer-

---

[1] This phenomenon could be particularly effective in those economies such as the Italian one, where households keep most of their financial wealth invested in fixed interest rate securities (Treasury bonds).

tain by following the standard approach found in most recent economic literature (Dixit - Pindyck [12]), (Bertola - Caballero [6]).

We consider a risk neutral firm to be one that produces a single final good with technology[2].

(1) $Y^\beta f(K)$

such that $f' = (.) > 0$ and $f'' = (.) < 0$. Moreover, we assume that
there is no depreciation and that the capital price (q) is constant
and known. In equation *(1)* Y is a demand shock and β is a positive constant. If we also assume that interest rates are uncertain,
then the firm's optimal investment can be determined by maximizing its market value $V = (.)$ or, equivalently, the expected present
value of its cash-flows:

$$(2) \quad V(Y, r, K) = \max_{\{dK\}} E_t \left\{ \int_t^\infty \exp\left(-\int_t^s r(u)\,du \right) \left[Y^\beta f(K)\,ds - qdK \right] \right\}$$

where r is the interest rate, dK is net investment and E_t denotes
the expectation conditional on information available at time t.

However, in what follows, we will analyze the effect of the two
sources of uncertainty on investment separately, so as to keep the
analytical problem tractable and to obtain closed-form solutions
which allow us to draw clear-cut conclusions.

2.1 Interest Rate Uncertainty

2.1.1 Interest Rate Uncertainty and Reversible Investment

To keep our analysis simple, here we assume that $q = 1$ and,
in order to eliminate the effect of demand shocks, that $\beta = 0$.
Therefore, equation *(2)* becomes:

---

[2] Equation *(1)* can be obtained from a set-up with a technology $F(L, K) = L^a K^b$
and a constant elasticity demand curve of the type $Q = Y P^{-\varepsilon}$. Maximizing away
labor, it can be shown that the operating profit of the firm, i.e., revenue minus
the cost of the variable factors of production, is given by $CY^\beta K^\alpha$ where $\beta = 1/\varepsilon +$
$a(1-\varepsilon)$ and $\alpha = b(\varepsilon-1)/\varepsilon + a(1-\varepsilon)$ and C is a constant (ABEL A. - EBERLY J. [2]).

(3) $V(r, K) = \max_{\{dK\}} E_t \left\{ \int_t^\infty \exp\left(-\int_t^s r(u)\, du \right) \left[f(K)\, ds - dK \right] \right\}$

Now, we also assume that r follows a Brownian stochastic process of the type:

(4) $$dr = \sigma r^{3/2} dz$$

where z is a Wiener process and σ is a constant that represents the interest rate volatility and is assumed to be less than 1[3].

The first order condition *(FOC)* for this problem is:

(5) $E_t \left\{ \int_t^\infty \exp\left(-\int_t^s r(u)\, du \right) f_K ds \right\} = 1$

where f_K represents capital marginal productivity. Equation *(5)* is a standard result for a firm's intertemporal decision problem. It states that, in equilibrium, the price of capital is to be equal to the expected value of the future flow of revenues, discounted at the market interest rate which we assume to be variable over time.

Given the stochastic process *(4)*, it can be shown that equation *(5)* becomes (Saltari - Calcagnini [17]):

(6) $$\frac{f_K}{r_t (1 - \sigma^2)} = 1$$

Equation *(6)* has two important implications. The first implication is that in a deterministic environment with a known interest rate (i.e. with $\sigma = 0$) firms demand capital up to the point where its price ($q = 1$) is equal to the ratio between the marginal revenue product of capital and its user cost. The second implication is that $\partial K / \partial \sigma^2 > 0$ for $\sigma^2 > 0$; i.e. an increase in uncertainty will lead to an

---

[3] This assumption constrains a firm's value to be finite (Cox J. - INGERSOLL J. - Ross S. [10]) and the interest rate to take on only positive values: if r goes to zero, it remains there. In other words, zero is an absorbing barrier for the assumed process.

increase in investment demand. Technically, this is due to the fact that firms' expected present value is a convex function of the interest rate. In this case, according to Jensen's inequality, an increase in σ^2 determines a higher expected firm value. Intuitively, this result means that very high and very low interest rate values are more likely to occur, and convexity ensures that the benefits of the low values more than offset the losses incurred at high values.

2.1.2 Interest Rate Uncertainty and Irreversible Investment

Here we assume that investment decisions are irreversible, meaning that scrapping is never profitable in the case that firms' past decisions turn out to be wrong. This also means that investment cannot be negative, i.e. $dK > 0$.

In this case the Bellman equation for problem *(2)* becomes:

$$(7) \qquad r_t V(r, K)\, dt = \max_{\{dK\}} \left[f(K_t)\, dt - q dK_t + E_t (dV(r, K)) \right]$$

subject to $dK > 0$ for every t. Equation *(7)* states that at the optimum the expected return, which is the sum of its cash-flow plus its expected capital gain (or loss), must be equal to the market return calculated at the current interest rate.

Applying Ito's Lemma to obtain an expression for $E_t(dV(r, K))$, given the stochastic process assumed for r (see equation *(4)*), and substituted in equation *(7)* we obtain a differential equation, the solution to which is:

$$(8) \qquad \frac{f_K}{r_t(1-\sigma^2)} + A_1 r_t^{n_1} = 1$$

where A_1 is an arbitrary constant to be definitized and $n_1 < 0$ is one of the two roots of the characteristic equation (Saltari - Calcagnini [17]).

Solution *(8)* contains two terms. The first is equal to solution *(6)* which we call fundamentals. The second term is the option value. The optimal acceptance rate[4] ($r*$) is determined by satisfying the value-matching condition and the smooth-pasting condition and a project is undertaken (i.e. the option is exercised) for $r \leq r*$. It can be shown that:

(9)
$$\frac{f_K}{(1-\sigma^2)}\left(1+\frac{1}{n_1}\right) = r_t^* = \rho_t\left(1+\frac{1}{n_1}\right) < \rho_t$$

where ρ_t is the optimal acceptance rate of the model with investment reversibility; we can note that ρ_t is larger that $r*$ since $n_1 < 0$.

Equation *(9)* states the traditional inverse relationship between the desired capital stock and the interest rate level. It also shows that, for a given capital stock, firms require a lower interest rate when irreversibility is present than when it is not.

Equation *(9)* also allows us to analyze how changes in interest rate uncertainty affect investment demand. Indeed, it can be shown that $\partial\rho/\partial\sigma^2 > 0$ and $\partial n_1/\partial\sigma^2 > 0$; therefore, in general, the total effect of an increase in σ^2 is not determined. However, given the stochastic process *(4)* that drives r_t, the option value effect is dominant (i.e. $\partial r*/\partial\sigma^2 < 0$) so that an increase in interest rate uncertainty reduces the desired capital stock or makes it more profitable to keep the option alive and to delay investment.

2.2 *Demand Uncertainty*

2.2.1 Demand Uncertainty and Reversible Investment

In this section, in order to isolate the effect of demand uncertainty, we will assume that r_t is known with certainty, that Y follows a geometric Brownian diffusion process of the type:

---

[4] $r*$ is the equivalent of what is traditionally known as marginal efficiency of capital or internal rate of return.

(10)
$$\frac{dY}{Y} = \mu dt + \sigma dz$$

where z is a Wiener process, μ is the istantaneous mean of dY/Y and σ is a constant that represents demand volatility, and finally that $q = 1$. Accordingly, equation *(2)* becomes:

(11) $$V(Y, K) = \max_{\{dK\}} E_t \left\{ \int_t^\infty \exp\left(r(s-t)\right)\left[Y^\beta f(K) ds - dK\right] \right\}$$

and the correspondent Bellman equation is:

(12) $$rVdt = \max_{\{dK\}} \{Y^\beta f(K) dt - dK + E_t(dV(Y, K))\}$$

Given the stochastic process *(10)*, and making use of Ito's Lemma to evaluate $E_t(dV(Y, K))$, we obtain the following solution for the firm's problem *(11)*:

(13) $$V = A_1 Y^{n1} + A_2 Y^{n2} + \frac{Y^2 f(K)}{\phi(\beta)}$$

where A_1 and A_2 are two constants to be definitized, and $n_1 > 0$ and $n_2 < 0$ are the two roots of the characteristic equation (Calcagnini - Saltari [9]).

    In equation *(13)* $Y^\beta f(K)/\phi(\beta)$ is the expected present value associated with K since $[\phi(\beta)]^{-1} = 1/r - m$ is a discount factor with r equal to the market interest rate and m the expected growth rate of profits. Moreover, $Y^\beta f(K)/\phi(\beta)$ is the fundamental value of the firm since $A_1 Y^{n1}$ can be eliminated based on the no arbitrage condition (there are no speculative bubbles in our model) and $A_2 Y^{n2}$ gives rise to a solution with no economic meaning.
Given the *FOC* for problem *(11)*, $V_K = 1$, and equation *(13)*, we obtain that:

(14)
$$\frac{Y^{\beta} f'(K)}{\phi(\beta)} = 1$$

or since $n = \beta\mu + \sigma^2/2\ \beta\ (\beta - 1)$

(15)
$$r = Y^{\beta} f'(K) + \beta\mu + \frac{\sigma^2}{2}\beta(\beta - 1)$$

Since r is an exogenous variable for the firm, equation *(15)* determines the optimal or desired capital stock. From equation *(15)* we see that *a)* an increase in the expected demand growth rate always increases firms' desired capital stock; *b)* an increase in demand volatility will determine a higher (lower) capital stock when $\beta > 1$ ($\beta < 1$)[5]. Finally, an increase in σ^2 will have no effect on K when $\beta = 1$.

In the case of a Cobb-Douglas production technology $f(K) = K^{\alpha}$ ($\alpha < 1$)[6] it can be shown that firms' demand for capital is:

(16)
$$K = \left(\frac{\phi(\beta)}{\alpha}\right)^{\frac{1}{\alpha-1}} Y^{\frac{\beta}{1-\alpha}} \equiv cY^{\gamma}, \gamma = \frac{\beta}{1-\alpha}$$

and that, by applying Ito's Lemma to equation *(16)*, the expected capital growth rate is (Calcagnini - Saltari [9]):

(17)
$$\frac{1}{dt}\frac{E_t(dK)}{K} = \gamma\mu + \gamma(\gamma - 1)\frac{\sigma^2}{2}$$

Equation *(17)* shows that an increase in the expected demand growth rate always has a positive effect on investment, while the precise effect of demand volatility on investment depends on γ: if $\gamma = 1$, that is $\alpha + \beta = 1$, I will be independent of σ^2. In particular,

---

[5] β should also be less than n_1 otherwise it can be shown that $\phi(\beta) = r - m$ becomes negative.
[6] See also footnote 2.

it can be shown that this holds when returns to scale are constant[7]. Diversely, when returns to scale are increasing (decreasing) we have that $\alpha + \beta > 1$ $(\alpha + \beta < 1)$ and $\gamma > 1$ $(\gamma < 1)$ meaning that a higher (lower) σ^2 will positively (negatively) affect investment.

2.2.2 Demand Uncertainty and Irreversible Investment

Here we assume that there is no secondary market for capital, or that reducing K is infinitely costly. Consequently, the firm's problem can still be represented by equation *(11)*, subject to the additional constraint $dK > 0$. In this case, the solution for the Bellman equation that corresponds to equation *(11)* is:

$$(18) \qquad V = \frac{Y^{\beta} f(K)}{\phi(\beta)} + BY^{n_1}$$

where n_1 is the positive root of the characteristic equation, as in the previous case (Calcagnini - Saltari [9]) and B is a function of K. According to the solution *(18)*, the firm's value has two terms: the first is once again the fundamental, while the second term represents the option value.

To determine the level of the marginal product at which making an investment is profitable, we make use fo the value matching condition and the smooth pasting condition:

$$(19) \qquad V_K = \frac{Y^{\beta} f'(K)}{\phi(\beta)} + B'(K) Y^{n_1} = 1$$

$$(20) \qquad V_{KY} = \beta \frac{Y^{\beta-1} f'(K)}{\phi(\beta)} + B'(K) n_1 Y^{n_1} - 1 = 0$$

---

[7] Given α and β as in footnote 2, it can be easily shown that $\alpha + \beta = 1$ if $a + b = 1$.

From equation *(19)* and *(20)* we obtain:

$$(21) \qquad \frac{n_1}{n_1 - \beta} \phi(\beta) = Y^\beta f'(K^*)$$

Given our assumption of capital irreversibility, equation *(21)* still does not allow us to determine the expected accumulation rate. Indeed, in the presence of negative demand shocks we obtain that:

$$(22) \qquad Y^\beta f'(K^*) < \frac{n_1}{n_1 - \beta} \phi(\beta)$$

but firms' capital stock cannot be adjusted. In the opposite case, firms will adjust capital to the new demand level and investment occurs.

If we specify firms' production technology as we did earlier:

$$(23) \qquad f(K) = K^\alpha$$

with $\alpha < 1$, and making use of the theory of Brownian motions, we are able to determine the long-run distribution of the marginal product of capital and the correspondent accumulation rate. Indeed, in this case, it can be shown that the expected accumulation rate is (Dixit - Pindyck [12]; Harrison [14]):

$$(24) \qquad \frac{1}{dt} \frac{E_t(dK)}{K} = \gamma \left(\mu - \frac{\sigma^2}{2} \right)$$

where, as before, γ is a parameter that depends on production returns to scale (Calcagnini - Saltari [19]).

Equation *(24)* shows that, given a Cobb-Douglas technology and investment irreversibility, in the long-run: 1) an increase in the expected demand growth rate always has a positive effect on expected investment; 2) an increase in demand uncertainty has always a negative effect on expected investment.

3. - The Empirical Evidence

3.1 *Investment and Uncertainty: Some Descriptive Measures*

In this section we will describe some uncertainty measures and analyze their influence on investment demand in Italy for the period 1970-1995.

We decided to concentrate on demand uncertainty, firstly, because firms seem to pay more attention to conditions regarding demand than other economic variables and, secondly, because we will then make use of results from this analysis as a benchmark for interpreting the influence of interest rate uncertainty on investment.

Table 1 shows results from a bi-annual survey carried out by ISCO (Istituto Nazionale per lo Studio della Congiuntura, Rome) among Italian industrial firms. The importance of demand conditions on investment is generally greater than financial or technical factors; but it becomes more important during recessions when, as we should expect if investment is irreversible, firms find it harder to adjust their capital stock to the new product demand level (Table 1)[8].

Other reasons why we started from analyzing demand uncertainty are that, *a*) it is generally not a simple task to identify which (short-term or long-term) interest rate is relevant for investment decisions (Abel [1]) and *b*) a simultaneity problem may exist between shifts in the marginal product of capital and the interest rate. As a consequence, the expected negative relationship between interest rates and investment might be masked by the positive relationship between *r* and investment, in response to exogenous shifts in the investment function (Black [7], Calcagnini [9], Abel [1]). Finally, as we said in the Introduction, investment is more

---

[8] The importance of demand conditions for firms' investment decisions also emerges from a survey periodically carried out by Banca d'Italia (BARCA - CANNARI - BENEDETTO - GAVOSTO - MENDOLIA [4]).

TABLE 1

FACTORS AFFECTING INVESTMENT
(PERCENTAGE DISTRIBUTION OF ANSWERS)

Year	Demand evolution	Access to capital markets	Technical factors
1987	83	80	59
1988	88	79	56
1989	89	73	59
1990	53	42	51
1991	46	43	54
1992	38	33	41
1993	86	29	34
1994	91	31	31
1995	93	34	36

Source, Isco, *Inchiesta semestrale sugli investimenti*, various years.

likely affected by interest rates through the financial accelerator than directly by its level or volatility.

To avoid one of the most common shortcomings associated with uncertainty measures, i.e. they are *ex-post* volatility indicators, we once again made use of results from another monthly survey carried out by ISCO among industrial firms. In particular, we took into consideration two types of answers referring to entrepreneur expectations on orders and production over the 3-4 months to come. Data refer to the whole sample of firms and are provided as a percentage distribution broken down into three types of answers: increase, stability, decrease.

Using this distribution of values we constructed a first demand uncertainty indicator (σ_Y^2) for orders (but we did the same for production) as the inverse of the percentage of firms that expect a stable level of orders[9]. In this case, an increase in σ_Y^2 means that the number of firms (in percentage values) that expect higher and lower orders increased. However, this piece of information

---

[9] More precisely, by σ_Y^2 we mean $E_{t-1}\,(\sigma_Y^2)$, that is the expected value at time t -1 of demand volatility prevailing at time t.

is similar to a mean preserving spread, that is it attaches the same weight to extreme values[10].

However, in the economic literature concerning irreversible investment, it has been shown that «only bad news matters» (Bernanke [4]). In other words, firms' willingness to invest would depend on the likelihood that only positive states of nature occur next period. Then, following this approach, we constructed a new demand uncertainty indicator (σ_Y^2+) as the inverse of increase in their orders.

As we would have expected, we notice that both σ_Y^2 and σ_Y^2+ are anticyclical, but the latter shows a greater variability than the former (Table 2). Moreover, σ_Y^2+ shows a stronger correlation with the investment rate than σ_Y^2, a result that seems to support the «only bad news matters» approach, and in most of the cases the effect of uncertainty on investment is the strongest at $t = 0$ (Table 3 and footnote 9)[11].

TABLE 2

CYCLICAL INDICATORS

	1980.2–1983.2 recession	1983.3–1992–2 expansion	1992.3–1994.1 recession
Investment rate[a]	9.92	10.70	9.68
Degree of capital utilization	72.10	76.37	74.41
σ_Y^2 [b]	1.08	1.02	1.07
σ_Y^2+ [b]	1.09	0.89	0.96

[a] Ratio between equipment and value added, whole economy.
[b] Base 1975.4-1977.1 = 1.00. Both volatility indicators refer to industrial firms' demand.
Source, Our calculations Isco and Istat, based on data.

---

[10] As an alternative indicator we explicitly estimated the variance of the distribution of answers following (DASGUPTA D. - LAHIRI K. [11]; PARIGI G. - SCHLITZER G. [16]). However, results are qualitatively the same as with the use of σ_Y^2.

[11] Besides the type of demand uncertainty indicators described above, the ISCO investment survey allows us to construct an investment revision index (*IRI*). In another paper we constructed it as the difference between planned and realized investment and we noticed that *IRI* showed a strong positive correlation with σ_Y^2+. We interpreted this result as another piece of evidence in favor of irreversible investment theories (CALCAGNINI G. - SALTARI E. [9]).

TABLE 3

CORRELATION ANALYSIS BETWEEN THE INVESTMENT
RATE AT TIME *t* AND UNCERTAINTY AT TIME *t*, *t*–1
AND *t*–2, 1970.1-1995.2

	Quarter *t*	Quarter *t*–1	Quarter *t*–2
Orders			
σ_Y^2	–0.40	–0.34	–0.13
σ_Y^2 +	–0.43	–0.32	–0.10
Production			
σ_Y^2	–0.27	–0.17	–0.16
σ_Y^2 +	–0.49	–0.33	–0.06

Source, Our calculations on Isco and Istat data.

3.2 *Investment and Uncertainty: the Econometric Results*

In this section we test the relationship between investment
and uncertainty using as a benchmark model *(17)* or, equivalently, model *(24)*. Indeed, both models state that investment reacts
positively to the growth rate of demand and negatively to its volatility, even if we require more stringent assumptions in the case
of reversibility (see above). In particular, we should require that γ
< 1 in order to always find a negative effect of demand uncertain-
ty on investment. This restriction can be easily tested looking at
the estimated coefficient of the growth rate of demand (μ).

From preliminary tests, we found that the investment rate
(*dK/K* = *I/K*) is integrated of order 1, i.e. *I* (1), while the value added growth rate (μ and our uncertainty measures (for orders and
production, respectively) are all stationary (i.e. *I* (0))[12].

---

[12] Quarterly capital stock data are constructed using a perpetual inventory and
a constant rate of depreciation (10% for equipment and 16.5% for means of transport), starting from the 1970 value published in ANNUNZIATO P. - MANFRONI P. - RO-
SA G. [3].

Therefore, since I/K and Y are also not cointegrated, we adopted the following specification:

$$(25) \qquad \Delta\left(\frac{I}{K}\right)_t = b_0 + b_1\mu_t + b_2 (\sigma_Y^2)_t + \varepsilon_t$$

where all variables have been previously specified and ε_t is an error term with the usual properties, and estimates are IV (Instrumental variables) in order to avoid the well known simultaneity problem between I and μ[13].

Results are shown in columns 1 and 2 (for orders and production respectively) of Table 4, and strongly support model (25): expected demand growth rate has a positive effect on the investment rate, while demand volatility has a negative effect. Moreover, $b_1 < 1$ and $b_1 > b_2$ as can be checked by looking at the beta coefficients corresponding to b_1 and b_2 : $\tilde{b}_1 = 0.217$ and $\tilde{b}_2 = -0.064$ respectively, for orders, and $\tilde{b}_1 = 0.226$ and $\tilde{b}_2 = -0.051$ for production[14].

In the short run changes in I/K are largely due to changes in I, therefore we re-estimated equation (25) after substituting I/K with ΔI ($ln\ I_t - ln\ I_{t-1}$). Since both series I and Y are I (1) and cointegrated (with a cointegration vector equal to $[1, -1.249]$), we also added an error correction term ($\lambda_t = ln\ I_t - 1.249\ ln\ Y_t$) to the r.h.s. variables. Consequently, equation (25) became:

$$(26) \qquad \Delta I_t = b_0 + b_1 \mu_t + b_2 (\sigma_Y^2)_t + b_3 \lambda_{t-1} + \varepsilon_t$$

and its corresponding IV estimates are shown in Table 5.

Estimated coefficients of equation (26) all have the expected sign and they confirm the positive effect of the demand growth rate and the negative one of demand volatility as in model (25). In particular, within model (26) σ_Y^2 seems to play a greater role than within model (25): its beta coefficient is one-half of the one

---

[13] As instruments we used the constant and all the variables on the r.h.s. of equation (25) up to lag 4.

[14] However, we also note that $\tilde{b}_1 > 1/2\ \tilde{b}_2$ as implied by equation (24).

TABLE 4

IV ESTIMATES FOR MODEL *(25)*, 1971.2-1995.3*

	Model A: orders 1. $\Delta I/K$	Model B: production 2. $\Delta I/K$
Constant	0.194	0.194
	(1.40)	(1.09)
μ_t	0.137***	0.145***
	(4.87)	(5.85)
$(\sigma_Y^2)_t$	−0.243***	−0.256**
	(−2.55)	(−1.91)
R^2	0.460	0.444
SE	0.124	0.127
DW	2.090	2.072
Nobs	98	98

* Student-t values are in parentheses;
significance level: ** = 0.10, *** = 0.05.

TABLE 5

IV ESTIMATES FOR MODEL *(26)*, 1971.2-1995.3*

	Model A: orders 1. ΔI	Model B: production 2. ΔI
Constant	−33.643	−38.030**
	(1.44)	(1.92)
μ_t	2.404***	1.952***
	(2.90)	(3.04)
$(\sigma_Y^2)_t$	−6.629***	−11.787***
	(−2.46)	(−3.83)
λ_{t-1}	−7.69	−9.690***
	(−1.57)	(−2.34)
R^2	0.476	0.519
SE	2.640	2.489
DW	1.810	1.754
Nobs	98	98

* Student-*t* values are in parentheses;
significance level: ** = 0.10, *** = 0.05.

for demand growth rate (–0.306 and 0.629, respectively) in the case of orders, and –0.394 and 0.511 in the case of production. Moreover, the negative value of b_3, even if it is not always statistically significant, means that adjustments in the equilibrium ratio I/Y mainly occur through changes in I, or that investment volatility is higher than demand (or production) volatility, as is historically documented in all national accounts[15].

As for the effect of interest rate uncertainty on investment, and in order to empirically analyze equations *(6)* and *(9)*, we first need to specify the production function $f(K)$: here we assume again that firms' technology can be represented as in equation *(23)*. In this case $f_K = \alpha Y/K$ and, consequently, equation *(6)* can be re-written as:

$$(27) \qquad \ln K_t = \ln \alpha + \ln Y_t - \ln t_t - \ln (1 - \sigma_t^2)$$

while in the case of equation *(9)* we have:

$$(28) \qquad \ln K_t = \ln a + \ln Y_t - \ln r_t - \ln (1 - s_t^2) + \ln \left(1 + \frac{1}{n_1} \right)$$

Remembering that $\partial n_1/\partial \sigma^2 > 0$ and that $n_1 < 0$, the last two terms of equation *(28)* show that demand for capital depends both positively and negatively on interest rate volatility, respectively: which of the two effect prevails is an empirical matter. In order to obtain empirical estimates, the two models can be nested in the following specification:

$$(29) \qquad \Delta \left(\frac{I}{K} \right)_t = \ln c_0 + c_1 \mu_t + c_2 \ln r_t + (c_3 - c_4)(\ln \sigma_r^2)_t + \varepsilon_t$$

where $\Delta (I/K)_t$, μ_t and ε_t have been previously defined and $c_0 = \ln \alpha$.

Moreover, r_t is calculated as the nominal interest rate on long-term bonds issued by private companies minus the inflation rate, while σ_r^2 is the standard error of the monthly real interest rate for

---

[15] This adjustment mechanism has been tested by a traditional Granger causality test. Indeed, at the 5% probability level, we accept the hypothesis that Y causes I, but we can reject the opposite hypothesis that I causes Y.

each quarter of our sample. While we expect that $c_1 > 0$, $c_2 < 0$, we cannot say anything about the sign of the coefficient of σ_r^2: it all depends on whether the positive effect of the interest rate volatility (due to the convexity of the firm's value function and to the well known effect of Jensen's inequality) is greater, equal to or smaller than the negative effect (due to the option value). IV estimates of equation *(29)* are shown in Table 6.

In order to correctly interpret estimates in Table 6, it should be pointed out that we replaced r_t with $1/1 + r_t$ since our real interest rate series contains negative values[16]. Consequently, we should correctly expect $c_2 > 0$.

TABLE 6

IV ESTIMATES FOR MODEL *(25)*, AUGMENTED WITH THE INTEREST RATE AND ITS VOLATILITY, 1971.2-1995.2*

	Model A: orders		
	1971.2-1995-2		1979.1-1995.2
	1. $\Delta\,I/K$	2. $\Delta\,I/K$	3. $\Delta\,I/K$
Constant	−0.139***	0.485**	1.124***
	(−3.05)	(1.78)	(4.24)
μ_t	0.159***	0.103***	−0.002
	(6.39)	(3.56)	(−0.04)
$(\sigma_Y^2)_t$		−0.406***	−0.825***
		(−2.18)	(−4.44)
$1/1+r_t$	−0.141	−0.051	1.296***
	(0.29)	(−0.09)	(2.05)
$(\sigma_r^2)_t$	−0.013	0.062**	0.073***
	(−0.31)	(1.89)	(1.97)
R^2	0.387	0.480	0.434
SE	0.135	0.121	0.094
DW	1.984	1.957	1.362
Nobs	97	97	66

* Student-t values are in parentheses; significance level: ** = 0.10, *** = 0.05.

---

[16] We also estimated equation *(29)* without taking the log of r_t and σ_r^2. Results and their correspondent interpretation do not change significantly.

Two different versions of model *(29)*, with or without demand volatility (Table 6, columns 1 and 2), have been estimated, since results which exclude σ_Y^2 are disappointing (only μ significantly affects investment demand). Therefore, the augmented version of model *(29)* can also be seen as a test of the robustness of model *(25)*. This augmented version was estimated over the entire sample and over the last seventeen years (Table 6, column 3) during which firms likely perceived as more credible the stance of the monetary policy mainly oriented towards controlling inflation (Saltari - Calcagnini [17]).

Results for the period 1971-1995 confirm our previous estimates according to which investment seems more affected by demand variables than financial variables. The interest rate level is not statistically significant[17], while its volatility has a positive and statistically significant effect on capital accumulation (Table 6). However, if we look at the beta coefficients (–0.42 for σ_Y^2 and 0.32 for σ_r^2, respectively), the total effect of uncertainty (demand plus the interest rate) on investment is still negative. Among all variables, the demand growth rate has the largest and positive effect: indeed, its beta coefficient is equal to 0.62.

As for the period 1979-1995, firms seem to have traded off the increase in the real interest rate with a lower demand growth rate: c_1 and c_2 are statistically not significant and significant, respectively, as opposed to their estimates over the whole period 1971-1995. Instead, no changes are observed in the estimated coefficients of demand and interest rate volatility. However, the role of the former is reinforced: indeed beta coefficients are –0.84 and 0.42, respectively. All together these results give us the idea that firms mainly paid attention to demand variables as long as they had access to cheap funding, while in the presence of high and increasing real interest rates their investment decisions were affected by both real (especially demand volatility) and financial fac-

---

[17] Indeed, for most of the 1970s, our calculated real interest rate is negative. This fact may also explain why our empirical results are not much in accordance with our theoretical conclusions: equations *(6)* and *(9)* were obtained under the assumption that r_t follows a stochastic process as described by equation *(4)* which does not admit negative values for the real interest rate.

tors. In other words, during the most recent period, firms' likelihood of going bankrupt due to demand uncertainty increased because of tighter financial equilibrium conditions. Indeed, in the presence of high interest rates and shocks to demand growth rate, firms may not be able to generate enough cash-flow to meet their financial obligations and, therefore, their likelihood to go bankrupt will increase.

Finally, we carried out an experiment to check for possible interactions between real and financial shocks. In particular, according to a simple Granger causality test, σ_r^2 seems to significantly affect σ_Y^2, while the opposite (i.e. $(\sigma_Y^2 \to \sigma_r^2)$ is not supported by empirical evidence. This result seems to increase the importance of financial shocks in determining investment, not only directly but also indirectly (and negatively) through its influence on demand volatility.

4. - Conclusions

In this paper we studied a stochastic model of investment in the presence of interest rate and demand uncertainty, which allowed us to analyze the role of variable levels together with their volatility in affecting firms' accumulation decisions.

From a theoretical point of view it is important to distinguish between the case of reversible investment from that of irreversible investment.

In the first case, while an increase in interest rates and expected demand has the traditional effect on investment (negative and positive respectively), an increase in σ_r^2 always has a positive effect and the effect of σ_Y^2 depends upon the type of returns to scale assumed: a higher demand volatility determines a higher (lower) investment demand when returns are increasing (decreasing). When returns to scale are constant, σ_Y^2 will have no effect on I.

In the second case, while the effect of the two variable levels is the same as in the previous case, an increase in σ_r^2 will generally have an undetermined effect on investment demand. However, we showed that given a particular stochastic process (but also often-used in the finance literature) for r, an increase in σ_r^2 will determine a lower I. Conversely, an increase in σ_Y^2 will always reduce investment.

From an empirical point of view, our results show that investment in Italy mainly responds to changes in the level and volatility of demand, while r and σ_r^2 seem to have a more explanatory role since 1980. However, the latter may be the result of two shortcomings of the most traditional approach to investment analysis. The first, form which our study is also not exempt, is the use of reduced-form models; the second is the attempt at detecting a direct channel through which r, or monetary policy, affects investment demand without taking into account the existence of many capital market imperfections. We find this last unresolved question a promising avenue for future research.

BIBLIOGRAFY

[1] ABEL A., *Consumption and Investment*, vol. II, Chapter 14, Amsterdam (The Netherlands), North Holland, 1990, pp. 725-78.

[2] ABEL A. - EBERLY J., «Optimal Investment With Costly Reversibility», *Review of Economic Studies*, vol. 63, n. 217, 1996, pp. 581-93.

[3] ANNUNZIATO P. - MANFRONI P. - ROSA G., «La stima del capitale per settore e area geografica e alcuni indici di produttività», *CSC Ricerche*, n. 66, 1992.

[4] BARCA F. - CANNARI L. - BENEDETTO C.D. - GAVOSTO A. - MENDOLIA A., «Metodi e risultati dell'indagine sugli investimenti delle imprese industriali», Supplemento al *Bollettino Statistico*, vol. 59, 1996.

[5] BERNANKE B., «Irreversibility, Uncertainty and Cyclical Investment», *Quarterly Journal of Economics*, n. 98, 1983, pp. 85-106.

[6] BERTOLA G. - CABALLERO R., «Irreversibility and Aggregate Investment», *Review of Economic Studies*, n. 61, 1994, pp. 223-46.

[7] BLACK F., *Exploring General Equilibrium*, London, MIT Press, 1995.

[8] CALCAGNINI G., «Debito pubblico e decisioni di investimento, quali i riflessi sulle imprese italiane?», *Moneta e Credito*, vol. XLV, n. 180, 1992, pp. 451-72.

[9] CALCAGNINI G - SALTARI E., «Un'analisi del principio dell'acceleratore in condizioni di incertezza», in CALCAGNINI G. - RODANO G. - VERCELLI A. (eds.), *La dinamica complessa dell'economia italiana: cicli e trend*, forthcoming, Roma, ISCO, *Rassegna di Lavori*, 1997.

[10] COX J. - INGERSOLL J. - ROSS S., «An Analysis of Variable Rate Loan Contracts», *Journal of Finance*, n. 35, May 1980, pp. 389-403.

[11] DASGUPTA D. - LAHIRI K., «On the Use of Dispersion Measures from Napm Surveys in Business Cycle Forecasting», *Journal of Forecasting*, n. 12, 1993, pp. 239-53.

[12] DIXIT A. - PINDYCK R., *Investment Under Uncertainty*, Princeton, Princeton University Press, 1994.

[13] FAZZARI S., «Monetary Policy, Financial Structure, and Investment», chapter 3, *Economic Policy Institute Series*, Armonk (NY), Sharpe, Inc., 1993, pp. 35-63.

[14] HARRISON J., *Brownian Motion and Stochastic Flow Systems*, New York, J. Wiley.

[15] HENDEL I., «Competition Under Financial Distress», *The Journal of Industrial Economics*, vol. XLIV, n. 3, 1996, pp. 309-24.

[16] PARIGI G. - SCHLITZER G., «Indicatori ciclici e modelli econometrici», in BANCA D'ITALIA, *Ricerche quantitative per la politica economica*, vol. I, 1993, pp. 1-52.

[17] SALTARI E. - CALCAGNINI G., «Instabilità dei mercati finanziati e decisioni di investimento», *Rivista Internazionale di Scienze sociali*, vol. CIII, 1995, pp. 333-52.

II - RISK MANAGEMENT, BANKING SYSTEM AND FINANCIAL MARKETS

Measuring Credit Risk in Bank Loans: Pricing and Risk Management Implications

Pier Luigi Gilibert*

European Investment Bank, Luxembourg

1. - Introduction

Applied research in finance has offered new tools (e.g. «value-at-risk») to intermediaries having to cope with certain forms of market exposures. This research has been, at least partly, motivated by the wish to influence legislation in the area of capital requirements. This objective seems to have been attained, as regulators now look more leniently towards in-house risk assessment models and seem ready, within limits, to countenance their use for meeting solvency standards.

However, credit (or default) risk incurred by banks in their ordinary lending operations has received comparatively less attention, even though capital regulations for credit-risk taking are generally deemed unsatisfactory for their «rule-of-thumb» risk-weighting approach. Particularly resented is that they do not sufficiently distinguish within classes of borrowers (e.g., an AAA-rated international corporation is considered as risky as a start-up firm),

---

* The author, Economist, wishes to thank E. Barone of Istituto Mobiliare Italiano for his useful comments on an earlier draft, and for contributing the Appendix. Of course, the author only is responsible for the opinions expressed in the paper, as well as for any remaining errors.

N.B.: the numbers in square brackets refer to the Bibliography at the end of the paper.

across them (e.g., it is always safer to lend to a bank than to an industrial concern), or among loans with different cash-flow (e.g., it is as much hazardous to lend for 3 months as for 10 years) or legal features (e.g., a subordinated loan implies the same loss expectation as a senior-ranking one extended to the same borrower). As a result, the link between the amount of risk taken on by a lender and its minimum required capitalisation is tenuous at best.

A related issue concerns the valuation of third-party credit support to bank loans (or, more generally, to debt instruments), which current bank solvency legislation recognises only to the extent that it is supplied by another credit institution. Yet, there is hardly a solid foundation for such a regulatory choice. Ideally, the added value provided by an external credit enhancer to the lender seeking protection against default risk should be assessed within a valuation framework encompassing both the third party's intrinsic solvency, as exemplified by its rating (i.e., a measure of its capacity to absorb general operating risk), and its relationship with the main obligor (i.e., its ability to shoulder a specific type of credit risk). Such a framework should be able to tell which of these two considerations is the more relevant in any situation, and how they combine. The problem can be looked at under at least two related angles.

The first can be resumed in the following question: where should the lending bank (i.e., the purchaser of financial insurance) primarily look when evaluating the attractions of different external loan support structures, and how should it account for the risk-transfer they allow? To approach this issue, the lender can be looked at as a consumer «shopping» for insurance services, and therefore in need for a tool to discriminate good from bad bargains on a price/quality basis. This is not an idle question, since minimising the cost of financial insurance (or maximising its benefits) is, for any lender, an important part of efficient credit-risk management.

The second aspect is more general, and involves the future directions the banking industry might take. If, as it has been argued (see, for instance. Crane - Bodie [9]), the institutional structure of banking is moving towards a stronger functional specialisation, then the supply of funds to borrowers can be separated from the activities of risk-assessment and risk-bearing. Credit support structures, alongside other risk-hedging mechanisms, could then be provided by specialised firms, rather than bundled into financial packages made up of heterogeneous components, with hidden cross-subsidies running from one to the other. Any such evolution presupposes a keen understanding of risk-measuring methodologies and risk-transferring mechanisms. All the more so in economies, such as Europe's, where the corporate bond market is of scant significance and cannot be relied upon to offer valuable information on credit risk.

In short, credit-risk assessment, allocation of capital and its remuneration are both major regulatory problems and important bank management issues. Their solution requires a unified and coherent framework, which this paper attempts to provide. It starts by introducing the familiar concept of «expected loss», in conjunction with historic (bond) default frequencies and the assumption of risk-neutrality. This framework is tested over a range of loan features impinging on credit-risk, and then extended to the valuation of loan guarantees. Several analogies with option pricing are drawn along the way, and then used in explaining the nature of credit risk. The paper closes with a discussion of the «unexpected loss», a useful concept when trying to capture the different degrees of risk aversion of bank managers and regulators.

2. - Risk-Neutral Loan Pricing

Following an often made assumption, a world of risk-neutral agents (lenders, borrowers, and credit insurers) is posited. In equilibrium, the following «break-even» relationship will then hold for a one-period, $ 1 loan:

$$q (1 + R^*) \, rr + (1 - q) (1 + R^*) = (1 + R)$$

where R is riskless rate (e.g., a government bond yield), rr stands for the «recovery rate» (that is, the fraction of a defaulted loan that is recovered by the lender)[1], q is the borrower's default probability over the loan's life, and R^* is the risky lending rate we want to find. In other words, in equilibrium, the end-of-period expected value of the loan must be worth as much as a sure sum of cash, of size equal to the loan's face value, invested in a risk-free instrument. Solving for the risky lending rate, we obtain:

$$R^* = (1 + R)/[q \; rr + (1 - q)] - 1$$

It is easily shown that if either q or R increase, R^* also increases, while if rr falls R^* rises. Of course, if $q = 0$ and/or $rr = 1$, then $R^* = R$, for the loan is riskless. The loan's «expected loss» (E^*) is defined as:

$$E^* = q \; (1 + R^*) \; (1 - rr)/(1 + R)$$

while the expected (i.e., risk-adjusted) revenues from the loan are found by subtracting the future value of the expected loss, or $E^* (1 + R)$, from that of the promised (i.e., contractual) revenues $(1 + R^*)$. Since this difference is equal to $(1 + R)$, one can write:

$$R^* = R + E^* (1 + R)$$

In other words, the equilibrium risk-spread $RS = (R^* - R)$ charged to the borrower is such that the revenues from it are just sufficient to offset the lender's expectation of loss. Hence, the risk-adjusted return on the loan is equal to that obtainable on an investment yielding the riskless rate. Put differently, if the lender's

---

[1] It is also common to conduct the expected loss analysis in terms of «loss severity» $(1 - rr)$ rather than using the recovery rate. It should be noted that, while the default probability is borrower-specific, the recovery rate is more appropriately referred to the asset (i.e., loan, bond) whose risk is being assessed. As such it will be used to characterise the loan's seniority, its legal structure and its level of collateralisation.

debt is risk-free, the anticipated returns on the lender's debt and equity are the same[2].

We now extend these results to the more general case where there is a whole yield curve, different timings of possible defaults, and the loan is paid back gradually over time. The model's structure is similar to those developed by Fons [10] and Jonkhart [14], and is set out in more detail in the Appendix.

---

[2] In ordinary banking practice, a more common formulation for the lending rate is obtained by substituting the riskless rate R with the (after-tax) rate of return the lender feels it can obtain on alternative investments, often called the «hurdle» rate, or H. As will be seen. H is the lender (after-tax) risk-adjusted average cost of funds. Anyway, H replaces R in the above formula for the lending rate R^*, and the risk-pricing decisions may simply be recast in terms of H (one for each maturity). Furthermore, if F ($> R$; $< H$) is the lender's all-in borrowing cost and «c» is the fraction of the loan funded with equity ($0 < c < 1$), then the end-of-period dollar value of the contractual net revenues C (NR) on the $ 1 loan is equal to $[(1 + R^*) - ((1 + F)(1 - c)]$. Subtracting from C (NR) the end-of-period value of the expected loss, one obtains the expected (or, risk-adjusted) net revenues, that is:

$$E(NR) = (H - F) + c(1 + F)$$

The lender's promised return on equity (ROE) is obtained by noting that c ($1 + ROE$) = C (NR), therefore obtaining $ROE = F + (R^* - F)/c$. The corresponding expected measure is likewise found starting from c ($1 + E(ROE)$) = $E(NR)$, so that:

$$E(ROE) = F + (H - F)/c$$

where the second term on the right-hand-side denotes the gains from debt financing (or leverage). Furthermore, one may define the lender's nominal return on assets as: $ROA = [C(NR) - c]$, so that $ROA = R^* - (1 - c)F$. Subtracting the end-of-period value of the expected loss from ROA one obtains the expected ROA, namely:

$$E(ROA) = (H - F) + cF$$

In case of an all-equity bank ($c = 1$), $E(ROA) = E(ROA) = H$. If $R = H = F$, which is the special case treated in the text, then $E(ROE) = R$ and $E(ROA) = cR$. Finally, the risk-adjusted average cost of funds for the lender (assuming «c» is both the marginal and the «target» capital ratio of the lender) is:

$$E(ACF) = (1 - c)F + c(F + (H - F)/c) = H$$

As Merton R.C. [9] stresses in a survey of certain credit-risk issues («junk» bonds and loan guarantees), one should always be careful to distinguish among promised, expected and realised returns, where the first provides a ceiling of the other two. In what follows, the term «expected» is used in the meaning of «risk-adjusted». In common parlance. $E(ROE)$ is also known as risk-adjusted return on capital ($RAROC$), while the acronym for $E(ROA)$ is $RAROA$. These concepts will be referred to again in paragraph 2.3.

Pier Luigi Gilibert

2.1 *The Loan's Expected Loss*

We shall now consider a $ 100, junior subordinated unsecured 3-year bank loan, extended to a borrower having a Moody's/Standard & Poor's rating of *Ba1/BB* +, and to be paid back in two equal instalments at the end of the second and third years. The risk-free, par yield-to-maturity (*YTM*) curve is assumed to start at 7% for 1-year «bullet» loans, and step up by 0.25% for each additional year of final maturity (column (*i*) of Table 1). The risk-free par *YTM* applying to this loan (that is, *R*) is then 7.40% and its Maculey duration is 2.36 years[3]. The default probabilities are taken from the historical default table compiled by Lucas ([15], Exhibit 8A) drawing from Moody's research (see also: Carty - Lieberman [7]), and are shown in column (*ii*)[4]. The 3 year cumulative default rate is 5.38%. Due to the low seniority of the loan, the recovery rate is conservatively set at zero. Column (*iii*) shows the present value (*PV*) of the loan's total expected cash-flows (i.e. its future nominal cash-flows multiplied by the probabilities of survival derived from the historic default frequencies and discounted to present at the zero-coupon rates implied in the risk-free par *YTM* curve) when the lending rate (*R**) is set at 9.27%[5].

---

[3] To find the risk-free rate corresponding to this loan, it is first necessary to derive, from the risk-free par *YTM* curve, the relevant zero-coupon rates. Using the standard boot-strapping methodology, one obtains: $Z1 = 7.00\%$, $Z2 = 7.26\%$ and $Z3 = 7.53\%$ for 1, 2 and 3 years respectively. Next, a present value calculation is performed by discounting, at these rates, the loan's annual capital repayments (of $ 0.00, $ 50.00 and $ 50.00 respectively) augmented by coupon income at the unknown rate *R*. This present value is set equal to $ 100. Solving for *R* yields 7.40%.

[4] Alternatively, the default probabilities can be extracted from market data, for instance from bond market quotes. For an exposition of this methodology, see ALTMAN E.I. - BENCIVENGA J.C. [1].

[5] The probabilities that the borrower survives (i.e., remains solvent) through a given year, having survived the previous ones, are equal to $S1 = (1 - 0.0137) = 0.9863$, $S2 = (1 - 0.0319) = 0.9681$ and $S3 = (1 - 0.0538) = 0.9462$ for the first, second and third years respectively. The 9.27% risky lending rate (*R**) is found in the same way as the riskless rate *R*, but after having multiplied the contractual cash-flows (both principal – C1 = C2 = $ 50 – and interest repayments) by the respective survival probabilities, that is:

$$100 = 100R^*S1/(1+Z1) + (100\,R^* + C1)S2/(1+Z2)^2 + [(100 - C1)R^* + C2]S3/(1+Z3)^3$$

where $\wedge$ = exponential. Of course, if $S1 = S2 = S3 = 1$, then $R^* = R = 7.40\%$. For a more general treatment, see formula *(11)* in the Appendix.

Column (*iv*) repeats these same calculations, but uses the risk-less rate 7.40% as the loan's coupon rate. It can then be seen that the sum of the *PV* of these expected (that is, risk-adjusted) cash-flows is now only worth $ 96.00. It is as if the lender is granting a loan of $ 100 at a rate of 7.40%, while expecting to receive back $ 96 only. Put differently, the «fair» (or, «market») value of the risky loan, when disbursed at the 7.40% riskless rate, is only $ 96 instead of $ 100. This is so because the riskless rate, employed as lending rate, is insufficient to recoup the loan's expected losses, which are now wholly unprovided for, showing up as a $ 4 loss expectation. Only by lending at 9.27% will the bank expect to be repaid back, in *PV* terms, the $ 100 it has loaned out. Hence, the differences between column (*iii*) and (*iv*) are the loan's expected losses, reported in column (*v*). These losses are cumulatively equal to $ 4.00. Finally, column (*vi*) shows the *PV* of the revenues generated by the 1.87% (i.e., 9.27% less 7.40%) risk-premium which, by construction, is designed to offset the risky loan's expected losses.

TABLE 1

THE LOAN

Risk-free YTM in %	Annual default probabilities in %	PV of expected cash-flows:		PV of exp. losses	PV of risk-premium revenues
		a) 9.27%	a) 7.40%		
(*i*)	(*ii*)	(*iii*)	(*iv*)	(*v*)=(*iii*)–(*ii*)	(*vi*)
7.00	1.37	8.54	6.82	1.72	1.72
7.25	1.82	49.87	48.30	1.57	1.57
7.50	2.19	41.59	40.88	0.71	0.71
Total	5.38	100.00	96.00	4.00	4.00

For ease of illustration, the borrowing and lending operations described above can be reduced to their zero-coupon equivalents. If so, then it is as if the lender borrows $ 100 at 7.40% from depositors for a period of 2.36 years, promising to pay them back $ 118.35 (= $ 100 (1.074)^2.36). He then lends the same amount to the borrower at a 9.27% lending rate. At maturity, the borrower returns $ 118.35 (that is, $ 123.28 = $ 100 (1.0927)^2.36, less the future value of the expected loss of $ 4.93 = $ 4 $(1.0927)^{2.36}$)), with the lender will extinguish his deposit liabilities.

Therefore, if no «surprises» take place (i.e., in case of a zero variance of the credit losses), a risk-neutral lender able of achieving a lending spead of 1.87% would not need to set aside a risk-reserve, as the net revenues generated by the loan will provide the adequate cushion against expected losses. That is, in a risk-neutral world there would be no need to «pre-commit» an equity buffer in the form of a risk reserve. The necessary «cushion» would be provided by the risk-spread. However, when uncertainty is present, it is neither true that the lender will always achieve this pricing target, nor that the actual loss will always be the expected one. As this uncertainty as to the actual level of the expected loss is what justifies the need for bank capital, we postpone the discussion of this topic to paragraph 2.6[6].

Naturally, should the borrower's financial conditions deteriorate during the life of the loan, then the loan's equilibrium risk-spread would increase above 1.87% and, unless the lending rate can be renegotiated according to contractual clauses, the «fair» value of the loan would fall below par. Thus, the lender would in effect be facing a «virtual» loss which, in principle, would have to be recognised by writing down the loan's book value, or by increasing risk-reserves[7].

2.2 *Expected Loss and Option Pricing*

Notice that, as an alternative procedure, the loan could have been disbursed at $ 96 and serviced at the 7.40% riskless rate on a face value of $ 100. The lender would then invest the balance of $ 4.00 in risk-free securities of a duration of 2.36 years, and this

---

[6] In this ideal risk-neutral world where nothing happens which is unexpected, there is no substantive difference between debt and equity, and any concept of optimal leverage is undefined. It is only introducing uncertainty, that is «risk», that capital takes on a meaning.

[7] To quantify this loss (and the required increase in risk provisions) it is sufficient to apply the same methodology used in Table 1, with suitably higher default rates.

reserve would be held against future expected losses. Its end-of-period value would be $ 4.73 (= $ 4 (1.1074)^2.36). The borrower will return $ 113.62 (that is, $ 118.35 = $ 100(1.074)^2.36, less $ 4.73, the future value of a $ 4 expected loss compounded at the lending rate of 7.40%). Added to the sum released from the risk reserve, the overall amount of $ 118.35 will be returned to depositors.

In so doing, the lender would self-insure against default risk. By the same token, a risk-neutral credit insurer would demand a $ 4.00 up front fee to guarantee the loan, which the lender would be ready to pay if the guarantor is risk-free (that is if he invests this sum in risk-free securities with a maturity of 2.36 years). As, following Merton [20], a guarantee can be interpreted as an over-the-counter (OTC) put option, the expected loss can also be seen as the price of a «credit derivative», or as the cost of hedging the lender's credit-risk exposure. This line of reasoning will be taken on again later on in discussing bank solvency requirements (paragraph 2.6) and loan guarantees (Section 3).

Following Ambarish and Subrahmanyam 1990, the risky loan can also be seen as a portfolio of a long position in an «equivalent» risk-free loan (B - using the symbols in the Appendix) and a short position in a put option on the market value of the firm (project) the lender has sold to the firm's shareholders (project's sponsors). This intuition follows the (by now, standard) result from modern option pricing theory, according to which a share of common equity can be seen as a call option: «stockholders have the equivalent of an option on their company's assets. In effect, the bond holders own the company's assets, but they have given options to the stockholders to buy the assets back» (Black - Scholes [6], pp. 649-50). This result can be extended to corporate debt because, due to the limited liability nature of the firm's equity, the shareholders of an enterprise will default on the firm's debt if the value of the corporate equity (i.e., its net asset value) falls short of the nominal value of its debt. That is, shareholders will «put» the firm to the lenders, who will bear a loss equal to the difference between the face value of debt and the defaulted firm's market value (the recovery rate, in this paper's terminology). If B^* is

the value of the risky loan evaluated at the riskless interest rates,
then:

(1) $B^* = B = E^*$

where E^* is the option value. In the example described in Table
1, one might be led to think that $B = \$ 100$ and $B^* = \$ 96$, while
the option value is nothing else than the \$ 4 expected loss. As it
will be shown, this is indeed the case. Moreover, if the borrower
is lowly rated, or the loan is «long», the value of the embedded
option will account for a large proportion of the loan's «fair» market price (Table 3). Anyway, the value of the risky loan is affected by two sets of variables: those influencing its value in a non-
default world, and those affecting the chances and recovery possibilities in case of default. A similar property holds in derivative
valuation when counterparties may default (Hull - White [12])[8].

2.3 *Loan Collateral, Seniority and Covenants*

The expected loss framework also assists in evaluating the
risk-reduction and risk-transfer capabilities of certain types of risk
mitigants, such a collateral, the degree of debt priority in the
borrower's liability structure, and contractual covenants.
The function of collateral is to increase the loan's recovery

---

[8] Note also that E^* changes proportionately to the default rates. For instance,
with respect to the loan described in Table 1, if the cumulative default rates goes
up uniformly across time by 1% to 6.38% all else being equal, E^* increases by \$
0.80 to \$ 4.80. If the cumulative default rate increases by an additional 1% to
7.38%, then E^* again increases by a further \$ 0.80 to \$ 5.60, and so on. Since B
is unchanged, B^* falls by the same amount as E^*. However, due to the convexity
of bond (here: of «fair» loan) prices, the changes in the risky rate (R^*) will be progressively larger. That is, the relationship between default rate and credit spreads
is non-linear. Thus, after increasing by 0.38% to 9.65% when the cumulative default rate increases by the first 1%, R^* will increase by 0.43% to 13.30% when the
cumulative default rates increases from 14.38% to 15.38%. This corresponds to the
often remarked circumstance that open-market credit spreads widen substantially
in response to sudden and severe downgrades of borrowers («event risk»), to the
point that credit may cease to be available. Absence of market liquidity both blurs
the real extent of the ensuing credit losses, and prevents a prompt disposal of the
distressed assets.

rate, thereby reducing loss severity. This being the case, the valuation of the expected loss on a collateralised loan cannot proceed on the assumption of a nil recovery rate. By now much it will have to be increased shall depend on the nature, quality and size of the collateral relative to the loan. If risk-free securities of a market value equal to, or higher than, the loan's principal are offered as collateral, the loss severity falls to zero and the risk spread as well. More generally, however, any risk-accounting system must be able to recognise that collateral does not, in general, reduce risk, but shifts it from the obligor to the collateral itself[9].

Similarly, different degrees of debt priority will have to be reflected in the recovery rate. Indeed, default statistics are normally standardised to the common denominator represented by senior unsecured debt. Yet companies generally issue various types of liabilities characterised by diversified priority levels (e.g., junior, subordinated, convertible debt). Accommodating different seniority levels requires adjusting recovery rates according to higher or lower debt priorities (for instance, the average recovery rate for senior unsecured loans is estimated at 49%, see Table 5 in Carty

---

[9] Estimates of the recovery rate (or of loss severity) should take into account that the recovery process may both be long and uncertain in its results (much depending on the working of the judiciary system), and that during this period lenders may not receive interest payments. The loss severity experiences by Citibank's North American corporate loan portfolio covering 831 defaulted commercial and industrial loans in the period 1970-1993 has been of about 35%, implying a 65% recovery rate, which is higher than what reported by CARTY L. - LIEBERMAN D. [7] for defaulted public bonds. A recent research for Italy has found that, on average between 1985 and 1993, the length of formal bankruptcy proceedings has been five years, and that unsecured creditors lose about 80% of their claims (BARONTINI R. [4]. With interest rates in the region of 10%, this means that the present value of the recovered sums may be as low as 10% of nominal principal. By contrast, in informal work-out proceedings, the main losses derive from debt restructuring operations, where the distressed debtor may be offered a reduced interest rate (or interest payments are simply waived for a certain period). The ensuing shortfalls have been estimated, for the 1993-1994 period, in 20-30% of the nominal value of rescheduled debts (BELCREDI M. [5]). Creditors have also to shoulder the direct costs of bankruptcy and work-out procedures (about 4-5% of nominal obligations). Recovery rates, of course, depend heavily on the existence (and the type of) security available, as well as on the nature of the legal procedures employed for dealing with the borrower's distress (e.g., formal bankruptcies or informal work-outs). Based on a survey of recent experiences of Italian banks, GENERALE A. - GOBBI G. [11] report recovery rates in the region of 10-30% for unsecured loans, and of around 60-70% for those secured with real estate. In general, formal bankruptcy proceedings take longer to close, and return less to the lenders, than informal ones.

- Lieberman [7]. Altman - Bencivenga [1] offer estimates of recovery rates for high-yeld bonds according to seniority over the period 1985-1994.

With reference to the loan described in the previous section, Table 2 shows the expected loss and the risk spread associated with different levels of the recovery rate. As can be seen, their effect is nearly proportional.

TABLE 2

IMPACT OF THE RECOVERY RATE
ON THE EXPECTED LOSS AND RISK SPREAD

Recovery rate	0%	25%	50%	75%	100%
Expected loss (in $)	4.00	3.00	2.00	1.00	0.00
Risk spread	1.87%	1.40%	0.93%	0.46%	0.00%

As to loan covenants, their contribution to reducing anticipated losses can be evaluated in terms of the likely reduction in default probabilities they allow. By compressing the room of manoeuvre available to the management of the borrowing company, and by constraining their ability to take actions to the detriment of the interest of creditors (e.g., paying out large dividends; selling key assets; increasing leverage), the risk profile of a borrower may be reduced. Of course, the quantification of any such effect is itself subjective, and much will depend on the lender's capacity to monitor the borrower and enforcing its rights in case of non compliance.

2.4 *The Loan's Cash-Flow and Interest Rates*

It is generally agreed that the higher the risk accepted by the lender. When the expected loss is used as a metric for credit risk, this remains the case. However, for lowly rated borrowers for which marginal default rates tend to diminish for progressively more distant years, the risk spread tends to fall as the loan's duration increases. Table 3 shows the expected losses (risk spreads are in parenthesis) associated with a $ 100 senior unsecured loan extended to borrowers in the main rating classes. The yield curve is the same as in Table 1, and it increases by 0.25% for each additional year. A 50% recovery rate has been used together with bullet maturities[10].

The effect of a changing level of risk-free interest rates on a loan's expected loss is in principle ambiguous, as two opposing effects are at work. Although the higher risk-free rates, the lower will be the present value of all future expected losses on the outstanding loan's principal, higher riskless rates also increase the break-even lending rate and, with it, the expected losses on future interest service. However, the first effect will normally prevail, and higher riskless rates will reduce expected losses.

These considerations can be reinterpreted in terms of option pricing. From *(1)*, we can write:

$$d\ B^*/d\ R = d\ B/d\ R - d\ E^*/d\ R$$

where, of course, $(d\ B/d\ R)$ is negative. As to $(d\ E^*/d\ R)$, the option's «rho», it is also negative, since — all else being equal — a put option's value falls when interest rates increase, the reason being that the option writer can reinvest the premium at higher yields and thus needs a lower price to match a given future loss stemming from the option's exercise (Chance [8])[11]. Theorefore, the market value of a risky loan (bond) is less sensitive to changes in risk-free rates than a riskless one, all the more so if its option component (i.e., its expected loss) is large.

---

[10] The risk-spreads presented in Table 3 would seem to be huge. However, consider that ALTMAN E.I. - BENCIVENGA J.C. ([1]; Table 6 and Graph 3), report aggregate yield-spreads over US treasuries as high as 1066 bp in January 1991 for the so-called high-yield bonds (*BB, B* and *CCC*-rated issues). For the *CCC*-rated bonds alone, the risk-premium shot up to 1.600 bp. The same authors provide an estimate for the overall recovery rate on bonds rated *BBB* or below of the order of 40-50% (Table 3 of their paper).

[11] In principle, one would have to take into account the effect of higher risk-free rates on the value of the firm. If the correlation between the two is sufficiently negative (i.e., if higher interest rates strongly increase the chances of default), the sign of $(d\ E/d\ R)$ could be positive. For a discussion of this topic, see HULL J; - WHITE A. [12].

The impact of risk-free rates on the risk spread, however, is less clear, and will in general depend on the loan's cash-flow distribution. This is so because, higher (lower) rates will (as just argued) most likely reduce (increase) the present value of expected losses to be offset, but will do the same to the net revenues from the risk spread designed to offset them. For all practical purposes, however, this effect is generally negligible.

TABLE 3

EXPECTED LOSSES, RISK SPREADS AND LOAN MATURITY
(dollar values for $ 100 of loan principal - basis points in
parenthesis - recovery rate set at 50%)

Moody's/S & P ratings	3-years	5-years	7-years	10-years
Aaa/AAA	0.01 (0)	0.02 (1)	0.03 (1)	0.04 (1)
Aa3/AA-	0.05 (1)	0.09 (3)	0.14 (4)	0.22 (5)
Aa3/A-	0.20 (9)	0.37 (12)	0.57 (16)	0.88 (20)
Baa3/BBB-	1.10 (50)	1.68 (58)	2.28 (65)	3.10 (72)
Ba3/BB-	5.42 (260)	7.37 (273)	9.03 (281)	10.92 (286)
B3/B-	16.82 (942)	20.31 (924)	22.68 (905)	24.90 (878)

2.5 *Risk Accounting, Aggregation and Performance Monitoring*

It is now possible to advance a few broad considerations on risk control and risk-adjusted performance. Suppose the loan in Table 1 is junior subordinated, for which the recovery rate is assumed to be nil, but offers a collateral conservatively valued at 25% of the loan's face value. Furthermore, the borrower accepts a limitation-of-indebtedness covenant (i.e., a contractual clause setting the maximum amount of debt the borrower may take on during the loan's life). Bank's management assess the contribution of this covenant in a 20% reduction of default rates. Following negotiations, the loan is disbursed at 8.55%, a spread of 1.15% over the 7.40% riskless yield.

Evaluated in the expected loss framework, the required spread on this loan is 1.12%, while its expected loss is $ 2.41. These values compare with the 1.87% and $ 4.00 respectively for the loan with no risk mitigants. Their contributions to risk-reduction can now be quantified.

First, the collateral shifts $ 25-worth of nominal exposure from the obligor to the collateral, in the process reducing the expected loss from $ 4.00 to $ 3.02 (indeed, 3.02/4.00 = 0.75) and the required risk spread from 1.87% to 1.40%. As to the covenant, it further reduces the expected loss by 0.61 cents to $ 2.41, and the risk spread by 0.25% to 1.15%. Therefore, the covenant's contribution to risk reduction in terms of nominal exposures can be evaluated at $ 15, for $ 60 is the loan's principal for which $ 2.41 represents a loss of 4.00% (i.e., $ 60 = $ 2.41/0.04). In risk-accounting terms, this means that the lender's exposure to the borrower has been reduced to $ 60 only, as $ 25 has been transferred on to the collateral and $ 15 has been eliminated by the covenant. Of course, the bank will have to account for, and keep track of, its exposures to the collateral[12].

A related issue is represented by risk aggregation. One major problem inherent in risk aggregation is the existence of non-zero correlations among individual exposures in a portfolio. In what follows, however, it will be naively assumed that individual risks are independent, and another topic will be explored: namely that of finding a «common unit of account», or «numeraire», in which to express different types of credit risks. In current bank capital regulation this is done via risk-weights. Fundamentally, they are designed to reduce credit exposures to a «common denominator», after which a comparison with available capital becomes permis-

---

[12] The reader might have noted that, although the end-result is the same (namely $ 60 worth of exposure left with the principal obligor), how risk is redistributed (and the various credit enhancements valued) depends on the sequencing with which risk-mitigants are approached. Had one started by assessing the covenants, followed by the collateral, then $ 20 worth of exposure would have been absorbed by the covenant (for the expected loss of the unsecured covenanted loan would be $ 3.21), and an additional $ 20 (25% of $ 80) by the collateral. In practice, the most appropriate ordering will depend on the negotiating process, or on the lender's a-priori views as to the relative strengths of the available risk-mitigants. In short, the expected loss framework can be used to evaluate the contribution of each additional risk-mitigant, to judge the trade-offs among them, and between them and loan pricing.

sible. It was already hinted at the fact that such risk-weights are generally thought to be somewhat arbitrary, and unable to fully capture different degrees of default risk. The expected loss approach allows to perform this aggregation with a higher level of realism. It is however first necessary for bank management (regulators) to define an «acceptable exposure», that is a level of credit risk they feel comfortable with and which can thus be used as «risk numeraire». Such definition will of course depend on matters such as the bank's client base and other operational circumstances, as well as to its risk appetite. Assume that the loan described in Table 1 fits the definition of «acceptable» exposure. Then, the risk-weight assigned to the collateralised and covenanted loan discussed in this section is 60%. Risk-weights computed in this way will react correctly to changes in the borrower's credit standing, in loans' durations, and to the use of collateral and covenants.

Finally, the lending bank might wish to assess the risk-adjusted rates of return on the loan implied by the achievable lending rates. For this purpose, assume it is funding itself at the 7.40% riskless rate and that it capitalises the \$ 100 loan with \$ 8 of equity. Assume that, being risk-neutral, it sets its «hurdle» lending rate at 8.52% against an actual lending rate of 8.55%. Then, the realised risk-adjusted return on assets (*RAROA*) is equal to 0.61%, which is higher than the «hurdle» level of 0.59% implied by the risk-neutral lending rate. Alternatively, the «required» risk-adjusted return on capital (*RAROC*) on the loan is equal to 7.40%, while the actual one turns out to be 7.65%[13]. In either case, the more severe the risks incurred, the higher the «required» rates of return that need to be passed in order for the loan to be seen as feasible. Risk-taking without appropriate compensation should be discouraged.

---

[13] From footnote 2, setting $H = R = F$, we have that $RAROA = [(H - F) + cF]$ = cf, where here $c = 0.08$ and $F = 7.40\%$. Thus the «required» $RAROA$ is 0.08 x 7.40% = 0.59%. However, the bank lends at 8.55%, not 8.52%, and the actual $RAROA$ is thus 0.02% higher at 0.61%. Equally, the required $RAROC$ has been expressed as $[F + (H - F)/c] = F$, that is 7.40%. However, given that the lending rate is 2 bp over the required level, the actual $RAROC$ is 0.02%/0.08 = 0.02% x 12.5 = 0.25% higher than required, namely, 7.65%.

2.6 *Capital Adequacy*

So far the lender's funding mix (i.e., the proportion of debt and equity in his liability structure) has not been discussed. It was as if loans were fully funded with either debt or equity – both yielding the same expected rate of return – or with any combination of the two. The lender's choice as to the capital ratio was therefore immaterial. In other words, a higher leverage (a lower equity base) would increase the promised return on shareholders' funds but, being matched by a higher incidence of the expected loss, would represent a higher risk venture for equity holders, and thus offer an unchanged yield in risk-adjusted terms[14].

We now move away from this ideal world of perfect foresight and consider a few real-life imperfections. One is, of course, the fact that there are no assurances that the actuarially fair lending rate will be achieved, for instance because market conditions would not allow. A second complication is the circumstance that actual credit losses have a volatility, that is they are more or less widely dispersed around their expected value. For instance, the borrower may be downgraded during the loan's life, thereby increasing the chances of default over and above those originally assumed.

These uncertainties generate the need for a solvency cushion. This is particularly true if, to protect systemic financial stability, bank regulators run a deposit insurance fund or operate an implicit lender-of-last resort policy towards the banking system. They may thus wish to see lending operations backed by an «adequate» capital cushion, so as to minimise the chances that a bank default due to poor private credit choices has a negative impact on the public budget. The problem is, of course, how much capital is «adequate».

Since the expected loss is the actuarially fair cost of credit insurance, one could say that it represents the amount of capital

---

[14] «An essential message of the M&M proposition as applied to banking, in sum is that you cannot hope to lever up a sow's ear into a silk purse. You may *think* you can during good times; but you'll give it all back and more when bad times roll around» MILLER M.H. [21], p. 486, italics in the original.

which, as a minimum, should be committed up-front by bank shareholders. Any positive risk spread would then provide additional solvency cover. In the example of Table 1, a capital of $ 4.00 combined with a risk spread of 1.87% would provide an equity buffer worth $ 8, or 8% of principal. True, the equity pre-commitment would be a type of bank capital (call it *Tier*-1) of higher quality than the one embedded in the risk-spread (*Tier*-2). However, should the loan be disbursed at $ 96, the two types of equity would be very close.

Suppose the loan is indeed disbursed at $ 96 and further backed by $ 4.00 of shareholder equity. Then, if the actual loss is lower than $ 4.00, bank shareholders would enjoy a rate of return above the 7.40% riskless rate. If higher than this, but lower than $ 8.00, they would still obtain a positive return, but one less than the risk-free rate. In case of a loss larger than $ 8.00, bank shareholders would lose all, and the insurance fund would shoulder the balance. The consequence is twofold: banks, facing a cost of equity higher than that of (essentially risk free) debt, would wish to reduce the amount of equity injected in loans to the minimum possible; bank regulators would want banks to pre-commit an «adequate» equity cushion so as to reduce the insurance fund's potential losses.

As currently applied, the requirement to commit «adequate» capital means that at least $ 8.00 of equity should back each $ 100 worth of loans. It is easily seen that the results may not be those intended. Assume, in the example above, that the lender is forced to provide $ 8.00 of equity. With a $ 4.00 disbursement discount, this would generate a solvency cover of three times the expected loss ([8 + 4]/4). However, had the borrower had been rated *B1* instead, the loan's expected loss would have been $ 16.17, and a flat 8% capital requirement, coupled with actuarially fair lending yield, would have allowed for an equity buffer of 1.5 times the expected loss ([8 + 16]/16) only. In other words, the effective capitalisation of the first loan is double that of the second. Put differently, a flat undifferentiated capital ratio as currently applied might well end up providing both excess or insufficient coverage of credit losses.

Combine now the fact that bank equity can be significantly more expensive than bank debt with the existence of only mildly risk-sensitive capital ratios, and the end result might well be an incentive towards bank imprudence. This is so because, being allowed to economise on expensive equity, banks could be drawn to attract borrowers with high risks (e.g., expected losses) by quoting «low» lending spreads, while better rated clients would be offered relatively «high» lending rates, or else left to less regulated lenders.

In Graph 1, if left free to provision according to the actuarial expectation of loss, a lender would create an equity cushion equal to *OA* when lending to a low-risk borrower[15]. It is instead required to reserve *OB*, that is $ 8. The lender would thus face an opportunity loss equal to the difference between its cost of equity and debt times the amount *AB*. On the contrary, when lending to a high-risk client the lender would reserve *OB* instead of the more prudent *OC*, with a corresponding saving in funding costs. This would allow lenders to quote comparatively (i.e., compared with expected losses) lower credit spreads for high-risk clients, and comparatively higher ones for better credits. These is some empirical evidence that this might indeed be the case (Lustig *et* Al., [17], pp. 7-8).

In other words, current credit-risk bank capital regulations, to the extent that they try to strike a difficult balance in the risk profile of the average bank lender, might create an incentive for banks to prefer high risk operations for which capital ratios are not binding (e.g., corporate loans with expected losses in excess of 8%), and to provide capital in the (by definition) insufficient amount (e.g., 8%)[16]. This may result in a worsening of asset quality, in insufficient reserves, and in a push towards securitisation of debt issued by more finely rated borrowers.

---

[15] For simplicity, the argument is here developed in terms of expected losses. However, the conclusions would be the same if banks set equity capital also in terms of unexpected losses (see later), or according to some other parameter reflecting the «true» level of risk of the individual credit transaction.

[16] Table 5 above seems indeed to suggest that a minimum capital ratio of 8% is some average of the expected losses on low and high-risk operations.

GRAPH 1

LENDING RISKS AND REQUIRED CAPITAL

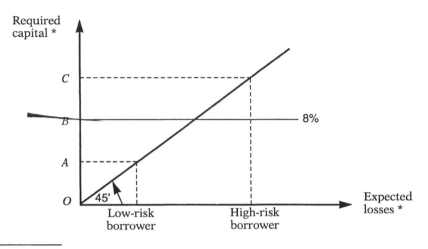

* In percent of the loan's par value.

In sum, from a normative viewpoint, a loan's expected loss seems, under at least two respects, a reasonable benchmark for an «adequate» level of credit risk provisioning. Firstly, it represents an actuarially fair estimate of the possible credit loss and, secondly, it can be interpreted as the cost of hedging the loan exposure, that is as the market price to pay for eliminating the downside volatility of the loan's value. Although this argument will be more comprehensively pursued below within the analysis of loan guarantees, it should be intuitively clear from relationship *(1)* that, if the creditor can perfectly hedge the short position $(-E^*)$ he has in the put option, he will be left with a riskless asset B which in principle needs no capital buffer. If he can do so by going long (i.e., purchasing) an «equivalent» put option (let us call its value G), then it seems reasonable that the equity cushion he is asked to pre-commit be commensurate with what he would have to spend for an hedging operation resulting in a complete disposal of risk (i.e., if $E^* = G$). In other words, the higher the cost of eliminating credit risk, the higher must be the risk itself. The link between capital adequacy and put option pricing, in the context of market risk, has been highlighted by Barone - Bragho' [3].

3. - Guarantee Valuation

Loan pricing and credit support valuation are, of course, two sides of a same coin. Should the credit-enhanced loan be riskless, either because the enhancement is sufficiently strong, or because the borrower-insurer combination is (e.g., due to a low correlation between the two's default probabilities), then the lender should be prepared to forego any risk-premium it would otherwise have collected[17].

In such a case, the borrower pays the riskless rate to the lending bank, while offering the provider of external credit support (i.e., the party ultimately bearing the risk of default) a compensation for the risk assumed. Equivalently, the borrower pays the full risky rate to the lender, who in turn will pay the guarantee fee to the guarantor (because the insured party is the lender, in the following we shall use this second presentation). But if the combination of borrower and credit-enhancer is not as strong as to render the secured loan completely safe, then the lender would still keep a part of the risk premium, reflecting the fact that only a fraction of the exposure has been transferred. At the same time, the credit support fee will be lower, and in principle equal to the difference between the risk-premium retained by the lender, and the one reflecting the loan's default risk.

After these introductory remarks, we now consider in more detail the valuation framework for third-party credit support arrangements (e.g., letters of credit, surety bonds, corporate guarantees) drawing on the notion of expected loss. Specifically, the questions we want to address are: how much should the lender be prepared to pay

---

[17] In case the credit enhancement is provided by a collateral, then the relevant correlation would be that between the probability distribution of the borrower's defaut risk and that of the resale price of the collateral. For instance, if the borrower is an airline company and the collateral is an aircraft, then one may be led to think that a downturn in air traffic is liable to increase both the chances of the borrower defaulting and of the collateral fetching a low price. Hence, this particular collateral would offer scant protection. Put differently, it does not diversify lending risks.

for a full, irrevocable and unconditional external credit support («guarantee», from now on?) And how would this cost relate to the quality of the credit enhancement offered, that is to the amount of risk effectively transferred from the borrower to the provider of credit support («guarantor», for brevity?)[18]. Given loan guarantees' already remarked nature of *OTC* put options, this analysis will give an additional perspective on the pricing of these instruments, whose valuation in a typical option pricing setting may pose problems due to lack of data, of market trading and of a clearing-house capable of eliminating counterparty risk in *OTC* transactions.

3.1 *The Default Correlation*

To explore this subject, three possible guarantors for the above loan are considered: the first has a rating of *Aa2/AA*, that is a credit-standing substantially higher than the borrower's; the second has a rating of *Baa1/BBB*, or just above that of the principal obligor, while the third is rated *B2/B*, that is lower than the borrower. Again, Moody's historic default rates will be used to characterise the default risks of these guarantors. However, while a guarantor's rating captures his general solvency, a second, more specific, «dimension» of credit risk has to be assessed: the guarantor's independence from the borrower, or the combination of factors which tie the fate of the guarantor to that of the main obligor. This is measured by the correlation between the default risks of the two: the higher this correlation, the higher the possibility that, the borrower having defaulted, the guarantor also defaults, thereby forcing the lender into a loss.

All else being equal, therefore, the higher the correlation between the borrower's and the guarantor's default risks, the less valuable is the guarantee. A high positive correlation can be due to the fact that the borrower is legally tied to the guarantor (par-

---

[18] Guarantees are here assumed to cover the whole credit exposure (principal plus interest), although in practice they may cover only a part of it. This is so in order to avoid moral hazard behaviour on the part of the lender. However, as will be seen, the lender will generally maintain an interest in monitoring both the principal obligor and the guarantor as, in financial terms, the risk-transfer properties of even a full, irrevocable and unconditional guarantee may not be total.

ent or subsidiary), that both operate in the same business sector (or are anyway adversely affected by the same set of circumstances), or that one has a large exposure towards the other (e.g., the guarantor is a bank with large credits to, or is an important supplier/client of, the borrower). A low and, at the limit, a negative correlation is, on the contrary, a sign of independence.

Two logical requirements bound the feasible values the default correlation may take on the upper and lower side. First, the default probability of the guaranteed loan cannot be negative. Second, this same probability cannot be higher than that of the more risky between the borrower and the guarantor[19]. In what follows, for practical purposes, we shall assume, for each individual guarantor, a correlation equal to the maximum, the minimum and the average feasible levels (as defined in footnote 19). These values, referred to the end of the third year of loan's life, are set out in Table 4 below.

---

[19] To clarify, consider that a default can be described by the Bernoulli distribution, which applies to events where only two outcomes are possible: either outcome «1» (e.g., a default occurs) with probability P, or outcome «0» (e.g., the borrower remains solvent) with probability $(1 - P)$. The mean of this distribution is P and the standard deviation $SQRT (P \times (1 - P))$, where $SQRT$ = square root. If P is the borrower's probability of default and S the guarantor's, the joint probability of both defaulting (that is, the default probability of the guaranteed loan) is:

$$P \times S + SQRT [P \times (1 - P)] \times SQRT [S \times (1 - S)] \times Corr (P, S)$$

where $Corr (P, S)$ is the correlation between the default risks of the borrower and the guarantor. Statistically, the correlation can vary between $- 1$ (when the two default probabilities always perfectly move in opposite directions) and $+ 1$ (when their relationship is perfect, but positive), in other words when one default risk is a linear function of the other. In case of zero correlation, the default probability of the guaranteed loan is simply $P \times S$. However, in financial terms, there an upper bound to default risk correlation (LUCAS D.J. [15]). This is so because the default probability of the guaranteed loan cannot be higher than that of the better rated party. We may thus write:

$$Corr (P, S) < [\min (P, S) - P \times S] / \{ SQRT [P \times (1 - P)] \times SQRT [S \times (1 - S)]\}$$

Moreover, this same probability cannot fall below zero. Thus:

$$Corr (P, S) > - P \times S / \{ SQRT [P \times (1 - P)] \times SQRT [S \times (1 - S)]\}$$

Another way to interpret these two restrictions on the default correlation is in terms of the requirements that the expected of the guaranteed loan ($E°$) be non negative and no higher than $E*$.

TABLE 4

FEASIBLE CORRELATION VALUES

Guarantor's rating	*Aa2/AA*	*Baa1/BB*	*B2/B*
Correlation levels			
Max	0.145	0.406	0.396
Average	0.069	0.192	0.126
Min	−0.009	−0.023	−0.144

3.2 *The Fair Values of Loan Guarantees*

Going back to the example introduced in Section 2, and considering that the expected loss on the unsecured loan was $ 4.00, it is evident that the maximum price the lender would be willing to pay for the guarantee is the difference between this amount and the expectation of loss on the guaranteed loan. If this zero (i.e., the guaranteed loan is riskless), then the value of the guarantee would be $ 4.00 (or alternatively, 1.87% per year)[20]. But if the guaranteed loan is not itself risk-free, because there is a chance that both the guarantor and the borrower default simultaneously, then the value of the guarantee will be less than $ 4.00. This is so

---

[20] MERTON R.C. ([19], p. 8, formula *(4)*, derives a formula expressing the value of a loan guarantee as percent of the loan's principal based on the definition that the value of the guarantee (G) plus that of the risky loan (i.e., its certainty-equivalent cash-flow discounted to present at the risk-free rate - that is B^*) must equal that of an «equivalent» guaranteed loan (B°). That is: $(G + B^*) = B^\circ$, or $G/B^\circ = (1 - B^*/B^\circ)$. Allowing for the fact that Merton deals with zero-coupon loans and continuous compounding, this formula can be approximately rewritten as:

(i) $G/B^\circ = 1 - [(1 + R^\circ) / (1 + R^*)]^T$

where $\wedge$ = exponentiation, R° is the rate on the guaranteed loan (i.e., the riskless rate R if the guarantor is default risk-free, or if the correlation of its default risk with that of the borrower is such that their joint probability of default is zero - see later), R^* is the risky loan rate, and T the loan's duration (i.e., the zero-coupon equivalent of final maturity). If the guaranteed loan is default-free, then $R^\circ = R$. Thus, in the case of Table 1, if $R^\circ = 7.40\%$, $R^* = 9.27\%$ and $T = 2.36$, G/B° is equal to 4.00%. However, suppose the guaranteed loan is not default free, and $R^\circ > R$. For istance, assule $R^\circ = 7.69\%$. Then $G/B^\circ = 3.38\%$ (Table 5 first row, second column).

Notice also that, by substituting *(i)* above into $B^*/B^\circ = (1 - G/B^\circ)$, we can express the value of the risky loan as a function for the guaranteed one:

(ii) $B^* = B^\circ [(1 + R^\circ) / (1 + R^*)]^T.$

because not all risk is being shifted on to the guarantor, a portion of it remaining with the lender; more specifically that part corresponding to the non-zero probability of joint default[21].

Based on this reasoning. Table 5 quantifies the «fair» values of full, unconditional and irrevocable guarantees issued by the three possible guarantors, with the three different correlation values of Table 4. These values correspond to the reduction of the expected loss to the lender, which is thus prepared to pay the guarantor up to this lowered expectation of loss. The table presents guarantee values both in terms of a dollar up-front fees and of percent annual premia (in parenthesis).

TABLE 5

FAIR VALUES OF LOAN GUARANTEES
(figures in $ - % in parenthesis)

Guarantor's rating	*Aa2/AA*	*Baa1/BBB*	*B2/B*
Correlation levels			
Max	3.93 (1.83%)	3.38 (1.58%)	0.00 (0.00%)
Average	3.97 (1.85%)	3.69 (1.73%)	2.01 (0.95%)
Min	4.00 (1.87%)	4.00 (1.87%)	4.00 (1.87%)

---

[20] note continued
Proceeding in the same way, one finds:

(iii) $$B° = B [(1 + R) / (1 + R°)]^T$$

so that after substitution of *(iii)* in *(ii)*, we finally have:

(iv) $$B^* = B [(1 + R) / (1 + R^*)]^T.$$

[21] Following the considerations developed in footnote 19, the corresponding default probabilities for the guaranteed loan are set out below:

DEFAULT PROBABILITIES OF THE GUARANTEED LOAN
%

Guarantor's rating	*Aa2/AA*	*Baa1/BBB*	*B2/B*
Correlation levels			
Max	0.12	0.93	5.38
Average	0.06	0.47	2.69
Min	0.00	0.00	0.00

They can be compared with a default probability of 5.38% for the unsecured loan (second column of Table 1).

As expected, the value of a guarantee (i.e., the reduced expected loss for the secured lender) decreases as the rating of the guarantor falls (moving from left to right along the lines in Table 5). This decline in the value of the guarantee may be interpreted as reflecting an increase in the «generic» counterparty risk, that is the possibility that the guarantor may not be able to perform in case of default of any borrower it may guarantee. Equally, the value of the guarantee also falls as the correlation increases (moving from bottom to top along the columns of Table 5). This decline reflects a rise in the «specific» counterparty risk, that is the probability that the guarantor is unable to perform when that particular borrower defaults.

If there are grounds to think that default correlation is as feasible, one may just as well ignore the guarantor's rating, as the guarantees would anyway be as highly valuable as possible. It can also be seen that a guarantee from a highly rated party is nearly (but not totally) insensitive to the assumed level of correlation, and is generally apt to absorb most of the risk, therefore commanding a high price under any circumstance. Hence the importance attached by specialised financial guarantors to reaching and preserving a top credit-rating. Not so when the guarantor is lowly rated: if such a guarantee is indistinguishable from that offered by a highly-rated guarantor when the default correlation is at its lowest possible level, it is worthless when the correlation is as high as it can possibly be. In this case, the guarantee adds nothing to the solidity of the loan, and its value is zero (upper-right corner in Table 5).

3.3 *Loan Guarantees as Options*

All the above can be now easily translated into the language of option pricing. By acquiring a guarantee, the lender buys insurance cover against default risk, as he effectively purchases the right to sell the loan at a strike price equal to par to the guarantor when a default occurs. For this purpose, it will pay an insurace fee, that is an option premium represented by the guarantee's price. Therefore, the value of the guaranteed loan ($B°$) is the same as that of a portfolio in which the lender is long in both the risky loan ($B*$) and in the put option representing the guarantee (G):

$$B° = B* + G$$

However, substituting *(1)* in the above, we also have:

(2) $$B° = B - (E* - G)$$

which shows that the guaranteed loan is a portfolio in which the lender is long in the «equivalent» riskless loan, and short and long in two put options with the same exercise period and strike price. Indeed, $E*$ is both the risky loan's expected loss and the put option the lender has sold to the equity-holders of the borrowing company, and which is embedded in the risky loan. G is the price of the guarantee, a function of the guarantor's default risk and of the default correlation. Since it is also true that:

(3) $$B° = B - E°$$

then, combining *(2)* and *(3)*, we may write:

(4) $$G = E* - E°$$

that is, the value of the guarantee is the difference between the expected loss on the unguaranteed loan and that on the guaranteed one. Based on what argued above, the guarantee's price can also be characterised as the difference between the prices of two put options, having the same exercise period and strike price, but with different volatilities of the underlying.

If the guarantor/option-writer cannot default (the standard assumption in option princing), then the guaranteed loan is riskless, $E° = 0$ and $B° = B$. Therefore, from *(4)*, the price of the guarantee equals the loan's expected loss ($G = E*$). However, if the guarantor can fail to meet his obligation to provide cash against the delivery of the defaulted loan, then the guaranteed loan has a positive default probability. It then follows that $E° > 0$, $G < E^*$ and $B°$ $< B$. Moreover, since G is an option price, it must be non negative, and one could also write:

(5) $G - \text{Max}[0; (E^* - E°)]$

In practice, however, given the upper and lower-bound constraints imposed on the default correlation, $E°$ can neither be higher than E^*, nor be negative. Therefore, *(4)* and *(5)* are equivalent[22].

4. - Loan Guarantees and Credit Risk Accounting

A different way to look at the same phenomenon is by quantifying the share of loan exposure which, by virtue of the guarantee, is transferred from the lender to the guarantor. This is presented in Table 6 below. To understand how these results are obtained, consider the guarantee supplied by a *Baa1/BBB*-rated counterparty when its default correlation with the borrower is at its maximum feasible level. From Table 5 we know that, for the ef-

---

[22] Note that for European options, the put-call parity states that:

$$C + X/(1 + R)^\wedge T = P + S$$

where C = call price, X = exercise price, R = interest rate, T = length of the exercise period, P = put price and S = current market value of the underlying. To give a meaning to this relationship in the current context, consider the example of Table 1, and assume that the guaranteed loan is granted at $ 96. Its promised end-of-period value after 2.36 years is $ 118.35 (for an effective yield of 9.27%) with no interest paid in between. If the guarantor is riskless, then $P = $ 4$. In addition, if the guaranteed loan is correctly priced, we have: $T = 2.36$, $R = 7.40\%$, $S = 96$ and $X = 113.62$. Since, $S = X/(1 + R)^\wedge T$, $C = P = $ 4$. An investor could then borrow $ 100 at the risk-free rate of 7.40% for 2.36 years promising to repay $ 118.35 (or else, he uses own funds). He then buys the call for $ 4 from the lender, and invests the remaining $ 96 in risk-free securities maturing 2.36 years from now. The call is to purchase the loan at $ 113.62 at the end of a 2.63 years period. At maturity, the placement in riskless securities has grown to $ 113.62, and the investor uses this sum to buy the loan, whose value is $ 118.35. With this sum he extinguishes his liabilities. The lender has disbursed $ 96, and has purchased the guaranteed loan for $ 4, which he has financed by selling the call. When the call is exercised, he receives $ 113.62 which he uses to pay bank his depositors ($ 96 (1.074)^2.36).

fect of the guarantee, the loan's expected loss is reduced by $ 3.38, that is from $ 4.00 to $ 0.63. It thus seems natural to ask: what is the loan's principal amount for which an expectation of loss of $ 0.63 represents 4%? The answer is $ 15.75 (that is $ 0.63/0.04). Put differently, $ 15.75 is the «equivalent» exposure towards the main obligor left with the lender once the guarantee is issued, while the balance $ 84.25 is shifted onto the guarantor in exchange for the guarantee's price. It is as if, from a pure risk perspective, of the $ 100 loan, about $ 16 is provided by the lender, and $ 84 by the guarantor, each of them bearing a proportional risk[23].

TABLE 6

PERCENTAGE OF THE LOAN'S
EQUIVALENT EXPOSURE SHIFTED ONTO THE GUARANTOR

Guarantor's rating	*Aa2/AA*	*Baa1/BBB*	*B2/B*
Correlation levels			
Max	97.93	84.25	0.00
Average	98.96	92.04	50.00
Min	100.00	100.00	100.00

Clearly, a guarantee which shifts the entire exposure onto the guarantor, simultaneously discharging the lender of any risk, is surely highly valuable for the latter, which should be prepared to pay more for it. Moreover, if the guarantor is highly rated, con-

---

[23] These arguments can be restated in terms of the symbols introduced in Section 3.6. If «*a*» is the share of the loan exposure left with the principal obligor, then $a = E°/E* = (B - B°)/(B - B*)$, where $B* < B° < B$. Then, if $B° = B$, $a = 0$. Furthermore, from footnote 20, we can also write:

$$E*=(B–B*)=B\{1–[(1+R)/(1+R*)]^T\} \quad \text{and} \quad E°=(B–B°)=B\{1–[(1+R)/(1+R°)]^T\}$$

Therefore, $G = (E* - E°)$ can also be written as: $G = B\{[(1 + R)/(1 + R°)]^T - [(1 + R)/(1 + R*)]^T\}$.

Which is equivalent to *(i)* in footnote 20. Note, however, that for $T = 1$, the above formula for $E*$ does not exactly coincide with that reported in Section 2, but will be: $E* = Q (1 - RR)/(1 + R)$. The reason is that, implicitly, we are here dealing with zero-coupon loans where $R*$ is zero and all the return (cost) is in capital appreciation.

siderations regarding the default correlation can safely be ignored: the guaranteee is solid anyway. Much the same can be said if the guarantor can be deemed to be fully independent from the principal obligor. Its guarantees would always achieve the end result of freeing the lender from any risk-exposure to the borrower. In other words, the left column and the bottom row of Table 6 indicate cases where guarantees are undoubtedly «strong».

These considerations have an importance in terms of internal management of credit risk exposure limits. a guarantee from an *Aa2/AA* guarantor would suggest that the lending bank may assign nearly the whole exposure against the guarantor's credit limit, almost totally discharging that of the principal obligor. But a guarantee from a *B2/B* rated guarantor, showing an «average» default correlation with the borrower, would require that only one half of the total exposure be imputed against the guarantor's credit limit, the difference remaining with the borrower.

It is also possible to put guarantees in a dynamic risk management perspective. For instance, suppose that, in the average default correlation case, the guarantor's rating fall, from *Aa2/AA* to *Baa1/BBB* soon after the loan is granted. Then the value of the guarantee would decline by 28 cents to $ 3.69 (see Table 5 - and this should also be the reduction in the «fair» value of the loan), while about 7% (= 0.28/3.97) of the exposure would be shifted back from the guarantor to the main obligor. Individual credit risk exposures should be adjusted accordingly.

These results can be used to throw some light on the implications of current bank capital regulations concerning guarantees. Under present rules, a bank lender receiving a full, irrevocable and unconditional guarantee from another bank on a corporate loan will see the minimum capital adequacy requirement fall from 8% to 1.6% of the loan's face value (that is, from a 100%-weighted risk, requiring at least a minimum capital reserve of 8%, to a 20%-weighted one). Applying the same framework of Table 6, this means that 20% of the credit risk exposure is left with the original lender (as $ 20 is the equivalent full-risk exposure for which $ 1.6 represents an 8% capital requirement), the remaining 80% being shifted on to the guarantor. No explicit concession is made either for the guarantor's creditworthiness or for the borrower-guarantor default correlation. It may however be said that a rough-and-ready allowance for these aspects is surreptitiously introduced via the (questionable) proviso that no regulatory capital (and risk) reduction is permitted should the guarantor be a non-bank entity (e.g., an insurance or industrial company). This could well have the effect of concentrating risk in the banking sector, and more generally represent an obstacle to efficient risk-spreading throughout the whole economy.

Another perplexing result is that, should the guarantee be issued by another bank, this will be counted as a full-risk item for the guarantor, thereby requiring an $ 8 minimum capital allocation (instead of one of $ 6.4 - or 8% of $ 80 - only). We have therefore a situation where, in effect, the addition of a bank guarantee not only redistributes a given amount of credit risk across different players within the banking system (presumably to those better able to bear it), but also multiplies it by a factor of 1.2. That is, a risk-mitigation measure has the end-result of increasing by 20% the aggregate amount of (regulatory) risk banks have to provide for, and therefore the amount of resources an economy has to devote to bank intermediation.

In principle, a more rational distribution of loan-loss reserves (i.e., bank capital) in case of bank-guaranteed loans would have to look at the specific risk-transfer properties of guarantees on a case-by-case basis, as illustrated above. Take the situation where the guarantor is rated *B2/B*. Then, from Table 5 above, it is clear that, in case of minimum default correlation between the borrower and the guarantor, the guaranteed loan is risk-free, and the lender would not need to provide any capital against the loan. By contrast, the guarantor bank will shoulder the whole risk, and would have to crease a loan-loss reserve, let us say one equal to the $ 4.00 expectation of loss[24]. In the opposite case of maximum feasible correla-

---

[24] The considerations developed in paragraph 2.6 on the lender's capital adequacy extend to the guarantor. Thus an up-front equity commitment equal to the expected loss would cover a loss larger than that if the lender pays a guarantee fee, particularly if this is paid as lump-sum at the time of issuance. On this point, it should be noted that, while US monoline bond guarantors generally receive the whole of their guarantee fees up-front, banks normally bundle the payment of the risk-spread with the regular loan service.

tion no risk would be transferred on the guarantor, and it would be up to the bank lender to provide the whole $ 4.00. In the intermediate case of average correlation, the lender would reserve $ 2.00, while the balance of $ 2.00 would be provided by the guarantor.

5. - The Unexpected Loss

So far, we have proceeded under the simplifying assumption that loan and guarantee pricing were established on the basis of expected losses, and that the risk-profile of the borrower remained unchanged during the life of the loan. This is probably an acceptable assumption whenever pricing considerations are concerned. Expected loss calculations thus performed allow for an estimate of the «fair» value of a loan. They can thus play a role in loan structuring and negotiations, but whether the lending officer is indeed able to eventually transform these a-priori calculations into actual results will depend, inter alia, on the loan (or guarantee) market structure and its current conditions.

Moreover, accepting the «expected loss» as a credit risk metric may be resisted by risk-averse bank management and regulators. For both, what could be more relevant is the distribution of the possible credit losses around their expected value, rather than the latter alone. This is all the more important if the approach described earlier is to be extended to credit risk management issues, such as the assessment of level of bank capital. A few indications as to such a use have already been given, but a somewhat more detailed investigation of the statistical properties of the random variable «credit loss» is necessary in order to add precision to the proposed application of this risk-management methodology.

For this purpose, one could evaluate a set of possible future distributions of the loss variable, one for each future instant of time deemed relevant. There are several ways to accomplish this. One involves «stressing» specific future default rates (e.g., those relating to years when possible adverse occurrences for the borrower may take place - such as large loan repayments) by increasing the average historic default frequencies by some multiple of their standard deviations[25]. Here, however, we shall explore a more general method based on the concept of «rating drift», namely on the observation that a borrower's rating may «drift» over time according to certain statistical «laws» characterised by a set of «rating-transition probabilities» and described by the well-known stochastic processes called «Markov chains». These «transition probabilities» are the (historically observed) likelihood that a borrower, starting with a given credit rating when the loan is granted, ends up, at the end of a given period, with a different one, implying higher or lower default probabilities, and thus expected losses for the lender. Such probabilities are summarised in a «rating-transition matrix»[26].

---

[25] On a very intuitive level, one might draw a parallel between measures of interest rate and credit risks. For instance, a metric of interest rate risk for a traded fixed-income instrument is «duration», which is a first-degree approximation of the instrument's yield sensitivity. A second-order approximation is «convexity». Here, the «expected» and «unexpected» losses coincide with or depend on, respectively, the first and second-moments of the statistical distribution of the random variable «credit loss».

[26] The generic element a $(i:j)$ of the «rating-transition matrix» A represents the probability that the borrower's rating changes from «i» to «j» at in the course of a given time period. Then, assuming such probabilities are independent from their past realisations, the generic element of the n-power of this matrix gives the probability that, starting with an «i» rating when the loan is granted, the borrower ends up with a rating of «j» after «n» periods. This fact allows the extension of the above «scenario analysis» to any time horizon. Notice that the «rating-transition matrix» is square (the nulber of initial rating - shown in the rows - must equal that of final ratings - shown in the columns), that all its elements are non-negative, and that the sum of the elements in each row equals one (a construction known as «Markov matrix»). For instance, assume the following «rating-transition matric»:

	Aaa	Aa1
Aaa	70%	30%
Aa1	40%	60%

Then there is a 70% probability that a borrower rated *Aaa* at the beginning of the year will keep this rating to yearend, and one of 30% that it will be downgraded to *Aa*1. Equally, there is a 60% probability that a borrower initially rated *Aa*1 will still be rated *Aa*1 at the end of the year, and one of 40% that the rating is upped to *Aaa*. Then, the «rating-transition matrix» referring to a 3-year period will be:

	Aaa	Aa1
Aaa	58.3%	41.7%
Aa1	55.6%	44.4%

As an example, we have shown, in the third row of Table 7 labelled «Unsecured», the expected losses of the unsecured loan described in Table 1 under the assumption that, at the end of the first year, the borrower shall be re-rated higher or lower, or will be declared insolvent, according to a given set of empirically estimated rating-transition probabilities shown in the second row of Table 7 (Lucas [15]). As usual, these expected losses are based on the historical default frequencies associated with each of these possible new ratings (applied only to the loan's last two years of life). For brevity, we shall refer to them as *One-Year-Ahead Expected*

---

[26] note continued

Therefore, the three-year-ahead mean and standard deviation of the expected loss distribution on a loan where the borrower's initial rating is *Aaa* (*Aa*1) can be computed as in Table 7, using the probabilities in the first (second) row of the above matrix to weight each expected loss associated with each of two possible future ratings. It could also be interesting to compute the limit distribution of the transition probabilities $P1$ and $P2$ (that is, the values of the transition probabilities as the nulber of periods considered - i.e., the length of the loan - increases). In the example above, these are found by solving the following system:

$$0.7\,P1 + 0.4\,P2 = P1$$
$$0.3\,P1 + 0.6\,P2 = P2$$

which can also be written as:

(1a) $AP = P$

where P is the column vector of the limit transition probabilities $P1$ and $P2$. A general method for solving *(1a)* consists in considering the following system of equations:

(1b) $(A - u\,I)\,P = 0$

where the scalar u is called the «characteristic root» (or eigenvalue) of matrix A, I is the identity matrix and P is now referred to as the «eigenvector» corresponding to u. A non zero solution *(1b)* exists only if the matrix $(A - u\,I)$ is non-singular, that is if:

(1c) $det\,(A - u\,I) = 0$

where *det* = determinant. Given A as in the example above, there will be two values for u, namely $u' = 1$ and $u'' = 0.3$ Selecting the larger of them, and substituting it into *(1a)*, yields $P1 = 0.4/0.3\ P2$. This result, associated with the normalising condition $(P1 + P2) = 1$, yields the economically relevant solution, namely $P1 = 57.14\%$, $P2 = 42.86\%$. In other words, as the length of the loan increases, the probability that the borrower shall keep his initial rating at the end of it is 57.14% while there is a 42.86% chance that he will not (for the worse or the better). Note that these limiting transition probabilities are independent from the initial rating, that is, the rows of the limit transition matrix will be the same. As an empirical remark, it is easily shown that this limiting probability distribution is reached in about 9 periods.

Losses. There is thus a 73.8% probability that the borrower's present rating is confirmed at the end of the first year, implying an unchanged expected loss of $ 4.00, as well as a probability of 1.4% that it shall default, inflicting an «exceptionally» large loss on the lender (keep in mind that the highly conservative hypothesis of a nil recovery is maintained).

TABLE 7

DISTRIBUTION OF ONE-YEAR-AHEAD EXPECTED LOSSES
(figured in $)

New ratings	A3	Baa1	Baa2	Baa3	Ba1	Ba2	Ba3	B1	B2	B3	Caa	Def
Probabilities	0.9%	0.8%	3.3%	6.2%	73.8%	4.6%	4.7%	2.6%	0.3%	1.2%	0.2%	1.4%
Unsecured	1.68	1.86	2.17	2.82	4.00	5.22	7.94	10.74	13.69	18.51	23.72	100
Baa1-Guar	0.23	0.32	0.32	0.32	0.32	0.32	0.32	0.32	0.32	0.32	0.32	0.32

Source, the rating transition probabilities shown in the second row above are from the one-year rating-transition matrix reproduced in Exhibit 7 of Lucas D.J. [15]. For the *Baa1*-guaranteed loan, the default correlation values between borrower and guarantor are kept at their average feasible levels.

As can be seen, while the median value for this one-year-ahead distribution of expected losses is still $ 4.00, its weighted average is now $ 5.84 (for a standard deviation of $ 11.47). One interpretation of this fact could be that $ 1.83 (i.e., $ 5.84 less $ 4.01) represents a sort of «unexpected» or «excess» credit loss, in the sense of embedding a measure of the volatility of the borrower's credit rating one year from now. In other words, it is an «add-on» a lender (and regulator) might wish to consider when allocating equity capital to the loan (and, market permitting, the lending rate) to face unexpected adverse future circumstances.

This analysis also allows us to conclude that there about 90% chances that the actual loss shall be no more than $ 10.74, while there is a 97% probability that it will be lower than $ 13.69. Thus, if the bank's management operates on the basis of a 90% confidence level for the one-year-ahead loss, it might still decide to price the loan according to an expectation of loss of $ 4.00, but to prudentially set risk provisions as high as $ 6.74 (i.e. $ 10.74 less $ 4.00), reflecting the possibility that an «exceptional» loss may occur[27].

Notice also that there are about 95% chances that the loss shall be below $ 8, that is the minimum required regulatory capital. However, if in this case a capital ratio of $ 8 offers the reasonable confidence of keeping the lender solvent in 95% of the possible future outcomes regarding the loan, these may diminish dramatically, or soar to close to 100%, if the borrower's initial rating was much lower or higher. Thus, even if the notion of expected/unexpected loss is rejected as unreliable or inadequate for setting risk-based capital ratios in favour of some other definition of worst-case loss, the fact remains that a flat capital requirement runs the risk of either being insufficient or redundant. Anyway, this sort of exercise can yield useful insights, both for the lender or the guarantor (and, for that matter, a bank supervisor) when deciding the appropriate general risk-provisioning against credit exposures[28].

---

[27] It has been reported (JACKSON P. [13], p. 179) that, in banking practice, the lending spread is counted upon to absorb the expected loss. Therefore, the equity injected by the lender should only reflect the unexpected loss. For a more formal treatment of loan-loss provisions, see McKENZIE G. [18]. However, as already remarked, one is never certain that the lending spread achieved will be sufficient to cover the expected part of the loss, while, unless the loan is disbursed below par, in case of default the lender will not recover the whole value of the lending spread. All in all, it would seem more appropriate to have the lender «pre-commit» an up front equity reserve at least equal to the expected loss, and then leave the lending spread (whatever it might be) to provide for any unexpected loss.

[28] Should a rating-transition-matrix not be readily available, there are other techniques for estimating the loan's unexpected loss. One is base on the Poisson stochastic process. For instance, starting from the 1-year default frequency of 1.37% (see the second column of Table 1), and assuming the frequency of default is Poisson distributed, then the mean and standard deviation of the 3-year comulative default rate are both equal to 4.11%. Furthermore, there is a 99% a-priori probability that the 3-year cumulative default rate shall not be higher than 9%. Distributing this cumulative probability of insolvency over the loan's 3-year life proportionally to the annual default rate statistics (i.e. proportionally to the second column of Table 1), one arrives at an expected loss of $ 6.70. Therefore, $ 2.70 (or $ 6.70 less $ 4.00) is the unexpected loss corresponding to a 99% confidence level. Had one started with the average annual default frequency of 1.79% instead (i.e., 5.38% divided by 3), the unexpected loss at the 99% confidence level would have been $ 4.20 (so that a capital cushion of $ 8 would have been sufficient to face the total loss on this loan in 99 out of 100 cases).

The same exercise can be performed by a lender evaluating a guaranteed loan. In other words, the «fair» value of the guarantee (Table 5) can be recomputed under different scenarios as to the future rating of the guarantor. In this case, however, another dimension has to be added: namely, the possibility that the guarantor-borrower default correlation also changes. This is done in Table 8 for a guarantor with an initial rating of *Aa2/AA*. Again, we have assumed that after one year, the rating of the guarantor may be revised (with the probabilities expressed by the rating-transition matrix), while the default correlation may either settle at its average, or move to its lowest/highest possible levels. Similarily, we shall refer to these various guarantee prices (expressed in terms of up-front fees, only) as «one-year-ahead guarantee values».

TABLE 8

DISTRIBUTION OF ONE-YEAR-AHEAD GUARANTEE VALUES
(figures in $)

New ratings Probabilities	*Aaa* 1.0%	*Aa1* 2.7%	*Aa2* 77.2%	*Aa3* 9.7%	*A1* 6.5%	*A2* 1.7%	*A3* 0.9%	*Baa1* 0.2%	*Baa2* 0.1%	*Avg.*	*St Dev*
Correlation levels											
Max	3.93	3.92	3.88	3.87	3.80	3.78	3.63	3.45	3.14	3.87	0.05
Average	3.93	3.93	3.91	3.91	3.87	3.86	3.78	3.69	3.54	3.91	0.02
Min	4.00	4.00	4.00	4.00	4.00	4.00	4.00	4.00	4.00	4.00	4.00

Source, see Table 7. For simplicity, the probabilities of the *Aa2/AA* guarantor being rated below *Baa1/BBB*, or defaulting, after one year are ignored. The cumulative value of this probabilities (0.223%) has been redistributed proportionally on the other rating changes. In the simulations, the first-year default rate for the guarantor has been kept unchanged at its *Aa2* level of 0.02%.

First we consider the case where a change in the guarantor's rating occurs without a modification in the default correlation, that is we move horizontally along the rows of Table 8. For instance, if the assumption is that the correlation remains at the average of its maximum and minimum feasible levels when the one-year-ahead guarantor's rating changes, then the worst case situation will be a 37 cent increase in the secured loan's expected loss (i.e. the difference between $ 3.91, the original value of the guarantee, and $ 3.54, its new value). If the correlation is kept at its maximum level, the worst case additional loss transferred to the guaranteed lender will be 74 cents (i.e. $ 3.88 less $ 3.14)[29].

The mirror-image situation is when the guarantor rating is unchanged (at *Aa*2 here) but, for the effect of certain economic events (e.g., the guarantor acquires an «exposure» to the borrower), the default correlation is affected. We thus move vertically along the columns of Table 8. As we already know (Table 5), a variation in the default correlation is bound to affect the value of the guarantee. In general, this change will be the higher the lower is the guarantor's rating. In the example of Table 8, the value of the guarantee drops at most (and, in principle, the lender's risk provisions should be increased) by 12 cents, from $ 4.00 to $ 3.88.

In general, the worst-case is represented by an increase in the correlation from the lowest to its highest feasible value, accompained by a simultaneous «large» downgrading of the guarantor, from *Aa*2 to *Baa*2 in the example. The value of the guarantee would then drop by a maximum of some 22%, that is from $ 4.00 to $ 3.14. This will inflict an opportunity loss of 86 cents on the secured lender, which should therefore increase risk reserves by at least this amount. Additionally, the share of exposure shifted on the guarantor will fall from the original 100% to 78.35%.

There is also the possibility that, while the future creditworthiness of the guarantor and its relationship with the borrower remains unchanged, the borrower's solvency is modified, for the better or the worse. The effect on the loan's expected loss of this possibility occurring at the end of the first year is shown in the bottom row of Table 7. For sake of simplicity, these figures refer to only one of the several possible cases, namely when the guarantor is originally rated *Baa*1 and its default correlation with the borrower is kept at the mean of the feasible minimum and maximum levels. As can be seen, the result is that nothing really chang-

---

[29] Of course, if the default correlation is kept at its lowest possible level when the guarantor's rating is modified, the value of the guarantee remains unaffected. This is so by construction, since a minimum level for the correlation simply implies that the default probability of the guaranteed loans is set at zero. The bottom row of Table 8 may have just as well been omitted. It is shown only for sake of completeness.

es, as the expected loss of the guaranteed loan is only marginally affected[30].

Finally, the guaranteed lender may wish to combine the effects of the two situations described above, namely a future simultaneous deterioration in the financial conditions of both the borrower and the guarantor. In practice, however, since we have just seen that the changes in the credit standing of the guarantor, and in its default correlation with the borrower, dominate the final results, this analysis does not seem to add important insights as to credit risk management. In plain words, we have the numerical demonstration of the common sense conclusion that, when the guarantee is full, irrevocable and unconditional, the guaranteed lender needs only to monitor the guarantor, while the latter monitors the principal obligor.

What this kind of sensitivity analysis also permits to do is for the lender or the guarantor to use any additional private information they may have obtained from close contacts with the borrower to modify the generic default probabilities derived from the available default frequency tables, thereby arriving at a more precise assessment of the risk involved in a lending or guarantee operation.

6. - Conclusions

This paper has argued that a loan's expected loss, supplemented by a number of considerations pertaining to its statistical distribution, is a useful benchmark on which to price loans and build internal risk monitoring systems. The notion of expected loss is

---

[30] Indeed, because the correlation is here left to adapt to its new average level when the rating of the borrower changes, the expected loss of the guaranteed loan never increases over its original level of 32 cents. It falls, however, to 23 cents when the borrower's rating exceeds that of the guarantor. in other words, if the guarantor's rating does not change over time, and the default correlation is also fixed (not in absolute terms, but in relative ones, that is at the – changing – average of the minimum and maximum values), the expected loss of a guaranteed loan can only improve following modifications in the creditworthiness of the principal obligor.

intuitive, and can be easily computed. It can also accomodate several loan features which shape credit risk. Making recourse to the expected loss as a guide for setting lending rates and risk-provisions should bring banks to emphasise the need for adequate risk-adjusted returns and internal capital generation. Used for devising in-house systems for risk-adjusted performance monitoring, it should restrain lending desks' incentives to maximise lending growth at the expense of asset quality. In short, it holds a number of attractions as a benchmark for bank solvency policy.

The paper has also given special attention to loan guarantees. Following Merton [19], a loan guarantee can be seen as an over-the-counter (*OTC*) put option on a credit-risk exposure (i.e., a «credit derivative»), purchased by the lender from the guarantor against a price. This option gives the lender the possibility, to be excercised up to a specified future date (the loan's maturity), of transferring the loan to the option's writer (the guarantor) in exchange for a predetermined price (the loan's face value plus interest). Traditionally, however, the exercise of this option is made conditional on a well-specified default event occurring, rather than it being exercisable, as would be the case with ordinary American put options, any time the loan's market value falls below par, for instance following a downgrading of the borrower (whereupon the rational lender would put the loan to the guarantor). Indeed, in cases falling short of outright default (such as the missing of an interest payment), it is more common to renegotiate lending terms than to draw on the guarantor. Moreover, the ways a guarantee is exercised are also non-standard, and depend on the nature of contractual provisions. For example, there may or not be an acceleration clause, while the degree of enforceability and timeliness of payments under the guarantee contract may also vary.

However, an important feature loan guarantees have in common with *OTC* options (and, more generally, with *OTC* derivatives) is the lack of a formal assurance, such as that provided by the interposition of a clearing house, of the option seller's ability to perform. This paper has developed an approach in which this particular form of counterparty risk is explicity priced by taking into account both the counterparty's general riskiness (as exemplified by its rating) and the risk specific to the underlying financial claim (as encapsulated in its relationship with the guaranteed borrower). Although loan guarantees may be tailor-made in several other ways, all of which shall ultimately be reflected in their market price, the identity of guarantor, and its ability to perform as expected, are by far the most relevant ones.

1) The valuation of the «fair» market price of a loan extended to a borrower subject to default risk can be pursued following two equivalent procedures, namely by: *(i)* discounting to present, using interest rates adjusted for default risk, the loan's promised (i.e., contractual) cash-flows, or by: *(ii)* discounting to present using the risk-free rates, the loan's promised cash-flows adjusted for default risk (i.e., the certainty-equivalent, or «expected», cash-flows).

If the adjustmments to the interest rates (under *(i)*) and to the cash-flows (under *(ii)*) are mutually coherent, the results (i.e., the «market price» of the loan) will be the same. The approach *(ii)* above has been used in the main text (Table 1).

2) In symbols, these two equivalent approaches can be represented as:

$$(6) \qquad B^* = SUM\,(P_j^*\, a_j) \quad \text{or} \quad B^* = SUM\,(P_j\, a_j^*)$$

where the summation (*SUM*) extends over the loan's maturity ($j = 1, 2, \ldots, m$), and: B^* is the market value of the risky loan; a_j^* is the j-th cash-flow adjusted for risk (i.e., the «expected» cash-flow); P_j^* is the current price of a risky zero-coupon bond promising to pay \$ 1 at time j; a_j is the j-th risk-free cash-flow; P_j is the current price of a riskless zero-coupon bond promising to pay \$ 1 at time j.

3) Besides, we also have the following relations:

$$(7) \qquad P_j^* = (1 - hj\,Lj)\,P_j \quad \text{and} \quad a_j^* = (1 - hj\,Lj)\,a_j$$

where: hj is the default probability corresponding to the j-th cash-flow; Lj is the loss severity affecting the j-th cash-flow in case of insolvency.

4) Since the value of a risky loan is equal to that of an «equivalent» (i.e., for the same term structure, cash-flow, etc.) risk-free one less the expected loss, we may write:

(8) B* = SUM (P_j (1 – hj Lj) a_j) = SUM (P_j a_j) – SUM (P_j hj Lj a_j) =

$$B – SUM (P_j \, hj \, Lj \, a_j).$$

where *B* is the value of the equivalent risk-free loan.

5) Let us now assume that the riskless loan is issued at par (*B* = 1). Then from *(8)*, we can derive the present value of the expected loss (*E**) on the risky loan, namely:

(9)   *E* = (1 – B) = SUM (P_j hj Lj a_j).*

6) In the case of a riskless loan, with a general amortisation plan, we also have:

$$a_j = R \, D_j + K_j$$

where: *R* is the nominal risk-free coupon rate to be found; D_j is the debt outstanding before the *j*-th instalment of principal ($D1 = 1$; *Dm* + 1 = 0); K_j is the *j*-th instalment of principal ($K_j = D_j – D_j + 1$).

7) Therefore, for a riskless loan's issue price to be set at par, it must be that:

(10) $1 = SUM ((P_j (R \, D_j + K_j)) = R \, SUM (P_j \, D_j) + SUM (P_j \, K_j)$

Solving *(10)* for the contractual par coupon rate on the riskless loan, we obtain:

$$R = (1 – SUM (P_j \, K_j)) \, SUM (P_j \, D_j)$$

expressing the risk-less par coupon rate as a function of the loan's cash-flows (K_j and D_j), and the risk-free term structure (P_j).

8) The analogous condition for a risky loan is:

(11) $R* = (1 – SUM (P_j^* \, K_j)) \, SUM (P_j^* \, D_j)$

which shows how the risky loan's coupon rate depends, through P^*_j, on the default probabilities and the severity of loss *(7)*.

9) Finally, the risk-spread $RS = (R^* - R)$ applied to the risky loan can be seen, with a few manipulations, to be exactly sufficient to generate net revenues with a present value equal to the loss expectation, that is:

$$RS \; SUM \; (P^*_j \; D_j) = E^*.$$

BIBLIOGRAPHY

[1] ALTMAN E.I. - BENCIVENGA J.C., «A Yield Premium Model For the High-Yield Debt Market», *Financial Analysis Journal*, September-October 1995, pp. 49-56.

[2] ASARNOW E. - EDWARDS D., «Measuring Loss on Defaulted Bank Loans: A 24-Year Study», *Journal of Commercial Lending*, March 1995.

[3] BARONE E. - BRAGHÒ A., «An Integrated System for the Management of Interest Rate Risk», paper presented at the IV Financial Conference organised by the Faculty of Economics of the University of «Tor Vergata» on: *Asymmetric Information, Risk Management, Financial and Banking Innovation*, Rome, 30 November-2 December 1995.

[4] BARONTINI R., *Costi del fallimento e gestione della crisi nelle procedure concorsuali*, Milano, Università Cattolica del S. Cuore - Centro Studi Finanziari, April 1996.

[5] BELCREDI M., *Le ristrutturazioni stragiudiziali delle aziende in crisi in Italia nei primi anni '90*, Milano, Università Cattolica del S. Cuore - Centro Studi Finanziari, April 1996.

[6] BLACK F. - SCHOLES M., «The Pricing of Options and Corporate Liabilities», *Journal of Political Economy*, Vol. 81, n. 3, May-June 1973, pp. 637-54.

[7] CARTY L. - LIEBERMAN D., «Corporate Bond Defaults and Default Rates 1938-1995», *Moody's Investors Service*, January 1996, pp. 1-37.

[8] CHANCE D.M., «Translating the Greek: The Real Meaning of Call Option Derivatives», *Financial Analysts Journal*, July-August 1994, pp. 43-9.

[9] CRANE D.B. - BODIE Z., «The Transformation of Banking. Form Follows Function», *Harvard Business Review*, March-April 1996, pp. 109-17.

[10] FONS J.S., «Using Default Rates to Model the Term Structure of Credit Risk», *Financial Analysts Journal*, September-October 1994, pp. 25-32.

[11] GENERALE A. - GOBBI G., «Il recupero dei crediti: costi, tempi e comportamenti delle banche», Roma, Banca d'Italia, *Temi di Discussione*, n. 265, March 1996.

[12] HULL J. - WHITE A., «The Price of Default», *Risk*, vol. 5, n. 8, September 1992, pp. 101-3.

[13] JACKSON P., «Risk Measurement and Capital Requirements for Banks», *Bank of England Quarterly Bulletin*, May 1995, pp. 177-84.

[14] JONKHART M., «On the Term Structure of Interest Rates and the Risk of Default: An Analytical Approach», *Journal of Banking and Finance*, n. 3, September 1979, pp. 253-62.

[15] LUCAS D.J., «The Effectiveness of Downgrade Provisions in Reducing Counterparty Risk», *The Journal of Fixed Income*, June 1995, pp. 32-41.

[16] — —, «Default Correlation and Credit Analysis», *The Journal of Fixed Income*, March 1995, pp. 76-97.

[17] LUSTING J. - GUINEE C.L. - DOMMERMUTH M. - WATSON JR. M. DOUGLAS, «Moody's Bank Loan Ratings: Pricing Implications and Approach», Global Credit Research, *Moody's Investors Service*, April 1996, pp. 1-29.

[18] MCKENZIE G., «Loan-Loss Provisions and Bank Buffer-Stock Capital», *Applied Financial Economics*, n. 6, 1996, pp. 213-23.

[19] MERTON R.C., «An Analytic Derivation of the Cost of Deposit Insurance and Loan Guarantees», *Journal of Banking and Finance*, n. 1, June 1977, pp. 3-11.

[20] — —, «The Financial System and Economic Performance», *Journal of Financial Servicies Research*, 1990, pp. 263-300.

[21] MILLER M.H., «Do the M&M Propositions Apply to Banks?», *Journal of Banking and Finance*, n. 19, 1995, pp. 483-89.

A Model for Measuring Financial Risks

Emilio Barone - Antonio Braghò*

Istituto Mobiliare Italiano, Roma

Introduction

Banks will soon be called upon to apply special capital requirements for market risks, in addition to those for credit risks,
in accordance with the prescriptions of the Basle Committee. Some banks will choose the internal models method to determine
these requirements with the aim of optimizing the use of their
own capital.

In this paper, after reviewing the regulatory conditions for the
use of internal models, such as the specification of market risk
factors, quantitative standards (including backtesting) and stress
testing, we put forward a general continuous-time model. This is
used to determine measures of volatility and «turbulence» that serve as synthetic instruments for monitoring the riskiness of a
portfolio. We then look at the significance of value-at-risk (VAR)
and propose an analytical approximation. A discussion follows of
the reasons (including the empirical evidence contrary to the assumption of normality) which led the Basle Committee to pre-
scribe a multiplicative factor for VAR in determining the capital
requirement for market risks. VAR is then compared with the va-

---

* The authors are in charge of the Analysis of Financial Risks.

N.B.: the numbers in square brackets refer to the Bibliography at the end of
the paper.

lue of a put option guaranteeing a minimum level of shareholder's equity. This leads to a call for the present regulations to be developed in the direction of an integrated approach that will determine the value of a portfolio and its volatility as a function of the various financial and credit factors (and of the concentration of exposures towards given sectors/ borrowers). The paper concludes with the presentation of some applications showing how the proposed approach can be implemented in practice.

1. - Capital Requirements for Credit and Market Risks

The *Amendment to the Capital Accord to Incorporate Market Risks*, published in January 1996 by the Bank for International Settlements (BIS - Basle Committee on Banking Supervision), states that «As from the end of 1997, or earlier if their supervisory authority so prescribes, banks will be required to measure and apply capital charges in respect of their market risks in addition to their credit risks. Market risk is defined as the risk of losses in on- and off-balance-sheet positions arising from movements in market prices. The risks subject to this requirement are: the risks pertaining to interest rate related instruments and equities in the trading book; foreign exchange risk and commodities risk throughout the bank»[1].

The application of the *Amendment* is the responsibility of the supervisory authorities of the Group of Ten countries[2]. The capital requirements for market and credit risks will be determined in the following manner:

---

[1] Specifically, «The trading book means the bank's proprietary positions in financial instruments (including positions in derivative products and off-balance-sheet instruments) which are intentionally held for short-term resale [...], and positions in financial instruments arising from matched principal brokering and market making, or positions taken in order to hedge other elements of the trading book». (BANK FOR INTERNATIONAL SETTLEMENTS [3], p. 1, paragraph 2).

«The capital charges for foregn exchange risk and for commodities risk will apply to bank's total currency and commodity positions, subject to some discretion to exclude structural foreign exchange positions». (BANK FOR INTERNATIONAL SETTLEMENTS [3], p. 2, paragraph 6).

[2] Benelux, Canada, France, Germany, Italy, Japan, Sweden, Switzerland, United Kingdom, United States.

a) the capital requirement for market risk (R_M) is calculated as the sum of the requirements for general market risk (R_{GM}), the risk of loss arising from «adverse changes in market prices», and for specific risk (R_S), the risk of loss arising from «an adverse price movement of a security due principally to factors related to the issuer of the security» (Bank for International Settlements [2], paragraph 23, p. 7).

b) the capital requirement for market risk is multiplied by 12.5 (i.e. the reciprocal of the minimum capital ratio of 8%) and the result added to the sum of risk-weighted assets (A_p) compiled for credit risk purposes ($R_C = 8\% \times A_p$)[3];

c) the ratio between the capital eligible for supporting risk (P_I) and the term given above at point *b)* is then calculated. This capital ratio must exceed 8%.

In symbols:

(1)
$$\frac{P_I}{(R_{GM} + R_S) \times 12.5 + A_p} > 8\%$$
$$P_I = P_1 + P_2 + P_3$$
$$P_2 \le P_1$$
$$P_{3M} < 2.5 P_{1M}$$

where: $P_1 = P_{1C} + P_{1M}$ is the tier 1 capital (share capital plus retained earnings) available to support credit and market risk; $P_2 = P_{2C} + P_{2M}$ is the eligible tier 2 capital (medium and long-term subordinated debt, credit loss provisions, etc.) available to support credit and market risk; $P_3 = P_{3M}$ is the eligible tier 3 capital (short-term subordinated debt) available to support market risk ($P_{3C} = 0$).

For both components of market risk the Committee has proposed its own – simplified – method of calculation (the «standar-

---

[3] As regards risk-weighted assets, the Committee provides for credit risk to be measured «excluding debt and equity instruments in the trading book and all positions in commodities, but including the credit counterparty risk on all over-the-counter derivatives whether in the trading or banking books». (BANK FOR INTERNATIONAL SETTLEMENTS [3], p. 4, paragraph 13).

dized» approach), but has left banks free to use measurement systems they have developed internally (the «internal models» approach)[4].

The use of internal models has been made conditional on approval by the national supervisory authority, which will be granted subject to seven sets of conditions: 1) general criteria concerning the adequacy of the risk management system; 2) qualitative standards for internal oversight of the use of models; 3) guidelines for specifying market risk factors; 4) quantitative standards for measuring market risk; 5) guidelines for stress testing; 6) validation of models by external auditors and/or supervisory authorities; 7) rules for the use of a mixture of the internal models and standardized approaches.

For the present purposes it is sufficient to provide a summary review of the conditions laid down for (1.1) the specification of market risk factors, (1.2) the quantitative standards, including backtesting, and (1.3) stress testing.

1.1 *Specification of Market Risk Factors*

Models must comply with the following guidelines:
1) for interest rates, there must be a set of risk factors corresponding to interest rates in each currency in which the bank has interest-rate-sensitive on- or off-balance sheet positions. [...] For material exposures to interest rate movements in the major currencies and markets, banks must model the yield curve using a minimum of six risk factors. [...] a bank with a portfolio of various types of securities across many points of the yield curve and that engages in complex arbitrage strategies would require a greater number of risk factors to capture interest rate risk accurately.

---

[4] «The Committee has accordingly decided [...] a modelled treatment of specific risk would be allowed subject to an overall floor on the specific risk charge applicable under the standardized approach. Banks whose models take little or no account of specific risk will be subject to the full specific risk charges of the standardized approach». (BANK FOR INTERNATIONAL SETTLEMENTS [2], p. 6, paragraph 19).

[...] The risk measurement system must incorporate separate risk factors to capture spread risk (e.g. between bonds and swaps)[5];

2) for exchange rates (which may include gold), the risk measurement system should incorporate risk factors corresponding to the individual foreign currencies in which the bank's positions are denominated;

3) for equity prices, [...] at a minimum, there should be a risk factor that is designed to capture market-wide movements in equity prices; [...] a somewhat more detailed approach would be to have risk factors corresponding to various sectors of the overall equity market; [...] the most extensive approach would be to have risk factors corresponding to the volatility of individual equity issues;

4) for commodity prices, [...] a straightforward specification of risk factors [...] would likely entail one risk factor for each commodity price to which the bank is exposed. In cases where the aggregate positions are quite small, it might be acceptable to use a single risk factor for a relatively broad sub-category of commodities (for instance, a single risk factor for all types of oil); for more active trading, the model must also take account of the variation in the «convenience yield» [...].

1.2 *Quantitative Standards*

The Basle Committee leaves banks some flexibility in defining their models, but establishes value-at-risk (VAR) as the measure of risk and lays down eleven quantitative standards that must be complied with: 1) value-at-risk must be computed on a daily basis; banks are nonetheless expected «to maintain strict management systems to ensure that intra-day exposures are not excessive» (Bank for International Settlements, [3], p. 5, paragraph

---

[5] Consider also the difference between the interest rate observable on Treasury bills and Libor for the same maturity. In this case reference is sometimes made to «basis risk» or «parameter risk». It is often forgotten that, in addition to monetary interest rates for the loan of money, there are specific interest rates for the loan of goods other than money, including securities. The existance of positive interest rates for such loans may sometimes explain the misalignment between the interest rates observable on different markets for the same maturity.

14); 2) a 99th percentile, one-tailed confidence interval is to be used in calculating VAR; 3) the minimum holding period will be ten trading days. Value-at-risk numbers may nonetheless be calculated according to shorter holding periods provided they are scaled up to ten days by the square root of time; 4) the historical observation period must be at least one year. However, this constraint is less restrictive than it might appear since the Basle Committee «has also reviewed the question of how to address different weighting schemes for the observation period. It concludes that banks should have some flexibility in this area, subject to the constraint that the "effective" observation period be at least one year». (Bank for International Settlements, [2], p. 4, paragraph 12); 5) the data sets of risk factors, observed on a daily basis, must be updated at least once every three months; 6) VAR may be calculated using models based, for example, on historical simulations or Monte Carlo simulations or analytical methods based on variance-covariance matrices; 7) in calculating VAR, account may be taken of empirical correlations both *within* and *across* broad risk categories; 8) the model must take account of the non-linear price characteristics of options with respect to the price of the underlying security. The risk measurement system «must have a set of risk factors that captures the volatility of the rates and prices underlying options positions [...]»; 9) the capital requirement for market risk is the higher of the VAR of the previous day and the average of the VAR measures on each of the preceding sixty business days, multiplied by a multiplicative factor; 10) the multiplicative factor, «set by individual supervisory authorities on the basis of their assessment of the quality of the bank's risk management system» may not be less than 3; banks may be required to increase the multiplicative factor by adding a «plus» of between 0 and 1 if the performance of the model is not deemed to be satisfactory. In fact, internal models will be subjected to backtesting on a quarterly basis. If the actual daily losses exceed the potential losses 10 times in one year (250 business days), the supervisory authorities may disallow the model[6]; 11)

---

[6] See the section on backtesting below.

the capital requirement for specific risk of interest rate related instruments and equity securities may never be less than half the requirement calculated according to the standardized methodology. Such requirement will be applied in full where specific risk is not incorporated in the model.

1.2.1 Backtesting

Banks are required to carry out backtesting on a quarterly basis for the most recent twelve months (250 business days) in order to compare the daily estimates of VAR (with reference to a one-day holding period) and the actual overall trading outcomes. (The definition of VAR to be used for backtesting is different from that based on ten-day holding periods used to determine the capital requirements for market risks)[7].

The comparison is to be made using both actual trading outcomes and the hypothetical outcomes that would have been obtained by assuming no change in the end-of-day composition of the trading portfolio compared with the previous day[8]. «In combination, the two approaches are likely to provide a strong understanding of the relation between calculated risk measures and trading outcomes». (Bank for International Settlements, [4], p. 4).

The formal calculation of the number of «exceptions», the number of days on which the VAR estimates do not cover the trading outcome, gives an indication of the reliability of the internal model which will be assessed according to the grid shown in Table 1.

---

[7] «[...], comparing the ten-day, 99th percentile risk measures from the internal models, capital requirement with actual ten-day trading outcomes would probably not be a meaningful exercise. In particular, in any given ten-day period, significant changes in portfolio composition relative to the initial positions are common at major trading institutions». (BANK FOR INTERNATIONAL SETTLEMENTS [4], p. 3).

[8] «[...], there is a concern that the overall one-day trading outcome is not a suitable point of comparison, because it reflects the effects of intra-day trading, possibly including fee income that is booked in connection with the sale of new products». (BANK FOR INTERNATIONAL SETTLEMENTS [4], p. 3).

TABLE 1

RESULTS OF BACKTESTING AND INCREASES
IN THE MULTIPLICATIVE FACTOR

Zone	Number of exceptions:[a] (x)	Increases of the multiplicative factor	Exact % probability:[b] (p)	Cumulative % probability:[c] (P)	I-type error % probability:[d] (Q)
Green	0	0	8.11	8.11	91.89
	1	0	20.47	28.58	71.42
	2	0	25.74	54.32	45.68
	3	0	21.49	75.81	24.19
	4	0	13.41	89.22	10.78
Yellow	5	0.40	6.66	95.88	4.12
	6	0.50	2.75	98.63	1.37
	7	0.65	0.97	99.60	0.40
	8	0.75	0.30	99.89	0.11
	9	0.85	0.08	99.97	0.03
Red	≥ 10	1	0.02	99.99	0.01

[a] In a sample of $n = 250$ observations and with a confidence level of $1 - \alpha = 99\%$.
[b] Probability of obtaining a number of exceptions equal to that indicated

$$p\,(x) = \frac{n!}{x!\,(n-x)!}\;\alpha^x\,(1-\alpha)^{n-x}.$$

[c] Probability of obtaining a number of exceptions less than or equal to that indicated:

$$P\,(x) = \sum_{k=0}^{x} p\,(k).$$

[d] Probability of obtaining a number of exceptions greater than that indicated:

$$Q\,(x) = 1 - P\,(x).$$

Source, BANK FOR INTERNATIONAL SETTLEMENTS [4].

Models with a small number of exceptions (≤ 4) will be «rewarded» by not having to increase the VAR multiplicative factor to obtain the capital requirement for market risk (green zone). Models with a large number of exceptions (≥ 10) will, instead, be «punished» by having to use a multiplicative factor of 4 and, in the most serious cases, by having the model disallowed by the supervisory authority (red zone). Between these two extremes (yellow zone, from 5 to 9 exceptions), the model will be subject to discretionary assessment by the supervisory authority and the size of the increase in the multiplicative factor (the «plus») will depend on the number of exceptions found. The Committee indicatively suggests a value in the range 0.4-0.85.

The last column of Table 1 shows the probability of a type I error, i.e. the probability that, given the number of exceptions found in a period of 250 business days, an accurate model is classified as inaccurate. It can be seen that the probability of an accurate model falling in the red zone is 0.01%.

1.3 *Stress Testing*

Provision is made for stress testing in order to take account of low-probability events «in all major types of risks» that could «create extraordinary losses or gains in trading portfolios, or make the control of risk in those portfolios very difficult»[9]. Stress testing scenarios must be able to «shed light on the impact of such events on positions that display both linear and nonlinear price characteristics»[10]. Two major goals of stress testing are «to evaluate the capacity of the bank's capital to absorb potential large losses and to identify steps the bank can take to reduce its risk and conserve capital»[11].

The stress-testing prescribed by the Basle Committee is to be carried out in three types of scenario:

1) supervisory scenarios requiring no simulations by the bank: banks will be required to make information available on the largest losses experienced during the reporting period to enable their supervisory authority to determine «how many days of peak day losses would have been covered by a given value-at-risk estimate»;

2) supervisory scenarios requiring a simulation by the bank: these scenarios could include testing the current portfolio against past periods of significant disturbance (e.g. the 1987 equity crash, the ERM crises of 1992 and 1993 and the fall in bond markets

---

[9] MERTON R.C. - PEROLD A. ([24], p. 2, footnote 4) give five examples of hard-to foresee «event risks» in areas external to the bank: the «scandals» at E.F. Hutton (check writing), Merrill Lynch («ticket in drawer»), Salomon Brothers (Treasury auction), Drexel Burnham Lambert (FIRREA/collapse of high-yield debt market) and T. Rowe Price Associates (money-market-fund credit loss).

[10] BANK FOR INTERNATIONAL SETTLEMENTS ([3], p. 46).

[11] The results of stress testing must be routinely communicated to senior management and periodically to the board of directors.

in the first quarter of 1994) and periods marked by brusque changes in volatilities and correlations;

3) scenarios developed by banks to capture the specific characteristics of their portfolio: such scenarios should identify highly unfavourable situations in the light of the characteristics of the bank's portfolio (e.g. problems arising from a sharp move in oil prices).

2. - A Valuation Model

In order to define and measure the risks a bank incurs, it is first necessary to define and measure its current value[12]. Three different standpoints offer three different views of the value of the bank for shareholders: the accounts show the book value, the stock exchange determines the market value and the model gives the theoretical value. Only the last approach permits the evaluation of the risks to which the bank is exposed.

Following Merton ([23], p. 450-7), a continuous-time model can be defined that makes it possible to assign a theoretical value to the portfolio and, *inter alia*, to determine the expected value and standard deviation of its rates of return.

2.1 *The Dynamics of Risk Factors*

Consider a model with n risk factors, each of which follows the dynamics described by a particular Ito process. In symbols,

$$(2) \qquad dF_i = \alpha_i (F_i, t) \, dt + \beta_i (F_i, t) \, dz_i \qquad 1 \leq i \leq n$$

where F_i is the current value of the i-th risk factor, α_i is the

---

[12] This first step is of fundamental importance. According to the GROUP OF THIRTY ([15], p. 3): «Incorrect valuation leads not only to inaccurance income recognition, but also to inaccurate hedging». See also BARONE E. - BRAGHÒ A. [6].

drift rate, i.e. the expected change in F_i per unit of time, β^2_i is the variance rate, i.e. the variance of dF_i per unit of time, and dz_i is a Wiener process $[E\,(dz_i) = 0,\ E\,(dz_i)^2 = dt,\ E\,(dz_i\,dz_j) = \rho_{ij}dt]$[13].

2.2 *Current Value, Expected Return, Volatility and Turbulence of a Portfolio*

The value of the whole portfolio W is given by

$$(3) \qquad W = \sum_{k=1}^{m} V_k \qquad 1 \le k \le m$$

where V_k is the value of the k-th contract.

Since the value of each contract depends on the n risk factors considered and on time, we have[14]:

$$(4) \qquad W \equiv W\,(F_1, F_2, ..., F_n, t).$$

Accordingly, the dynamics of the value of the portfolio is obtained by applying a generalization of Ito's lemma:

$$(5) \quad dW = \left(\sum_{i=1}^{n} \frac{\partial W}{\partial F_i}\,\alpha_i + \frac{\partial W}{\partial t} + \frac{1}{2}\sum_{i=1}^{n}\sum_{j=1}^{n} \frac{\partial^2 W}{\partial F_i\,\partial F_j}\,\beta_i\,\beta_j\,\rho_{ij} \right) dt + \sum_{t=1}^{n} \frac{\partial W}{\partial F_i}\,\beta_i\,dz_i$$

where ρ_{ij} is the correlation coefficient between dz_i and dz_j.

---

[13] For a simple introduction to Ito processes and stochastic calculus, see HULL J.C. ([17], Chapter 10, pp. 209-27). Specifically, it should be noted that dF_i is distributed normally, while ΔF_i may be distributed non-normally (HULL J.C. [17], p. 222).

[14] Time is not a risk factor. It follows that the theta (or time decay of a portfolio) plays no role in measuring the risk of a portfolio. «Traders would often add other Greek letters, such as the theta ... Theta is better viewed as a cost, not a risk factor, since it is a known quantity ...» (LITTERMAN R. [20], footnote 10, p. 7).

The expected return on the portfolio, $E(dW)$, is given by the term in dt on the right hand side of (5), while the variance of the return, VAR (dW), is equal to

$$(6) \quad VAR(dW) = VAR\left(\sum_{i=1}^{n} \frac{\partial W}{\partial F_i} \beta_i \, dz_i \right) = \sum_{i=1}^{n}\sum_{j=1}^{n} \frac{\partial W}{\partial F_i} \frac{\partial W}{\partial F_j} \beta_i \beta_j \rho_{ij} \, dt.$$

Accordingly, the volatility of the portfolio, defined as the standard deviation of its instantaneous rate of return, is equal to:

$$(7) \quad \sigma\sqrt{dt} \equiv std\left[\frac{dW(F_1, F_2, \ldots, F_n, t)}{W} \right] = \sqrt{\frac{VAR(dW)}{W^2}} =$$

$$= \sqrt{\frac{1}{W_2} \sum_{i=1}^{n}\sum_{j=1}^{n} \frac{\partial W}{\partial F_i} \frac{\partial W}{\partial F_j} \beta_i \beta_j \rho_{ij} \, dt} =$$

$$= \sqrt{\sum_{i=1}^{n}\sum_{j=1}^{n} \eta_i \eta_j \sigma_{ij} \, dt}$$

where η_i is the elasticity of the portfolio's value with respect to the i-th risk factor

$$(8) \qquad\qquad \eta_i \equiv \frac{\partial W}{\partial F_i} \frac{F_i}{W}$$

and σ_{ij} is equal to

$$(9) \qquad\qquad \sigma_{ij} = \frac{\beta_i}{F_i} \frac{\beta_j}{F_j} \rho_{ij} .$$

Since the volatility of a portfolio consisting of derivatives may vary sharply, it is worth defining a measure of the «volatility of the volatility», which we call «turbulence» and denote by the greek letter ψ *(psi)*[15]. The turbulence of a portfolio is defined as follows:

(10)
$$\psi \sqrt{dt} \equiv std \left[\frac{d\sigma(F_1, F_2, \ldots, F_n, t)}{\sigma} \right].$$

Applying Ito's lemma again, we obtain:

(11) $$d\sigma = \left[\sum_{i=1}^{n} \frac{\partial \sigma}{\partial F_i} \alpha_i + \frac{\partial \sigma}{\partial t} + \frac{1}{2} \sum_{i=1}^{n} \sum_{j=1}^{n} \frac{\partial^2 \sigma}{\partial F_i \partial F_j} \beta_i \beta_j \rho_{ij} \right] dt + \sum_{i=1}^{n} \frac{\partial \sigma}{\partial F_i} \beta_i dz_i .$$

The expected change in volatility, $E(d\sigma)$, is given by the term in dt on the right hand side of *(11)*, while the variance of the instantaneous change in volatility, VAR $(d\sigma)$, is equal to:

(12) $$\mathrm{VAR}(d\sigma) = \mathrm{VAR}\left(\sum_{i=1}^{n} \frac{\partial \sigma}{\partial F_i} \beta_i dz_i \right) = \sum_{i=1}^{n} \sum_{j=1}^{n} \frac{\partial \sigma}{\partial F_i} \frac{\partial \sigma}{\partial F_j} \beta_i \beta_j \rho_{ij} dt .$$

Accordingly, the turbulence of the portfolio, defined as the standard deviation of the instantaneous rate of change in volatility, is equal to:

(13)
$$\psi \sqrt{dt} \equiv std \left[\frac{d\sigma(F_1, F_2, \ldots, F_n, t)}{\sigma} \right] = \sqrt{\frac{\mathrm{VAR}(d\sigma)}{\sigma^2}} =$$

$$\sqrt{\frac{1}{\sigma^2} \sum_{i=1}^{n} \sum_{j=1}^{n} \frac{\partial \sigma}{\partial F_i} \frac{\partial \sigma}{\partial F_j} \beta_i \beta_j \rho_{ij} dt} = \sqrt{\sum_{i=1}^{n} \sum_{j=1}^{n} \lambda_i \lambda_j \sigma_{ij} dt}$$

---

[15] If all contracts were linear, hedging operations would be relatively simple, since they would only involve the calculation of delta (the first derivative of the value of the contract with respect to the underlying asset). However, in the case of non-linear contracts such as options, the function linking the value of the contract to the underlying asset is decidedly non-linear. Non-linearity implies that gamma (the second derivative with respect to the underlying asset) is important, because it measures how quickly a portfolio protected against a source of risk may lose its protection.

where λ_i is the elasticity of the volatility with respect to the i-th risk factor

$$(14) \qquad \lambda_i = \frac{\partial \sigma}{\partial F_i} \frac{F_i}{\sigma}.$$

2.3 VAR of a Portfolio

As mentioned earlier, the Basle Committee refers to VAR (value-at-risk) to define the capital requirements for market risks where the internal models approach is adopted. VAR is the estimate of the maximum potential loss a portfolio is likely to incur in a given period of time and in a given percentage of cases.

VAR can be calculated by means of simulations (using historical data or the Monte Carlo method) or analytically, as in the approach followed so far[16]. In general, the VAR of a portfolio is defined by the following expression:

$$(15) \qquad \text{Prob} \left(- \text{VAR} \le \Delta W \right) = \varepsilon$$

where ΔW is the change in the portfolio's value in an interval Δt and ε is the confidence level chosen.

From *(15)* we obtain:

$$(16) \qquad \text{Prob} \left(\frac{\dfrac{-\text{VAR}}{W} - \mu \Delta t}{\sigma \sqrt{\Delta t}} \le \frac{\dfrac{\Delta W}{W} - \mu \Delta t}{\sigma \sqrt{\Delta t}} \right) = \varepsilon$$

----

[16] The fundamental difference between simple scenario analysis ($\pm$ 100, $\pm$ 200, $\pm$ 300 p.b., non parallel shifts, etc.) and a Monte Carlo approach is that, with the latter, the future is not arbitrarily specified. On the contrary, the future time paths of the risk factors are constructed on the basis of the probability distributions defined by the model. See, for example, SMITHSON C. [26], [27]. For an analysis of VAR by means of simulations based on historical data, see BARONE-ADESI G. - GIANNOPOULOS K. [5].

where:

(17) $$\mu\Delta t = E\left(\frac{\Delta W}{W}\right) \text{ and } \sigma\sqrt{\Delta t} = std\left(\frac{\Delta W}{W}\right).$$

Accordingly, on the basis of (16)

(18) $$\text{Prob}(-x_\varepsilon \le X) = \varepsilon$$

with:

(19) $$-x_\varepsilon = \frac{\dfrac{-VAR}{W} - \mu\Delta t}{\sigma\sqrt{\Delta t}} \qquad X = \frac{\dfrac{\Delta W}{W} - \mu\Delta t}{\sigma\sqrt{\Delta t}}.$$

For (19) to be satisfied, it is necessary that

(20) $$VAR = \left(x_\varepsilon\sigma\sqrt{\Delta t} - \mu\Delta t\right)W.$$

It will be assumed that X is distributed according to a standardized normal distribution and the rate of return expected in the short interval Δt ($\mu\Delta t = 0$) prudently taken to be equal to zero. Following the prescriptions of the Basle Committee, we obtain: *a)* $x_\varepsilon \cong 2.33$, since in (18) $\varepsilon = 0.99$ (the confidence level chosen); *b)* $\sqrt{\Delta t} = \sqrt{10/250} = 0.2$, since the time horizon is ten business days (out of the approximatively 250 in a year); and hence, on the basis of (20),

(21) $$VAR \cong 2.33\sigma0.2W = 0.466\sigma W.$$

Alternatively, on the basis of (17) and (20), VAR can be analytically defined as the product of a multiplier (an increasing function of the confidence level chosen), x_ϵ, and the standard deviation, $std\,(\Delta W)$, the value the portfolio may experience in the interval Δt[17]:

$$(22) \qquad \text{VAR} \cong 2.33 \times std\,(\Delta W).$$

The estimate of the VAR of a portfolio is clearly not univocal, since it depends crucially on the current value of the portfolio itself, W, and its volatility, σ. It is therefore hardly surprising that some simulations should have led to very different VAR for the same portfolio, with scale factors as large as $14:1$[18].

It should also be noted that VAR shifts attention to the estimate of the market risk of the trading portfolio with respect to the determination of its current value. It would be desirable in this respect for the regulatory authorities to verify the consistency between the methods for determining VAR and the methods for determining the value of the portfolio, especially in the case of unlisted assets (e.g. OTC swaps and options), which should use the same estimates of volatility and correlations.

Lastly, both the confidence level (99%) and the time horizon (10 days) fixed by the Basle Committee for the calculation of VAR are questionable. As regards the time horizon, in line with the Basle Committee's own comments on backtesting, it would be better to consider the volatility of the portfolio in the next instant of time rather than over a finite time horizon, since the composition of the portfolio can vary (and very substantially) from one moment to another. It would thus appear preferable to interpret the VAR given by *(21)* as the product of a multiplication factor, 0.466, the instantaneous volatility (on a annual basis), σ, and the current value of the portfolio, W.

As seen earlier, the Basle Committee prescribes a capital re-

---

[17] Goldman, Sachs & Co. use a multiplier of 4 (for linear products). «Given the non-normality of returns that we find in most financial markets, we use as a rule of thumb the assumption that four-standard-deviation events in financial markets happen approximately once per year. Given this assumption, the daily once-per-year VAR for portfolios whese payoffs are linear is approximatively four standard deviations». (LITTERMAN R. [20], p. 3).

[18] See BEDER T.S. [8].

quirement for market risks (R_M) equal to at least 3 times VAR. Accordingly, on the basis of *(21)*, we have:

$$(23) \qquad R_M = 3 \times 0.466\sigma W = 1.398\sigma W.$$

To conclude, the capital requirement for market risks is equal to the product of a multiplicative factor (an increasing function of the risk aversion of the regulatory authorities), the instantaneous volatility and the current value of the portfolio.

The multiplicative factor is justified, *inter alia*, by the following considerations: 1) the assumption of normality is not supported by empirical evidence. If the actual distribution is leptocurtic (has fatter tails than the normal distribution), the probability of large losses increases[19]; 2) the volatilities and correlations are unstable (can change suddenly); 3) VAR calculated at the end of the day does not take account of the risks incurred in respect of the operations carried out during the day.

2.3.1 The Assumption of Normality

The assumption of normality for the rate of change in the risk factors is not supported by empirical evidence. «The point is well made by the Federal Reserve Board which observes that: «Assuming a normal distribution, the probability of experiencing a four standard deviation event is approximately three in 100,000 – in trading terms, about once in 130 years. In practice, however, such unusual market movements are seen in most major markets on average almost every year»[20].

Actually, if X is a standardized normal distribution, the probability of observing a 4-standard deviation event is equal to

---

[19] The October 1987 crash, for instance, when the Dow Jones index of the shares listed on the New York Stock Exchange fell by 23% in just one day. According to the usual volatilities of share index (15-20% on annual basis), the probability of such an event occuring was virtually nil.

[20] See BAGG J. [1].

around 3 in 100,000 (Prob $(X \geq 4\sigma)$ = 0.00003167). Moreover, if X is taken to be the rate of daily change in a market variable and the number of business days to be 250, a 4-standard deviation event should occur about 3 times in 100,000 days, i.e. 3 times in 400 years (approximately once in 130 years).

In reality such events occur much more frequently. Consider, for example, the exchange rate of the lira against the dollar in the period from 9 February 1973 to 22 October 1996. The volatility on a daily basis was 0.71%, corresponding to 11.26% on an annual basis. In the more than 23 years considered, the daily changes exceeded 4σ, i.e. were larger than 2.85%, on 27 occasions. Accordingly, on average, a 4-standard deviation event occurred once every 1.14 years.

But even if the rates of change in risk factors were distributed normally, the rates of change in the value of a portfolio could still be distributed far from normally if the portfolio included contracts with non-linear characteristics and if the time horizon were extended beyond the next instant of time.

The non-normality of the actual distribution is likely to lead to excessively large or even unrealistic capital requirements. Consider the following extreme case of a portfolio consisting exclusively of a European call option. Assume, for example, that $S = 100$, $K = 100$, $r = 10\%$, $\sigma_S = 20\%$ and $T = 0.04$ (10 business days).

The distribution of the rates of return of the portfolio is markedly non-normal, since there is a very high probability of the bank losing all its capital (in the event that exercising the option is not advantageous). According to Black-Scholes [9], the current value of the portfolio is equal to 1.8, the delta is 0.54776 and hence, on the basis of *(7)*, the volatility is 608.61% ($\sigma = 0.54776 \times 0.2 \times 100/1.8$). The maximum potential loss is 1.8, an event that will occur if the option is not exercised. By contrast, on the basis of *(21)*, VAR is equal to 5.1051 (= $0.466 \times 6.0861 \times 1.8$) and hence the capital requirement is 15.315 (= 3×5.1051), about 8.5 times higher than necessary.

Even though it is an extreme case, this example shows how VAR may sometimes send highly distorted signals.

2.4 An Alternative to VAR: the Put Approach

As an alternative to the approach adopted by the Basle Committee, the capital requirements for credit and financial risks could be determined by means of a method that requires neither the specification of a confidence level nor the distinction between credit and financial factors.

The method involves determining the capital requirements as a function of the value of a *Put* written on the bank's net assets, with an exercise price in line with the level of protection desired. This is the approach adopted by Merton and Perold [24].

The analogy between capital requirements and insurance are evident. If shareholders wish to be sure that the value of the bank will not fall below a predetermined limit, they can take out an insurance policy. In financial terms it would be a question of acquiring a *Put* option guaranteeing the owners a minimum amount of shareholders' equity at a given maturity, for example after a year.

If the *Put* expires after a year and is at-the-money forward, i.e. if its exercise price is equal to the current value of the portfolio capitalized at the riskless interest rate over the entire life of the option, its pricing formula is approximated very closely by the following expression[21]:

$$(24) \qquad\qquad Put \cong 0.4\sigma W.$$

The value of the *Put* coincides with VAR when the confidence level chosen for the latter is equal to 97.72%. In this case, in (20), $x_\varepsilon = 2$ (the area of the standardized normal distribution between $-\infty$ and $+2$ is equal to 97.72%) and hence:

$$(25) \qquad\qquad VAR = 2\sigma \sqrt{10/250} \ W \cong 0.4\sigma W.$$

The *Put* approach is equivalent to the VAR approach for a confidence level of 97.72%, but is independent of the choice of a confidence level.

---

[21] See BRENNER M. - SUBRAHMANYAM M.G. [10], [11].

The two measures of risk are thus very similar and both depend on the current value of the portfolio and its volatility. With a view to complete integration, it would be necessary for both financial and credit factors to be included among the risk factors whose volatility and correlations are to be calculated. The volatility of the portfolio depends, in fact, on the volatility of the financial variables (interest rates, exchange rates, etc.), the volatility of the credit variables (credit spreads, relationship between credit losses and total loans disbursed, etc.) and on their correlation.

Today's rules should therefore evolve towards a single measure of risk that would take account of financial risks, credit risks and the concentration of exposures towards given sectors/borrowers.

2.5 *Estimating the Model*

The model described in sections 2.1 and 2.2 is a generic continuous-time model. In the applications that will be described below, the risk factors specified are the instantaneous interest rates of the various currencies, share prices and exchange rates.

The following assumptions are made regarding their dynamics: 1) the instantaneous interest rates of the various currencies follow a square root process[22]; 2) share prices and exchange rates follow a geometric Brownian motion[23].

---

[22] This is the dynamics assumed by Cox J. - INGERSOLL J.E. - ROSS S.A. [12]. The application of this model to different types of contract is described in BARONE E. - BRAGHÒ A. [6]. The Cox J. - INGERSOLL J.E. - ROSS S.A. (CIR) [12] model is also used internally by J.P. MORGAN (FODY S.A. [13]), but the estimates are not made public in *RiskMetrics*™ (this is the trademark used by J.P. Morgan for its method of calculating risk and the matrix of variances and covariances proposed for the measurement of VAR): «*RiskMetrics*™ is based on, but differs significatively from, the system developed by J.P. Morgan for the measurement, management, and control of market risks in its trading, arbitrage, and own account investment activities» (LONGERSTAEY J. [21], p. 1). The growing acceptance of the Cox, Ingersoll and Ross model for risk management purposes appears to be confirmed by some recent attempts to integrate it in the methodology underlying *RiskMetrics*™ (PHELAN M.J. [25]).

[23] This is the dynamics assumed by BLACK F. - SCHOLES M. [9] and by GARMAN M.B. - KOHLHAGEN S.W. [14].

In general, the models can be estimated on the basis of historical data (time-series approach), current data (cross-section approach) or both (panel data). The (currently insurmountable) difficulty of managing the database means that the latter approach has to be excluded, while the cross-section approach appears to be better than that based on time series, which would not allow the structural changes that occur in the economy to be captured. However, not all the parameters required by the model can be estimated using the cross-section approach (owing to estimation difficulties or lack of data), so that time series also have to be used.

The rules proposed by the Basle Committee appear to presume that internal models must necessarily use the historical volatilities and correlations of risk factors rather than those implicit in market prices. However, the approach based on historical series may be inconsistent with the methods financial institutions use to value their trading portfolios. Consider, for example, the case of options whose value, calculated on the basis of the historical volatilities of the underlying asset rather than the implicit volatility, may diverge very significantly from their market prices.

The historical approach is the one most commonly used. For example, according to J.P. Morgan: «The evidence points towards the superior forecasting ability of historical volatility over implied. [...] Based on these observations, we decided in the first edition of *RiskMetrics*™ to focus on the second source for volatility and correlation estimates: history»[24].

This approach, however, may result in prices of options that are systematically different from their market prices in cases where historical volatility does not coincide with implied volatility. It is based, moreover, on a premise with which not all agree[25]. It would be preferable (wherever possible) to estimate the volatili-

---

[24] See J.P. MORGAN ([19], p. 16).

[25] For a different opinion on the validity of the premise found in the *Technical Document* of *RiskMetrics*™, see HULL J.C. ([17], pp. 385-6): «Chiras and Manaster have carried out a study using CBOE data comparing the weighted implied standard deviation from options on a stock at a point in time with the standard deviation calculated from historical data. They found that the former provides a much better forecast of the volatility of the stock price during the life of the option. The study has been repeated by other authors using other data and has always given similar results».

ties and correlations implicit in contracts rather than have re-course to time series.

A mixed cross-section/time series approach, that allows the value of the portfolio and its volatility to be determined, is as follows: 1) estimate the model on cross-section data, assuming the risk factors to be independent[26]; 2) calculate the variance/covariance matrix on the basis of the time series of the parameters estimated.

In the first step we obtain the theoretical values of the contracts and the elasticity with respect to the risk factors, in the second the additional elements (variances and covariances) needed to estimate the volatility of the portfolio[27].

3. - Applications

As shown earlier, whichever measure of risk is adopted (VAR or *Put*), it is necessary to determine the current value of the portfolio and its volatility. The manner of proceeding in practice will now be described with some applications.

The case of a single risk factor is distinguished from those in which more than one risk factor is considered. Reference is also made to portfolios consisting of shares and bonds, denominated in domestic or foreign currency.

---

[26] The model should be estimated so as to minimize a specific loss function (the sum of the squares of the deviations – weighted appropriately – between market and theoretical prices), considering the largest possible number of contracts. In general, the estimates are based exclusively on linear contracts (forward contracts, futures and swaps, etc.). However, in order to obtain reliable estimates for some of the parameters of the model, the model should also be estimated on the basis of non-linear contracts (futures options, swaptions, caps and floors, etc.), whose prices are found to be more sensitive to such parameters; if this procedure is not followed, there is the risk of obtaining combinations of parameters that are not consistent with non-linear contracts, even though they are consistent with linear contracts.

[27] In order to obtain an *ex ante* estimate of the volatility of a bank's portfolio, it is necessary to have a valuation model. To obtain an *ex post* estimate, it is sufficient to have a (homogeneous) time series of the bank's (balance sheet, market or theoretical) value. Consequently, the *ex ante* volatility of the total portfolio (σ) can be compared with its historical value, estimated *ex post* on the basis of the time series of the value of the portfolio (after eliminating every possible source of unhomogeneity).

3.1 *One Risk Factor*

In the case of a single risk factor, the volatility of a portfolio, defined by *(7)*, is equal to the product of the absolute value of the elasticity with respect to the risk factor and the standard deviation of the proportional changes in the risk factor.

In symbols, if W is the current value of the portfolio and S the current level of the risk factor, we have $\sigma = std(dW/W) = |\eta| \times \sigma_S$ where $\eta = (\partial W/\partial S)\, S/W$ and $\sigma_S = std\,(dS/S)$.

3.1.1 Volatility and Turbulence of a Share Portfolio

Consider a portfolio consisting of a long position in a share with current price $S = 100$ and volatility $\sigma_S = 0.25$. Naturally, since the elasticity is equal to one, the volatility of the portfolio is equal to that of the share. Consider now a short position in a call, written on the same share, with a delta equal to 0.4. If the current value of the call is equal to 8, the volatility of the portfolio is equal to 125% (= $|0.4 \times 100/8| \times 0.25$).

The overall volatility of the portfolio consisting of the share and the short position in the call is equal to 16.3% [= $|(1 - 0.4) \times 100/(100 - 8)| \times 0.25$], i.e. less than the original 25%, since the sale of the call has reduced the exposure to the risk factor (the price of the share).

Consider now a portfolio consisting of a long at-the-money call, with a maturity of one year, written on a security A that does not pay dividends. We assume that the current price of the share is 100, the riskless (continuously compounded) interest rate 10% on an annual basis and the volatility of the share 20% on an annual basis. In other words, $S_A = 100$, $X = 100$, $T = 1$, $r = 0.1$ and $\sigma_A = 0.2$.

According to the Black-Scholes [9], model, the call has a theoretical value (c_A) of 13.27, a delta (Δ_A) of 0.72575 and a gamma (Γ_A) of 0.16665. Assuming risk neutrality, the probability of the option being exercised, p_A, is equal to 65.542%. The current value of a one-year zero-coupon bond, with a face value of $X = 100$, is equal to 90.484.

The portfolio equivalent to the call thus consists of a long position in $\Delta S_A = 0.72575$ shares, whose value is 72.575, and a short position in $p_A = 0.65542$ one-year zero-coupon bonds, whose value is -59.305 ($= 0.65542 \times 90.484$). Naturally, the current value of the equivalent portfolio, 13.27 ($= 72.575 - 59.305$), is equal to that of the call.

On the basis of equations *(7)-(9)*, the volatility of the call is equal to 109.38% on an annual basis ($dt = 1$)[28]:

$$(26) \qquad \sigma_{c_A} = std\left(\frac{dc_A}{c_A}\right) = \sqrt{\eta_A^2 \sigma_A^2} = 5.4692 \times 0.2 = 1.0938$$

where η_A is the elasticity of the call with respect to the underlying share:

$$(27) \qquad\qquad \eta_A \equiv \Delta_A \frac{S_A}{c_A} = 5.4692 \ .$$

The turbulence of the portfolio, ψ_A, caused by the leverage implied by the call, is equal to 43.458% on an annual basis. In fact, on the basis of equations *(13)* and *(14)*, we have:

$$(28) \quad \psi_A \equiv std\left(\frac{d\sigma_{c_A}}{\sigma_{c_A}}\right) = \sqrt{\lambda_A^2 \sigma_A^2} = \sqrt{(-2.1729)^2 \times 0.2^2} = 0.43458$$

where λ_A is the elasticity of the volatility of the call with respect to the underlying share:

$$(29) \qquad \lambda_A \equiv \frac{\partial \sigma_{c_A}}{\partial S_A} \frac{S_A}{\sigma_{c_A}} = 1 - \left(\frac{\Delta_A}{c_A} - \frac{\Gamma_A}{\Delta_A}\right) S_A = -2.1729.$$

Graph 1 and Graph 2 show the volatility and turbulence of the call as a function of the price of the underlying share. As can be seen, the volatility of the call decreases monotonously as the price

---

[28] The formula of BLACK F. - SCHOLES M. [9] postulates that the risk factor, $F = S_A$, follows a geometric Brownian motion. Consequently, the generic diffusion coefficient β, present in *(2)*, is equal to $\sigma_A S_A$.

of the share increases and, when it becomes deep in the money, tends towards the same level of volatility as the underlying share. By contrast, the turbulence, which is a funcion of gamma, peaks when the option is at the money: very small changes in the price

GRAPH 1

VOLATILITY OF A CALL AS A FUNCTION OF THE SHARE PRICE

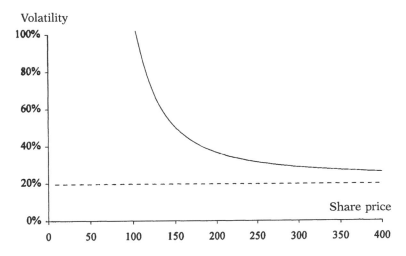

GRAPH 2

TURBULENCE OF A CALL AS A FUNCTION OF THE SHARE PRICE

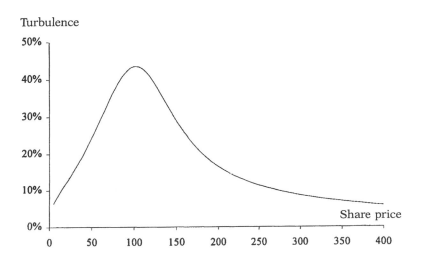

of the underlying share cause large changes in the probability of the option being exercised and hence in the volatility of the call.

Graph 3 and Graph 4 show the volatility and turbulence of the call as a function of the maturity of the option. Both the volatility and the turbulence decrease as the maturity of the option increases: the volatility of the call tend towards that of the underlying share and the turbulence tends towards zero. As seen earlier, for a given maturity, the volatility of an out-of-the-money call is greater than that of the corresponding at-the-money and in-the-money calls, in that order. The turbulence of an at-the-money call is greater than that of the corresponding in-the-money and out-of-the-money calls.

Equations *(26)-(29)* show that the volatility of a call is a function of its delta and that the turbulence is a function of both delta and gamma. The two measures (volatility and turbulence) might thus appear redundant to market participants who base their hedging operations on the *Greeks*. However, their usefulness is clear when one considers complex portfolios consisting of options written on different shares. In this case there is a need for synthe-

GRAPH 3

VOLATILITY OF A CALL AS A FUNCTION OF MATURITY

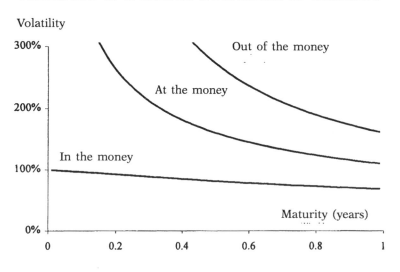

GRAPH 4

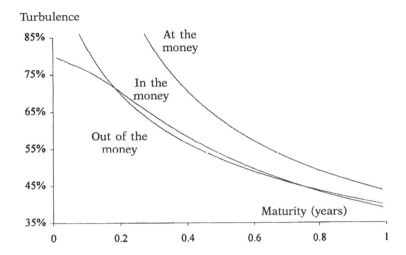

TURBULENCE OF A CALL AS A FUNCTION OF MATURITY

tic measures, functions of delta and gamma, that take account of the portfolio diversification.

Suppose, for example, that the portfolio consists not only of the call written on security A but also of a call written on security B, which does not pay dividends. The characteristics of the second call are the same as those of that already examined: $S_B = 100$, $X = 100$, $T = 1$ and $\sigma_B = 0.2$. Suppose, moreover, that the correlation coefficient between the instantaneous rates of change in S_A and S_B is equal to zero ($\rho_{AB} = 0$). It follows that the current value of the portfolio is equal to twice that found above; however, owing to the diversification, the volatility is significantly lower.

In fact, on the basis of equations *(7)-(9)*, the portfolio volatility is equal to 77.346% on an annual basis (as against 109.38%):

$$(30) \quad \sigma = std\left(\frac{dW}{W}\right) = \sqrt{\eta_A^2 \sigma_A^2 + \eta_B^2 \sigma_B^2 + 2\eta_A \eta_B \sigma_A \sigma_B \rho_{AB}} =$$

$$= \sqrt{2\eta_A^2 \sigma_A^2} = 5.4692 \times 0.2 \times \frac{\sqrt{2}}{2} = 0.77346$$

where η_A and η_B are the elasticities of the portfolio value with respect to the price of the shares A and B:

$$(31) \qquad \eta_A = \eta_B \equiv \frac{1}{2} \Delta_A \frac{S_A}{c_A} = 2.7346.$$

By contrast, the portfolio turbulence, ψ, remains unchanged at 43.458% on an annual basis, given the invariance of the leverage. In fact, on the basis of equations *(13)* and *(14)*, we have:

$$(32) \quad \psi \equiv std\left(\frac{d\sigma}{\sigma}\right) = \sqrt{\lambda_A^2 \sigma_A^2 + \lambda_B^2 \sigma_B^2 + 2\lambda_A \lambda_B \sigma_A \sigma_B \rho_{AB}} =$$

$$= \sqrt{2\lambda_A^2 \sigma_A^2} = \sqrt{(-2.1729)^2 \times 0.2^2} = 0.43458$$

where λ_A and λ_B are the elasticities of σ with respect to the price of the shares A and B:

$$(33) \quad \lambda_A = \lambda_B \equiv \frac{\partial\sigma}{\partial S_A} \frac{S_A}{\sigma_A} = \left[1 - \left(\frac{\Delta_A}{c_A} - \frac{\Gamma_A}{\Delta_A}\right)S_A\right]\frac{\sqrt{2}}{2} = -2.1729\frac{\sqrt{2}}{2}.$$

3.1.2 Volatility and Turbulence of a Bond Portfolio

To give an example of a bond portfolio, consider a long position in 100 one-year zero-coupon bonds, with a face value of one, current price (P) equal to 0.91239, delta (Δ) equal to -0.76165 (delta is the first derivative with respect to the instantaneous rate r) and gamma (Γ) equal to 0.63582 (gamma is the second derivative with respect to the instantaneous rate r).

If the current level of the risk factor r is 8.661% and its volatility parameter $s = 19.247\%$, the volatility of r is 65.4% [= std $(dr/r) = s/\sqrt{r}$][29]. It follows that the portfolio volatility, σ, is equal to 4.73% (= $|-0.76165 \times \sqrt{0.08661}/0.91239| \times 0.19247$).

---

[29] It is assumed that r follows a square-root process.

The portfolio turbulence, ψ, is equal to 32.7% on an annual basis. In fact, on the basis of equations *(13)* and *(14)*, we have:

$$(34) \quad \psi \equiv std\left(\frac{d\sigma}{\sigma}\right) = \sqrt{\lambda^2 \frac{\sigma^2}{r}} = \sqrt{0.5^2 \times \frac{0.19247^2}{0.08661}} = 0.327$$

where λ is the elasticity of the portfolio volatility with respect to r

$$(35) \qquad \lambda \equiv \frac{\partial\sigma}{\partial r}\frac{r}{\sigma} = \frac{1}{2} - \left(\frac{\Delta}{P} - \frac{\Gamma}{\Delta}\right) r = 0.5$$

3.2 *n Risk Factors*

In the case of n risk factors, the portfolio volatility, defined by *(7)* or by *(52)*, is equal to the square root of the variance/co-variance matrix of the proportional changes in the risk factors, premultiplied and postmultiplied by the vector of the elasticity with respect to the risk factors.

3.2.1 Volatility of a Bond Portfolio in Foreign Currency

Consider a 3-year Treasury note. Its current value in dollars is P, the derivative with respect to the instantaneous interest rate in dollars, r, is P_r, and the lira/dollar exchange rate is E. The value of the security in lire is $W = PE$. Denoting the vector of the elasticity by **u** and the variance/covariance matrix of the (continuously compounded) rates of change of r and E by **C**, we have:

$$(36) \qquad \sigma = std\left(\frac{dW}{W}\right) = \sqrt{\mathbf{u'Cu}} =$$

$$= \sqrt{[W_E E / W \quad W_r r / W]\begin{bmatrix} \sigma_E^2 & \sigma_{Er} \\ \sigma_{rE} & \sigma_r^2 \end{bmatrix}\begin{bmatrix} W_E E / W \\ W_r r / W \end{bmatrix}}$$

Since $W_r = P_r E$ and $W_E = P$, it follows that $\mathbf{u}' = [1 \; rP_r/P]$. If the input data are as follows[30]

(37) $E = 1596 \quad P = 106.26 \quad P_r = -298.12 \quad r = 5.18\%$

$$\mathbf{u}' = [1 - 0.1452999] \quad \mathbf{C} = \begin{bmatrix} 0.0032883 & -0.0007039 \\ -0.0007039 & 0.1366653 \end{bmatrix}$$

the portfolio volatility, σ, is equal to 7.99% on an annual basis:

(38)

$$\sigma = \sqrt{1^2 \cdot 0.0032883 + 2 \cdot 1 \cdot (-0.1452999) \cdot (-0.0007039) + (-0.1452999)^2 \cdot 0.1366653} = 7.99\%$$

The risk measure can be disaggregated into its different components (exchange rate risk, interest rate risk, diversification effect).

If interest rates are assumed constant, i.e. if the elasticity with respect to r is annulled, the portfolio volatility becomes:

(39) $\sigma = \sqrt{1^2 \cdot 0.0032883} = 5.73\%$

i.e. it is equal to the volatility of the lira/dollar exchange rate.

If, instead, the exchange rate is assumed constant, i.e. if the elasticity with respect to E is annulled, the portfolio volatility becomes

(40) $\sigma = \sqrt{(-0.1452999)^2 \cdot 0.1366653} = 5.37\%$

i.e. it is equal to the interest rate risk on its own.

The sum of the two volatilities, exchange rate risk (5.73%) and interest rate risk (5.37%), is equal to 11.11%. This level of risk corresponds to the case of perfect (negative) correlation between E and r, when the diversification effect is annulled[31]. Naturally,

---

[30] The variance/covariance matrix on an annual basis has been obtained by multiplying the daily matrix by 250.

[31] The volatility of the 11.11% is obtained by putting the covariances in $\mathbf{C}$ equal to the square root, with the sign changed, of the product of the two variances:

$$\sigma = \sqrt{1^2 \cdot 0.0032883 - 2 \cdot 1 \cdot (-0.1452999)\sqrt{0.0032883 \cdot 0.1366653} + (-0.1452999)^2 \cdot 0.1366653} = 11.11\%$$

the difference between the sum of the volatilities (11.11%) and the overall volatility (7.99%) gives the measure of the diversification effect (3.12%).

3.2.2 Volatility of a Bond Portfolio in Domestic Currency

Consider now a portfolio that is sensitive only to lira interest rates. Its current value is W, delta (the sensitivity with respect to the instantaneous interest rate r) is W_r, rho (the sensitivity with respect to the long-term asymptotic interest rate R) is W_R, vega (the sensitivity with respect to the volatility parameter s) is W_s, phi (the sensitivity with respect to velocity of adjustment - β - of the instantaneous interest rate towards its long-term mean) is W_β[32]. Denoting the vector of the elasticity by **u** and the variance/covariance matrix of the (continuously compounded) rates of change in r, R, s and β by **C**, we have

$$(41) \qquad \sigma = std\left(\frac{dW}{W}\right) = \sqrt{\mathbf{u'Cu}} =$$

$$= \sqrt{[W_r/W \ \ W_R/W \ \ W_s/W \ \ W_\beta/W] \begin{bmatrix} \sigma_r^2 & \sigma_{rR} & \sigma_{rs} & \sigma_{r\beta} \\ \sigma_{Rr} & \sigma_R^2 & \sigma_{Rs} & \sigma_{R\beta} \\ \sigma_{sr} & \sigma_{sR} & \sigma_s^2 & \sigma_{s\beta} \\ \sigma_{\beta r} & \sigma_{\beta R} & \sigma_{\beta s} & \sigma_\beta^2 \end{bmatrix} \begin{bmatrix} W_r r/W \\ W_R R/W \\ W_s s/W \\ W_\beta \beta/W \end{bmatrix}}$$

If it assumed that only r is variable (R, s and β are constant and their variances and covariances cancel out) the portfolio volatility is equal to $|W_r|r/W\sigma_r = |W_r|r/W \times std\ (dr/r) = |W_r|/W \times std\ (dr) = |W_r|/W \times s\ \sqrt{r}$.

For example, consider the Italian Treasuries reported in Table

---

[32] The parametrization of the CIR model in terms of r, R, s, β (and k for floaters) is that adopted by BARONE E. - RISA S. [7].

2, which shows the actual and theoretical cum-coupon prices, the deviations between the two prices and the complete set of sensitivities.

The last three columns show two *ex ante* volatilities and the historical volatility (for the period from 1 September 1995 and 28 February 1996). The first of the two *ex ante* volatilities is that implicit in the model (which assumes R, s and β to be constant), while the second has been calculated on the basis of the elasticity of the securities with respect to r, R, s and β and the historical variance/covariance matrix of r, R, s and β.

Specifically, the two volatilities for the first security have been calculated in the following manner. The first is simply equal to:

$$(42) \quad \sigma = \frac{|W_r|}{W} s \sqrt{r} = \frac{|-0.79|}{1.0095} \cdot 0.19247 \cdot \sqrt{0.08661} = 4.43\%$$

since $W_r = -0.79$, $W = 1.0095$, $s = 0.19247$ and $r = 0.08661$.

The second is obtained from:

$$(43) \qquad \sigma = std\left(\frac{dW}{W}\right) = \sqrt{\mathbf{u'Cu}} = 1.80\%$$

where:

$$(44) \qquad \mathbf{u'} = [W_r r / W \quad W_R R / W \quad W_s s / W \quad W_\beta \beta / W] =$$

$$= [-0.0677780 \quad -0.0170112 \quad -0.0019066 \quad 0.0000000]$$

$$(45) \quad C = \begin{bmatrix} \sigma_r^2 & \sigma_{rR} & \sigma_{rs} & \sigma_{r\beta} \\ \sigma_{Rr} & \sigma_R^2 & \sigma_{Rs} & \sigma_{R\beta} \\ \sigma_{sr} & \sigma_{sR} & \sigma_s^2 & \sigma_{s\beta} \\ \sigma_{\beta r} & \sigma_{\beta R} & \sigma_{\beta s} & \sigma_\beta^2 \end{bmatrix} \begin{bmatrix} 0.06650224 & 0.00275516 & 0.00212669 & -0.00006835 \\ 0.00275516 & 0.03459147 & 0.01161009 & -0.00050637 \\ 0.00212669 & 0.01161009 & 0.00414006 & -0.00017685 \\ -0.00006835 & -0.00050637 & -0.00017685 & 0.00000763 \end{bmatrix}$$

and $r = 0.08661$, $R = 0.10733$, $s = 0.19247$, $\beta = 0.36177$.

TABLE 2

TREASURIES: MARKET VALUE, THEORETICAL VALUE,
SENSITIVITIES AND VOLATILITY*

Bond	Maturity	Current Coupon	Actual	Theor.	Dev.	δ	ρ	λ	ϕ	Volat 1	Volat 2	Hist Volat
BTP	5/1/96	5.75	100.95	100.96	−0.01	−0.79	−0.16	−0.01	0.00	4.43	1.80	0.78
BTP	8/1/04	4.25	83.55	83.78	−0.23	−1.69	−3.69	−0.09	−0.01	11.46	10.25	10.90
BTP	1/1/05	4.75	89.98	89.39	0.59	−1.77	−3.94	−0.09	−0.02	11.14	10.12	10.89
BTP	11/1/23	4.50	75.52	75.44	0.07	−1.52	−5.69	−0.08	−0.01	11.40	16.07	15.00
CCT	10/1/00	5.45	100.20	100.13	0.07	−0.52	−0.19	−0.01	0.00	2.94	1.25	1.77

* Quotes of 23 May 1995 on MTS (the screen-based secondary market for Italian government securities). The theoretical values and sensitivities have been obtained on the basis of the following CIR model parameters (net payments): r = 8.661%, R = 10.733%, s = 19.247%, β = 0.36177, k = 0.90527.

The divergences between the *ex ante* and *ex post* measures are rather small. In particular, the first of the two measures of *ex ante* volatility appear to be more accurate than the second for the second and third securities and less accurate in the other three cases.

The calculation of the volatilities is easily extended to portfolios. For example, suppose that the quantities of the 5 securities in a portfolio are [10, −13, 20, 5, −22]. The portfolio's sensitivities (δ, ρ, λ, ϕ) are obtained as linear combinations of the sensitivities of the individual securities. Accordingly, $\delta = -17.49$ [$= -0.79 \times 10 - 1,67 \times (-13) - 1.77 \times 20 - 1.52 \times 5 - 0.52 \times (-22)$], $\rho = -56.70$, $\lambda = -0.91$, $\phi = -0.32$.

Given the theoretical prices of the securities [100.96, 83.78, 89.39, 75.44 and 100.13], the portfolio value is -1.174 [$= 1.0096 \times 10 - 0.8378 \times 13 + 0.8939 \times 20 + 0.7544 \times 5 - 1.0013 \times 22$] and its elasticities with respect to r, R, s and β are equal, respectively, to 1.2902972, 5.1836550, 0.1491888 and 0.0986085.

Accordingly, σ = 104.66%. The portfolio, which is highly levered, has a very high volatility[33].

---

[33] Under the traditional approach, in a scenario analysis, it would be possible to calculate the value the overall portfolio would lose in the event of an (upward) shift of r and R equal to 100 b.p. This would be equivalent to determining the volatility of the portfolio, σ, on the assumption that: *a)* there are only two risk factors (r and R); *b)* their rates of change are perfectly and positively correlated; *c)* the standard deviation of their changes is equal to 100 b.p. on an annual basis. In symbols: $\sigma = [(|W_r| std (r) + |W_R| std (R)]/W = (|W_r| \times 0.01 + |W_R| \times 0.01)/W$.

4. - Conclusions

The model proposed in this paper provides a set of methodologies for the comprehensive treatment of issues that are normally addressed separately. The starting point is the view that the management of a complex portfolio can be reduced to the management of a relatively simple portfolio containing only traded assets.

The model makes it possible, in fact, to value portfolios even when most of the assets and liabilities are not traded in organized secondary markets. Moreover, the whole exposure to risk in respect of derivatives can be expressed in terms of the exposure to risk in respect of the underlying securities and of securities providing a riskless interest rate. This exposure changes continuously even where the composition of the portfolio remains unchanged. By supplying a mix of «bullish» and «bearish», «convex» and «concave» products, it is possible to reduce the volume of transactions in traded securities needed to ensure the immunization of the portfolio.

The risk of a portfolio is measured in terms of the instantaneous volatility and turbulence (defined as «volatility of volatility»). The latter measure of risk reflects the leverage of a portfolio, obtained sometimes by including non-linear products, and takes account of the second derivatives with respect to the risk factors. On the basis of these two measures trading limits can be established for individual desks and their performances evaluated.

Volatility and Turbulence of a Portfolio: Matrix Notation

In matrix terms the dynamics of the risk factors are represented by the following system of n stochastic differential equations

$$(46) \qquad d\mathbf{F} = \mathbf{a}\,(\mathbf{F},\,t)\,dt + \mathbf{b}\,(\mathbf{F},\,t)\,d\mathbf{z}$$

where

$$(47) \qquad \mathbf{F} = \begin{bmatrix} F_1 \\ F_2 \\ \cdots \\ F_n \end{bmatrix} \quad \mathbf{a} = \begin{bmatrix} \alpha_1 \\ \alpha_2 \\ \cdots \\ \alpha_n \end{bmatrix} \quad \mathbf{b} = \begin{bmatrix} \beta_1 \\ \beta_2 \\ \cdots \\ \beta_n \end{bmatrix} \quad d\mathbf{z} = \begin{bmatrix} dz_1 \\ dz_2 \\ \cdots \\ dz_n \end{bmatrix}$$

and $\mathbf{W}$ is the matrix of the Wiener process correlation coefficients

$$(48) \qquad \mathbf{W} = \begin{bmatrix} 1 & \rho_{12} & \cdots & \rho_{1n} \\ \rho_{21} & 1 & \cdots & \rho_{2n} \\ \cdots & \cdots & \cdots & \cdots \\ \rho_{n1} & \rho_{n2} & \cdots & 1 \end{bmatrix}.$$

The dynamics of the value of the portfolio are given by

$$(49) \quad dW = \left[\mathbf{a}'\frac{\partial W}{\partial \mathbf{F}} + \frac{\partial W}{\partial t} + tr\left(\mathbf{BWB}\frac{\partial^2 W}{\partial \mathbf{F}\partial \mathbf{F}'} \right) \right] dt + \left(\frac{\partial W}{\partial \mathbf{F}} \right)' \mathbf{Bdz}$$

where:

(50)

$$\frac{\partial W}{\partial \mathbf{F}} = \begin{bmatrix} \dfrac{\partial W}{\partial F_1} \\[2mm] \dfrac{\partial W}{\partial F_2} \\[1mm] \cdots \\[1mm] \dfrac{\partial W}{\partial F_n} \end{bmatrix} \qquad \frac{\partial^2 W}{\partial \mathbf{F} \, \partial \mathbf{F}'} = \begin{bmatrix} \dfrac{\partial^2 W}{\partial F_1^2} & \dfrac{\partial^2 W}{\partial F_1 \partial F_2} & \cdots & \dfrac{\partial^2 W}{\partial F_1 \partial F_n} \\[3mm] \dfrac{\partial^2 W}{\partial F_2 \partial F_1} & \dfrac{\partial^2 W}{\partial F_2^2} & \cdots & \dfrac{\partial^2 W}{\partial F_2 \partial F_n} \\[1mm] \cdots & \cdots & \cdots & \cdots \\[1mm] \dfrac{\partial^2 W}{\partial F_n \partial F_1} & \dfrac{\partial^2 W}{\partial F_n \partial F_2} & \cdots & \dfrac{\partial^2 W}{\partial F_n^2} \end{bmatrix}$$

(51)

$$\mathbf{B} = \begin{bmatrix} \beta_1 & 0 & \cdots & 0 \\ 0 & \beta_2 & \cdots & 0 \\ \cdots & \cdots & \cdots & \cdots \\ 0 & 0 & \cdots & \beta_n \end{bmatrix}.$$

The volatility of the portfolio is given by

(52)

$$\sigma \equiv std\left[\frac{dW(\mathbf{F}, t)}{W(\mathbf{F}, t)}\right] = \sqrt{\mathbf{u}'\mathbf{C}\mathbf{u}}$$

where the vector $\mathbf{u}$ contains the elasticities of the value of the portfolio with respect to each risk factor

(53)

$$\mathbf{u} \equiv \begin{bmatrix} \eta_1 \\ \eta_2 \\ \cdots \\ \eta_n \end{bmatrix} = \begin{bmatrix} \dfrac{\partial W}{\partial F_1}\dfrac{F_1}{W} \\[3mm] \dfrac{\partial W}{\partial F_2}\dfrac{F_2}{W} \\[1mm] \cdots \\[1mm] \dfrac{\partial W}{\partial F_n}\dfrac{F_n}{W} \end{bmatrix}$$

and $\mathbf{C}$ is the matrix of the variances and covariances of the instantaneous rates of change of the risk factors

(54)

$$C \equiv \begin{bmatrix} \sigma_{11} & \sigma_{12} & \cdots & \sigma_{1n} \\ \sigma_{21} & \sigma_{22} & \cdots & \sigma_{2n} \\ \cdots & \cdots & \cdots & \cdots \\ \sigma_{n1} & \sigma_{n2} & \cdots & \sigma_{nn} \end{bmatrix} = \begin{bmatrix} \dfrac{\beta_1^2}{F_1^2} & \dfrac{\beta_1\beta_2}{F_1F_2}\rho_{12} & \cdots & \dfrac{\beta_1\beta_n}{F_1F_n}\rho_{1n} \\ \dfrac{\beta_2\beta_1}{F_2F_1}\rho_{21} & \dfrac{\beta_2^2}{F_2^2} & \cdots & \dfrac{\beta_2\beta_n}{F_2F_n}\rho_{2n} \\ \cdots & \cdots & \cdots & \cdots \\ \dfrac{\beta_n\beta_1}{F_nF_1}\rho_{n1} & \dfrac{\beta_n\beta_2}{F_nF_2}\rho_{n2} & \cdots & \dfrac{\beta_n^2}{F_n^2} \end{bmatrix}$$

The turbulence of a portfolio is defined by the following expression

(55)
$$\psi \equiv std\left[\frac{d\sigma(\mathbf{F}, t)}{\sigma(\mathbf{F}, t)}\right] = \sqrt{\mathbf{v'Cv}}$$

where the vector $\mathbf{v}$ contains the elasticities of the volatility with respect to each risk factor

(56)
$$\mathbf{v} \equiv \begin{bmatrix} v_1 \\ v_2 \\ \cdots \\ v_n \end{bmatrix} = \begin{bmatrix} \dfrac{\partial\sigma}{\partial F_1}\dfrac{F_1}{\sigma} \\ \dfrac{\partial\sigma}{\partial F_2}\dfrac{F_2}{\sigma} \\ \cdots \\ \dfrac{\partial\sigma}{\partial F_n}\dfrac{F_n}{\sigma} \end{bmatrix}.$$

BIBLIOGRAPHY

[1] BAGG J., «Taking the Wider View», *International Derivative Review*, June 1996, pp. 12-4.

[2] BANK FOR INTERNATIONAL SETTLEMENTS (Committee on Banking Supervision), *Overview of the Amendment to the Capital Accord to Incorporate Market Risks*, Basle, January 1996.

[3] — — (Committee on Banking Supervision), *Amendment to the Capital Accord to Incorporate Market Risks*, Basle, January 1996.

[4] — — (Committee on Banking Supervision), *Supervisory Framework for the Use of «Backtesting» in conjunction with the Internal Models Approach to Market Risk Capital Requirements*, Basle, January 1996.

[5] BARONE-ADESI G. - GIANNOPOULOS K., «A Simplified Approach to the Conditional Estimation of Value at Risk (VAR)», Alberta (Canada), Faculty of Business, *Working Paper*, 1996.

[6] BARONE E. - BRAGHÒ A., «Un sistema integrato per la gestione del rischio di interesse», *Bancaria*, vol. 51, n. 11, November 1995, pp. 18-31.

[7] BARONE E. - RISA S., «Valuation of Floaters and Options on Floaters under Special Repo Rates», *Working Paper*, IMI, November 1994.

[8] BEDER T.S., «VAR: Seductive but Dangerous», *Financial Analysts Journal*, September-October 1995.

[9] BLACK F. - SCHOLES M., «The Pricing of Options and Corporate Liabilities», *Journal of Political Economy*, vol. 81, n. 3, May-June 1973, pp. 637-54.

[10] BRENNER M. - SUBRAHMANYAM M.G., «A Simple Formula to Compute the Implied Standard Deviation», *Financial Analysts Journal*, vol. 44, n. 5, September-October 1988, pp. 80-3.

[11] — — - — —, «A Simple Approach to Option Valuation and Hedging in the Black-Scholes Model», *Financial Analysts Journal*, vol. 50, n. 2, March-April, 1994, pp. 25-8.

[12] COX J. - INGERSOLL J.E. - ROSS S.A., «A Theory of the Term Structure of Interest Rates», *Econometrica*, vol. 53, n. 2, March 1985, pp. 385-407.

[13] FODY S.A., *J.P. Morgan Term Structure Model: Technical Appendix*, April 1992.

[14] GARMAN M.B. - KOHLHAGEN S.W., «Foreign Currency Option Values», *Journal of International Money and Finance*, vol. 2, December 1983, pp. 231-7.

[15] GROUP OF THIRTY, *Derivatives: Practices and Principles, Appendix I: Working Papers*, July 1993, p. 3.

[16] HULL J.C., *Introduction to Futures & Options Markets*, 2nd edn., Englewood Cliffs (NJ) Prentice Hall, 1995.

[17] HULL J.C., *Options, Futures, and Other Derivatives*, 3rd edn., Englewood Cliffs (NJ) Prentice Hall, 1997.

[18] HULL J.C. - WHITE A., «Pricing Interest-Rate-Derivative Securities», *Review of Financial Studies*, vol. 3, n. 4, 1990, pp. 537-92.

[19] MORGAN J.P., *RiskMetrics™ - Technical Document*, 3rd edn., New York, May 26, 1995.

[20] LITTERMAN R., «Hot Spots and Hedges», *Working Paper*, Goldman, Sachs & Co., July 1996.

[21] LONGERSTAEY J., *Introduction to RiskMetrics™*, 3rd edn., New York, J.P. Morgan, March 15, 1995.

[22] MASERA R.S., «Rischio controparte e rischio finanziario in mercati integrati: separatezze e intrecci», *Bancaria*, vol. 49, n. 6, June 1993.

[23] MERTON R.C., *Continuous-Time Finance*, Oxford - Cambridge (MB), Basil Blackwell, 1990.

[24] MERTON R.C. - PEROLD A., «Management of Risk Capital in Financial Firms», Harward Business School, *Working Paper*, n. 93-038, 1993.

[25] PHELAN M.J., «Probability and Statistics Applied to the Practice of Financial Risk Management: The Case of JP Morgan's RiskMetrics™», Wharton, *Working Paper*, 1995.

[26] SMITHSON C., «Value at Risk», *Risk*, vol. 9, n. 1, January, 1996.

[27] — —, «Value at Risk (2)», *Risk*, vol. 9, n. 2, February, 1996.

Macroeconomic Effects of Corporate Macroeconomic Exposure: Conceptual Issues and Estimation

Clas Wihlborg*

Göteborg University

The literature on corporate exposure to exchange rate and interest rate risk has been expanding rapidly in recent years in the finance and the financial management literature. Macroeconomists have also paid attention to the subject, because one of the claimed benefits of a European Monetary Union (EMU) would be reduced exchange rate uncertainty. Hardcore proponents of the EMU even argue that the general level of (real) interest rates would fall as á result of a reduced risk premium in interest rates. The benefits in the absence of such an interest rate effect would be caused by less resources (manpower and investment in flexibility) devoted to the management of exchange rate risk in corporations, and greater informativeness of prices.

The analysis and estimation of exchange rate and interest rate exposure in the finance literature do not necessarily imply that firms should devote resources to risk-management. The focus is often on whether investors in financial assets need to consider the exchange rate an independent risk-factor in portfolio management. The question whether exchange rate and interest rate risk is priced

---

* Clas Wihlborg is Professor of Banking and Financial Economics, School of Economics and Commercial Law.

N.B. the numbers in square brackets refer to the Bibliography at the end of the paper.

in financial markets is also asked, however. The results are ambiguous for exhange rate risk while interest rate risk seems to be priced. The interest rate is also more consistently found to be a factor that affects the stock market values of firms in a somewhat systematic way.

In spite of these results non-financial firms seem to devote substantial attention and resources (manpower and investment in flexibility) to exchange rate exposure management but less attention to interest rate exposure. Banks, on the other hand, are strongly concerned with interest rate exposure. This can be explained by banks' involvement in the payment systems. Their customers (or the government as their agent) require a very low probability of bankruptcy.

One possible explanation for the ambiguous results of the studies of exchange rate exposure is that firms often eliminate exposure, i.e. they devote resources to exchange rate risk management. If this is the case, then we would expect reduced exchange rate uncertainty to contribute to an expansion in international trade and the efficiency of the capital stock by reducing the costs of having unbalanced currency positions in the normal course of business, as well as of having «real options» when exchange rates change.

The empirical evidence on the impact of exchange rate uncertainty on international trade is at least as ambiguous as the empirical evidence on stock-market effects of exchange rate changes, however.

In this paper, an explanation is offered for the ambiguities of the empirical results about exchange rate effects on stock-maket values of firms and on international trade, and the empirical literature is reviewed. The main point being made is that both exchange rate and interest rate exposures are aspects of macroeconomic exposure. Such exposure emanates from disturbances in the macroeconomic environment, which affect exchange rate, interest rates, and inflation rates simultaneously. Evidence on strong effects of exchange rate uncertainty per se on stock market valuations, and on international trade and investment is lacking.

Section 1 asks under what conditions reduced exchange rate uncertainty in, for example, a monetary union can be compared to a reduction in tax on foreign currency positions. The information value of prices is discussed in Section 2. Empirical work on the relation between exchange rate regime, and international trade investments is reviewed in Section 3. In Section 4, effects of changes in exchange rate and related variables in the Swedish stockmarket are analysed. The purpose here is to ascertain whether Swedish investors require a risk-premium to accept exchange rate risk in their protfolios.

1. - Is Exchange Rate Uncertainty Costly?

There are three commonly used microeconomic arguments for a monetary union to increase economic efficiency. First, a monetary union leads to a reduction of direct transactions costs in trade. These costs are ignored here. Second, if reduced exchange rate uncertainty can be likened to a reduction in a tax on financial positions in foreign currency, then the fixing of exchange rates in a monetary union increases economic efficiency. Third, the information value of prices could increase when there are no fluctuations in exchange rates.

These gains of reduced exchange rate uncertainty are not as obvious as they may seem. One reason is that the exchange rate is one of several variables that to a large extent reflect disturbances in the economic environment occurring independently of the exchange rate regime. Another reason is that hedging of exchange rate risk in financial markets can be obtained at very low costs.

The costs of exchange rate uncertainty must ultimately be determined by empirical analysis. Even if in theory costs are low, it is possible that firms and households do not act in the way they are assumed to in theory.

The answer to both of the following questions must be «yes» for the comparison between exchange rate uncertainty and a tax on foreign currency positions to be valid: 1) are exchange rate fluctuations independent of fluctuations in macroeconomic disturbances that simultaneously influence interest rates, inflation rates, and aggregate demand and supply?; 2) is the risk caused by independent exchange rate changes systematic in financial terminology meaning that it cannot be diversified away? The consequence of a «yes» is that households or firms demand compensation to accept exchange rate risk in their portfolios.

The first question is familiar to a macroeconomist thinking in terms of models of exchange rate determination with changes in «fundamentals» causing changes in the exchange rate. The exchange rate regime determines the extent to which different variables are influenced by the changes in fundamentals but there is no obvious relation between the regime and the total risk facing firms and households. A monetary union leads to fewer sources of disturbances since one monetary authority substitutes for up to 12 central banks in today's EU. On the other hand, the aggregate effect of a certain action by the single central bank is likely to be larger than the effect of the actions of twelve central banks acting with little coordination. There is a kind of diversification effect of having twelve central banks working independently. Against this advantage of many central banks there are advantages associated with a well-coordinated policy or one central bank behaving in a stabilizing manner.

Econometric studies indicate that only a small faction of short-term exchange rate changes are explained by contemporaneous changes in fundamentals. One reason for this is that expectations play an important role in exchange rate determination and that the relation between changes in fundamentals and in expectations about future changes in these fundamentals is not stable over time. The econometric studies underestimate the role of fundamentals in exchange rate determination, because they do not capture exchange rate changes caused by changes in expectations about fundamentals.

One source of exchange rate fluctuations independent of changes in fundamentals, as well as of expectations about fundamentals, is so called bubbles in prices of financial assets. A bubble occurs when, for example, a large number of market participants buy a currency on the grounds that each one individually believes that others will push up the price of the currency, even though each market participant knows that the expected price increase does not correspond to developments in fundamentals. Frankel [19] has argued that the strong dollar in 1984 and early 1985 was the result of a bubble. The stock-market crash in October 1987 and the rise in Swedish property values in 1989 and 1990 have been seen as bubbles by many observers.

If bubbles are common under freely floating rates, then exchange rate flexibility adds a source of risk to those risks caused by uncertainty about fundamentals. Empirical work on bubbles is inconclusive because it is impossible for the researcher to distinguish between a bubble and exchange rate changes caused by expectations about fundamentals. There are reasons to be very skeptical about claims about the existence of long lasting bubbles when the claims occur only in hindsight. A price increase caused by widespread false expectations about fundamentals cannot be distinguished from a bubble. The price path caused by, for example, widespread excessive optimism cannot be considered mispricing, however.

A second type of exchange rate changes independent of fundamentals are the daily, weekly or monthly changes classified as «noise» by the finance literature. Noise is caused by fluctuations in supply and demand related to, for example, variations in the need for liquidity and in the demand for hedge positions. There is little doubt that «noise» is an important factor explaining the short-term volatility in exchange rates.

This reasoning leads to the preliminary conclusion that exchange rate fluctuations are often independent of macroecoonomic fundamentals in the short term. However, the longer the time-period the more likely it is that exchange rate changes are caused by changes in fundamentals or expectations about fundamentals. Therefore, the answer to the first question above is a partial yes. We must therefore turn to the second question whether it is costly to hedge exchange rate risk.

One way to phrase the second question is whether the expected return on a portfolio designed to diversify away or hedge exchange risk is lower than the return on a portfolio designed independently of exchange rate risk-consideration.

If exchange rate risk cannot be diversified completely, then exchange rate risk premia should be observed in rates of return on similar securities denominated in different currencies. Financial economists have devoted much time to evaluate whether exchange rate risk-premia exist[1]. Without going into detail the evidence indicates that on the average over time there is no risk-premia but there is also convincing evidence that there are fluctuating deviations from parity between interest rate differentials and measures of expected exchange rate changes. This evidence could be consistent with a time-varying risk-premia except that there are no plausible explanations for the variation over time. Factors that theoretically should determine the variation in risk-premia have no explanatory value (Rogoff [44]). A more plausible explanation for the observed relations between exchange rate changes, interest rate differentials, and forward premia is that market participants require periods of learning actual patterns and relations among variables, because these patterns change when, for example, monetary authorities change their rules for interest rate, money supply, and exchange rate targeting. Thus, expectations are not captured correctly in many empirical models.

In Section 4 below results of regressions of the return on the Swedish stock-market on exchange rate changes and other macroeconomic variables are discussed. The results indicate that Swedish investors do not require a risk premium to accept exchange rate risk. If so, the answer to the second question above is «no». Besides costs of hedging in financial markets, exchange rate uncertainty may induce investment in flexibility creating «real options» for a firm. Costs associated with such investments are considered in Section 3. Thus, even if exchange rate uncertainty is an independent source of risk on short-term financial positions there are no or negligible costs associated with diversifying and hedging this risk.

---

[1] In Sweden, HÖRNGREN L. - VREDIN A. [30] and OXELHEIM I. [42] have studied this issue. The international literature is summarized in several textbooks such as MACDONALD R. [40].

2. - Exchange Rate Changes and the Information Value of Prices

Prices in a market economy convey information. In order for prices to perform this role efficiently for the benefit of consumers and firms, observable prices must be comparable, reglect resource use in products, and adjust with reasonable speed to changes in demand and supply. The existence of more than one currency can disturb the pricing mechanism in two ways. First, it is harder to make price comparisons across currencies when individuals have little intuitive sense for the units of foreign currencies. In this case, producers find it easier to price-discriminate among markets (Gros and Thygesen [28]). Second, rigidities of prices imply that relative prices among commodities produced in different countries are influenced by nominal exchange rate changes.

Even if the argument that exchange rate fluctuations reduce the information value of prices is accepted, it does not follow that there is less mispricing under fixed rates. Again, it is necessary to ask whether there is less mispricing caused by macroeconomic disturbances under one regime than another. Thus, the relevant question here is whether short-term fluctuations in exchange rates cause mispricing and misinformation.

The quantitative effect of short-term misinformation in relative prices among countries is hard to evaluate. Unless bubbles are common, the mispricing should not be long-lasting. If individuals know this, then they would disregard a large proportion of short-term exchange rate fluctuations when allocating resources.

Exchange rate fluctuations can have a positive informational role as well. Glick, Kretzmer and Wihlborg [23] find evidence that exchange rate changes convery information about disturbances in comparison to fixed exchange rates between countries with different currencies. In a monetary union both the number of sources of disturbances (central banks) and the number of exchange rates conveying information are reduced. The net effect on the information conveyed by prices cannot be evaluated without knowledge about the variability of different kinds of shocks and the responsiveness of prices to these shocks.

3. - Risk, International Trade and Investment

The hypothesis that exchange rate volatility has a negative influence on international trade flows has been subject to empirical testing in numerous papers[2]. However, these empirical studies have in general been unable to establish a significantly negative relationship between measured exchange rate volatility and the volume of international trade in time-series regressions. Hooper and Kohlhagen [29], estimating effects on bilateral US trade flows, rejected the hypothesis that exchange risk discourages the volume of trade. This was supported by an International Monetary Fund survey, 1984, of work in the early 1980s. Cusman [14] estimated 16 bilateral trade equations and found evidence that exchange risk had a significantly negative effect on trade in 6 cases and a significantly positive effect in 2 cases. In a later study (1986), he analyzed the effect of exchange rate risk for US bilateral exports to its 6 major trading partners, while controlling for risk associated with third-country currencies.

Across various specifications and sample periods, less than half of the coefficients on exchange rate risk were ever significantly negative. The evidence from gravity models of bilateral trade flows are more mixed. Thursby and Thursby [45] find some support for the hypothesis that exchange rate flexibility discourages the volume of trade; however, Brada and Mendez [9] reject the hypothesis.

Some have argued that by focusing on multilateral rather than bilateral trade flows misspecification problems can be avoided arising from not including in the estimated trade equations relative prices involving third country importers and exporters. However, papers using multilateral trade flows have provided no more conclusive evidence. Ahktar and Hilton [3] reported significantly negative effects of exchange rate risk on US and German multilateral exports and German multilateral imports, while Gotur [26], after updating their work, found a significant negative effect for

---

[2] EDISON H.I. - MELVIN M. [17] provide a critical survey of the empirical literature on exchange rate volatility and international trade.

German imports only, and significantly positive effects on multi-lateral US exports and Japanese imports. Kenen and Rodrik [32] analyzed multilateral manufacturing imports for 11 industrial countries and found a significantly negative effect in only 4 cases[3]. Bailey, Tavlas, and Ulan [6] found no significant effect of exchange rate volatility on multilateral exports of industrial countries.

Some have suggested the need to disaggregate trade by goods sectors in order to avoid the aggregation problems that arise when sectors are exposed to exchange risk to different degrees. Maskus [41], for example, examined real exchange risk effects on US bilateral trade with 4 countries, disaggregated into 9 industry sectors. Of his 64 estimated equations, only 26 had significantly (at a 10 percent level) negative coefficients on exchange rate risk. Klein [33] analyzed the effects of real exchange rate variability on the proportions of US bilateral exports to 7 major trading partners, disaggregated into 9 goods categories. In contrast to the results of Maskus, he found that in 5 of 9 categories the volatility of the real exchange rate significantly and positively affected the value of exports; this effect was significantly negative only in one category.

Others have argued that the empirical trade effects of exchange rate risk are sensitive to the statistical techniques employed and have suggested alternative methodologies. However, these results are nonrobust as well. For example, Koray and Lastrapes [35] and Lastrapes and Koray [38] estimate vector autoregression of trade levels and their determinants; they find little or no effect of exchange rate volatility on trade. Utilization of time series techniques that take account that international trade and its determinants may be nonstationary integrated variable has not provided unambiguous results either. For example, Asseery and Peel [5] and Arize [4] estimate error correction models with cointegrating long-run relationships between trade, output, and relative prices. In the former paper, exchange rate risk was found to have a positive ef-

---

[3] Nevertheless KENEN P. RODRIK D. [32] interpreted their findings as evidence in support of arguments for greater exchange rate fixity.

fect on exports, while the effect was found to be negative in the latter. Gagnon [21] parameterizes a theoretical model of trade under uncertainty and demonstrates that exchange rate variability of the magnitude typical among industrial countries during the floating rate period has an insignificant effect on the level of international trade.

This brief review of the empirical literature indicates that time-series analyses have not been successful in establishing a robust relation between exchange rate risk and international trade. As noted above, there are several reasons for the lack of an unambiguous relationship between the exchange rate regime, exchange rate risk, and trade, First, an increase in (nominal or real) exchange rate risk need not be associated necessarily with an increase in uncertainty about macroeconomic conditions. For example, an increase in exchange rate variability associated with the shift to a more flexible exchange rate regime may be accompanied by a reduction in other kinds of risk in the form of lower inflation, interest rate, or output variability. Conversely, while exchange rate variability may be low under a fixed exchange rate regime, uncertainty about inflation, interest rates, or aggregate demand may be relatively higher instead. Thus, overall uncertainty about macroeconomic conditions is reflected in different variables under different regimes, and is not necessarily correlated with (unconditional or conditional) exchange rate variability[4]. The problem of properly measuring exchange rate regime-related risk is compounded by difficulties in constructing a time-series measure of exchange rate risk, since expectations are inherently difficult to measure.

Perl and Wihlborg [43] analyze effects of different sources of macroeconomic risk on sectoral trade between the USA and four countries listed in Table 1. In this study, exchange rate risk is measured by the variation in the real exchange rate that cannot be explained by money supply and industrial production changes.

Table 1 shows the total effect on all sectors' trade of macroeconomic risk measured by the variances of unexpected changes in a number of macroeconomic variables. The results indicate that

---

[4] Oxelheim and Wihlborg, 1987 explore the corporate finance implications of this view.

TABLE 1

EFFECTS OF EXCHANGE RATE AND MACROECONOMIC
UNCERTAINTY IN INTERNATIONAL TRADE BETWEEN
USA AND CANADA, GERMANY, UNITED KINGDOM AND JAPAN**

Variance of	Japan	Canada	Germany	UK
Exports from USA to				
US money supply	0.11*	−0.01	0.00	0.00
US industrial prod.	0.03*	0.00	0.02	−0.07*
Partners' money supply	−0.05*	−0.05	−0.02	−0.41
Partners' industrial prod.	0.01	0.03*	−0.07*	−0.36*
Real exchange rate	0.22*	0.07*	0.13	−0.02
Total	0.32	0.04	0.06	−0.86
Imports to USA from				
US money supply	−0.03	−0.05*	−0.05*	0.02
US industrial prod.	−0.02	−0.02	0.00	−0.01
Partners' money supply	0.03	0.04	−0.04*	−0.21
Partners' industrial prod.	0.06*	−0.02	0.10*	−0.07
Real exchange rate	−0.06	0.03	0.18*	−0.02
Total	−0.02	0.02	0.19	−0.29

* Coefficient in regression for exports and imports was significantly different from zero at 80% level of confidence.

** The figures show cumulative effect of variances of money supply, industrial production and real exchange rates during period 1975:4-1984:4 in relation to trade at lowest observed variance (percent). Figures are summations over seven sectors.

effects on trade are very small or even negligible, although they hide larger effects in some sectors. These effects are sometimes positive and sometimes negative. The magnitude of these coefficients are representative for most studies. It can also be noted that the largest trade effects are caused by other sources of macroeconomic risk than real exchange rate uncertainty.

The effects of exchange rate risl on foreign direct investments is expected to be dominated by substitution of foreign investments for domestic investments in production capacity for exports. However, if the effects on trade are small or negligible the effects on foreign investment are expected to be small, as well. A few studies by, for example, Chang and Kogut [12] and Goldberg and Kostad [25] have identified coeffcients. As expected, the effects are small relative to the total variation in foreign direct investments.

The relation between risk of different kinds and investments in a country is more complex. On the one hand, the present value of a cash flow stream increases as its variance increases. On the other hand, an investment that is planned but not yet done has an option value, if invested resources cannot be sold at their initial prices (Abel [1]). The relation between option values and exchange rate regimes is discussed below.

Campa and Goldberg [11] analyze effects of exchange rate variability on investments in sectors such as electrical machinery and transport equipment in the USA. They calculate whether each sector is a net exporter or a net importer and each sector's profit margin. The hypothesis is that exchange rate changes and exchange rate risk are relatively important for sectors with large net exports or imports and small profit-margins.

The hypothesis with respect to effects of exchange rate changes are supported by the data but the hypothesis that increased exchange rate variance leads to a decrease in investment is only weakly supported in some industries. Coefficients are not different from zero with 90% significance. The authors calculate, however, that in the one industry with the largest effects of exchange rate variability, a 10% increase in the standard deviation of exchange rate changes causes a 0.3% reduction in investments.

All the studies reviewed above employ time-series analysis. Measuring risk as it is perceived by market participants by using actual variability during quarters or half-years is bound to be subject to serious doubt. Glick and Wihlborg [24] propose that cross-section measures of variability over longer period may better capture risk. They also suggest that a measure of degree of exchange rate flexibility should better capture risk associated with an exchange rate regime, whether the source of risk is exchange rate risk, or risk related to macroeconomic disturbances. Their hypothesis is that the risk facing exporters declines with increasing exchange rate flexibility.

Exchange rate flexibility is measured as the variance of a country's bilateral exchange rate relative to the USD as a fraction of the variance that would have occurred without foreign exchange market intervention. Table 2 contains definitions and it lists this measure of flexibility for 30 countries.

TABLE 2

CROSS-COUNTRY REGIME CHARACTERISTICS*

Country	Abbreviation	Sample range		XRVAR	XRFLEX	OPEN
Canada	CAN	80.1	93.12	0.15	0.08	0.46
Japan	JAP	80.1	93.12	1.00	0.94	0.19
Mexico	MEX	80.1	93.12	3.69	0.28	0.21
Japan	JAP	80.1	93.12	1.00	0.94	0.19
United Kingdom	GBR	80.1	93.12	1.23	0.53	0.40
Germany	DEU	80.9	93.12	1.11	0.51	0.48
France	FRA	80.1	93.12	1.12	0.48	0.36
Netherlands	NLD	80.1	93.12	1.14	0.37	0.95
Korea	KOR	80.1	93.12	0.21	0.08	0.58
Singapore	SIN	80.1	93.12	0.16	0.04	2.97
Japan	JAP	80.1	93.12	1.00	0.94	0.19
Australia	AUS	80.1	93.12	0.84	0.27	0.27
Belgium	BLX	80.1	92.12	1.17	0.33	1.23
Italy	ITA	80.1	93.9	1.01	0.78	0.34
Brazil	BRA	80.1	92.12	3.31	0.30	0.16
Switzerland	CHE	80.1	93.3	1.32	0.60	0.57
Malaysia	MAL	80.1	93.12	0.15	0.02	1.05
Spain	ESP	80.1	93.12	1.10	0.68	0.28
Venezuela	VEN	80.1	93.12	9.13	0.46	0.42
Sweden	SWE	80.1	93.12	1.02	0.12	0.29
Thailand	THA	80.1	93.12	0.24	0.10	0.49
Ireland	IRL	80.1	93.12	1.08	0.10	0.98
Israel	ISR	80.1	93.9	1.10	0.47	0.56
Philippines	PHI	80.1	93.12	0.98	0.17	0.40
Argentina	ARG	80.1	90.12	41.52	0.79	0.12
Colombia	COL	80.1	93.9	0.01	0.00	0.25
Chile	CHI	80.1	93.12	0.88	0.52	0.42
Indonesia	IDN	80.1	93.12	1.35	0.264	0.39
Norway	NOR	80.1	93.12	0.87	0.04	0.56
Denmark	DNK	80.1	93.12	1.06	0.04	0.53
New Zealand	NZL	80.1	93.12	1.12	0.01	0.43
Greece	GRC	80.1	91.3	1.01	0.56	0.37

Legend:
XRVAR: variance of monthly percent exchange rate changes.
XRFLEX: variance of monthly percent exchange rate changes/variance of monthly percent exchange rate changes plus the variance of incipient exchange rate changes.
The incipient exchange rate change during a month is calculated as the change in the foreign exchange reserves as a percent of the monetary base.
OPEN: exports plus imports/GDP.
* XRVAR, XRFLEX, and OPEN denote the variance of exchange rate changes, the degree of exchange rate flexibility, and multilateral openness, respectively, calculated over the sample range indicated. See the Data Appendix for details of calculation. XRVAR figures are multiplied by 1,000.
Source, GLICK R. - WIHLBORG C. [24].

Table 3 shows the results of pooled regressions for US exports of manufactured goods to 30 countries 1980-1993. Each importing country's exchange rate regime (*XRFLEX*) affects the elasticity of US exports with respect to the real exchange rate (*P*) and the importing country's GDP (*Y*). The importing country's openness (-*OPEN*) is also included interactively and measured as total exports plus imports relative to GDP.

Table 3 shows that the export volume elasticities with respect to the real exchange rate and foreign GDP have the expected positive sign and are strongly significant in all specifications. For the full sample of countries, both of the interactive terms involving the degree of flexibility (*XRFLEX*) are positive and significant across specifications without and with the openness interaction terms (though including Y_{US} does lower the significance level for the interactive term with foreign GDP). Thus, both the real exchange rate elasticity of US exports as well as the elasticity of US exports with regard to foreign GDP increase (in absolute value) as the degree of exchange rate flexibility rises, as is expected when greater flexibility is associated with lower risk. For OECD countries alone, the interactive term with the degree of exchange rate flexibility is significant and positive only in its effect on the elasticity with regard to foreign GDP. The finding of a positive effect of exchange rate flexibility on US exports and the interpretation that greater exchange rate flexibility is associated with lower risk is supported by the observation that most of the variation in the exchange rate flexibility measure is atributable to differences in incipient exchange rate changes offset by central bank intervention, rather than to differences in exhange rate variability per se. The cross-country variation in the latter variability is relatively low.

The irreversibility of investment provides one argument why the return elasticity of investment (dK_j/dR_j) (R_j/K_j) and hence the price elasticity of export supply declines with greater uncertainty about the returns to exporting. If investment is irreversible, there is an «option» value of waiting which renders firms cautious about exiting and giving up on investments in foreign matters or investing in entering new markets. With greater uncertainty about the exchange rate and other determinants of investment and supply,

TABLE 3

POOLED BILATERAL US MANUFACTURED EXPORTS[1]

Explanatory variables	All countries				OECD countries			
	(1)	(2)	(3)	(4)	(5)	(6)	(7)	(8)
P	0.61 (0.10)***	0.66 (0.10)***	0.70 (0.13)***	0.36 (0.12)***	0.84 (0.13)***	0.98 (0.14)***	1.18 (0.23)***	1.10 (0.21)***
Y	1.45 (0.07)***	1.38 (0.07)***	1.28 (0.09)***	1.15 (0.09)***	1.83 (0.16)***	1.56 (0.21)***	1.25 (0.27)***	0.30 (0.23)
$P.\,XRFLEX$	0.79 (0.19)***	0.52 (0.20)**	0.44 (0.22)**	1.10 (0.21)***	0.30 (0.22)	-0.05 (0.25)	-0.18 (0.27)	-0.02 (0.25)
$Y.\,XRFLEX$		0.69 (0.18)***	0.82 (0.20)***	0.35 (0.19)*		0.70 (0.29)**	0.91 (0.31)***	1.09 (0.25)***
$P.\,OPEN$			0.02 (0.11)	0.14 (0.10)			-0.30 (0.27)	-0.35 (0.24)
$Y.OPEN$			0.09 (0.05)*	0.09 (0.04)*			0.77 (0.41)*	0.91 (0.30)***
$Trend$	0.03 (0.00)***	0.03 (0.00)***	0.03 (0.00)***	-0.00 (0.01)	0.03 (0.01)***	0.03 (0.01)***	0.02 (0.01)***	-0.0 (0.01)**
Y_{US}				1.34 (0.17)***				2.00 (0.21)***
R^2	0.71	0.71	0.72	0.75	0.74	0.74	0.74	0.79
DW	1.75	1.78	1.78	1.56	1.84	1.84	1.84	1.73
SEE	1.23	1.23	1.23	1.29	1.22	1.22	1.22	1.22

[1] The dependent variable is (logged) real bilateral manufactured exports X. P, Y and Y_{US} denote the (logged) real dollar price of foreign exchange, foreign GDP, and US GDP, respectively. $XRFLEX$ and $OPEN$ denote the degree of exchange rate flexibility and multilateral openness, respectively. Heteroscedastic-adjusted standard errors in parentheses;
   * denotes significance at the 0.10 level;
  ** denotes significance at the 0.05 level;
 *** denotes significance at the 0.01 level.
Source: GLICK R. - WIHLBORG C. [24].

the option value of not acting increases. The increased reluctance of firms to deviate from the status quo implies in the aggregate a decline in the elasticity of the capital stock and export supply with respect to the real exchange rate (P_j) and the importing country's GDP (Y_j)[5].

4. - Exchange Rate Changes, and the Pricing of Macroeconomic Risk in the Swedish Stock Market

By studying the effects of exchange rate changes and other macroeconomic variables on stock-market returns, it should be possible to observe the impact on a firm of the factors influencing the firm's trade and investments through a variety of channels. There is a problem analyzing stock-market prices since they incorporate information about management's activities as well. Thus, if the firm's policy is to hedge all exchange rate risk, then we will not observe any relation between the exchange rate and the firm's value if management is successful. Fortunately, few firms follow such a stategy primarily because they do not have information systems that allow an evaluation of exposure, and even if they had the information, it is unlikely that firms would want to remove all risk.

Another reason to study the relation between exchange rate changes and stock-market prices is to answer the question whether exchange rate and other macroeconomic risks are priced in financial markets.

Wihlborg [48] analyzes daily and monthly returns for 28 individual firms on the Stockholm stock exchange for the period 1987 through February 1992. The stock market returns were regressed on changes in the market index, exchange rates and the interest rate. In addition, the standard deviation of exchange rate

---

[5] See, for example, DIXIT A. [15], [16] and BALDWIN R. - KRUGMAN P. [8]; a particularly accessible variation of this argument can be found in KRUGMAN P. ([8], Ch. 2). AIZENMAN J. [2]. GOLDBERG L. - KOLSTAD C. [25], and GOLDBERG, 1996, explore the international direct investment implications of variable exchange rates more formally.

changes implicit in options prices were used as proxies for exchange rate risk.

The Swedish market index was not significantly influenced by daily exchange rate changes. Using monthly data, a one per cent depreciation of the Swedish krona was associated with a two per cent fall in the market index. Returns for a few individual firms rose in response to a depreciation. If exchange rate changes were independent of macro-shocks, we would expect that the stock market return increases in response to a depreciation as it did at the time of the large depreciation when the SEK started to float in 1992. One interpretation of the opposite result is that both the Swedish currency and the stock market responded in the same direction to a common underlying factor. In other words, the regression results for monthly data indicate that the coefficient for exchange rate changes captures effects of macroeconomic disturbances.

The proxy for exchange rate risk enters in regressions for many firms, but the sign is sometimes negative, sometimes positive. The results are hard to interpret, but the observed effects and the explanatory value of the risk variables are small.

Finally, significant coefficients for one more exchange rates in the regression for the market index using monthly data indicates that the risk captured by the exchange rates was not completely diversifiable within the Swedish market during the period 1987-1991.

Table 4 presents the results of a study by Ibrahimi, Oxelheim and Wihlborg [31] indicating that Swedish households do not require a premium to accept exchange rate risk before 1987. The study has been extended to other countries with similar results.

There are results for three different specifications in Table 4. First, the nominal return on the Swedish stock market index is regressed on nominal exchange rate changes (*SEK/USD*). Second, real returns and real exchange rates are used. Third, other macroeconomic price variables such as interest rates and inflation are incorporated in order to identify exchange rate changes that occur independently of other macroeconomic price variables. Regressions are also performed for three sub-periods of the full period 1970-1987.

Clas Wihlborg

TABLE 4

PERCENT MONTHLY RETURNS ON SWEDISH STOCK MARKET
(GENERAL INDEX) EXPLAINED BY EXCHANGE RATE CHANGES,
INTEREST RATE CHANGES AND INFLATION.
UNDERLINED COEFFICIENTS ARE SIGNIFICANTLY DIFFERENT
FROM ZERO AT 90% LEVEL OF CONFIDENCE

Year	1970-1987	1970-1973	1974-1979	1980-1987
a) *Nominal returns explained only by nominal exchange rate changes (percent changes)*				
Coefficient Kr/$	0.101	−0.443	−0.187	0.259
[*T*-value]	[0.73]	[−1.19]	[−0.90]	[1.23]
b) *Same as* a) *but real and real exchange rate changes*				
Coefficient Kr/$	0.078	−0.021	−0.062	0.168
[*T*-value]	[0.56]	[−0.06]	[−0.34]	[0.74]
c) *Real returns explained by unexpected changes in exchange rates, interest rates and inflation**				
Coefficient Kr/$	0.107	0.203	−0.044	0.402
[*T*-value]	[0.79]	[0.61]	[−0.18]	[1.50]
Swedish long rate	−3.39	4.08	0.513	−3.607
[*T*-value]	[−1.93]	[0.19]	[0.07]	[−1.50]
USA's long rate	−1.92	−8.71	−6.77	2.402
[*T*-value]	[−1.64]	[−1.62]	[−1.57]	[−1.24]
Swedish inflation	−1.35	−3.27	−2.58	−3.27
[*T*-value]	[−2.94]	[−2.37]	[−1.99]	[−2.24]
USA's inflation	0.562	2.05	0.362	1.344
[*T*-value]	[0.97]	[1.39]	[0.16]	[−0.50]

* Regressions also include measures of expected values for the explanatory variables but these are of less interest. Expected values of each regressor are included with with lagged values. All regressions are corrected for heteroskedasticity.
Source, IBRAHIMI F., OXELHEIM L., WIHLBORG C. [31].

As noted, one interpretation of the results is that households could diversify exchange rate risk by holding the Swedish market portfolio through 1987. The table shows also that other macroeconomic risks causing interest rate changes and inflation are very important sources of risk and households demand compensation to accept these risks.

The results reported above with respect to the diversifiability of exchange rate risk in the Swedish stock market indicate that after 1987 exchange rate risk was not diversified away by holding a Swedish stock market portfolio. The next question is whether households thereafter could diversify this risk by holding a more international portfolio.

Table 5 presents results of regressions that include the rate of return in dollars on a world portfolio as an explanatory variable for the monthly rate of return on the Swedish stock market index[6]. Other independent variables are changes of Swedish short and long interest rates, Swedish inflation in consumer prices, and

TABLE 5

RATE OF RETURN ON SWEDISH STOCK MARKET INDEX.
ALL VARIABLES IN PER CENT RATE OF CHANGE. OLS[a]

	97.03-95.03		87.03-92.92.10		93.02-95.03*	
Constant	0.01	[1.2]	0.004	[0.44]	0.02	[2.7]
World index in USD	1.12	[9.7]	0.97	[7.23]	1.47	[4.1]
SEK/USD	1.12	[6.2]	1.35	[4.3]	1.50	[3.0]
L1 SEK/USD	−0.11	[−0.7]	−0.03	[−0.1]	−0.79	[−2.0]
L2 SEK/USD	−0.29	[1.9]	−0.56	[2.2]	0.61	[1.6]
Short int. rate	−0.15	[−2.1]	−0.13	[−1.5]	0.19	[0.9]
Long int. rate	−0.21	[1.7]	−0.09	[−0.4]	−0.26	[−1.9]
CPI	0.33	[0.4]	1.50	[1.5]	−0.39	[−0.1]
L1 CPI	−0.51	[0.6]	−1.5	[1.0]	1.56	[1.0]
L2 CPI	−0.45	[−0.06]	−0.06	[−0.06]	−3.07	[−2.1]
SEK/Yen	−0.32	[−1.6]	−0.25	[1.0]	−0.54	[−1.9]
SEK/GBP	0.22	[0.8]	0.59	[1.4]	0.23	[0.4]
SEK/DM	−0.21	[−0.7]	0.14	[0.2]	−0.61	[−1.3]
L1 SEK/DM	−0.35	[−1.4]	−0.46	[−0.7]	0.41	[0.9]
L2 SEK/DM	−0.18	[−0.7]	0.77	[1.1]	−0.49	[−1.1]
DF	77		63		9	
R^2	0.69		0.62			
DW	2.08		2.0		2.3	

[a] Coefficients for exchange rate changes holding the SEK value of the world index constant:

Adj. to world index in *SEK**	1.12	0.97	1.47
Adj. to *SEK/USD***	0	0.38	0.03
Adj. to *SEK/FC***	−0.30	0.85	−0.79

* Yale-Walker estimates correcting for autocorrelation
** Coefficient for *SEK/USD* minus coefficient for world index.
*** Sum of coefficients for exchange rates using the coefficient on the previous line for *SEK/USD*.

[6] The world index was obtained from the MSCI data base.

changes of the Swedish currency (*SEK*) price of US dollars (*USD*), British pounds (*GBP*), Japanese Yen (Yen) and German marks (DM). Three lags (*L*1, *L*2, *L*3) were included for changes of the exchange rate relative to the USA and Germany. Thereby, autoroccelation was removed for the sub-period 1987.1-1992.10 but not for the period 1993.02-1995.03. Estimates were corrected for autocorrelation in the regressions for the full period and for the most recent shorter period.

During the first estimation period 1987.1-1992.10 the Swedish Krona was pegged to a trade-weighted basket or the ECU. The currency has been floating thereafter. Data for the last month of 1992 was excluded, because it was a period of adjustment of the exchange rate after a long period of «leaning against the wind» in defence of a pegged rate relative to the ECU.

The most striking result in Table 5 is that the coefficient for the dollar exchange rate is nearly identical to the coefficient for the world index expressed in dollars in the regression for the second sub-period, as well as for the full period. This similarity of coefficients implies that there is no independent effect of the exchange rate on the Swedish stock index return when the return on the world index is calculated in *SEK*. Thus, Swedish households holding an internationally diversified portfolio face no additional risk due to uncertainty about the dollar exchange rate.

The other exchange rates are not significant on the 5% level. The Yen is barely significant on the 10% level during the floating period.

The total effect on the Swedish index of a simultaneous one per cent depreciation of the *SEK* against all currencies, while the world stock market index remains constant, is presented in Table 3 as the effects of a change in *SEK/FC*. Although the coefficients for the exchange rate changes are not significant they have been used because they represent the best available estimates. It can be seen that the total effect of a depreciation is small for the full period in comparison with the effects of a one per cent change in the Swedish price level during the first sub-period or a one percentage point change in the long interest rate during the second sub-period[7]. (A one percentage point increase in the interest rate corresponds to 10% change in the interest rate). The effect of a depreciaton is positive for the first sub-period and negative for the second sub-period. This instability is an indication that effects of exchange rate changes depend on the fundamental sources of the changes.

The results for the second sub-period must be interpreted with caution. The number of observations is small and auto-correlation problems are severe. It can be observed in table 3, however, that the regression coefficients for the exchange rates for the last period are not very different from the implied coefficients that can be obtained for the same period by comparing the coefficients for the full period with the coefficients for the first sub-period.

In summary, the results of the empirical analysis of effects of exchange rate and macroeconomic disturbances on stock market values of Swedish firms do not contradict the results of the theoretical analyses. In other words, exchange rate changes are to a large extent reflections of changes in the macroeconomic environment and to the extent exchange rate changes are independent, the costs of hedging exchange rate risk are negligible. The results presented here indicate that interest rates and inflation are important risk factors, however. Thus, microeconomic benefits of a monetary union in the form of reduced risk facing firms and households are negligible, unless the union contributes to stability of general macroeconomic conditions.

---

[7] Swedish inflation was low and stable during the second sub-period.

BIBLIOGRAPHY

[1] ABEL A., «Optimal Investment Under Uncertainty», *American Economic Review*, January 1983.

[2] AIZENMAN J., «Exchange Rate Flexibility, Volatility, and the Patterns of Domestic and Foreign Direct Investment», IMF, *Staff paper*, n. 39, 1992, pp. 890-922.

[3] AKHTAR A. - HILTON R.S., «Effects of Exchange Rate Uncertainty on German and US Trade», Federal Reserve Bank of New York, *Quarterly Review*, Spring 1984, pp. 7-16.

[4] ARIZE A., «The Effects of Exchange-Rate Volatility on US Exports: An Empirical Investigation», *Southern Economic Journal*, n. 62, 1995, pp. 34-43.

[5] ASSERY A. - PEEL D., «The Effects of Exchange Rate Volatility on Exports: Some New Estimates», *Economic Letters*, n. 37, October 1991, pp. 173-7.

[6] BAILEY M. - TAVLAS G. - ULAN M., «Exchange Rate Variability and Trade performance: Evidence for the Big Seven Industrial Countries», *Weltwirtschaftliches Archiv*, n. 126, 1986, pp. 466-77.

[7] BALDWIN R.E., «On the Microeconomics of the European Monetary Union», *The Economics of EMU*, Special Edition, *European Economy*, n. 1, 1991.

[8] BALDWIN R. - KRUGMAN P., «Persistent Trade Effects of Large Exchange Rate Shocks», *Quarterly Journal of Economics*, n. 104, 1989, pp. 635-54.

[9] BRADA J. - MENDEZ J., «Exchange Rate Risk, Exchange Rate Regime and the Volume of International Trade», *Kyklos*, 41, 1988, pp. 263-80.

[10] BURDEKIN R. - WIHLBORG C. - WILLETT T., «A Monetary Constitution Case for an Independent European Central Bank», *The World Economy*, March 1992.

[11] CAMPA J. - GOLDBERG L., «Investment in Manufacturing, Exchange Rates and External Exposure», NBER, *Working Paper*, Series 1993.

[12] CHANG S.J. - KOGUT B., «Platform Investments and Volatile Exchange Rates: Japanese Direct Investment in US Electronic Industries», Wharton School, Working Paper, 1992.

[13] COMMISSION OF THE EUROPEAN COMMUNITIES, «One Market, One Money: An Evaluation of the Potential Benefits and Costs of Forming an Economic and Monetary Union», *European Economy*, October 1990.

[14] CUSHMAN D., «The Effects of Real Exchange Rate Risk on International Trade», *Journal of International Economics*, n. 15, August 1983, pp. 45-63.

[15] DIXIT A., «Entry and Exit of Firms under Uncertainty», *Journal of Political Economy*, n. 97, 1989, pp. 620-38.

[16] — —, «Hysteresis, Import Penetration, and Exchange-Rate Pass Through», *Quarterly Journal of Economics*, n. 104, 1989, pp. 205-28.

[17] EDISON H.J. - MELVIN M., «The Determinants and Implications of the Choice of an Exchange Rate System» in HARAF W.S. - WILLET T.D. (eds.), *Monetary Policy for a Volatile Global Economy*, American Enterprise Institute, 1990.

[18] EICHENGREEN B., «Should the Maastricht Treaty Be Saved?», *Princeton Studies in International Finance*, n. 74, 1992.

[19] FRANKEL J.A., «The Dazzling Dollar», *Brookings Paper on Economic Activity*, n. 1, 1985.

[20] FRANKEL J.A. - MACARTHUR A., «Political vs Currency Premia in International Real Interest Differentials», *European Economic Review*, 1988.

[21] GAGNON J., «Exchange Rate Variability and the Level of International Trade», *Journal of International Economics*, n. 34, 1993, pp. 269-87.

[22] GIOVANNINI A., «Currency Substitution and Monetary Policy», in WIHLBORG C. - FRATIANNI M. - WILLET T.D. (eds.), *Financial Regulation and Monetary Arrangements After 1992*, Amsterdam (The Netherlands), North Holland, 1991.

[23] GLICK R. - KRETZMER P. - WIHLBORG C., «Real Exchange Rate Effects of Monetary Disturbances under Different Degrees of Exchange Rate Flexibility», *Journal of International Economics*, forthcoming, 1995.

[24] GLICK R. - WIHLBORG C., «Exchange Rate Regimes and International Trade», in COHEN B. (ed.) *International Trade and Finance: New Frontiers for Research, Essays in Honor of Peter B. Kenen*, Cambridge, Cambridge University Press, 1997.

[25] GOLDBERG L - KOLSTAD C., «Foreign Direct Investment, Exchange Rate Variability and Demand Uncertainty», *International Economic Review*, n. 36, 1995, pp. 855-73.

[26] GOTUR P., «Effects of Exchange Rate Volatility on Trade: Some Further Results», IMF, *Staff Papers*, n. 32, 1985, pp. 475-512.

[27] DE GRAUWE P., *The Economics of Monetary Integration*, Cambridge, Cambridge University Press, 1992.

[28] GROS A. - THYGESEN N., «The Institutional Approach to Monetary Union in Europe», *Economic Journal*, September 1990.

[29] HOOPER P. - KOHLHAGEN S., «The Effect of Exchange Rate Uncertainty on the Prices and Volume of International Trade», *Journal of International Economics*, n. 8, 1978, pp. 483-511.

[30] HÖRNGREN L. - VREDIN A., *The Foreign Exchange Risk Premium - A Review of Evidence*, Stockholm, FIEF, 1986.

[31] IBRAHIMI F. - OXELHEIM L. - WIHLBORG C., «International Stock Markets and Fluctuations in Exchange Rates and Other Macroeconomic Variables», in AGGARWAL (ed.) *Global Portfolio Diversification*, New York, Academic Press, 1994.

[32] KENEN P. - RODRIK D., «Measuring and Analyzing the Effects of Short-Term Volatility in Real Exchange Rates», *Review of Economics and Statistics*, n. 68, May 1986, pp. 311-5.

[33] KLEIN M., «Sectoral Effects of Exchange Rate Volatility on United States Exports», *Journal of International Money and Finance*, n. 9, 1990, pp. 299-308.

[34] KOGUT B. - KULATILAKA N., «Operating Flexibility, Global Manufacturing, and the Option Value of A Multinational Network», *Management Science*, forthcoming, 1993.

[35] KORAY F. - LASTRAPES W., «Real Exchange Rate Volatility and US Bilateral Trade: A VAR Approach», *Review of Economics and Statistics*, n. 71, November 1993, pp. 708-12.

[36] KOTILAINEN M., «Is the EU an Optimal Currency Area?», Helsinki, ETLA, *Working Papers*, 1995.

[37] KRUGMAN P., *Exchange-Rate Instability*, Cambridge (MA), MIT Press, 1989.

[38] LASTRAPES W. - KORAY F., «Exchange Rate Volatility and U.S. Multilateral Trade Flows», *Journal of Macroeconomics*, n. 12, 1990, pp. 341-62.

[39] LOUREIRO J., *Foreign Exchange Intervention, Sterilization and Credibility in the EMS - An Empirical Study*, Göteborg University, Department of Economics, Dissertation, 1992.

[40] MACDONALD R., *Flexible Exchange Rates, Theory and Application*, 1989.

[41] MASKUS K., «Exchange Rate Risk and US Trade: A Sectoral Analysis», Federal Reserve Bank of Kansas City, *Economic Review*, n. 71, March 1986, pp. 16-28.

[42] OXELHEIM L., *International Financial Market Fluctuations*, Chichester, John Wiley and Sons., 1985.

[43] PERL T. - WIHLBORG C., «Sources of Exchange Rate Variability and US Sectoral Trade», *Gothenburg Studies in Financial Economics*, Göteborg University, 1991.

[44] ROGOFF K., «On the Effects of Sterilized Interventions: An Analysis of Weekly Data», *Journal of Monetary Economics*, 1984.

[45] THURSBY M. - THURSBY J., «Bilateral Trade Flows, the Linder Hypothesis, and Exchange Risk», *Review of Economics and Statistics*, n. 69, August 1987, pp. 488-95.

[46] VAUBEL R., «Currency Competition and European Monetary Integration», *Economic Journal*, September 1990.

[47] WIHLBORG C., «Interest Rates, Exchange Rate Adjustment and Currency Risks», *Journal of Money, Credit, and Banking*, February 1982.

[48] — —, «Mikroekonomiska Aspekter pa en Monetar Union», Bilaga 4 i EG konsekvensutredningen (Finansdepartmentet), 1993.

[49] — —, «EMU - Economic Substances or Political Symbolism?», *The World Economy*, September 1994.

[50] WIHLBORG C. - WILLETT T.D., «Optimum Currency Areas Revisited on the Transition Path to a Currency Union» WIHLBORG C. - FRATIANNI M. - WILLET T.D. (eds.), *Financial Regulation and Monetary Arrangements after 1992*, Amsterdam (The Netherlands) North Holland, 1991.

III - MONEY, FINANCE AND MACROECONOMICS

Economic Growth and Evolution of Credit Market's Structure

Luca G. Deidda*

School of Oriental and African Studies,
London University

1. - Introduction

There is a large literature documenting the existence of a relationship between the evolution of the financial intermediation system and the process of economic growth[1]. These studies suggest that the two dynamic processes are linked in two ways with economic development inducing the evolution of financial systems which, in turn, has a positive impact on the subsequent rate of growth of the economy. The presence of this two-way link results in two pieces of empirical evidence: *a*) periods of high economic growth seem to occur in countries with well-developed financial systems; *b*) the main indicators of the degree of evolution of financial systems are strongly correlated with the level of development.

* The author, PhD student (Department of Economics) is grateful to Laurence Harris, Ben Fine and Pasquale Scaramozzino for close supervision at all stages of this work and also wishes to thank Carlo Casarosa, Claudio Michelacci and Pier Mario Pacini for helpful discussions, and all the participants at the seminars held at the School of Oriental and African Studies, the University of Pisa, and at the XI Annual Conference of the European Economic Association held in Istanbul this summer. Financial support by Istituto S. Paolo di Torino, Fondazione «Luciano Jona» is gratefully acknowledged.

N.B. the numbers in square brackets refer to the Bibliography at the end of the paper.

[1] Traditional studies include GOLDSMITH R.W. [5]. Examples of more recent works are KING R.G. - LEVINE R. [8], [9], [10].

Traditional works on economic growth and development of financial intermediation lacked theoretical foundations. This is because within the traditional neoclassical growth theory, which has been the dominant analytical framework for long-run studies, financial intermediation could only be related to the level of capital per head and/or to the level of productivity, but not to their respective long run growth rates which depend on exogenous technical progress. During the 1980s, the development of endogenous growth theory has offered the theoretical underpinnings for the analysis of the relationship between economic growth and financial development. Endogenous growth models have shown that growth rates of per capita capital and productivity could be related to preferences, technology, and, more generally, to institutional settings.

These new theoretical insights stimulated a focus on the theoretical explanation of the regularities which characterize the relationship between financial and economic development. The resulting models produced so far are based on two general considerations[2]: 1) Economies are characterized by informational asymmetries between potential borrowers and lenders, indivisibilities, risky investment projects, and agents' risk aversion. Given these features financial intermediaries which economize on screening/monitoring costs and pool savings diversifying against idiosyncratic risks are able to improve the allocation of savings toward the most productive, and growth inducing investments, which are generally the most risky and illiquid; 2) Set up costs are associated with financial intermediaries. The resulting opportunity cost associated with the creation of such institutions decline as per-capita income grows, therefore financial institutions endogenously arise at a certain level of development. An implication of this argument is that if set up costs vary across types of financial institutions, each particular kind of financial institution develops at a particular stage of development.

---

[2] Among others, here we refer to BLACKBURN O. - HUNG Y.T. [3], BENCIVENGA V.R. - SMITH B.D. [2], GREENWOOD J. - JOVANOVIC B. [7], SAINT-PAUL G. [12]; LEVINE R. [11] and KING R.G. - LEVINE R. [10].

The existing models, while embedding these elements into various endogenous growth frameworks, have been able to offer appealing interpretations of the two-way link between financial intermediation and economic development.

However all these models are not completely satisfactory with respect to some relevant aspects. With respect to empirical evidence, they all end up with a unambiguously positive link between financial and economic development which is fixed over time. Looking at the empirical evidence suggests that the growth impact of financial intermediation tends, instead, to be not always significantly positive and quite variable in magnitude over time anyway. Moreover the link stressed by these models is discontinous. By this we mean that in these models, once financial intermediation is introduced the economy jumps to another long run equilibrium characterizated by an higher growth rate constant over time. Again, looking at cross sectional empirical evidence[3], the relationship between growth rates and development of financial intermediation seems to be pretty much a continous one. This suggests the impact of financial intermediation on growth (measured as the hypothetical difference between the growth rate under financial intermediation and that under financial autarky) changes as the process of financial deepening proceeds. From a theoretical point of view, in these models, the impact of the real costs, in terms of consumption of resources and capital requirements, associated with financial intermediation, is neglected when discussing the effects of financial intermediation on growth rates. Moreover, even if the evolution of the financial system is, in some sense, endogenized, there is no attempt to consider the relation between the evolution of the structure of each particular market for financial services and the process of economic development.

In this paper the relationship between development of financial intermediaries and economic growth is reconsidered, while accounting for both the consumption of resources for which financial institutions are responsible and the endogeneity of the structure of the credit market. The resulting model links the

---

[3] See for example KING R.G. - LEVINE R. [8], [9], [10].

growth impact of financial intermediation with the level of economic development achieved by the economy. The endogenous growth framework we use is a simple one based on the existence of learning by doing externalities which allow for aggregate constant returns to scale in accumulable inputs. Given this hypothesis physical capital accumulation becomes the source of sustainable positive long-run growth. Investment in physical capital accumulation is risky and agents are risk averse by assumption. Moreover, there is *ex ante* asymmetric information between borrowers and lenders. This raises the need for lenders to monitor borrowers. The monitoring cost structure implies the existence of economies to scale. Given these assumptions the standard argument put forward by modern theory of financial intermediation applies[4]. According to this, large scale financial intermediaries which avoid the duplication of monitoring costs constitute the Pareto-dominant solution to the problem of a missing market for risk rather than the implementation of a security market. Large scale intermediaries which pool savings from a large number of individuals and lend to a large number of firms are able to exploit the large numbers law so that they can commit themselves to deterministic repayment on their liabilities. When, given the monitoring costs faced by financial intermediaries, the safe return on these liabilities is high enough compared to the uncertain return on physical capital accumulation, agents will decide to save through deposits instead of through self-financing of investment projects. Therefore financial intermediaries will endogenously emerge in the economy. On the other hand, if the return on deposits financial intermediaries might offer is too low agents will save through self-financing. This means they will select a financial autarky equilibrium[5]. Whenever the economy is characterized by the existence of financial intermediaries which offer safe financial assets, the amount of savings channelled to investment will

---

[4] We refer here to the theory of delegated monitoring described by DIAMOND D.W. [4] for the case of state-independent monitoring, and by WILLIAMSON S.D. [14] for the case of state-dependent monitoring.

[5] Where according to the relevant literature, we call financial autarky a situation in which each agent funds his investments projects only through his own savings.

be greater with respect to the case of a financial autarky economy. This has, *ceteris paribus*, a positive effect on capital accumulation. On the other hand, financial intermediaries consume part of the pooled savings to perform the monitoring task and also employ a portion of the pooled savings to finance their capital requirements. This has, *ceteris paribus*, a negative effect on capital accumulation. The trade-off between these two partial effects working in opposite directions with respect to the process of capital accumulation is shown to be ambiguous. This means that, once the impact of the real costs associated with financial intermediation is considered, the overall impact of financial intermediation on growth becomes ambiguous as well. More precisely, inefficient financial intermediatiaries could arise spontaneously, such that their impact on the growth rate of the economy could be small or even negative. This first conclusion is somewhat new to the existing literature on financial intermediation and endogenous growth to the extent that the existing models usually only stress the beneficial consequences, for growth, which should arise, naturally and inevitably, from the emergence of a financial sector. The standard unambiguously positive link between financial intermediation and growth is recovered here, only in the limiting case where monitoring costs faced by the intermediary are zero.

When modelling the structure of the credit market we assume a spatial model of monopolistic competition[6]. So, what we do here is to use a spatial competition framework to model explicitly the non-perfectly competitive nature of the credit market. We assume that a certain amount of physical capital is necessary for financial intermediaries to operate. Moreover we assume the monitoring technology shows constant returns to scale combined with increasing returns to specialization. Notice that the presence of capital requirements means there are some fixed costs associated with

---

[6] Notice that this assumption regarding the non-perfectly competitive structure of the credit market is perfectly consistent with the essential assumption underlying Diamond's argument in favour of delegated monitoring. If monitoring delegation results in cost savings then, it must be the case that there are economies to scale in monitoring costs. In other words the cost function exhibits non-convexity. If so, the structure of the credit market cannot be perfectly competitive in a pure sense, because perfectly competitive equilibrium may not exist.

financial transactions. Economizing on these costs financial intermediaries constitute the pareto-dominant solution to the problem
of a missing market for risk. Given the assumptions about financial intermediaries' technology, we show that the structure of the
credit market, which is measured by the number of banks operating in the sector, depends on the level of economic development,
as measured by the stock of accumulated capital per head. As the
stock of accumulated capital increases, per capita income and savings rise, so that the market for deposits enlarges. This, given the
externality associated with physical investment, ensures that profitability of the banking sector increases, so that, given the absence
of barriers to entry, new banks enter into the market. As banks
enter the market, the monopolistic power of each intermediary is
reduced and so is the average consumption of resources made by
the financial system. As a consequence, the impact of financial
intermediation on the long run equilibrium growth rate of the
economy is a positive function of the level of development. The
financial system might have the power to magnify growth for the
real side of the economy but this power is conditional on the stage
of development achieved by the economy. This power is high if
the economy is fully developed and low if the economy is under-
developed. This means financial intermediation *per se* cannot be
considered an engine of growth. These results offer a theoretical
justification for both for the continuous dynamic link between financial and economic development, and the dynamic evolution of
the growth impact of financial intermediation along the process
of financial deepening, which is consistent with the two stylized
facts we mentioned and, as we show in the final part of the paper,
is also consistent with the empirical evidence produced by King-
Levine [8], [9], [10].

The paper is organized as follows. Section 2 describes the
structure of the model. In Section 3 we describe the economy
under financial autarky. Section 4 describes the economy under
financial intermediation. In Section 5 we compare the economy
with financial intermediation with the economy under financial
autarky. Section 6 deals with the link between economic development and evolution of credit market's structure. Section 7 de-

scribes the dynamic relationship between financial deepening and economic growth which emerges from the model. Section 8 deals with empirical evidence. The last section is left for final remarks.

2. - Structure of the Model

1) The economy has an overlapping generation structure with agents living for two periods. Each generation consists of a continuum of size $H > 0$ of identical agents. Each young agent is endowed with a quantity of labour $l_t = 1$ in his first period of life. Consequently the aggregate amount of labour available in the economy at each time t, is equal to H[7]. This amount of labour is inelastically supplied to firms. Firms operate under perfect competition.

They produce an homogeneous good which can be either consumed or converted into capital through the saving-investment process. Labour supplied to firms is paid a perfectly competitive salary w_t. This salary is either consumed or saved by young agents. Savings take the following possible forms: *a)* direct-funding of physical capital accumulation; *b)* indirect-funding of physical capital accumulation through financial intermediaries (if any exist). Physical capital accumulation is carried out by young agents and lasts one period. In their second period of life agents will eventually become entrepreneurs: in this case they run a firm: they hire labour and produce.

2) In each period t production takes place according to the following production function which is the same across agents[8]:

(1) $$Y_t = \psi \ \pi A_t K_t^\alpha l_t^{1-\alpha}$$

where: Y_t is the output produced by the single agent, K_t is the quantity of physical capital, and l_t is the quantity of labour, which are used in the production process. $\psi > 0$ is an exogenous produc-

---

[7] At each time t, the total supply of labour is given by following integral: $\int_0^H L_t dz = \int_0^H 1 dz = H$.
[8] Consistent with the assumption that agents are identical.

tivity parameter, A_t is an externality effect associated with the process of capital accumulation, and π is a time-invariant stochastic productivity shock with this probability distribution:

$$\pi = 1 \text{ with prob. } p$$
$$\pi = 0 \text{ with prob. } 1 - p$$

Resolution of uncertainty about the productivity of investments in physical capital accumulation takes place at the beginning of the second period of agents' life. Therefore, in period 1, investment is a risky activity. Young investitors do not know if their investments will be successful or not.

The externality A_t associated with the production function has the following expression:

$$A_t = k_t^{1-\alpha} \quad \text{where} \quad k_t = \frac{K_t}{l_t}$$

3) Agents make their consumption-saving and investment decisions when they are young, in order to maximize the expected value of their life time utility. For each member of generation t in the economy the utility function has the following form:

$$U_t = u\left(c_t^1\right) + v\left(c_{t,i}^2\right) \text{ with } i = G, B$$

where: U_t is the total life-time utility for the single agent, $u(.)$ is the utility associated with period 1 consumption, c_t^1, and $v^i(.)$ is the utility associated with period 2 consumption in good states of the world ($i = G$), and in bad states of the world ($i = B$), respectively. Period 2 consumption is equal to $c_{t,G}^2$ in the good states of the world (when investment made by the young agent is successful) and to $c_{t,B}^2$ in the bad states of the world (when the investment made by the young agent is unsuccessful). $u(.)$ and $v^i(.)$ are assumed to be strictly concave according to the assumption regarding agents' risk aversion and satisfy the following conditions:

$$u'(.),v'(.) \ > \ 0 \, \forall c_t^1, c_{t,i}^2 > 0$$

$$\lim_{c_t^1 \to 0} u'(.) = \lim_{c_{t,i}^2 \to 0} v^{i,'}(.) = \infty, \quad \lim_{c_t^1 \to \infty} u'(.) = \lim_{c_{t,i}^2 \to \infty} u'(.) = 0$$

$$v'^{,B}(c) \ > \ v'^{,G}(c) \, \forall c \ > \ 0$$

$$u''(.),v''(.) \ < \ 0 \, \forall c_t^1, c_{t,i}^2 > 0$$

The condition $v'^{,B}(c) > v'^{,G}(c)$, is meant to strengthen the assumption about agents' risk aversion. Agents care more about consumption in the bad states of the world than they do in the good states of the world[9]. Finally, u_t, is assumed to be homothetic.

In general for each agent, period 1 consumption, c_t^1, will be given by labour income, w_t, minus savings, S_t. Savings could be either in form of self-financing of investment projects, e_t, and/or in form of financial assets issued by a financial intermediary (deposits), b_t. Therefore $S_t = b_t + e_t$, holds. Period $t + 1$ accumulated capital, K_{t+1}, will be equal to self-financing, e_t, plus loans, f_t. If there are not financial intermediaries issuing deposits and financing firms through loans, as is the case under financial autarky, both b_t and f_t will equal zero.

For each single agent in the economy, period 2 consumption, will be given by the following expressions:

$$(2) \qquad c_{t,G}^2 = A_t \psi K_{t+1}^\alpha l_{t+1}^{1-\alpha} - w_{t+1} l_{t+1} - f_t r_t + r_t^d b_t \text{ with prob. } p$$
$$c_{t,B}^2 = r_t^d b_t \text{ with prob. } 1 - p$$

---

[9] Several justfications might be given for this assumption. One could be that the failure of the investment project associated with the bad states of the world is source of non-pecuniary losses which have a negative impact on the utility of the agent. In any case it should be stressed here that the assumption is not crucial for the results of the paper and it is made only to simplify matters. In fact it allows for the economy to reach a stage at which all savings are pooled by financial intermediaries. All the conclusions achieved in the paper will remain the same if we drop this assumption. The only difference being that we would then compare financial autarky equilibria with equilibria in which savings are part in form of deposits and part in form of self-financing. This involves more calculation but does not lead to different results from the case we discuss in the paper.

This means each agent's consumption in the second period will be given, with probability p, by the outcome of the production process, $A_t \psi K_{t+1}^\alpha l_{t+1}^{1-\alpha}$, minus the cost of labour, $w_{t+1} l_{t+1}$, minus the cost of loans, (if any), which is $f_t r_t^l$, plus the return on deposits, $r_t^d b_t$. Instead with probability $1 - p$ it will be equal to the return on deposits (if any), $r_t^d b_t$. Therefore in the bad states of the world, whenever deposits are equal to zero, agents are not able to consume in their second period of life. To mitigate this outcome we can assume that in this case agents are still able to get (somehow) a minimum (or subsistence) level of income $\bar{y}$ which they can, then, consume[10].

4) We assume there is asymmetric information between borrowers and lenders. Only the borrower knows the return on investment projects he operates without incurring some cost. This implies the existence of an *ex post verification* problem because the borrower funded at time t, will select this utility maximizing strategy: report at time $t + 1$ that the project was unsuccessful and consume the entire return eventually produced. This raises the need for lenders to monitor the borrowers. Monitoring is costly. Therefore the standard argument produced by Diamond [4] and Williamson [14] to justify the existence of financial intermediaries applies. By delegating the monitoring task to large size institutions, agents are able to economize on monitoring costs. The rate of return on lending is consequently higher than it would be under an arrangement characterized by direct debt contracts with many lenders financing and monitoring each borrower. Agents are consequently better off under financial intermediation with delegated monitoring than under indirect external finance.

However, as stressed by Diamond [4], delegated monitoring, in principle, does not work because the delegated agents need to be monitored as well. However if we assume rates of return on investment projects to be independent, large size institutions, which lend to many entrepreneurs and borrow from many savers,

---

[10] In other words we are assuming agents have access to an extra-amount of labour capacity which they find convenient to use only if they are starving. Using this extra-amount of labour capacity yelds a return $\bar{y}$.

are able to exploit the *Law of Large Numbers*. Such intermediaries can perfectly predict the fraction of entrepreneurs with good and bad outcomes. Consequently, they can commit themselves to make fixed payments to their depositors, without making such payments hinge on the outcomes of entrepreneurs' projects. Therefore, such a diversification process completely eliminates the problem of *ex post* verification between financial intermediaries and depositors so that financial intermediaries need not be monitored.

Notice that in our model we assume that more than one large size intermediary operates in the deposit-credit market. It is possible for more than a single large size intermediary to operate if each serves a different share of the credit market so that duplication of monitoring costs is, again, avoided. In order for that to be possible the density of the population has to be such that each portion of the entire population has the same potential for diversification as the total population itself. Since we assume a continuum of agents normalized to one, this property is satisfied.

Summing up, we assume large size financial intermediaries which, given our assumptions, constitute the Pareto-dominant solution to the problem of a missing market for risk, could be implemented to provide insurance against risks associated with funding investment projects.

As a final remark notice that we assume that if, for any reason, financial intermediaries are not present, agents will find it convenient to operate under financial autarky rather than under direct external financing. This means diversification through a system of direct debt contracts exchanged in a security market is always too costly to be implemented[11].

---

[11] This assumption is meant to simplify the analysis. Of course the existence of direct financial relationships could be an important phenomenon especially in small comunities in which the asymmetry of information between borrowers and lenders is not so relevant. Including this possibility would probably give a more realistic picture of the transition from financial autarky to equilibria characterized by the existence of a formal financial sector. However we think that within this more realistic picture the results we get in the paper will still hold and, even more, would be probably strengthened.

3. - The Economy Under Financial Autarky

Here we deal with the case in which there are no financial intermediaries providing external-funding for investment projects. Therefore, as discussed in the previous section, each young agent self-funds its own risky investment project.

3.1 *Agents' Behaviour*

By assumption, agents are identical. Therefore, here and in the following discussion, in order to derive the macroeconomic equilibrium, we refer to the maximization problem faced by the representative agent. Each young agent chooses the amount of savings, which is equal to the amount of self-financing of investment projects, e_t, and the quantity of labour to employ, l_{t+1}^d, in order to maximize the expected value of his life-time utility function. Considering the definition for period 1 and 2 consumption provided in the previous section this maximization problem can be written as follows:

$$(3) \quad \max_{\{e_t, l_{t+1}^d\}} E(U_t) = u(w_t - e_t) + pv^G (\psi A_{t+1} K_{t+1}^\alpha l_{t+1}^{d(1-\alpha)} - w_{t+1} l_{t+1}^d)$$

Where $K_{i+1} = e_t$. Notice that the utility term relative to the bad states of the world, $(1 - p) v^B (\bar{y})$, where $\bar{y}$ is the subsistence level of income, does not enter the maximization problem. This is because this term is completely exogenous and therefore completely irrelevant to the choice of the optimal values for e_t, and l_{t+1}^d. The first order condition associated with this maximization problem (in case of internal solutions[12]. $e_t^* > 0$, $l_{t+1}^{d*} > 0$) is the following:

$$(4) \qquad (e_t^* > 0): u'(c_t^{1*}) = v'^{,G} (c_{t,G}^{2*}) p\alpha A_{t+1} \psi K_{t+1}^{\alpha-1} l_{t+1}^{d(-\alpha)}$$

---

[12] The assumptions relative both to the utility function and the production function guarantee the existence of internal solutions with $e_t^* > 0$, $L_t^{d*} > 0$.

(5) $(l_{t+1}^{d*} > 0)$: $pv',^G (c^{2*}_{t,G}) [(1 - \alpha) \psi A_{t+1} K_{t+1}^{\alpha} l_{t+1}^{d1-\alpha} - w_{t+1}] = 0$

The condition determining the demand for labour by the single firm can be written as:

(6) $(1 - \alpha) \psi A_{t+1} k_{t+1}^{\alpha} = w_{t+1}$

Where $k_{t+1} = K_{t+1}/l^d_{t+1}$. It should be noticed that, as usual, the condition (6) could be rewritten as follows:

(7) $w_{t+1} = \psi A_{t+1} k_{t+1}^{\alpha} - \alpha \psi A_{t+1} k_{t+1}^{\alpha}$

Wages are equal to output per unit of labour, minus the payment to capital per unit of labour. Notice that both labour and capital are paid their marginal return consistently with the hypothesis of perfectly competitive behaviour of the agents. Rewriting the first order condition relative to the choice of e_t^*, we obtain the following saving function:

(8) $e_t^* = S_t = S_t (p\psi A_{t+1} k_{t+1}^{\alpha-1}, w_t)$

Where $\alpha p \psi A_{t+1} k_{t+1}^{\alpha-1}$, is the expected marginal rate of return on savings as perceived by the single agent. We assume preferences to be homothetic (see Section 2.3). Therefore the saving function is homogenous of degree 1 in labour income, w_t, so that we can write:

(9) $S_t = S_{FA} (p\alpha\psi A_{t+1} k_{t+1}^{\alpha}, 1) w_t$

where s_{FA} is the saving rate for the economy under financial autarky (*FA*). We assume gross substitutability. Therefore the saving rate will be an increasing function of the expected marginal rate of return on savings, $p\alpha\psi A K_{t+1}^{\alpha-1} l_{t+1}^{d(-\alpha)}$.

3.2 *Macroeconomic Equilibrium: Long-Run Growth*

At each time t the equilibrium of the economy is given by this system:

(10)
$$A_t = k_t^{1-\alpha}$$

$$w_t = \psi A_t k_t^\alpha - \alpha\psi A_t k_t^\alpha$$

$$S_t = w_t s_{FA} \left(p\alpha\psi A_{t+1} k_{t+1}^{\alpha-1}, 1 \right)$$

$$\frac{k_{t+1}}{p} = S_t$$

The first equation refers to the externality associated with capital accumulation described in the previous section (Section 2). The second one refers to the equilibrium price of labour which, according to equation *(6)*, is given by the total product per head y_t minus the remuneration of capital, which is k_t times its marginal product $\alpha\psi A k_t^{\alpha-1}$. The third is the saving function and, finally, the latter describes the equilibrium in the market for capital: period $t + 1$ capital per agent, K_t equals period t savings. As we know, at each time t, the population of young agents is endowed with a continuum of independent risky investment projects. Given the binomial probability distribution of each of these projects, the law of large numbers implies that, in each period t, exactly a fraction p of investment projects is successful. This means that the fraction p of the total population becomes final good producer. The total supply of labour is equal to the mass of the population, H. The population of entrepreneurs is equal to pH. Therefore, in equilibrium, each entrepreneur hires $1/p$ units of labour. But then $k_t = pK_t$ holds.

This system generates the equilibrium value of k_{t+1}, as function of k_t Precisely, the equilibrium level of k_{t+1} will be a function of k_t according to the following accumulation equation:

$$k_{t+1} = k_t \left[p\psi (1 - \alpha) \right] s_{FA} (p\alpha\psi)$$

Where: $k_t p\psi (1 - \alpha) s_{FA} (p\alpha\psi, 1, p)$, is the equilibrium level of savings for the economy. Notice that the equilibrium saving rate, $s_{FA} (p\alpha\psi)$, would have been higher if agents were remunerated for the positive externality generated in the process of capital accumulation[13].

Given this expression the growth rate of capital per head will be given by the following ewpression:

$$g^k_{FA} = \frac{k_{t+1} - k_t}{k_t} = s_{FA}\,\psi(1-\alpha)p - 1$$

Given the production function discussed in the previous section, the equilibrium level of output per unit of labour produced by the single agent is given by $y_t = \psi k_t$. Given the law of large numbers the aggregate amount of output per unit of labour will be equal to $pH\psi k_t$. Consequently, it follows that the growth rate of the economy, g_{FA} equals the growth rate of accumulated capital, g^k_{FA}[14].

Three qualitatively different dynamic patterns are possible depending on the saving rate of the economy: *a)* $s_{FA} < 1/\psi\,(1-\alpha)\,p = \overline{s}_{FA}$: the economy shrinks over time ($g_{FA} < 0$); *b)* $s_{FA} = 1/\psi\,(1-\alpha)\,p = \overline{s}_{FA}$: the economy is stuck in a no-growth trap; *c)* $s_{FA} > 1/\psi\,(1-\alpha)\,p = \overline{s}_{FA}$: the economy will grow indefinitely at the rate $g_{FA} > 0$.

$1/\psi\,(1-\alpha)\,p = \overline{s}_{FA}$, represents a critical level for the saving rate.

The cases of no growth traps and, even worse, of shrinking economies correspond to situations in which the propensity toward savings and/or the marginal return on investments are too low. Both the elements tend to lower the amount of resources saved and channelled to investment. In the no-growth trap, savings are constant over time. In the shrinking economy case, a vi-

---

[13] In that case the expected private marginal product of capital would coincide with the expected social marginal product of capital which is given by $p\psi$. Obviously $p\psi > \alpha p\psi$, since $\alpha < 1$. This means the return on savings would be higher once agents were remunerated for the externality they generate when accumulating physical capital. Since we assume savings to be a positive function of the rate of return on savings this would mean higher savings.

[14] In fact the growth rate of the economy is given by this expression:

$$\frac{y_{t+1} - y_t}{y_t} = \frac{p\psi H(k_{t+1} - k_t)}{p\psi k_t} = \frac{k_{t+1} - k_t}{k_t}$$

cious circle operates so that the level of investments decreases over time until the economy per capita income collapses toward a subsistence level. In the following discussion we assume the economy experiences positive growth. Notice that the growth rate of the economy will also depend on the probability p which affects the expected return on savings. As p grows the growth rate increases.

4. - The Economy Under Financial Intermediation

We now turn to the case in which large size financial intermediaries operate in the economy, pooling savings and funding investment projects. We allow for the possibility of financial intermediaries having some market power. In order to do so, we consider a standard model of spatial monopolistic competition for the financial sector. Regarding the terminology used in the following discussion notice that, as a matter of simplicity, we talk about banks referring to the financial intermediaries and therefore we use the term banking sector referring to the financial intermediation sector.

4.1 *Banks' Behaviour*

We assume the continuum of firms is uniformly distributed on the circumference of a circle with length H. The spatial model could be interpreted literally. If so a point in the circle could be either interpreted as a physical location or as one of the economy's sectors. However the characteristics space could be also given a location-free interpretation in terms of differentiation of other product attributes. Firms cannot change their location. Each bank chooses where to locate itself on the circle. Whatever the number of the banks operating in the market they locate at equal distances one from the others. There are positive monitoring costs associated with the supply of loans. We assume constant returns to scale in the monitoring technology. That is monitoring cost are a fraction c of the quantity of loans allocated by the bank. We assume monitoring costs are increasing but concave in the distance, z, between the financial intermediary and the firm, formally:

$$c'(z) > 0 \quad \text{and} \quad c''(z) > 0$$

The assumption about the first derivative, $c'(z)$, is meant to capture a sort of specialization effect: the closer is a firm to a particular bank the higher is the cost advantage of this particular bank with respect to the other banks. An implication of this assumption is that, as we will show later, as the number of banks increase, each bank specializes its behaviour and becomes (on average) more cost-efficent. The assumption about the second derivative, $c''(z)$, aims to mitigate the extent of returns to specialization in this way: the more a bank gets specialized the less it gains from further specialization. Moreover we assume each bank needs an amount E_t of capital to operate. We assume this amount of capital to be a function of the stock of accumulated capital in the economy according to the following expression:

(11)
$$E_t = h\frac{k_t}{n_t} + \frac{B}{n_t}$$

where: h, and B, are given parameters, and n_t, is the number of banks operating in the market. According to this expression capital requirements for the single bank are positively related to accumulated capital and negatively related to the number of banks. This assumption is meant to capture the idea that capital requirements are a positive function of per bank volume of deposits. Per bank volume of deposits is given by the total flow of deposits divided by the number of banks. The total flow of deposits in equilibrium is a positive function of the stock of accumulated capital. This legitimates our simplifying assumption about E_t depending on $h\frac{k_t}{n_t}$. Furthermore, according to *(11)*, the number of banks positively influences the capital requirements of the single bank, through the term B/nt. Here we intend to capture a positive externality associated with financial deepening of the economy. As the number of banks increase there could be technological progress in the banking sector, which, *ceteris paribus*, reduces the amount of capital requirements[15].

4.1.1 Banks' Pricing Rule

Banks act as price takers in the market for deposits. Therefore each bank takes the interest rate on deposits, r_t^d, as given. In the market for loans, banks play a Bertrand-competition game when setting the interest rate on loans which we now turn to describe. Each bank has some market power in the loans market, which comes from the cost advantage over nearby competitors. Given the number of banks, n_t, the distance between, say bank A, and bank B, will be H/n_t. All the banks being identical, bank A will have a cost advantage over bank B, with respect to all firms located to the left of $H/2n_t$ (see also Graph 1).

Banks seek an optimal pricing rule. They cannot implement perfect price discrimination because, *ex ante*, they do not know the location of each single firm. In principle each bank would set the interest rate on loans at the level which maximizes monopolistic rents. Call it r^m. However this pricing rule can be supported as an equilibrium pricing rule if and only if it coincides with the maximum interest rate chargeable by the single bank given its cost advantage over its competitors.

Consider again the case of banks A, and B. The monitoring cost faced by B when serving the marginal firm relative to the market share of A is $c\,(H/2n_t)$. The total faced by B, per unit of loan, would then be $[1 + c\,(H/2n_t)\,r_t^d$. The expected return per unit of loans is r^m times the probability that the project is successful, p

---

[15] We choose this specification for the capital requirements of banks because it seems to be realistic. However it should be noted that the results we achieve in this paper are consistent also with other specifications as well. For example the same analysis goes through if we assume capital requirements to be simply a constant K.

BANKS' BEHAVIOUR*

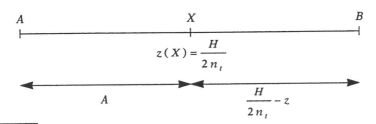

* Bank A and bank B are located at the same distance from x. Bank A has a cost advance over B over firms located to the left of x, because it is nearer to these firms than bank B is. The symmetric argument applies to bank B with respect to firms located to the right of x. x is the location of the marginal firms, the firm at the margin of the market share of both the banks.

(notice that, since a continuum of independent risky projects are funded by each bank, the law of large numers, operates so that the *ex-post* return per unit of loans equals its *ex-ante* value with probability 1). Therefore if A sets an interest rate on loans, r^m, such that: $r^m > [1 + c\,(H/2n_t)]\,r_t^d$, then B would have incentive to undercut its interest rate on loans thereby stealing some market share from A. The same argument then, applies to firm A and so on.

This Bertrand's price competition game played by banks leads to the conclusion that the maximum interest rate on loans chargeable by the single bank will be:

(12)
$$r_t^* = \frac{1}{p}\left[1 + c\left(\frac{H}{2n_t}\right)\right] r_t^d$$

It can be argued that the monopolistic interest rate, r^m, can be lower than r_t^*. In this case each bank has the incentive not to serve all the firms over which it has a cost advantage with respect to the other banks. However we assume that, independently of the number of banks, $r_t^* \le r^m$ holds. But then, r_t^* (equation *(12)*) which is maximum rate chargeable compatible with the Bertrand's game played by banks, turns out to be the optimal pricing rule to be followed by each bank.

4.1.2 Equilibrium Number of Banks

Even if there is no market left, potential entrants could still have some incentive to enter the market for credit tied to the possibility of stealing some market share from existing banks. Here the existence of capital requirements plays a key role. Banks will have an incentive to enter the market as long as the extra-profit opportunities do compensate for the opportunity cost $r_t^d E_t$ associated with the existence of the capital requirement. Otherwise, in absence of such capital requirements, new entrants will have always an incentive to enter the credit market. For each single bank the extra-profits are given by the following expression:

$$\pi_t^B = 2 \int_0^{\frac{H}{2n_t}} [pr_t - (1 + c(z)) r_t^d] dz] f_t^d$$

Where: f_t^d is the demand for loans by each firm served by the bank (determined as discussed in the following subsection), and r_t is the equilibrium interest rate determined according to equation *(12)* (we drop the star for simplicity).

As new banks enter the credit market the optimal rate of interest on loans set by each bank is, *ceteris paribus*, reduced. The interpretation of this outcome leads in the fact that as the number of banks increases the market power of each bank is reduced. Since $r_t \le r^m$ holds, a reduction in the loan interest rate reduces the extra-profits. Therefore each potential entrant perceives extra-profits opportunities as declining with the number of banks. However, as the expression for capital requirements suggests, also E_t declines as the number of banks increases. In order for the market to achieve an equilibrium number of banks we assume the first effect more than offset the second. This means that, starting from a disequilibrium situation in which $\pi^B > r_t^d E_t$, the entrance of new banks will finally lead to an equilibrium number of banks, n_t, such that:

(13) $r_t^d E_t = \pi_t^B$

At this stage potential entrants would no longer have any incentive to enter the credit market.

4.2 *Agents' Behaviour*

Young agents' choices will now regard the quantity of deposits, b_t, the quantity of self-financing of investment projects, e_t, and the quantity of loans to finance investment projects, f_t, and the demand for labour l^d_{t+1}. As in the previous section agents seek to maximize the expected value of their utility function as follows:

$$(14) \quad \max_{\{b_t, f_t, e_t, l^d_{t+1}\}} E(u_t) = u(w_t - e_t b_t) + pv^G (A_{t+1} \psi K^{\alpha}_{t+1} l^{d(1-\alpha)}_{t+1} -$$

$$- w_{t+1} l^d_{t+1} - r_t f_t + r^d_t b_t) + (1-p)v^B (r^d_t b_t)$$

where: $k_{t+1} = e_t + f_t$. The set of first order conditions associated with the problem will be the following:

$$(15) \quad (b^*_t) : u'(c^{t*}_1) \geq pr^d_t v^{',G} (c^{t*}_{2,G}) + (1-p) r^d_t v^{',B} (c^{t*}_{2,B})$$

$$(f^*_t) : pv^{',G} (c^{t*}_{2,G}) [A_{t+1} \psi \alpha k^{\alpha-1}_{t+1} -] \leq 0$$

$$(e^*_t) : u'(c^{t*}_1) \geq pv^{',G} (c^{t*}_{2,G}) A_{t+1} \psi \alpha k^{\alpha-1}_{t+1}$$

$$(16) \quad (l^{d*}_{t+1}) : v^{',G} (c^{t*}_{2,G}) [- \alpha) \psi A_{t+1} K^{\alpha}_{t+1} l^{d1-\alpha}_{t+1} - w_{t+1}] \leq 0$$

(each of the weak inequalities hold as a strict equality if the corresponding maximizing variable has an optimal level different from zero, and hold as a strict inequality otherwise).

Given the assumptions relative to the utility function, agents will always perform investment activity so that, according to the specification for the production function, the demand for labour will be strictly positive. Therefore, the first order condition relative to the demand for labour will give this expression:

$$w_{t+1} = \psi A_{t+1} k^{\alpha}_{t+1} - \alpha \psi A_{t+1} k^{\alpha}_{t+1}$$

This is exactly the same expression encountered in the previous section (equation *(7)*).

Similarly, from the set of first order conditions, whenever agents finance their investment through debt finance the following relationships hold about r_t (the rate of return on loans), r^e_t (expected rate of return on self-financing), and the rate of return on deposits, r^d_t, respectively[16]:

(17)
$$r_t = A_{t+1} \, \psi\alpha \, k_{t+1}^{\alpha-1}$$

(the rate of return on loans equals marginal product of capital);

(18)
$$r^d_t = \frac{p\psi\alpha A_{t+1} k_{t+1}^{\alpha-1}}{1 + c\left(\dfrac{H}{2n_t}\right)}$$

(This expression for the interest rate on deposits is found combining expression *(17)*, and *(12)*);

(19)
$$r^e_t = \psi\alpha p A_{t+1} \, k_{t+1}^{\alpha-1}$$

---

[16] In case of a financial intermediation equilibrium the first order condition relative to f^*_t, holds as a strict equality, therefore:

$$r_t = A_{t+1} \, \psi\alpha k_{t+1}^{\alpha-1}$$

Then:
$$r^d_t = \frac{p}{1 + c\left(\dfrac{H}{2n_t}\right)} A_{t+1} \, \psi\alpha k_{t+1}^{\alpha-1}$$

follows from the equilibrium relationship between interest rates on deposits and loans (equation *(12)*).

In case of financial autarchy, as explored in the previous section, given the hypothesis of perfect competition, the return on self-financing, r^e_t, is given by the expected marginal return on capital,

$$r^e_t = p A_{t+1} \, \psi k_{t+1}^{\alpha-1}$$

Finally, in case of mixed equilibrium, these equations describing rates of terurns on loans, deposits and self-financing hold simultaneously.

Then, considering that, in equilibrium, $A_{t+1} = k_{t+1}^{\alpha-1}$, we finally have:

(20)
$$r_t^d = \frac{p\psi\alpha}{1 + c\left(\dfrac{H}{2n_t}\right)}$$

$$r_t^e = p\psi\alpha$$

$$r_t = \psi\alpha$$

Given the set of first order conditions relative to the saving-financing decisions, and assuming agents cannot choose negative levels for e_t, and b_t, three possible types of equilibria exist: 1) each agent saves only through self-finance ($e_t > 0$, $f_t = b_t = 0$); 2) each agent saves partly through self-finance and partly through deposits and the also borrows from the financial intermediaries ($e_t > 0$, $f_t > 0$, $b_t > 0$); 3) each agent saves only through deposits and finances investment only through loans ($e_t = 0$, $f_t > 0$, $b_t > 0$).

The first kind of equilibria we mentioned above is that we called financial autarky. The second kind is referred as mixed equilibria. And, finally, the third kind will be called pure financial intermediation equilibria.

All these possible equilibria are compatible with the optimizing behaviour of the agents, given the hypothesis of risk aversion. As it appears from the equations *(18)*, and *(19)*, the return on self-financing is greater than the rate of return on deposits. Therefore, even if agents are risk averse the extra return on self-financing could be sufficiently high that agents either perceive deposits as equivalent to self-finance (in that case $e_t > 0$, $f_t > 0$, $b_t > 0$ will hold in equilibrium) or even, strongly prefer self-finance to deposits (and $e_t > 0$, $f_t = b_t = 0$ will hold in equilibrium). More precisely, given the degree of risk aversion, a critical value for the positive difference between r_t^e, and r_t^d, call it z, exists such that, for values of $r_t^e - r_t^d > z$, the agents will select a pure financial autarky equilibrium. On the other hand, for values of $r_t^e - r_t^d$

lower than a critical value z', agents will prefer an intermedia-
tion equilibrium. Notice that for values of $r_t^e - r_{t}^d$, such that $z' < r_t^e - r_t^d < z$, agents will save partly through deposits and partly
through self-financing. For a formal discussion see proof 1, in
the Appendix [17].

According to *(20)*, the rate of return on deposits depends, *ceteris paribus*, on the monitoring cost per unit of loan, $c\,(H/2n_t)$. As
this cost decreases, deposits will pay a higher rate of return. Therefore, given the degree of risk aversion of the agent two critical values for the monitoring costs, c_m, and c_M, with $c_M > c_m$ exist such
that: *a)* if monitoring costs are higher than c_M, then $r_t^e - r_t^d > z$,
holds, so that agents will prefer self-finance rather than deposits
and the system will end up in a financial autarky equilibrium; *b)*
if monitoring costs are higher than c_m, but lower than c_M, agents
will save partly through deposits and partly through external finance. In this case the lower are monitoring costs the higher will
be the portion of savings expressed in form of deposits; *c)* finally, if monitoring costs are lower than c_m, agents will save only
through deposits.

Here we focus on the case in which $c\,(H/2n_t) < c_m$, so that
deposits strongly dominate self financing and the economy is
in a pure financial intermediation equilibrium ($e_t = 0$, $f_t > 0$, $b_t > 0$).

In a pure financial intermediation equilibrium the optimality
condition relative to the saving behaviour, (system *(16)*), could be
rewritten as:

$$u'(c_1^{t*}) = r_t^d [v'^{,G}(c_{2,G}^{t*}) + v'^{,B}(c_{2,B}^{t*})]$$

---

[17] Notice that, as discussed in proof 1, the assumption according to which
agents care more about consumption in bad states of the world (prg. 2, in the section about the structure of the model) than about consumption in good states of
the world, is crucial to ensure the existence of equilibria where agents save only
through deposits exist. Dropping this assumption leads to an economy in which
the agents save only through self-financing of investment projects or through a
combinantion of self-financing and deposits (mixed equilibrium). As we said before, we use this assumption because the comparison of pure financial autarky situations with pure financial intermediation situation is simpler than a comparison
of a mixed equilibrium with financial autarky, even if this latter comparison does
not yield different conclusions to those we achieve in the paper.

The deposit-saving function associated with this optimality condition will, then, be:

$$D_t = w_t s_{FI}(r_t^d)$$

where $s_{FI}(.)$ is the saving rate under financial intermediation.

4.3 *Macroeconomic Equilibrium: Long Run Growth*

The aggregate demand for loans will be the following:

(21)
$$F_t^d = \int_0^H f_t^d \, di = Hf_t^d$$

The supply of loans by each single bank will be the following:

(22)
$$f_t^s = 2\int_0^{\frac{H}{2nt}} f_t \, dz = f_t \frac{H}{n_t}$$

Where f_t is the equilibrium quantity of loan supplied to the single firm. The agregate supply of loans by the banking sector will be:

(23)
$$F_t^s = \int_o^{n_t} f_t^s \, di = n_t f_t^s$$

Where we have used the fact that the supply of loans of the single bank is the same across banks.

In equilibrium demand for loans of the single firm equals supply for loans by the bank: $f_t = f_t^d = K_{t+1}$. At each time t the general equilibrium for the economy is described by the following system:

$$E_t = h\frac{k_t}{n_t} + \frac{B}{n_t}$$

$$w_t = \psi A_{t+1} k_{t+1}^{\alpha} - \alpha\psi A_{t+1} k_{t+1}^{\alpha}$$

$$A_t = k_t^{1-\alpha}$$

$$r_t^d E_t = 2\int_0^{\frac{H}{2n_t}} [\, pr_t - (1+c(z)) r_t^d \,] f_t^d \, dz$$

$$r_t = \frac{1}{p}\left[1 + c\left(\frac{H}{2n_t}\right)\right] r_t^d$$

$$r_t = A_{t+1} \psi\alpha k_{t+1}^{\alpha-1}$$

$$f_t = f_t^d = K_{t+1}$$

$$F_t^s = f_t^d = HK_{t+1}$$

$$D_t = H w_t s_{FI}(r_t^d)$$

$$pK_{t+1} = k_{t+1}$$

$$D_t = F_t^s\left(1 + 2\int_0^{\frac{H}{2n_t}} c(z)\,dz\right) + n_t hE_t$$

We have already discussed all the equations apart from the equilibrium expression in deposit-credit market. In equilibrium, the aggregate amount of deposits, D_t (which is given by the quantity of deposits relative to the single agent, $w_t s_{FI}(r_t^d)$, integrated over the interval $[0, H]$, equals the total supply of loans (which is equal to next period capital, which equals HK_{t+1}), plus the consumption of resources, $F_t^s\, 2\int_0^{H/2n_t} c(z)\,dz$, plus total capital requirements of the banking sector, $n_t hE_t$. After some substitutions we derive a reduced form of system (25):

$$(24) \qquad \frac{k_t}{n_t}h + \frac{B}{n_t} = 2\int_0^{\frac{H}{2n_t}}\left[c\left(\frac{H}{2n_t}\right) - (z)\right]dz\frac{k_{t+1}}{p}$$

$$k_{t+1} = \frac{k_t\, p\left[(1-\alpha)\psi s_{FI}\left(\dfrac{p\alpha\psi}{1+c\left(\dfrac{H}{2n_t}\right)}\right) - \dfrac{h}{H}\right] - p\dfrac{B}{H}}{[1+2]\int_0^{\frac{H}{2n_t}} c(z)dz}$$

This system gives the equilibrium values for the number of banks in the economy, n_t, and next period stock of capital, k_{t+1}, as a function of the accumulated stock of capital. Substituting back into the first equation for k_{t+1} we get the general equilibrium expression for the no extra-profit condition in the banking sector:

$$(25) \quad \frac{k_t}{n_t}h + \frac{B}{n_t} = 2\int_0^{\frac{H}{2n_t}}\left[c\left(\frac{H}{2n_t}\right) - c(z)\right]dz\; \frac{k_t\left[1-\alpha)\psi s_{FI}\left(\dfrac{p\alpha\psi}{1+c\left(\dfrac{H}{2n_t}\right)}\right) - \dfrac{h}{H}\right] - \dfrac{B}{H}}{\left[1+\int_0^{\frac{H}{2n_t}} c(z)dz\right]}$$

This expression gives the equilibrium number of banks given the stock of accumulated capital.

As we know from previous discussion the following relationships hold in equilibrium:

$$(26) \qquad r_t^d = \frac{p\psi\alpha}{1+c\left(\dfrac{H}{2n_t}\right)}$$

$$(27) \qquad r_t = \psi\alpha$$

Therefore, given the number of banks the equilibrium accumulation equation will be the following:

$$k_{t+1} = \frac{k_t p\left[(1-\alpha)\psi s_{FI}(r_t^d) - \dfrac{h}{H} - \dfrac{B}{Hk_t}\right]}{\left[1+2\int_0^{\frac{H}{2n_t}} c(z)\,dz\right]}$$

Where $s(r_t^d)$, is the equilibrium saving rate.

According to this expression the equilibrium growth rate for the economy at time t will be:

$$g = \frac{p\left[(1-\alpha)\psi s(r_t^d) - \dfrac{h}{H} - \dfrac{B}{Hk_t}\right]}{\left[1+2\int_0^{\frac{H}{2n_t}} c(z)\,dz\right]} - 1 =$$

$$= \frac{p\left[(1-\alpha)\psi s_{FI}(r_t^d) - \dfrac{h}{H} - \dfrac{B}{Hk_t}\right]}{\left[1+C(n_t)\right]} - 1$$

Where: $C(n_t) = 2\int_0^{H/2n_t} c(z)\,dz$ is the average monitoring cost per unit of loan.

The usual considerations about conditions for positive/negative growth and the possibility for the economy to be stuck in a «no-growth» trap ($g_{FI} = 0$) also apply here. Formally $g_{FI} \geq 0$ implies $s_{FI} \geq \bar{s}_{FI}$, where $\bar{s}_{FI} = p \ (h/H + B/Hk_t) + (1 + C \ (n_t))/p\psi \ (1-\alpha)^{18}$.

5. - Comparison Between the Financial Autarky Economy and the Economy Under Financial Intermediation

The goal here is to investigate if the presence of positive monitoring costs and capital requirements associated with the financial intermediation equilibrium matters when evaluating the impact of financial intermediation on growth.

If the agents prefer deposits to self-financing then it must be that they will save more under financial intermediation than under financial autarky (see Appendix, proof 2). Formally, the result $s_{FI} > s_{FA}$ holds. However, even if the saving rate has a positive effect on the growth rate, this does not automatically lead to the conclusion that the growth rate under financial intermediation would be greater than that relative to the financial autarky case. In fact, in order to evaluate the total effect on the process of capital accumulation we have to consider both the capital requirements and the consumption of real resources associated with the financial

---

[18] The reasoning is the same as in the financial autarky case:

$$g_{FI,t} = \frac{p \left[s_{FI} \ (r_t^d) \psi (1-\alpha) - \dfrac{h}{H} - \dfrac{B}{Hk_t} \right]}{\left[1 + C(n_t) \right]} - 1 \geq 0$$

$$\Leftrightarrow$$

$$\left[s_{FI} \ (r_t^d) \psi (1-\alpha) - \dfrac{h}{H} - \dfrac{B}{Hk_t} \right] p - \left[1 + C(n_t) \right] \geq 0$$

and therefore: $\quad s_{FI} \ (r_t^d) \geq \dfrac{(1 + C(n_t)) p + \left[\dfrac{h}{H} + \dfrac{B}{Hk_t} \right]}{\psi (1-\alpha) p} = \bar{s}_{FI}$

intermediation. Capital requirements and consumption of real resources reduce the net amount of savings channelled to investment by financial intermediaries. Therefore, in principle, even if the gross flow of savings associated with the economy under financial intermediation is greater than that relative to the economy under financial autarky, it is still possible that the net amount of resources which finally goes into investment could be lower in the former economy than in the latter one. This leads to the following proposition:

Proposition 1: given the cost of monitoring per unit of loans $c\ (n_t)$, there always exists a continuum of sets of individual preferences such that $s_{FI} > s_{FA}$, and $g_{FI} < g_{FA}$, so that even if the economy under financial intermediation saves more it will grow more slowly than the economy under financial autarky.

The proof emerges comparing the growth rate under financial intermediation, $g_{FI} = [s_{FI} \, \psi \, (1 - \alpha) - h/H - B/Hk_t] \, p/[1 + C\ (n_t)]$, with the expression for the growth rate under financial autarky, $g_{FA} = s_{FA} \, \psi \, (1 - \alpha) \, p - 1$. This comparison reduces to the expression:

$$g_{FI} \geq g_{FA} \iff s_{FI} \geq \left[1 + C(n_t)\right] s_{FA} +$$

$$+ \frac{\dfrac{h}{H} + \dfrac{B}{Hk_t}}{\psi(1-\alpha)} = \bar{C}$$

$(h/H + B/Hk_t)/\psi\ (1 - \alpha) > 0$, therefore $\bar{C} > s_{FA}$. Hence, clearly enough $s_{FI} > s_{FA}$ does not necessarily imply $g_{FI} > g_{FA}$. In fact $s_{CF} > s_{FA}$ is consistent with $g_{FI} < g_{FA}$ whenever $s_{FI} < C$.

This proposition leads to the following corollary: given α, ψ, and p, and $C\ (n_t)$ and assuming $s_{FA} > \bar{s}_{FA}$, there exists a set $S = \{s_{FI} : s_{FI} \in (\bar{s}_{FA}, \bar{s}_{FI})\}$ such that, for each saving rate $s_{FI} \in S$, the economy under financial intermediation will be either shrinking or stuck in a «no-growth» trap whereas the economy under financial autarky will grow indefinitely over time at the rate $g_{FA} > 0$.

Proof: we know from the previous section that $\bar{s}_{FA} = 1/\psi\ (1 - \alpha)p$.

On the other hand $\bar{s}_{FI} = [C\,(n_t) + 1]\,p + [h/H + B/Hk_t]/\psi\,(1 - \alpha)\,p$. Then it appears clearly that $\bar{s}_{FA} < \bar{s}_{FI}$.

Then the condition for the existence of a pure financial intermediation equilibrium, $s_{FI} > s_{FA}$ it is compatible with $s_{FI} \le \bar{s}_{FI}$, and $s_{FA} > \bar{s}_{FA}$.

Summing up, these results tell us that, once the impact of both consumption of resources and capital requirements associated with the banking system is taken into account, the global effect of financial intermediation on economic growth is the result of a trade off between positive and negative partial effects whose outcome is *a priori* ambiguous.

The result is even more interesting if we consider that, as shown in the model, financial intermediaries non-growth inducing could be supported by the optimizing behaviour of the agents. This also means (as we will discuss to a greater extent in the next section) the endogenous creation of financial intermediaries does not always induce significant or even unequivocally positive effects on the growth rate. This result is somewhat new to the literature on financial intermediation and growth to the extent that the existing models always stress the beneficial consequences, in terms of growth performances of the economy, which arise, naturally and inevitably, from the emergence of a financial sector. In our model financial intermediation would have an unambigous positive effect on growth performances only in the unrealistic limit case when it is costless for the banks to monitor firms' activity and there are no capital requirements (see also Appendix).

The result which emerges from our analysis has this economic interpretation: the economy lacks a market for risk diversification. Financial intermediaries arise to solve this problem. However financial intermediation is a costly solution both for the individual agent and for the economy as a whole. In this situation the trade off between costs and benefits from financial intermediation for the single agent and the whole economy respectively cannot coincide. This raises the possibility that even if such a trade-off is positive for private agents, so that the financial sector is spontaneously implemented, it could still be negative for the economy in terms of long run growth performance.

It should be noticed that the sign as well as the magnitude of the trade-off between costs and benefits of financial intermediation depends on the average monitoring cost per unit of loans $C\,(n_t)$. But $C\,(n_t)$, is not a given parameter, because it depends on the number of banks operating in the market. This variable, as the interest rate on savings, is endogenous and, as we will show in the next section, evolves according to the process of economic growth which characterises the economy. Therefore, the impact of financial intermediation on growth will be different at different stages of development. In order to analyse how it might evolve time we turn to the effects of economic growth on credit market structure.

6. - Economic Development and Evolution of Credit Market Structure

The equilibrium number of banks operating in the economy is a function of the accumulated stock of capital. In order to analyse this relationship we take the total differential of the general equilibrium expression for the no extra-profits condition in the banking sector, (equation *(25)*):

$$dk_t\delta + dn_t\beta = 0$$

Where δ is the derivative of the profits in the banking sector with respect to the stock of accumulated capital and β is the derivative of the profits of the banking sector with respect to the number of banks. Both the derivatives are calculated in equilibrium, which means for a level of extra-profits equal to zero. δ turns out to be unambigously positive. This means that, starting from a situation in which banks make no extra-profits an increase in the stock of accumulated capital induces an effect on banks' extra-profits which is, *ceteris paribus*, positive. In other words as the stock of capital increases banks experience positive temporany extra-profits. On the other hand β turns out to be ambiguous, it could be either positive or negative. In principle this tells us that the number of banks could either be a decreasing or an increasing function of the stock of capital. Formally we have:

$$\frac{dn_t}{dk_t} = -\frac{\delta}{\beta}$$

Since $\delta > 0$ for sure, we have $dn_t/dk_t > 0$ if $\beta < 0$, and $dn_t/dk_t < 0$ if $\beta > 0$. Apparently we have an ambiguity. However the ambiguity could be solved by looking at the stability of the equilibrium of the banking sector in the two cases.

When $\beta > 0$, in fact the equilibrium in the banking sector is not stable. As the stock of capital increases, banks experience positive extra-profits. Then, because of the free entry condition, new banks enter the credit market. But then, an equilibrium number of banks is never achieved. In fact as the number of banks increases, given $\beta > 0$, this leads to further increase in banks extra-profits so that the number of banks will grow without bound. This shows that the equilibrium is not stable. In order for an equilibrium to be achieved the number of banks should decrease, but market forces operate exactly in the opposite direction.

On the other hand when $\beta < 0$ the equilibrium is stable. As the stock of capital grows banks experience positive temporary extra-profits. Then new banks enter the credit market. But then, given $\beta < 0$, this has a negative effect on extra-profits so that the new entry of banks would finally lead to a new equilibrium in which banks experience no extra-profits.

This analysis shows that the only possible case in which the economy is dynamically stable is that in which $\beta < 0$ holds. In this case as the economy develops the number of banks increases. This result emerges because, as the stock of accumulated capital grows, per capita income grows as well, and therefore, given the saving rate, the market for deposits enlarges. This creates new extra-profit opportunities for potential entrants in the credit market which actually can enter the market due to the absence of barriers to entrance. As a result of the increased number of banks competition among banks themselves increases because, being closer to one another, the cost advantage of the single bank with respect to its next competitors falls.

The evolution of credit market structure as a consequence of economic development has important consequences on the impact that financial intermediation can have on economic growth itself.

7. - The Dynamic Link Between Economic Growth and Financial Deepening Reconsidered

In this section we analyse how, in the model described so far, financial intermediation endogenously arises as a consequence of economic development and how the trade off between costs and benefits from financial intermediation evolves accordingly to the changes in the credit market structure induced by economic development. In order to this we have to deal with the effects induced by capital accumulation on both the average cost of monitoring, $C(n_t)$, and the interest rate on deposits, r_t^d.

Deriving $C(n_t)$ with respect to n_t we have:

$$(28) \qquad \frac{dC(n_t)}{dn_t} = \frac{d2 \int_0^{\frac{H}{2n_t}} c(z)dz}{dn_t} = \frac{H}{n_t^2} c\left(\frac{H}{2n_t}\right) < 0$$

Similarly, deriving the equilibrium expression for the interest rate on deposits (equation *(26)*) with respect to n_i, we have:

$$\frac{dr_t^d}{dn_t} = -\frac{H}{2n_t^2} c'\left(\frac{1}{2n_t}\right) \frac{\psi \alpha p}{\left[1 + c\left(\dfrac{1}{2n_t}\right)\right]^2} > 0$$

Then, since a positive relationship between capital accumulation and the number of banks operating in the credit market exists, we can conclude that as the economy develops the average monitoring cost per unit of loans decreases and the interest rate on deposits increases. Formally:

$$(29) \qquad \frac{dC(n_t)}{dk_t} < 0$$

$$(30) \qquad \frac{dr_t^d}{dk_t} > 0$$

7.1 *The Endogenous Creation of the Financial Intermediation System as a Consequence of Economic Development*

We assume that in the limit, as the number of banks approaches infinity, the monitoring cost per unit of loans, $c\,(n_t)$, approaches a lower bound $\bar{c}$. Consequently the interest rate on deposits approaches an upper bound $r^d = \alpha\psi/1 + \bar{c}$. We assume r^d to be strictly greater than the level of interest rate on deposits r_M, associated with c_M. This means r^d is greater than the interest rate on deposits associated with c such that financial autarky is strongly preferred to financial intermediation by the agents (by this we mean a situation in which agents save only through self-financing). Moreover we assume $r^{\dot{d}}$ to be also greater than the level of interest rate on deposits associated with c_m. This means $r^{\dot{d}}$ is greater than the interest rate on deposits associated with c such that financial intermediation is strongly preferred to financial autarky (agents will save only through deposits)[19]. Therefore even if the economy starts with a level of accumulated capital such that $r_t^d <$

19

$$r_m = \frac{p\psi\alpha}{1+c_m}$$

$$r_M = \frac{p\psi\alpha}{1+c_M}$$

where c_m has been defined before as that critical level of monitoring cost per unit of loan such that, for all $c : c < c_m$ agents will select a pure financial intermediation equilibrium, and c_M has been defined as the critical level of monitoring cost per unit of loans such that, for all $c : c > c_M$ agents select a pure financial autarky equilibrium.

r_M so that it will spontaneously operate under financial autarky equilibrium, if the growth rate of this economy is positive, then a critical level of accumulated capital (i.e. economic development) will be reached such that $r_t^d = r_M$. At this stage the economy will shift from a pure financial autarky equilibrium to a mixed equilibrium in which agents save both through self-finance and deposits. Then, as economic growth proceeds, a level of economic development will be finally reached such that $r_t^d = r_m$. After this stage of development, the economy will move to a pure financial intermediation equilibria region in which all savings are processed by financial intermediaries. Notice that if we assume $r^{\bar{d}} < r_M$ then it follows that financial intermediaries will never arise.

7.2 *Dynamics of the Trade-Off Between Costs and Benefits of Financial Intermediation Along with the Process of Economic Development*

The trade-off between costs and benefits of financial intermediation reflects itself in the diference between the growth rate under financial intermediation and the growth rate under financial autarky,

$$g_{FI} - g_{FA} = \frac{p\left[s_{FI}(r_t^d)\psi(1-\alpha) - \frac{h}{H} - \frac{B}{Hk_t} \right]}{\left[1 + C(n_t)\right]} - s_{FA}\, p\psi(1-\alpha)$$

Notice that here we compare growth under financial autarky with growth under pure financial intermediation equilibrium. We leave the comparison between growth under financial autarky and growth under mixed equilibria where agents save both through financial autarky and financial intermediation as future work. We believe that this further comparison should give results in line with the results we obtain here. As we know from the above discussion (also expressions (29), and (30)) as the economy develops the interest rate on deposits increases and the average cost of monitoring decreases. This leads to the following proposition 3: the trade-off between

costs and benefits from financial intermediation evolves positively according with the process of economic development, formally: $d\,(g_{Fi} - g_{FA})/dk_t > 0$.

The result here emerges naturally once we consider that the
saving rate is increasing in the interest rate of deposits and that
expressions *(29)*, and *(30)* hold. Formally we have:

$$\frac{d\,(g_{FI} - g_{FA})}{dk_t} = p \left\{ \frac{\left[\dfrac{ds_{FI}\,(.)}{dr_t^d} \dfrac{dr_t^d}{dn_t} \dfrac{dn_t}{dk_t} + \dfrac{B}{Hk_t^2} \right]}{\left[1 + C(n_t) \right]} + \right.$$

$$\left. -\frac{\left[s_{FI}\,(r_t^d)\,\psi\,(1-\alpha) - \dfrac{h}{H} - \dfrac{B}{Hk_t} \right]}{\left[1 + C(n_t) \right]^2} \frac{dC(n_t)}{dn_t} \frac{dn_t}{dk_t} \right\} p > 0.$$

The economic intuition behind this result is quite clear. Financial intermediation systems eventually generated at low stages of development are comparatively less efficient than those generated at high levels of economic development. Inefficiency reflects
itself negatively in the trade off between costs and benefits of a
financial intermediation system. Therefore it must be the case that
this trade off will be better at high stages of development than it
is at lower stages of development.

From another perspective this result tells us that the magnitude of the positive effect of financial intermediation on the
growth rate of the real economy increases as the process of economic development proceeds. Comparatively, the impact of financial intermediation on growth will be lower at early stages of development than it would be once the economy has reached a high
level of development. This leads us to say that financial intermediation *per se* cannot be considered an engine of growth. In fact

financial intermediation might have the power to magnify the growth of an economy but this power still depends crucially on the stage of development of the economy itself.

Finally a technical remark. As the k_t approaches infinity having assumed that the monitoring cost has an upper bound we have:

with:
$$\lim_{k_t \to \infty} g_t = \frac{p(1-\alpha)\psi s(\overline{r_t^d}) - h/H}{\left[1+\overline{C}\right]} = \overline{g}$$

where:
$$\overline{C} = \lim_{k_t \to \infty} 2 \int_0^{\frac{H}{2n_t}} c(z)\,dz.$$

That is, the growth rate of the economy under financial intermediation which is increasing in the accumulated stock of capital approaches an upper bound $\overline{g}$.

8. - Empirical Evidence

As we have just shown, according to the model, the growth impact of financial intermediation depends positively on the stock of accumulated capital per head, k_t. k_t measures the level of economic development of the economy. In the model, output per head, y_t, is a function of k_t. Therefore also y_t can be used as a measure for the level of economic development of the economy.

The main implication of the model is that: *a*) financial intermediation has an impact on growth; *b*) this impact depends on the level of economic development.

In other words the level of economic development determines the level of financial intermediation which in turns affects the growth rate of the economy. This interpretation suggests that, in order for the model to be consistent with empirical evidence, the following regularities have to be found in the data: 1) a positive and significant correlation links the degree of financial deepening of an economy and the predetermined level of real gross domestic product; 2) a positive and significant correlation links growth indicators and the level of financial deepening; 3) the component of financial intermediation which is unrelated to the level of economic development has no relationship to the growth indicators.

We carry out this empirical investigation using the data set used by King-Levine [8], [9].

This data set includes 119 countries for the period 1960-1989. We refer to the cross section time series data set with data averaged each 10 years. As Graph 2 shows, these data show, coherently with King-Levine's [10] results, a strong positive correlation between the financial deepening indicator we refer to, which is *DCPTI* = credit erogated to the private sector/total credit, and the indicator of economic development we use, which is *RGDP* = real gross domestic product per capita (for each relationship of Graph 1, we indicate the correlation coefficient (corr. coeff.) and the associated *P*-value as an indicator of statistical significance). It should be said, here, that both these variables refer to the initial year of each ten year subperiod of the time series dimension of the sample. Moreover, once again, consistently with King-Levine's results, there is a positive and strongly statistically significant correlation between the growth indicators we refer to, which are *GYP* = real gross domestic product per capita growth rate, and *GK* = growth rate of capital stock per head, and the indicator of financial deepening, *DCPTI*. It should be noticed that the economic growth indicators reflect the average growth rate of *GDP* and capital stock per head in each of the 10 year subperiods of the sample. Finally, if we consider the part of the financial deepening indicator which is not explained by the economic development indicator, this variable, called *RESDCPTIN*, is not significantly correlated to either of the two growth indicators[20]. The fall in the lev-

---

[20] Technically this variable corresponds to the residuals of the following regression:

$$\log (DCPTI) = C (1) + C (2) \log ((RGDP) + \epsilon$$

We used a non linear specification because it guarantees a better fit of the data. However the same result is achieved if we go for a linear specification. The relationship between residuals and growth indicators is not statistically significant.

el of significance is dramatic, in both the cases. This exercise allows us to conclude that the predictions of our model are, at least in terms of corelation among variables, consistent with the empirical evidence derived according to King-Levine data.

9. - Conclusions

This paper shows that, once resources consumption imputable to financial intermediation is considered, the global effect of financial intermediation on growth becomes, *a priori*, ambiguous. Financial intermediaries positively affect the allocation of savings toward productive investment. But, in order to perform their role, they also employ part of the pooled savings, thereby reducing, *ceteris paribus*, the amount of savings finally channelled toward investments. These two partial effects affect capital accumulation in opposite directions. As a result non-growth inducing financial intermediaries could spontaneously arise in the economy. Assuming a spatial competition model for the banking sector we have shown that the structure of the credit market evolves along the process of economic development. As a consequence of development the number of banks operating in the credit market increases. As a result each intermediary specializes and gets more efficient. This evolution of the credit market structure affects the trade off between the positive and negative effects induced by financial intermediation on capital accumulation in a positive way. This leads to the conclusion that the growth inducing power that financial intermediaries might have is a positive function of the level of development. It is comparatively lower at early stages of development than it would be once the economy gets fully developed. In other terms financial intermediaries might have the power to magnify the growth of the economy but this power is crucially related to the level of economic development the economy has already achieved. For this reason considering financial intermediation as an engine of growth without looking at the state of the real economy could lead to misleading conclusions on its effectiveness.

GRAPH 2

RELATIONSHIP BETWEEN ECONOMIC DEVELOPMENT
AND FINANCIAL DEEPENING

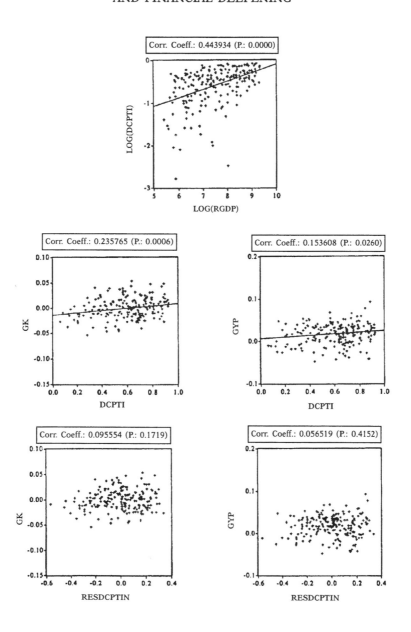

Comparison Between the Economy Under Financial Autarky and the Economy Under Costless Financial Intermediation

Where monitoring costs faced by large scale intermediaries were negligible, so that they could be set equal to zero, and so capital requirements, the market for credit operates under perfect competition. The no-extra profit condition would then imply this equilibrium relationship between interest rates on deposits and interest rates on loans:

$$r_t^d = pr_t^l$$

Agents will still behave as in the economy with monopolistically competitive banking system. As a result the equilibrium growth rate for the economy under costless financial intermediation would be:

$$g_f = sp\psi\,(1-\alpha) - 1$$

Where s is the saving rate under costless financial intermediation with no capital requirements. Under the costless hypothesis it is always true that $s > s_{FA}$ (proof 2). This leads to the following proposition: proposition 4: the long run growth rate of the economy under financial autarky, $g_{FA} = s_{FA}\,p\psi\,(1-\alpha) - 1$, will always be lower than the growth rate of the economy under costless financial intermediation.

The formal proof is trivial. In fact given a set of parameters (α, ψ, p) the inequality $g_f = sp\psi\,(1-\alpha) - 1 > g_{FA} = s_{FA}\,p\psi\,(1-\alpha) - 1$, reduces to $s > s_{FA}$.

The economic interpretation behind this standard result is immediate: agents are risk averse. Physical capital accumulation is risky. This means the rate of return of savings is risky as well. Agents will therefore seek for a market for risk in order to insure themselves against this riskiness. Due to our assumption, banks constitute the Pareto-superior solution to this problem. Given the limit assumption of zero monitoring costs for the banks, this solution corresponds to a first best solution. Delegating monitoring to banks each agent is better off without any cost. Therefore the economy as a whole must perform better. *Ceteris paribus*, the presence of a banking system guarantees agents will save more. The capital accumulation process will be consequently strengthened with positive effects on the long run growth performance of the economy. This is a standard result in the literature of endogenous growth and financial intermediation. However from our discussion this result holds only in the limit case of zero monitoring costs and no capital requirements for the banking sector.

Proof 1: assuming no constraints are imposed on the choice of the optimal values for e_t, and b_t, the first order conditions associated with this choice will be the following:

$$(31) \qquad (e_t^*) \, u'(w_t - b_t^* - e_t^*) = pr^e v^{,G} \, (r^e \, e_t^* + b_t^* \, r_t^d)$$

$$(b_t^*) \, u'(w_t - b_t^* - e_t^*) = pr_t^d v^{,G} \, (\alpha\psi \, e_t^* + b_t^* \, r_t^d) + (1-p) \, r_t^d v^{,B} \, (\, b_t^* \, r_t^d)$$

Where $r^e = \alpha\psi$, represents the equilibrium level of the rate of return on self-financing in the good states of the world, and $r_t^d = p\psi\alpha/(1 + c(H/2n_t))$, represents the equilibrium level of the rate of return on deposits, as described before. System *(31)* implies:

$$(32) \; pr^e v' \, (r^e \, e_t^* + b_t^* \, r_t^d) = r_t^d \, [pv^{,G} \, (\alpha\psi \, e_t^* + b_t^* \, r_t^d) + (1-p) \, v^{,B} \, (\, b_t^* \, r_t^d)]$$

We know that, since $c \, (1/2n_t) > 0 \; \forall \, n_t > 0$, $r_t^d < pr^e$, where pr^e is the expected rate of return on self-financing. The agents in the economy are risk averse. Risk aversion implies that in order to be preferred by the agents self-financing must guarantee a sufficiently higher expected return compared to the safe return on deposits. Consider equation *(32)*. Assume agents find it optimal to save both through self-financing and through deposits, which means $e^*_t > 0$, $b^*_t > 0$. This must imply the following equality holds:

$$(33) \qquad \frac{pr^e}{r^d_t} = \frac{pv'^{,G}(\alpha\psi e^*_t + b^*_t r^d_t) + (1-p)v'^{,B}(b^*_t r^d_t)}{pv'^{,G}(r^e e^*_t + b^*_t r^d_t)}$$

The *RHS* of this equation is a measure of risk aversion. Positive risk aversion implies this ratio to be greater than one. The higher is the ratio the higher is the degree of risk aversion. This equation therefore tells us which is the critical minimum level of the risk premium self-financing must guarantee, in terms of expected return, to induce risk averse agents to employ a positive fraction of their saving to finance their own investments directly, given their degree of risk aversion. Formally we have two limit cases. First if,

$$\frac{pr^e}{r^d_t} \le \frac{pv'^{,G}(b^*_t r^d_t) + (1-p)v'^{,B}(b^*_t r^d_t)}{pv'^{,G}(b^*_t r^d_t)}$$

then agents save only through deposits. (we assume $v'^{,B}(b^*_t r^d_t) > v'^{,G}(b^*_t r^d_t)$, so that $pr^e/r^d_t > 1$ holds also in this case)). This corresponds to the case in which $r^d_t \ge \alpha p\psi/1 + c_m$.

Second if:

$$\frac{pr^e}{r^d_t} \ge \frac{pv'^{,G}(\alpha\psi e^*_t) + (1-p)v'^{,B}(\bar{y})}{pv'^{,G}(r^e e^*_t)}$$

Agents will save only through deposits and self-finance.

Finally for values of pr^e/r^d_t within these two extrema agents will save partly through deposits and partly through self financing of investment projects.

Proof 2: assume that pure financial intermediation equilibria ($e^*_t = 0$, $b^*_t > 0$) strongly dominate financial autarky equilibria. Then the following relationship holds:

$$(34) \qquad (e_t^* = 0) \; u'(w_t - b_t^* - e_t^*) < pr^e v^{\wedge,G} \, (b_t^* \, r_t^d)$$

$$(b_t^* = 0) \; u'(w_t - b_t^* - e_t^*) = r_t^d \, [\, pv^{\wedge,G} \, (b_t^* \, r_t^d) + (1-p) \, v^{\wedge,B} \, (\, b_t^* \, r_t^d)\,]$$

Suppose that financial intermediation is not feasible.

Then agents save through self-finance. In that case the optimality condition implies:

$$(35) \qquad (e_t^* > 0) \; u'(w_t - b_t^* - e_t^*) = pr^e v^{\wedge,G} \, (e_t^* \, r^e)$$

Assume that agents save the same amount of resources they should have saved if financial intermediation was feasible, formally: $e_t^* = b_t^*$. Is this situation compatible with the conditions relative to agents' utility maximization?

From system *(34)* we know that:

$$pr^e v^{\wedge,G} \, (b_t^* \, r_t^d) < r_t^d \, [pv^{\wedge,G} \, (b_t^* \, r_t^d) + (1-p) \, v^{\wedge,B} \, (\, b_t^* \, r_t^d)]$$

Then, since $pr^e v^{\wedge,G} \, (e_t^* \, r^e) < pr^e v^{\wedge,G} \, (b_t^* \, r_t^d)$ holds, since we assume risk aversion (decreasing marginal utility) and $e_t^* \, r^e > b_t^* \, r_t^d$ given $e_t^* = b_t^*$, and $r^e > r_t^*$, it also follows that, for $e_t^* = b_t^*$, this inequality holds:

$$pr^e v^{\wedge,G} \, (e_t^* \, r^e) < r_t^d \, [pv^{\wedge,G} \, (b_t^* \, r_t^d) + (1-p) \, v^{\wedge,B} \, (\, b_t^* \, r_t^d)]$$

This means the answer to our previous question is: no, $e_t^* = b_t^*$, is not compatible with agents' utility maximization. In fact the optimal amount of e_t^* should satisfy this equality:

$$pr^e v^{\wedge,G} \, (e_t^* \, r^e) = r_t^d \, [pv^{\wedge,G} \, (b_t^* \, r_t^d) + (1-p) \, v^{\wedge,B} \, (\, b_t^* \, r_t^d)]$$

But, then, we conclude that the optimal values of e_t^*, has to be strictly lower than the optimal value of savings under financial intermediation, b_t^*.

This holds, of course, also in the case in which financial intermediation is costless.

Proof 3: nets profits of the bank, P^B, could be written as profits per unit of accumulated capital, Pk, times accumulated capital.

Then the derivative of P^B with respect to k could be written as:

$$\frac{dP^B}{dk_t} = \frac{dPk}{dk_t}k_t + Pk$$

In equilibrium profits per unit of capital are equal to zero. Therefore, in equilibrium the marginal change in banks' profits induced by a change in the stock of accumulated capital will be:

$$\frac{dP^B}{dk_t} = \frac{dPk}{dk_t}k_t$$

The expression for the net profits of the bank, is this:

$$P^B = \left\{ 2\int_0^{\frac{H}{2n_t}} \left[c\left(\frac{H}{2n_t}\right) + \right.\right.$$

$$pk_t \frac{\left[(1-\alpha)\psi s_{FI}\left(\frac{p\alpha\psi}{1+c\left(\frac{H}{2n_t}\right)}\right) - \frac{h}{H}\right] - p\frac{B}{H}}{\left[1+2\int_o^{\frac{H}{2n_t}} c(z)\,dz\right]} +$$

$$-c(z)]\,dz$$

$$-\frac{k_t}{Hn_t}h - \frac{B}{Hn_t}$$

Consequently the derivative of net profits with respect to the stock of accumulated capital taken at $P^B = 0$, will have this full expression:

$$\frac{dP^B}{dk_t} = 2\int_0^{\frac{H}{2n_t}} \left[c\left(\frac{H}{2n_t}\right) - c(z) \right] d\frac{B}{Hk_t^2} + \frac{B}{n_t Hk_t^2} = \delta > 0$$

That is, an increase in the accumulated stock of capital generates temporaneous extra-profits in the banking sector.

The derivative of net profits with respect to n_t will have the following expression:

$$\frac{dP^B}{dn_t} = -\frac{p\left[\frac{H}{4n_t^3} c'\left(\frac{H}{2n_t}\right)\right]\left[k_t \left\{(1-\alpha)\psi s_{FI} \left(\frac{p\alpha\psi}{1+c\left(\frac{H}{2n_t}\right)}\right) - \frac{h}{H}\right\} \frac{B}{H}\right]}{\left[1 + 2\int_0^{\frac{H}{2n_t}} c(z)\,dz\right]} +$$

$$+ \frac{2\int_0^{\frac{H}{2n_t}}\left[c\left(\frac{H1}{2n_t}\right) - c(z)\right] dzs'(r_t^d)\frac{dr_t^d}{dn_t}\psi p(1-\alpha)k_t}{\left[1 + 2\int_0^{\frac{H}{2n_t}} c(z)\,dz\right]} +$$

$$+ \frac{2\int_0^{\frac{H}{2n_t}}\left[c\left(\frac{H}{2n_t}\right) - c(z)\right] dzp\left[k_t(1-\alpha)\psi s_{FI}\left(\frac{p\alpha\psi}{1+c\left(\frac{H}{2n_t}\right)}\right) -\right]}{\left[1 + 2\int_0^{\frac{H}{2n_t}} c(z)\,dz\right]^2} +$$

Luca G. Deidda

$$+ \frac{-\dfrac{h}{H} - \dfrac{B}{H} \left. \dfrac{H}{2n_t^d} \, c\left(\dfrac{H}{2n_t}\right)\right]}{\left[1 + 2\int_o^{\frac{H}{2n_t}} c(z)\, dz\right]^2} + $$

$$+ \frac{B}{Hn_t^2} + \frac{B}{Hn_t^2 kt}$$

Given the behaviour of interest rate on deposits with respect to n_t, and the assumptions about the monitoring cost function this derivative, evaluated in equilibrium, at $P^B = 0$, has a value β, which is, *a priori* ambiguous.

BIBLIOGRAPHY

[1] AZARIADIS C., *Intertemporal Macroeconomics*, London, Basil Blackwell, 1992.

[2] BENCIVENGA V.R. - SMITH B.D., «Financial Intermediation and Endogenous Growth», *Review of Economic Studies*, vol. 58, April 1991, pp. 195-209.

[3] BLACKBURN K., - HUNG V.T.Y., *A Theory of Growth Financial Development and Trade*, mimeo, 1995.

[4] DIAMOND D.W., «Financial Intermediation and Delegated Monitoring», *Review of Economic Studies*, vol. 51, 1984, pp. 393-414.

[5] GOLDSMITH R.W., *Financial Structure and Development*, New Haven, Yale University Press, 1969.

[6] GEHRING T., *Excessive Risks and Banking Regulation*, mimeo, 1995.

[7] GREENWOOD J. - JOVANOVIC B., «Financial Development, Growth and the Distribution of Income», *Journal of Political Economy*, vol. 98, 1990, pp. 1076-107.

[8] KING R.G. - LEVINE R., «Financial Indicators and Growth in a Cross Section of Countries», World Bank, *Working Paper*, n. 819, 1992.

[9] — —, «Finance and Growth: Schumpeter Might be Right», *Quarterly Journal of Economics*, vol. 108, 1992, pp. 717-38.

[10] — —, «Finance, Entrepreneurship, and Growth», *Journal of Monetary Economics*, vol. 32, 1993, pp. 513-42.

[11] LEVINE R., «Stock Markets, Growth, and Tax Policy», *Journal of Finance*, vol. XLVI, 1992, pp. 1445-65.

[12] SAINT-PAUL G., «Technological Choice, Financial Markets and Economic Development», *European Economic Review*, vol. 36, 1992, pp. 763-81.

[13] SUSSMAN O., «A Theory of Financial Development», in GIOVANNINI A. (ed.), *Financial Intermediation and Economic Development: Issues and Experience*, New York-Cambridge University Press, 1993.

[14] WILLIAMSON S.D., «Costly Monitoring, Financial Intermediation and Equilibrium Credit Rationing», *Journal of Monetary Economics*, vol. 18, 1986, pp. 159-77.

Political and Economic News and Lira Fluctuations. The Recent Experience: 29 March 1994 - 29 December 1995

Massimo Tivegna*

Università «Tor Vergata», Roma

1. - Introduction

During the Berlusconi and Dini governments – the empirical basis for our study – the lira exchange rate reached the highest peaks of volatility since the end of the Second World War. What better opportunity than our reference period therefore to explore a possible method to attempt an empirical analysis of the effects of «political» noise on the exchange rate. As almost no empirical studies of this relationship are to be found in the literature[1], we wish to take advantage of this chance to use a period of particular turbulence to propose a empirical methodology which, albeit not particularly original technically, could be useful for studying

* The author would like to thank Dr. Fabio Fornari for his numerous suggestions as regards the econometric aspects of this paper and Dr. Irene Spada for her valuable research assistance. This paper was originally written in Italian.

N.B. the numbers in square brackets refer to the Bibliography at the end of the paper.

[1] Literature does include studies on the impact on share prices of political risks, AGMON T. - FINDLAY C. [1], DIAMONTE R.L. - LIEW J.M. - STEVENS R.L. [17], ERB C.B. - HARVEY C.R. - VISKANTA T.E. [25], and of the American presidential election, ALLVINE F.C. - O'NEIL D.E. [2], HOBBS G.R. - RILEY W.B. [32]. The methodology of all these studies is moreover very different from that adopted here. I would like to thank Professor Emilio Barone for bringing these works to my attention.

the impact of political events on exchange rates and their volatility[2].

This purpose of this paper is twofold: to revisit a period of much political and financial turbulence in Italy, namely from March 1994 to December 1995, and to attempt to explain the trend of the lira-DM exchange rate and more specifically its strong volatility. This is achieved by a very detailed reconstruction of the political and economic events which, day by day, accompanied the government headed by Silvio Berlusconi and that subsequent, which was headed by Lamberto Dini. This reconstructions is used to estimate the econometric equations which aim to measure the specific weight of the single events in determining the daily exchange rates. The estimated equations have a prevalently empirical base, but are situated in the theoretical framework of the impact of unexpected events (news) on the exchange-rate dynamics. They incorporate the known regularity shown by the lira during the period of free fluctuation, from September 1992, namely of appreciating against the DM when the dollar did similarly, and of depreciating against the former when the latter did.

This phenomenon is explained rather easily by the normal strategy of exchange dealers' trading which states that if there is an autonomous flow of funds from the dollar to the DM, the latter appreciates vis-à-vis both the former and, automatically, the other European currencies which are under the leadership of the DM. This movement is further compounded by the foreign exchange dealers' action, because it is worthwhile buying the currency which is appreciating, the DM, and it also protects the value of dealers' own stocks of dollars.

The basic econometric specification of this paper, which holds that it is mainly the movements of the dollar against the DM which determine those of the lira vis-à-vis the latter, has been integrated by the effects exercised by the various announcements concerning the behaviour of the Italian economy (public finances, infla-

---

[2] A more detailed version of this study with an analytical chronology of the period examined is to be found in TIVEGNA M. [45]. The political and economic events used are described and catalogued in a databank managed on an experimental basis by the DB5 program. See CHIOFI G. - TIVEGNA M. [9].

tion, economic activities, interest rates, and on economic policy guidelines *tout court*) and by the effects of the plethora of episodes of micro- and macro political tensions which characterised the two governments examined in this paper. These episodes, which are generically defined as «political noise», have been reclassified in this paper according to the fundamental factor which engendered them (in Section 3) and are summarised below.

For the period of the government headed by Silvio Berlusconi, we considered the effects produced by the general election, the conflicts within the Polo coalition which won the election, mainly between the Lega Nord and the other parties, the conflicts between the members of the Berlusconi government and the magistrates of the *Mani Pulite* ('Clean Hands') pool investigating corruption, the animated dialectic between leading figures of the Polo and the President of the Republic, other situations of institutional «conflict», principally between the government parties and Banca d'Italia, the frequent polemics generated by the potential conflicts of interest ascribed to Berlusconi when President of the Council of Ministers – generally for issues regarding television news – and, finally the polemics regarding the notices of judicial investigation served on Silvio Berlusconi when President of the Council of Ministers, and his brother Paolo. See Graph 1.

For the period of the Dini government, the political noise was determined mainly by the Polo's oscillating stance vis-à-vis the government – on the vote of confidence and on the «minibudget» designed to right the public accounts in Spring 1995 – by the various elections and referenda which were held during this period, and by the curious case of the hyperactivism of Minister of Justice Mancuso vis-à-vis magistrates of the *Mani Pulite* pool, which reproposed the effects produced previously by the polemics between the previous Minister of Justice, Biondi, and the pool. Much turbulence was generated during this period also by the Parliamentary passage of the pension reform and the 1996 Budget Law, basically as a result of the small majority on which the Dini government could count and the «political inconstancy» encountered in various factions of the Lega Nord. The final period of hypervolatility of the lira is, as is known, related to the Parliament's vote of no-confidence in Min-

GRAPH 1

LIRA-DM AND DM-$ IN 1994
(28 March 1994 = 100)

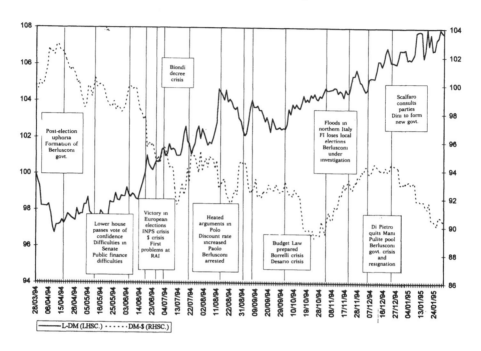

ster of Justice Mancuso and the subsequent attempt by the Polo to bring down the Dini government during the Parliamentary passage of the 1996 Budget Law. See Graph 2.

With regard to the period of the Dini government, this study can to some extent be considered as an analysis of the lira exchange rate volatility produced by the attempt to achieve fiscal stabilization with a narrow parliamentary majority.

The following section contains an overview of the theories of the effects of news on the foreign exchange markets. It is frequently pointed out here also that there exists no empirical literature on the effect of political events on exchange rates, although various authors are aware (well represented, for all, by the work of Hallwood-Macdonald [30], pp. 251-2, quoted at length in Section 2) that these are an important explanatory component in exchange rate dynamics. Section 3 describes the classification criteria for the individual

GRAPH 2

LIRA-DM AND DM-$ IN 1995
(28 March 1994 = 100)

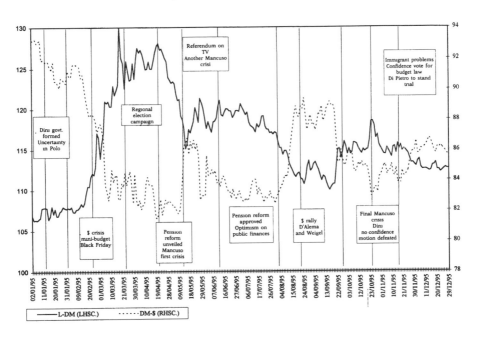

economic and political events of the period, which are given in full in the appendix to Tivegna [45] and, in more detail, in Chiofi-Tivegna [9]. Section 4 describes the construction of the explanatory political variables and the results of the econometric estimations made firstly by ordinary least squares and then by correcting the standard error for heteroscedasticity using White's [48] technique. Confirmation of these results will be sought using *GARCH* models, more suited to cope with this volatility in models which use financial variables. the final section contains some conclusions.

2. - News in the Foreign Exchange Markets

As is known, macro-economic modelling of the determination of exchange rates lies along two main theoretical paths in macroeconomics: the Keynesian path, in which lies the Mundell-Fleming model for determining exchange rates, and the monetarist path, which furnishes the theoretical base of the monetary approach to exchange rate determination[3].

It is also known that these models contain differing mechanisms which transmit changes in economic activity and interest rates to the exchange rate dynamics (here understood as the unit of domestic currency per unit of foreign currency).

In the Mundell-Fleming model, an increase in the 'domestic' country's economic activity causes a depreciation of the exchange rate through the disequilibrium of the balance of payments, while an increase in interest rates causes a appreciation of the exchange rate as a result of capital inflows from abroad.

In the monetary model, on the other hand, an increase in domestic economic activity is associated with a revaluation of the exchange rate while an increase in domestic interest rates engenders, on the contrary, a depreciation. This because both income and interest rates are two variables of the demand for money. An increase in the former, assuming constant circulation speed, is equivalent to an increase in the demand for money for transactions purposes which, money supply remaining unchanged, allows a reduction in prices and an appreciation of the exchange rate, by purchasing power parity. The interest rate is also to be found in the money demand and an increase in the former reduces the latter and hence gives rise to a surplus of money circulation – supply by central banks remaining unchanged – which triggers price increases and, via this, a devaluation of the exchange rate[4].

These differentiated exchange rate responses to variations of the «fundamental» variables are reinforced, in a stochastic version

---

[3] There are numerous reference texts in this field. See, of the more recent, COPELAND L.S. [13], chapters 5-10 and HALLWOOD P.C.-MACDONALD R. [30], Chapters 5, 8, 9 and 10.
[4] In the monetary models which produce this effect, the economic activity is always assumed to be close to full use and hence a surplus of money inevitably causes an increase in prices. It should be noted, moreover, that an increase in interest rates should have the effect of depressing domestic demand, also quite rapidly on stocks and on the most interest-sensitive part of consumption. This can produce a reduction in money demand for transaction purposes and hence can further accentuate the surplus of money in the economy and therefore inflation.

of the structural models which generate the reduced forms of the two models (Mundell-Fleming and monetary), also by effects which are temporally variable on the exchange rate dynamics stemming from the relative changes in the variances of the terms of error in these equations and from the latters' covariances[5].

These differentiated effects help create that particular mood of the financial markets – which we define as market sentiment – in which the same variations of the «fundamentals», by direction and intensity, give rise to reactions in the exchange rate which can differ considerably.

2.1 *Interest and Exchange Rates*

We shall now examine in more detail the relation between interest rates and exchange rates, which are a further example of differentiated responses. As we have seen, in Mundell-Fleming's Keynesian model, a relative increase in domestic interest rates produces univocally a revaluation of the domestic country's exchange rate; while in the monetary model, on the other hand, a similar increase produces a devaluation. But these are not the only differentiated effects, particularly in the Italian and, e.g., US international institutional contexts, of market reactions to changes in interest rates. These responses can be further strengthened by the possible overlapping of effects which can take place when the market operators believe that a reputation effect[6] is also at work, particularly in the presence of formal oscillation bands, such as those of the European Exchange-Rate Mechanism[7] (ERM) or when exchange rate objectives are announced[8].

In the Italian context, with its high public debt, the markets have generally shown negative reactions – selling lire spot or purchasing

---

[5] See, on this matter, Tivegna M. [45], pp. 3-7.

[6] This is a body of literature which uses the game theory and belongs to contributions on the international co-ordination of economic policies in vogue in the 1980s. See Buiter W.H. - Marston R.C. [8] and Macdonald R. - Milbourne R. [39].

[7] The relevant literature is that on target zones. See Svensson L.E.O. [44].

[8] Such as that of President of the Council of Ministers Dini in the re-entry of the lira into the ERM.

DM forward – to increases in interest rates, whether official or market, or to macro-economic developments which could push rates in the same direction, such as higher inflation[9]. The reason can here be traced to an increase in the risk premia of Italian assets.

Another atypical response – at least for the two schemes discussed here of exchange rate responses to changes in interest rates – is that observed for example in the US market of late whereby an increase (effective or expected) of interest rates is perceived by the markets as bearish for the dollar while their reduction (effective or expected) is instead considered to be bullish. Here also, it would appear that the monetary model is at work, but there is no trace of this (and of other related arguments on the relation between money and inflation) in the market comments. Note is merely taken of the «sympathy» between the US bond markets and the dollar exchange rates in the terms illustrated above. The probable explanation for this atypical relation between, for example, reductions in interest rates and the strengthening of the dollar derives in part from the positive impact which these reductions have on the price of securities – or on the prices of futures on the 30Y bond – and hence on the yield of the stock of dollar-denominated securities via the capital gain generated by the reduction of interest rates. In this case we once again find ourselves in the Mundell-Fleming model, as a reduction in short-term interest rates implies an increase in the yield of US securities in portfolio. Hence the dollar rally ahead of the expected cuts in interest rates and the consequent increase in the expected yield of securities.

2.2 News Models

The literature on the impact of news on the exchange rate generally follows the monetary model. Edwards ([20], [21], [22])

---

[9] As noted above, this reaction could be determined – according to the monetary model of exchange rate determination – by the markets' fear of a surplus money stock in circulation with the consequent loss in the lira's value. Moreover, this would not appear to have been the tone of the market when Italian interest rates were increased, also because the money stock has been at a record low level for some years now.

was the first author to propose a news model, deriving it from a structural model of this type. The news in this case consisted of deviations between the values produced by the model and those actually observed on the variables which appear in the structural form of the monetary model, in addition to the variance-covariance ratios between these errors.

The expected values are projected by an unrestricted VAR model which simulates the process of formation of operators' expectations. The results of these studies confirm the explanatory power of news.

Edwards, approach was followed[10] by various authors with a variety of results, using either purely autoregressive models, to generate expected values on a single variable[11] or expected values on several variables, modelling the economy with a VAR or seeking a somewhat structural explanation of the news[12]. The theoretical model used in this strand of literature was always the monetary model, with the exception of Branson [7], who used his own model.

A slightly different strand of literature links the dynamics of the exchange rate to the deviations between the monetary objectives announced by the central banks and the actual monetary values[13]. The result of this latter group of contributions is that operators expect a correction in the opposite sense of, say, an overshooting of the monetary target and hence the exchange rate will respond to the latter by appreciating, and not depreciating as the monetary model postulates, as a result of an expansion of money circulation.

A final group of contributions which has provided the principal inspiration for this study makes direct use of the differences between the value expected by the markets (and recorded by specialised bodies first and foremost of which the Money Market Ser-

---

[10] And in fact preceded by his thesis advisor FRENKEL J. [26] who introduced an expected interest rate, produced by a autoregressive model, in an exchange rate efficiency equation. It is worth noting here that the use in regression of an auxiliary variable obtained by another statistical procedure can produce distortions of the relative coefficient and losses of efficiency. See PAGAN A.R. [14].

[11] See COPELAND L.S. [12], EDWARDS S. [20], BOMHOFF E.J. - KORTEWEG P. [6].

[12] See BRANSON W.H. [7], EDWARDS S. [21], MACDONALD R. [36] and [37], FIORENTINI R. [27], CIFARELLI G. [10] and [11].

[13] See URICH T.J. - WACHTEL P. [47], CORNELL B. [14], ENGEL C. - FRANKEL J.A. [23], MACDONALD R. - TORRANCE T.S. [38].

vice of Redwood California) and the values observed *ex post* on
the explanatory variables in the exchange rate models – which as
we saw above are the same but with different signs – to explain
the daily[14] and the infra-daily[15] changes in exchange rates. The results obtained – which refer solely to the American and Japanese
experience – are very encouraging and indicate statistically significant effects of various macro-economic variables – trade balance,
factory-gate and consumer-price inflation, changes in employment
rate, retail sales, orders of durables, etc. – to explain exchange-
rate fluctuations. In the empirical verifications given below we
have studied with varying fortune the effects of the deviations of
the economic variables from their expected values (or from the
values observed during the previous periods as proxies of the expected values).

It is important to emphasise, in commenting the results of
this literature, that the effects of a particular news on the exchange
rate varies in time according to the current market sentiment and
the differing importance which the markets ascribe in time to this
news: from the afore-mentioned studies we note that the impact
of announcements regarding the trade balance is, for example,
very high between 1984 and 1987, when the revaluation of the dollar, which culminated in 1985, and the subsequent overvaluation
(which lasted for several years even during the period of dollar
depreciation) caused a significant deterioration in the USA's trade
position. The markets therefore attribute every announcement regarding this variable which is worse than expectations or in any
case worsens the existing situation, with an unequivocal devaluation message, either because it increases the probability of direct
intervention by the monetary authorities, or because the exchange
rate should move in that direction in view of the excess supply of
dollars which would come into being should the deficit not be reduced[16].

---

[14] See DERAVI M.K. - GREGOROWICZ P. - HEGJI C.E. [16], HARDOUVELIS G. [31],
IRWIN D. [34], HOGAN K. - MELVIN M. - ROBERTS D. [33], DOUKAS S. - LIFELAND D.
[18], SPADA I. [43].
[15] See ITO T. - ROLEY V.V. [35], EDERINGTON L. - LEE S. [19].
[16] This is naturally the implication of the portfolio balance model for the determination of exchange rates. HALLWOOD P.C. - MACDONALD R. [30], Chapter 10.

We encounter a similar effect in our empirical verifications, in which inflation exercises a different weight in the two periods of our analysis, that of the Berlusconi government, 28 March-22 December 1994, when inflation first decreased and then stabilised, and that of the Dini government, 16 January-29 December 1995, when inflation started to climb again from February 1995 and which was immediately followed by an increase in the discount rate. In line with these two differing market sentiments, the news on inflation was not significant during the Berlusconi government, while it was during the Dini government.

While this literature has furnished mixed results from the statistical point of view, it has however highlighted both the limits of traditional models for determining exchange rates[17], and also, above all, the actual *modus operandi* of the markets. Hence the validity of the considerations advanced in a recent textbook of international economics and finance, which contains an excellent collection of all the recent results in this sector, that of Hallwood - Macdonald [30]: «The above results (on the empirical efficiency of news) suggest that the new approach to the determination of the exchange rate is reasonably well supported by the data, and future research on this topic should usefully extend the range of news items considered and the methods of generating news. Nevertheless, a difficulty remains: the volatility of exchange rates appears to be greater than the volatility of the conventional news items. How can this be explained? It may be possible to supplement the news approach in a number of ways.

First of all it is quite possible that non-quantifiable news elements, such as political announcements and rumours, dominate the quantifiable elements which researchers use in their news models.

Second, a high relative volatility of exchange rates may be due to the presence of rational speculative bubbles.

A third rationalisation for the greater volatility of exchange rates relative to the news is that market participants may be using

---

[17] As regards empirical verification of the various monetary models, see for a summary consideration BAILLIE R.T. - McMAHON P. [13], Chapter 8 and PENTECOST E.J. [42], Chapters 2 and 4.

a different economic model from that prescribed by international economists» (Hallwood P.C. - Macdonald R. [30], pp. 251-2).

The first point, i.e. that the markets often tend to overshoot the values implicit in their fundamentals, has been commonly observed and received much empirical confirmation, for example by Davidson [15] and Flood-Rose [28]. In our study, which refers to an experience limited to the Italian lira, we integrate the explanations furnished by economic news with those of political news, of which there was no shortage, and indicated in the reference cited above as potentially dominant vis-à-vis economic explanations. In this experience we shall verify that the weight of political news played a significant role in the fluctuations of the lira and that the weight and sign of the various families of news – both economic and political – is not constant in time[18].

This is our interpretation of the third consideration formulated above by Hallwood and MacDonald who state that there may exist in the mind of operators interpretative models of various types and in any case different from those proposed by international economists. This is the spirit of the models typically present in the background of market operators, the Mundell-Fleming model, of Keynesian inspiration, and the monetary model. Our purpose is to underscore the differencies between the models used by market operators and the forming of a market sentiment which can cause deviations, even quite significant ones, in exchange rate trends vis-à-vis the prevalent (or those considered as such) interpretative models. Furthermore, the actual trend of exchange rates, while moving within the same interpretative model, can experience parametric alterations which modify the stochastic part of the model (Tivegna M. [45], paragraph 2). Finally, wholly economic determinants may not suffice to explain the hypervolatility of exchange rates in some specific phases and hence political vari-

---

[18] TIVEGNA M. [45] paragraph 2 noted that this non-constancy is produced by the continuous parametric – and perhaps also distributive – alterations of the terms of error present in the reduced forms of the Mundell-Fleming and monetary models. These can both effectively produce themselves in the dynamics of the markets and be subjectively processed by the traders. The political cycle probably transmits to the markets in time differing sentiments which produce quite differentiated reactions.

ables also have to be introduced into the explanatory model. This study takes all these elements into account.

3. - Classification of Events

In this section we shall examine the classification criteria we adopted for grouping the information in homogeneous categories to build variables representative of families of events.

There is an objective difficulty in selecting the qualitative events (of politics and concerning market events) which are really significant in determining the exchange rate dynamics from the many to which foreign exchange dealers and financial market operators, in general, attribute particular importance. Furthermore, it is rather arbitrary to give an appropriate quantification to their effects on the exchange rate.

To resolve the problem of choosing the important events, we have followed the following strategy. We carried out a preliminary selection on the basis of the importance which market operators attributed to the events we selected. The sources of this «importance» are Italian and international economic and financial publications. We then further reduced the events selected according to this principle: its presence in the first two pages of Italy's leading financial newspaper *Il Sole 24 Ore*.

As already noted, this study examines economic and political events. The economic events refer only to those on inflation and public finances. The former are grouped in a variable which refers to the news on inflation in the broadest sense. The latter refer to changes in the interest rate on the public debt (whatever the source of the news) and announcements on the trend of the public finances made by the institutional bodies responsible for collecting such statistics. News on interest rates and news on government accounts were grouped together as they are perceived in a homogeneous manner by the markets as significant for Italy's financial stability.

The political events were divided into several categories according to their nature as perceived by the markets. The different types of event are shown below grouped according to the type of event and with a brief description of the classification criteria. The groups of events from one to eight refer to events of a strictly po-litical-institutional type, while the last two groups refer to eco-nomic news. For each of the groups of news below, we indicate the code of the variable which is used in the empirical part of this study.

1) ELECTION RESULTS (VE). This group includes the results of the general, European, local (regional, provincial and local coun-cil) elections and referenda which took place during the reference period. The results of these elections had differing effects on the lira exchange rate according to the political backdrop against which they took place. During the Berlusconi government, the victories of the Polo coalition produced a strengthening of the exchange rate and vice versa, during the Dini government the exact opposite was the case, as is particularly evident in the markets' response to the defeat of the Polo in the regional elections at the end of April 1995. Many commentators place the lira's turning point, from devalua-tion to revaluation, precisely at the end of April (see Graph 1.2 for an overall view of the Dini government period).

2) CONFLICTS WITHIN THE POLO DELLE LIBERTÀ (CP). The Polo coalition was the winner of the March 1994 general election and formed the government which remained in office until 22 Decem-ber 1994, and fell after the defection of the Lega Nord. This fam-ily of events groups the political contrasts regarding government appointments and programme which preceded the formation of the Berlusconi government and that which subsequently charac-terised the difficult co-habitation in the Polo of the Lega Nord with the other coalition parties which culminated in the Lega quit-ting the majority and the consequent government crisis.

3) CONFLICTS ON INSTITUTIONAL ISSUES (CI) between authorita-tive members of parties of the Polo coalition – and of the Berlus-coni government – and the President of the Republic Scalfaro. The financial markets reacted negatively to the frictions and strong dif-ferences of judgement on some key issues of public life during the reference period (for example as regards the guide-lines for the Italian state broadcasting company RAI, the possible conflict of

interest engendered by Berlusconi holding the position of President of the Council of Ministers while simultaneously remaining sole (direct or controlling) shareholder of the commercial TV group Fininvest). This category also includes the long period required to ratify the appointment of a new Director General for the Banca d'Italia to replace Lamberto Dini.

4) JUDICIAL TROUBLES OF THE BERLUSCONI BROTHERS (CR) which saw the direct involvement of the President of the Council of Ministers Silvio Berlusconi or his brother Paolo. The events included here are the summons served on Paolo Berlusconi for his construction activities in June 1994 and those in which Silvio Berlusconi was directly involved, in November of the same year. This type of events was only marginally significant in the OLS estimates of the Berlusconi period and this result has not been confirmed in the *GARCH* estimates. Hence, the empirical part of our study gives no estimates regarding the impact of this type of news.

5) EVENTS RELATED TO THE ADMINISTRATION OF JUSTICE (CG), consisting of differences between members of the Berlusconi government, including the President of the Council of Ministers together with exponents of his Forza Italia party, and the investigating magistrates of the *Mani Pulite* pool: from the so-called Biondi Decree, with the differences engendered both inside and outside the government, to the frequent skirmishes in the press between the sides, including the sending of Ministry of Justice inspectors to Milan, etc. Once again, naturally, up to the fall of the Berlusconi government, from which date this type of news is included in that described immediately below.

6) ACTIONS OF MINISTER OF JUSTICE MANCUSO (MA): polemical announcements and inspections, negative reactions to both by those forces which supported the Dini government, in complete contrast to the approval of the parties of the Polo coalition which were by now in opposition. From 9 May 1995 to the traumatic epilogue of 19 October 1995.

For the last two families of events, which had judicial and institutional significance and no direct importance for the financial markets, it is difficult to identify a specific *a priori* – or «theoretical» if one prefers – link between the event and the anomalous variation in the lira exchange rate. This is particularly true for the reactions to Minister Mancuso's most controversial actions. The statistical evidence in this study confirms in part (see the subsequent section) the statistical significance of these two classes of events on the exchange rate variations. The markets probably consider this type of events as being representative of the solidity of the government and the continuity of economic policies.

7) ACTIONS OF DINI GOVERNMENT (GD) this category groups numerous events, which are not necessarily homogeneous with each other. These events include, by way of a very cursory summary: all the phases of the presentation of the government to Parliament, from the reactions to the appointment to those which unravelled during the various phases of the vote of confidence, with the see-saw attitude of the Polo; the events related to the drafting, preliminary discussion and Parliamentary approval of the Dini government's three major tasks: the minibudget, approved in March, the reform of Italy's pension system, agreed with the trade unions at the start of May and approved by Parliament in August, and the 1996 Budget Law. This category includes the failure of the vote of no-confidence in the Dini government in October 1995.

8) EASING OF TENSION BETWEEN THE POLO AND ULIVO COALITIONS (SC). This category encompasses a small group of events relating to the uncertainties on holding a «conference on rules» (tavolo delle regole) in addition to a couple of events within the Polo delle Libertà which appear to have influenced the lira exchange rate.

9) PUBLIC FINANCE AND INTEREST RATE ANNOUNCEMENTS (FP). This is another heterogeneous group of events which is basically quantitative in nature but which the reaction of the financial markets to the news makes appropriate for inclusion among the qualitative events. This type of events includes both announcements regarding the trend of public finances, and also increases and reductions in interest rates, and as such were directly relevant for the public finances as a result of the consequences on the public debt interest service.

10) NEWS ON INFLATION (PC). This item groups the headlines of «*Il Sole 24 Ore*» which largely give notice of the various press

releases on consumer and factory-gate inflation and in part furnish indirect news on inflation, such as, for example, the case of the very quick conclusion, without strikes, on a new national wage agreement for engineering workers in spring 1994.

4. - An Empirical Model of Impact of News on the Lira-DM Exchange Rate

In Section 2 we examined the prevalent theories regarding the influence of news on exchange-rate variations. We started to speak of this argument from somewhat «far off», i.e., referring to two well-known theoretical formulations used to specify exchange rate equations, those of Mundell-Fleming and of the monetary model. In these two formulations, exchange rates are explained by the relative levels of economic activity, interest rates, the money supply and inflation. The variables influence the exchange rates with a positive or negative sign according to the body of theory to which they refer. The opposite effect that the same variables can produce in the exchange-rate dynamics is the main reason for our approach «from afar», to draw the reader's attention immediately to the fact that the high-frequency exchange-rate fluctuations do not have unequivocal determinants.

Again for the same reason, concluding that section, we also recalled the influence of non-economic variables, in particular those of political news, speculative bubbles, with the possibility that, in specific market phases, the operators follow trading strategies which it is difficult to derive from those proposed in economic theory and elaborate interpretative models of the market dynamics in which economists can identify much *ad-hockery*. This sort of «theoretical anarchy» is aggravated by the heterogeneity of the expectation formation mechanisms, mentioned in Section 2 and originally elaborated in Tivegna [45]. Included in this context is also the role of the market sentiment in determining different exchange rate dynamics or movements of differing intensities in response to the same stimuli, but in different phases of the markets' life.

In this section we study the interpretative validity of the classes of events we drew up in the previous section for a model to determine the lira-DM exchange rate (lire per DM) estimated on daily data with an elementary specification in which the percentage variation of the lira-DM exchange rate is explained by the percentage variation in the DM-dollar exchange rate (DMs per dollar) and by a rather long series of political and economic news, with the former prevailing.

The base specification of the estimated linear model is as follows:

$$(1) \quad £/DM = \gamma_0 + \gamma_1 DM/\$ + \gamma_2 CP + \gamma_3 CI + \gamma_4 CG + \gamma_5 VE + \gamma_6 GD + \gamma_7 MA +$$

$$+ \gamma_8 SC + \gamma_9 FP + \gamma_{10} PC + \gamma_{11} CORR(-1) + \gamma_{12} DU17 + \gamma_{13} CR +$$

$$+ \gamma_{14} PCONS + \gamma_{15} PPRO + \gamma_{16} PROD + \gamma_{17} RBOT + \gamma_{18} M2 + \varepsilon$$

The values fo the symbols are given in Table 1 while the estimates of the coefficients from γ_1 to γ_{12} are given in Table 2. The economic-quantitative variables associated with the variables from γ_{13} to γ_{18} have produced mixed results and will require further fine-tuning in a second version of this study. The error term of *(1)* is distributed normally with zero mean and non-constant variance, as unequivocally confirmed by the heteroscedasticity tests shown in Table 2 (parts *A*, *B*, *C*). The model was estimated first by ordinary least squares (*OLS*) making the estimate of the standard error of the regression coefficients more «robust» by using White's [48] method to determine with greater precision the statistical significance of the variables included in the estimate and then by maximum likelihood attributing the variance a generalised autoregressive conditional heteroscedastic scheme (*GARCH*) (Bollerslev [4], [5]).

The *GARCH* estimates were made both directly, estimating the first 12 parameters of the equations *(1)* by maximum likelihood using the original historical series (corrected with the relative standard error to make the estimated parameters comparable amongst

TABLE 1

VARIABLES USED IN THE LIRE-DM EXCHANGE RATE
VARIABLE AND SOURCES[a]

1	*CI*:	Institutional conflicts, *.
2	*CG*:	Judicial conflicts, *.
3	*CORR*:	Difference between the exchange rate at Banca d'Italia's 14:15 fixing and that of Bankers Trust at 21:00 (Sources *S24O* and Datastream).
4	*CP*:	Conflicts within Polo coalition, *.
5	*CR*:	Judicial troubles of Berlusconi brothers, *.
6	*DM/$*:	DM-$ exchange rate, Banca d'Italia cross of 14:15, source *S24O*.
7	*DU*17:	Dummy for 17 March 1995, «Black Friday».
8	*DUAGO*94:	Dummy for 12/08/94.
9	*DUDIC*94:	Dummy for 8 and 9 December 1994.
10	*FP*:	Public finance news, *, source *S24O*.
11	*GD*:	Dini government, *.
12	*£/M*:	Lira-DM exchange rate, Banca d'Italia 14:15 fixing, source *S24O*.
13	*M2*:	Banca d'Italia's announcements on money supply, source *S24O*.
14	*MA*:	Actions of Minister of Justice Mancuso, *.
15	*PC*:	News on inflation[b], *.
16	*PCONS*:	ISTAT announcements on consumer-price inflation[b], source *S24O*.
17	*PPRO*:	ISTAT announcements on output prices[b], source *S24O*.
18	*PROD*:	Differences between Confindustria's «flash» estimates of industrial production and the final figures for the previous two months (source, CSC Confindustria.
19	*RBOT*:	Rates of three-month BOT notes at fortnightly auction, source *S24O*.
20	*SC*:	Lessening of political tension, *.
21	*VE*:	Electoral results, *.

[a] A lengthy description of the qualitative variables (which are included in the estimates as trichotomic variables, i.e., which can have a value of 0, +1 , and –1) is given in Section 3. The source for such variables is *Il Sole 24 Ore* (*S24O*) and they are indicated by *.
[b] The difference between *PC* and *PCONS* is as follows: the former includes various events regarding consumer-price, wholesale and factory-gate inflation reported by *S24O*, including ISTAT's quantitative monthly announcements on prices; the latter variable, on the other hand, includes only the quantitative announcements on the inflations variables.

them), and also by using instead of the DM-dollar exchange rate variable an instrumental variable consisting of the value of this variable forecast by a very simple *GARCH* model (1,1). This additional estimate was made in order to purify the direct estimates of possible distortions from simultaneity, as the model's two exchange rates could be influenced by the same unobserved component.

TABLE 2

EQUATIONS OF LIRA-DM EXCHANGE RATE:
ECONOMETRIC ESTIMATES
Part A: whole sample

Estimates	OLS		GARCH (1,1)		GARCH (1,1) INSTR. VAR.	
Equation no.	(1)	(2)	(3)	(4)	(5)	(6)
No. observations	444	440	444	440	444	440
COST	−0.0361	−0.0637*	−0.0619*	−0.0840*	−0.0597*	−0.0109
DM/$	−0.4299*	−0.4946*	−0.3692*	−0.3993*	−0.3527*	−0.4052*
CORR(−1)	−0.3777*	−0.3939*	−0.3664*	−0.4000*	−0.3841*	−0.4018*
CP	0.0783*	0.0906*	0.0852*	0.0954*	0.0870*	0.1023*
CI	0.1333*	0.1505*	0.0986*	0.1119*	0.0959*	0.1140*
VE	0.0968*	0.1097*	0.0789*	0.1179*	0.1052*	0.1169*
FP	0.1274*	0.1557*	0.1000*	0.1229*	0.1066*	0.1261*
DU17	0.2297*		0.3821*		0.3711*	
GD	0.1350*	0.1663*	0.1053*	0.1097*	0.0988*	0.1199*
MA	0.0780*	0.0902*	0.0668*	0.0771*	0.0696*	0.0752*
CG	0.0535[a]	0.0640*	0.0551*	0.0658*	0.0575*	0.0648*
SC	0.0318*	0.0346*	0.0383*	0.0404*	0.0362*	0.0402*
PC	0.0728*	0.1011*	0.0540*	0.0577*	0.0526*	0.0613*
W			0.0210*	0.0113*	0.0182*	0.0216*
AL			0.2006*	0.1284*	0.2009*	0.1436*
BE			0.7410*	0.8453*	0.7529*	0.7946*
R**2 corr	0.688	0.699				
Autoc.[b]	1.222	0.195				
Heter.[c]	66.509	45.271				
ARCH test CHI**2	41.697	27.021				
F	3.619	2.268				
Max-Likelihood value			109.839	79.519	110.743	76.764

* 99% significance
[a] 95% significance
[b] Godfrey LM test for autocorrelation
[c] Test based on regression of square residuals.

TABLE 2 *continued*

Part B: Berlusconi government

Estimates	OLS		GARCH (1,1)		GARCH (1,1) INSTR. VAR.	
Equation no.	(7)	(8)	(9)	(10)	(11)	(12)
No. observations	194	194	194	194	194	194
COST	−0.1155*	−0.1378*	−0.1183*	−0.1478*	−0.1219*	−0.1476*
DM/$	−0.4043*	−0.3462*	−0.4197*	−0.3454*	−0.4353*	−0.3357*
CORR(−1)	−0.4634*	−0.4971*	−0.5303*	−0.4977*	−0.5252*	−0.5321*
CP	0.2245*	0.2234*	0.2119*	0.2268*	0.2289*	0.1943*
CI	0.1538*	0.1444*	0.1631*	0.1486*	0.1736*	0.1541*
VE	0.1398*	0.1294*	0.2513*	0.1805*	0.2026*	0.2719*
FP	0.1438*	0.1123*	0.1669*	0.1099[a]	0.1813*	0.1294*
CG	0.1715*	0.1754*	0.1623*	0.1611[a]	0.1673*	0.1560*
PC	0.0333*	0.0273*	0.014*	0.029	0.0177	0.0023
DAGO94		2.6619*		0.0879*		0.1047*
DDIC94		2.2461*		0.0966		0.1355*
W			0.3750*	0.2988	0.0042	0.3393[a]
AL			0.0002	0.0005	0.0264	0.0375
BE			0.0001	0.0037	0.0009	0.0006
R**2 corr	0.622	0.68				
Autoc.[b]	0.819	0.32				
Heter.[c]	25.51	0.062				
ARCH test CHI**2	5.382	13.694				
F	0.411	1.082				
Max-Likelihood value			5.689	14.884	6.569	14.581

* 99% significance
[a] 95% significance
[b] Godfrey LM test for autocorrelation
[c] Test based on regression of square residuals.

TABLE 2 *continued*

Part C: Dini government

Estimates	OLS		GARCH (1,1)		GARCH (1,1) INSTR. VAR.	
Equation no.	(13)	(14)	(15)	(16)	(17)	(18)
No. observations	444	440	444	440	444	440
COST	–0.0047	–0.0382	–0.0263	–0.0399*a*	–0.0053	–0.0403
DM/$	–0.4771*	–0.5616*	–0.5525*	–0.6473*	–0.5435*	–0.6113*
CORR(–1)	–0.3078*	–0.3183*	–0.2318*	–0.2320*	–0.2670*	–0.2850*
CI	0.1260*	0.1393*	0.1957*	0.2302*	0.1809*	0.2093*
VE	0.0909*	0.1039*	0.0919*	0.1104*	0.1018*	0.1148*
FP	0.1357*	0.1714*	0.1169*	0.1394*	0.1216*	0.1397*
DU17	0.2519*		0.4636*		0.5000*	
GD	0.1419*	0.1803*	0.1510*	0.1854*	0.1504*	0.1744*
MA	0.0886*	0.1067*	0.0415	0.0557	0.0419	0.0522
SC	0.0373	0.0407	0.0567*	0.0625*	0.0456*	0.0515*
PC	0.0799*	0.1185*	0.0813*	0.0898*	0.0897*	0.1013*
W			0.0145*	0.0110*	0.0682*	0.0820*
AL			0.5364*	0.3038*	0.6522*	0.5494*
BE			0.4403*	0.5867*	0.1531*	0.2081*
R**2 corr	0.726	0.756				
Autoc.*b*	0.066	2.386				
Heter.*c*	32.754	28.219				
ARCH test						
CHI**2	20.645	16.24				
F	1.702	1.319				
Max-Likelihood value			104.816	82.798	98.642	77.165

* 99% significance
a 95% significance
b Godfrey LM test for autocorrelation
c Test based on regression of square residuals.

Equation *(1)* has a dummy variable positioned on 17 March 1996, the «Black Friday», when the lira fell 5.68% against the DM in one day, without any apparent reason. This anomalous data item disturbs the estimates considerably, particularly the *GARCH* estimates, which attempt to model the variance starting from the square of errors. For this reason, our estimates were made with two different samples: a sample with all the data used, including «Black Friday», which was «dummied», and a sample which did not include the data for 17, 20, 21 and 22 March 1995, when, as mentioned above, the lira fell on 17 March and then recovered ground in the following days. Furthermore, neither of the samples included the period between the resignation of Berlusconi and the appointment of Dini to form a new government – when President Scalfaro was consulting the political parties – as the lira «noise-driven» turbulence is somewhat anomalous. The estimates of the two samples indicated above vary quite considerably (Table 2) and in one case quite significantly transgress the conditions of stability implicit in the *GARCH* model.

The estimated model bears only a partial resemblance to the standard theoretical representations of the exchange rate determination models mentioned in Section 2 which, as already noted, intend to offer only a representation of the interpretative models which foreign exchange dealers follow in their actions, but with all the caveats indicated in Tivegna [45] on the asymmetries of the error terms and market sentiment. The two base models of Section 2 (the Fleming-Mundell and monetary models) represent two different theoretical reference models which are present – in unhomogeneous combinations and with differing approximations – in the mind of foreign exchange market participants (strategists and traders), while in the *(1)* model, the lira exchange-rate response to new information which flows into the market in time and which is evaluated and implemented by the operators in accordance with their own reference economic model – which, we reiterate, is not homogeneous for all – as regards economic news and in accordance with their own «instinct», operating experience and prevailing market sentiment as regards political news.

The model's most important driving variable is the DM-dollar exchange rate (DM/$) according to an empirical rule which is well known also to the «public at large» which states that «if the dollar is strong so is the lira». And vice versa. This phenomenon is explained rather simply by dealers' normal trading strategy according to which if, for example, there is an autonomous flow of funds from the dollar to the DM, the latter appreciates vis-à-vis the US currency and – automatically and without any arbitrage intervention – vis-à-vis the other European currencies which look to the DM for leadership. Moreover, this movement is compounded by the action of the dealers because it is worthwhile buying the currency which is appreciating, the DM, to protect one's own stock of dollars.

In estimating the parameters of model *(1)* we started out from the OLS which, not surprisingly, were affected by strong heteroscedasticity above all as a result of the violent fluctuations the lira experienced in our reference period and which our model could explain only in part. To eliminate the consequences of the heteroscedasticity, the model was re-estimated correcting the coefficient standard error estimate by White's [48] method. Finally, a *GARCH* (1,1) model was used to further verify the weight and significance of the news variables used and to model the stochastic variance of what could not be explained by the former. As we have already noted above, the *GARCH* estimates were carried out also with an instrument of the DM-dollar exchange rate.

Summarising the results, which we shall describe in greater detail below, almost all the political news variables were significant and with the expected sign while of the economic news, only the variable which measures the impact of public finance announcements maintained a high level of significance in the two types of empirical verification. The significance of news on the various types of inflation and industrial production was more fluctuating, while news on interest rates and money supply was not significant[19]. Announcements of increases in the interest rate of BOT Treasury notes at auction were included in the public finance news vector, as an increase in interest rates engenders a negative impact on the lira as it encourages fears for Italy's financial stability[20].

---

[19] For those reasons the coefficient estimates of the impact of industrial production, industrial prices and money were not included in our tables.

[20] As indicated in Section 2, the impact of changes in interest rates on the exchange rate can have either a positive or negative sign depending on the reference model (Fleming-Mundell or monetary). In the case of Italy, i.e., a country with a high public debt, an increase in interest rates should have a negative impact on the exchange rate. As noted above, movements of exchange rates are driven also by reputation effects. During the period of the lira revaluation subsequent to the conclusion of the Parliamentary passage of the 1996 Budget Law, there was a modest flow of funds into the lira, by virtue of the high yield of Italian lira-denominated notes and in expectation of a reduction in interest rates. Here again, the sign of the impact of changes in interest rates on the exchange rate was ambiguous. The lack of statistical significance of the pure and simple inclusion of changes in interest rates in our equations is therefore no surprise. A future re-formulation of our results would do well to take also into account the expected capital gains.

TABLE 3

RANKING OF THE IMPACT OF THE SINGLE VARIABLES*

	OLS		GARCH (1,1)		GARCH (1,1)	INSTR. VAR.
	Part A: whole sample					
	444 Obs.	440 Obs.	444 Obs.	440 Obs.	444 Obs.	440 Obs.
1.	*DM-$*	*DM-$*	*DM-$*	*CORR(−1)*	*CORR(−1)*	*DM-$*
2.	*CORR(−1)*	*CORR(−1)*	*CORR(−1)*	*DM/$*	*DM/$*	*CORR(−1)*
3.	*GD*	*GD*	*GD*	*FP*	*FP*	*FP*
4.	*CI*	*CI*	*FP*	*VE*	*VE*	*GD*
5.	*FP*	*FP*	*CI*	*CI*	*GD*	*VE*
6.	*VE*	*VE*	*CP*	*GD*	*CI*	*CI*
7.	*CP*	*CP*	*VE*	*CP*	*CP*	*CP*
8.	*MA*	*MA*	*MA*	*MA*	*MA*	*MA*
9.	*PC*	*PC*	*CG*	*CG*	*CG*	*CG*
10.	*CG*	*CG*	*PC*	*PC*	*PC*	*PC*
11.	*SC*	*SC*	*SC*	*SC*	*SC*	*SC*
12.	−	−	−	−	−	−
	Part B: Berlusconi government					
	194 Obs.**		194 Obs.**		194 Obs.**	
1.	*CORR(−1)*	*CORR(−1)*	*CORR(−1)*	*CORR(−1)*	*CORR(−1)*	*CORR(−1)*
2.	*DM-$*	*DM-$*	*DM-$*	*DM-$*	*DM-$*	*DM-$*
3.	*CP*	*CP*	*VE*	*CO*	*CP*	*VE*
4.	*CG*	*CG*	*CP*	*VE*	*VE*	*CP*
5.	*CI*	*CI*	*FP*	*CG*	*FP*	*CG*
6.	*FP*	*VE*	*CI*	*CI*	*CI*	*CI*
7.	*VE*	*FP*	*CG*	*FP*	*CG*	*FP*
8.	*PC*	*PC*	*PC*	*PC*	*PC*	*PC*
	Part C: Dini government					
	444 Obs.	440 Obs.	444 Obs.	440 Obs.	444 Obs.	440 Obs.
1.	*DM-$*	*DM-$*	*DM-$*	*DM-$*	*DM-$*	*DM-$*
2.	*CORR(−1)*	*CORR(−1)*	*CORR(−1)*	*CORR(−1)*	*CORR(−1)*	*CORR(−1)*
3.	*GD*	*GD*	*CI*	*CI*	*CI*	*CI*
4.	*FP*	*FP*	*GD*	*GD*	*GD*	*GD*
5.	*CI*	*CI*	*FP*	*FP*	*FP*	*FP*
6.	*VE*	*MA*	*VE*	*VE*	*VE*	*VE*
7.	*MA*	*VE*	*PC*	*PC*	*PC*	*PC*
8.	*PC*	*PC*	*SC*	*SC*	*SC*	*MA*
9.	*SC*	*SC*	*MA*	*MA*	*MA*	*SC*

* See Table 1 for the symbol legend.
** The two columns of this section refer to slightly different equations. See Table 2, Part B.

We will briefly discuss the construction of the variables for political and economic news (solely regarding public finances and inflation). Upstream of this there is a long and meticolous work reconstructing events, classifying and entering them in a data archive which could be used on other occasions for empirical verifications of phenomena for which «political noise» is significant (Chiofi - Tivegna [9]).

The estimates of the first equations and the interpretative analyses with them began in spring 1995 – to attempt to explain the violent fluctuations of the lira in February-March 1995 – with the news available at that time and have been repeatedly tested, even for forecasting, with the flow of new data. In this work of continuous updating, the criteria for identifying and classifying the significant events have been refined with the addition of new classes of types and with the transfer of individual events between the various classes, in a process of improvement which is still in progress, as the database (Chiofi - Tivegna [9]) from which all the information used in this study is taken, is continually updated.

This work commenced with a choice of events from the first two pages of «*Il Sole 24 Ore*» (*S24O*) – and occasionally from the first two of the newspaper's *Finance and Markets* section – and with the attribution of the various event to the relevant day (naturally the previous one to the date of publication of *S24O*). After having identified the individual events – particularly those of «political noise» – preliminary statistical analyses were carried out to verify the possible sign of the effect of a given political event on the exchange rate. The signs always conformed to those expected by market players and in particular to that type of economic theory described in Section 2. At times, only the statistical significance was lacking, but the sign maintained the expected value. Having done this, vectors were constructed for the «trinary» variables (+1, 0, –1) in which the value zero was attributed to the absence of the event, the value +1 if the event in question caused a weakening of the lira and the value –1 if it caused a strengthening. Equation *(1)* also contains the economic-quantitative variables which produced mixed results.

These were attributed with the relative values for the days in which they were announced while on other days zero was attributed.

And finally we come to a description of the empirical results. Econometric verification was carried out on two samples of daily data both between 28 March 1994, when the Polo coalition won the general election, and 29 December 1995, when the Dini government first resigned at the end of the Parliamentary passage of the 1996 Budget Law. The two samples differ from one another for four dates, 17 March 1995 (the «Black Friday» when the lira fell by 5.63% at the end of the approval of the minibudget for no apparent reason) and the three subsequent working days (when the lira partially recovered the ground lost on 17 March). The first sample includes 444 data items, the second 440. Neither sample includes the period of President Scalfaro's consultations for the formation of a new «truce» government, namely from 23 December 1994 (the day after the Berlusconi government's resignation) and 13 January 1995 (when, in the late evening, Dini was asked to form a new government).

These two samples, embracing both the Berlusconi and Dini governments, were further subdivided into two subsamples for each government. The first therefore embraces the period 28 March 1994-22 December 1994 (Berlusconi government), the second from 16 January 1995 to 29 December 1995 (Dini government). Only the Dini subsample, which includes the «Black Friday», gives rise in turn to a further two subsamples.

Three levels of empirical verification were carried out on all these samples. We started out with *OLS*, which proved to be very heteroscedastic, and the estimates of coefficient standard errors, distorted by heteroscedasticity, were therefore corrected using White's [48] method to obtain confirmation of the statistical significance already noted in the estimates using *OLS*. The second level of empirical verification sought to eliminate the problem of heteroscedasticity by modelling it: non-linear estimates were made using a model in which the variance was modelled according to a generalised autoregressive heteroscedasticity (the *Generalised Autoregressive Conditional Heteroscedasticity* model, *GARCH* of Bollerslev [4], [5])[21]. For the third level of empirical verification, an instrumental variable for the DM-dollar exchange rate was used in the *GARCH* model mentioned above to cleanse the relative variable from any possible bias of simultaneity. This instrumental variable was generated by a *GARCH* (1,1) model of the DM-dollar exchange rate.

Our purpose was threefold: first and foremost to verify at various levels and with an increasingly degree of sophistication, the significance of the different economic and political variables used in the model; secondly, to examine the volatility estimated by the *GARCH* models in the more turbulent phases experienced by the lira and finally to establish a ranking of the relative importance of the economic and political variables examined.

Table 2 (*A, B, C*) contains the *OLS* and *GARCH* (1, 1) estimates of equation *(1)* for the first 12 parameters only. The estimates were made using standardised variables with their respective standard error in order to facilitate comparison between the coefficients estimated in the same equation and with those of the other equations, in the spirit of traditional beta coefficients (see, for example, Goldberger [25], pp. 197-8). We note that the lira-DM exchange rate was explained to a considerable degree by the dollar's exchange rate with the latter and by the correction of the variations which took place the previous day between Banca d'Italia's fixing at 14:15 and that of New York, at 15:00 local time, by Bankers Trust, which generally corresponds to 21:00 in Italy.

The role of this latter regressor in our equation deserves some comment. In the period we studied, the turbulence of the lira was

---

[21] For further references see, for example, Mills T.C. [40], Chapters 3 and 4. The *GARCH* (1,1) model used for this study is as follows:

$$y_t = \gamma_0 + \sum_{i=0}^{n} \gamma_i x_{it} + \varepsilon_t$$

$$\varepsilon_t \approx N(0, \sigma_t^2)$$

$$\sigma_t^2 = \omega + \alpha \varepsilon_{t-1}^2 + \beta \sigma_{t-1}^2$$

where the x_is represent the model's independent variables (in our case the variables of the equation *(1)*).

at its peak and hence it is not surprising that there were some variations, sometimes quite significant, between the fixing in New York and that in Italy. Comparing, in terms of local time, the afternoon in Rome, we see that the overshooting is at its peak during the period of maximum turbulence (for example on 17 January 1995 the lira shed 11 points as the Polo announced first that it would abstain in any vote of confidence for the Dini government, and then changed its mind, or else the period 28 February-3 March 1995, when the Polo indicated its intention to vote the minibudget at the Senate on the 28th and 1st and then, on the 3rd, changed idea, with the lira shedding almost 50 lire overall, again vis-à-vis the dollar).

Let us now examine in more detail the estimates in Table 2 (*A, B, C*). We note, in general, that the test for the presence of autoregressive conditional heteroscedasticity (*ARCH*) confirms its presence in the models estimated with *OLS* for the entire sample and for the sample for the Dini government (Table 2, parts *A* and *C*) with both 444 and 440 observations, while it does not indicate the presence of *ARCH* errors in the various models estimated for the period of the Berlusconi government (Table 2, part *B*). This circumstance is somewhat surprising given that it is generally believed that this was a period of maximum turbulence for the lira exchange rate. The economic and political news variables used in the regression model for this period do manage, evidently, to furnish an exhaustive explanation of this turbulence, leaving no trace of any *ARCH* effects in the error terms.

A deeper investigation of the period of the Berlusconi government, in search of a final confirmation of the absence of *ARCH* effects, was estimated using a further model, which included two dummies on three days of particular turbulence in this period, the first on 12 August 1994 – at the end of strong tensions within the majority which formed the Berlusconi government, culminating with an increase in the discount rate – and the second on 8 and 9 December 1994, fraught with the tensions which had accumulated in the previous days with the serving of notice of judicial investigation on Berlusconi, the resignation of Di Pietro from the *Mani Pulite* pool and the start of the large-scale manoeuvres for the *ribaltone* (change of government majority) (Table 2, part *B*).

In all these models, as we mentioned above, no *ARCH* effects can be noted and, in fact, in estimating the *GARCH* (1, 1) model, the parameters for this model are not significant and the likelihood functions assume anomalous values at their peak (Table 2, part *B*).

As already observed for the *GARCH* (1, 1) models, the direct estimates on the coefficients of the models have been flanked by estimates made using an instrumental variable for the DM-dollar exchange rate (Table 2). The results are not significantly different and this indicates the robustness of the estimates and will allow us, below, to refer to the original *GARCH* models.

The significance of the coefficients of the economic and political news is in general good in all the models in Table 2. The variables *CR* (judicial troubles of Berlusconi brothers) and *PPI* (-split in *PPI* party) which should have been more significant for their possible repercussions on the government's stability, were either not significant or only moderately so. The results of these regressions are not shown. Note should be taken of the uncertain significance of the «political improvement» *SC*, the Mancuso variable *MA* and the inflation news variable for the period of the Berlusconi government only, when, moreover, inflation was stable or decelerating and the lira devaluation trend was still reasonable.

Graphs 3, 4 and 5 show the estimated volatility in the three equations (Table 2) which we have chosen to comment this phenomenon, respectively (4) for the entire period studied[22] (with a sample from which we have eliminated the observations for «Black Friday» and the three subsequent working days), (9) for the period of the Berlusconi government and (16) for the period of the Dini government which has experienced the same «amputation» as Graph 1 (equation 4). Graph 6 shows the volatility estimated by equation *(2)* for the entire sample (with the data for «Black

---

[22] All the complete samples, from 28 March 1994 to 29 December 1995, excluding the period between the resignation of the Berlusconi government, 22 December 1994, and 16 January 1996, when it was announced that Dini had been charged with forming a new government. The lira exchange rate in this period was in fact influenced by factors which it is difficult to model with the models which have managed to interpret the movements during the periods of the Berlusconi and Dini governments.

GRAPH 3

VOLATILITY OF LIRA-DM EXCHANGE RATE:
BERLUSCONI AND DINI GOVERNMENTS *GARCH* (1, 1) MODEL
Whole sample: 28.3.94-29.12.95 440 observations*

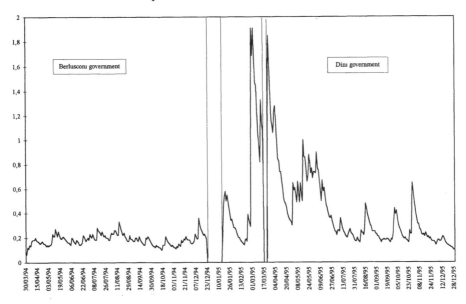

* Excluding 23.12.94-13.1.95: President Scalfaro's consultations and Black Friday (4 days).

Friday» and 3 subsequent working days); Graph 7 estimated by equation (8), shows the volatility for the Dini period similar to the previous graph.

Looking at Graph 3, it is immediately evident that the lira is much more volatile during the Dini period than that of Berlusconi. The graph's two peaks of volatility take place during the period from 27 February 1995 to the end of April. Volatility «takes off» on 28 February 1995 when the Polo indicated its willingness to support the minibudget in the lower house to then change its mind on 3 March 1995. Volatility then remains high in all the subsequent days and «explodes» between 14 and 15 March when the government loses a Parliamentary vote on the budget and is forced

GRAPH 4

VOLATILITY AND EXCHANGE RATES: BERLUSCONI GOVERNMENT
Exchange rate index: 28.3.94 = 100 Volatility: *Garch* (1, 1) from 28.3.94

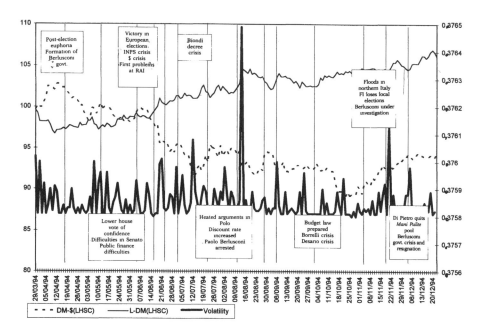

to resort to a vote of confidence to ensure the budget passes. These
events were examined with infra-daily frequency in Tivegna [46].
The budget then is approved but volatility remains high also in
the next few days. A similar trend can be seen also in Graph 6,
when volatility soars in the same days but peaks on «Black Friday». In this graph also, the volatility of the Dini period is much
higher than that of the Berlusconi period, albeit for more modest
values.

We shall now examine the volatility trends within the two periods, that of the Berlusconi government, in Graph 4, and that of
the Dini government, in Graph 5. Both the figures are related to
the same events as the graphs examined above.

During the Berlusconi period, volatility peaks around 12 August, at the end of a very difficult period of violent polemics in
the Polo which culminated in an increase in the discount rate on

GRAPH 5

VOLATILITY AND EXCHANGE RATES: DINI GOVERNMENT
Exchange rate index: 16.1.95 = 100
Volatility: *Garch* (1, 1) from 16.1.95-29.12.95*

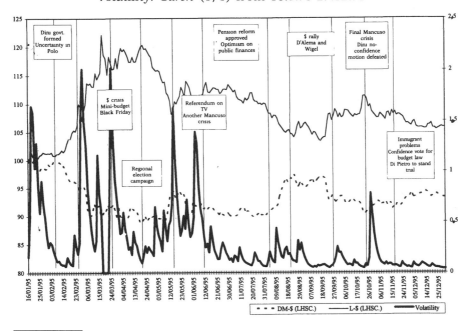

* Excluding Black Friday and the following days: 17.3.95-22.3.95

11 August. Prior to this, there was an initial increase in volatility: the market's initial euphoria for the victory of the Polo turned to delusion for the internal polemics between the Lega Nord and the other coalition parties. Later, volatility starts to increase again – after having diminished as a result of the successful conclusion of the negotiations within the Polo on the programme and distribution of ministerial posts – for the unexpected sentence of the Constitutional Court on pension reimbursements to be paid by the state pension institute INPS. Volatility then decreases, roughly around the time of the Polo's victory in the European Parliament elections, and then increases starting from mid-June to peak in August, as already mentioned, due to the strong increase in the level of political friction, both within and outside the government

GRAPH 6

VOLATILITY OF LIRA-DM EXCHANGE RATE:
BERLUSCONI AND DINI GOVERNMENTS *GARCH* (1, 1) MODEL
Whole sample: 28.3.94-29.12.95 444 observations*

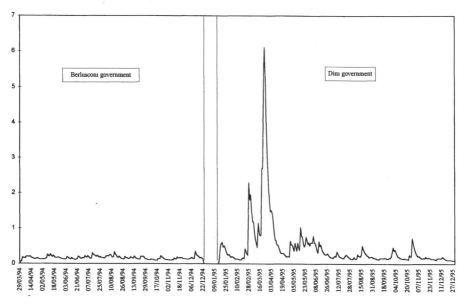

* Excluding 23.12.94-13.1.95: President Scalfaro's consultations.

majority. This period also saw the endless polemics concerning the Biondi Decree, the appointment of a new Board of Directors at the state broadcasting company RAI, the temporary arrest of Paolo Berlusconi, the government commercials broadcast by RAI and the conflict of interest engendered by Berlusconi's position as President of the Council of Ministers. After this peak, volatility falls until mid-November, only to increase again when notice of judicial investigation is served on Silvio Berlusconi and large-scale manoeuvres start to change the government majority.

The volatility of the lira during the period of the Dini government, Graph 5, is much more chequed, as already noted, compared with the period of the previous government headed by Silvio Berlusconi, Graph 4. There was a mini-peak between 30 Jan-

GRAPH 7

VOLATILITY OF LIRA-DM EXCHANGE RATE:
DINI GOVERNMENT *GARCH* (1, 1) MODEL
Whole sample: 28.3.94-29.12.95 444 observations

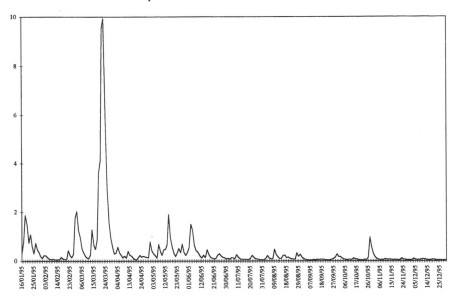

uary and 2 February, when the Senate was debating a vote of confidence for the Dini government, and in a period of strong friction between the President of the Republic and the Polo. There are later two peaks during the approval of the mini-budget in the lower house. Volatility then falls to a minimum in the period immediately preceding the European regional elections; it then starts to increase again during the final phase of the government-trade union negotiations on the reform of the pension system, reaching a pcak on 15 May when the lira rally comes to an end, also following the first signs of unease at the actions of Minister of Justice Mancuso. In early June there is a high peak of volatility caused probably by a strong and concentrated revaluation of the lira in parallel with a strengthening of the dollar produced by the co-ordinated intervention of the central banks

of the G-3. Volatility then decreases with another «small» explo-
sion during the mid-August intervention of the G-3 central banks
to support the dollar, which was not followed by an appreciation
of the lira. Small peaks, engendered by the imprudent statements
by Massimo D'Alema, general secretary of the Democratic Party
of the Left, and the German Minister of Finance Weigel preceded the final strong increase in volatility at the end of October
engendered by the vote of no-confidence in Minister of Justice
Mancuso and the Polo's attempt to pass a vote of no-confidence
in the Dini government right in the middle of the Parliamentary
passage of the 1996 Budget Law. The history of the volatility profile as shown in Graph 7 shows no substantial differences, this
graph uses the entire sample for the period of the Dini government, «Black Friday» included.

In conclusion, let us look at the ranking of the importance of
the economic and political variables in explaining the lira fluctuations. These are shown in Table 3 (parts *A, B, C*). As a summary
observation, we note that the DM-dollar exchange rate is principally the variable with the greatest weight while the variable correcting the greater (or lesser) exchange rate level in New York vis-
à-vis the Banca d'Italia's fixing (*CORR*) follows and in some cases precedes it. In the equations estimated for the entire period
(part *A* of Table 4), we see that the variables of the action of the
Dini government (*GD*), public finance announcements (*FP*) and
institutional conflicts (*CI*) and election victories carry the most
weight. The least important variables on the other hand are those
regarding judicial conflicts (*CG*), the consequences of the Mancuso case (*MA*) and the inflation rate (*PC*).

Table 4 also gives the results of equations estimated for the
periods of the Berlusconi (part *B*) and Dini (part *C*) governments.
Here the scenario undergoes a considerable change. In the Berlusconi period, the effects produced by conflicts within the Polo
(*CP*), by the election victories (*VE*) and by the judicial conflicts
(*CG*, mainly related to the Biondi Decree and tensions between
some leading members of the Polo and the investigating magistrates of the *Mani Pulite* pool) were to the fore. News on public
finance (*FP*) and inflation (*PC*) would appear to be less influent

than during the Dini period and the last variable is not even significant.

During the Dini period the hierarchy of the importance of effects changes completely and *pour cause*: leading the pack are the actions of the Dini government (*GD*), public finance news (*FP*) and institutional conflicts (*CI*). The variable *GD*, we would recall, contains a rather heterogeneous series of events which, however, revolve around the differences between the government's actions to stabilise the weight of the public debt on GDP and the Polo's oscillating attitude towards the government. The *FP* variable becomes significant during the Dini period because of the reasons indicated above and because of markets' increasing concern for the situation of Italy's public finances. We should not forget that the Dini government's principal task when appointed was to improve the state of Italy's public finances. The *CI* variable refers mainly to the animated polemics between members of the Polo coalition and President Scalfaro.

5. - Conclusions

This study has attempted to explain the recent fluctuations of the lira exchange rate with economic and political variables. The most important of the former is the DM-dollar exchange rate, as expected, followed by the corrections of the exchange rate and announcements on the trend of public finance variables and interest rates. The empirical results for the inflation rate show on average less significance.

The significance of this last variable turned out to be different in the two periods studied: those of the Berlusconi and Dini governments: greater in the latter than in the former. This results is no surprise given that in the first part of the Berlusconi period inflation had a descending trajectory and it remained low also during the second part of the period, even though it had begun to inch up. During the period of the Dini government however inflation had an ascending profile, the first strong increase was recorded in February 1995 and ran until autumn of that year, after which it fell only gradually. Thus, while the dynamics of inflation were not a problem during the Berlusconi period, during the Dini period the markets were more reactive to its trend.

Of the economic variables, the weight of changes in the lira exchange rate between that recorded by Banca d'Italia at its fixing of circa 14:15 vis-à-vis that at fixing at 21:00 by Bankers Trust in New York was very significant. This variable refers to the previous day and is included in the estimate with a negative sign, thus assuming the role of an «error correction» variable. The reason for this result lies in the high volatility of the lira exchange rate in the period studied in response to the political events identified in this study. The changes in the exchange rate which took place between 14:15 and 21:00 Rome time were, on days of particular turbulence, in excess of 15 lire per DM and these were in part corrected on the following day. On average, these corrections amounted to 40%, as indicated by the non-standardised coefficients of equations *(3)* and *(4)* (in Graph 2 the coefficients are standardised with the standard error).

The empirical verifications have been carried out in this study with the relation described in equation *(1)*, estimated on daily data with OLSs – using White's [48] correction to estimate the coefficients' standard errors and thus mitigate the effects of heteroscedasticity – and non-linear estimation methods for coefficients and error term variance whose movements were estimated using a generalised autoregressive heteroscedastic model (*GARCH*, Bollerslev [4], [5]) described in footnote 2). The *GARCH* estimate was also carried out in two stages, using an instrumental variable to eliminate possible distortion from simultaneity in the coefficient of the DM-dollar variable. Our model includes economic variables – mentioned above – and political variables: both are described and classified in Section 3 and are shown in detail on a day-to-day basis and by category, in Tivegna [45]. The estimates – discussed in Section 4 together with a description of the variable construction methodology – served first and foremost to establish the statistical significance of the political and economic news recorded during the periods of the Berlusconi and Dini governments. In the models, whose estimates are collected in Table 2, there appear only the variables (amongst those of equation *(1))* which turned out to be significant in either all or most of the equations estimated. These estimates were used to draw the conditional volatility of the *GARCH* models – in the graphs in Section 4 – and to establish a ranking for the economic and political variables taken into consideration (shown in Table 2).

A description of the empirical results of this study is given in Section 4. We shall merely summarise them here. The variables with the greatest explanatory power in the lira-DM exchange rate trend were the DM-dollar exchange rate and the correction of the overshooting of the exchange rate at 21:00 in New York compared with that at 14:15 in Rome. Of the economic variables considered in forms of non-quantitative announcement – derived from the headlines of the first two pages of *Il Sole 24 Ore* – those on public finances had the prevalent weight for the entire sample and for those of the Dini period (Table 3), and less significance during the period of the Berlusconi government. Of the political variables – recorded in the same form of event described in the first two pages of the newspaper – those with the greatest weight for the entire period examined were institutional conflicts *(CI)*, the Dini government's actions to stabilise the public accounts *(GD)* and the election victories *(VE)*. Those with the least weight were related to the improvement in the political climate *(SC)*, the actions of the Minister of Justice Mancuso *(MA)* and judicial conflicts *(CG)*.

This ranking is partially modified when one passes from the sample as a whole to the two subsamples for the Berlusconi and Dini periods. In the Berlusconi period, not surprisingly, the most important political variables are those of conflicts within the Polo coalition *(CP)* and between the latter and the *Mani Pulite* pool of investigating magistrates *(CG)*. The Dini period also reserves no surprises: the most important political news is that regarding economic policy measures *(CD)*, the mini-budget and reform of Italy's pension system, 1996 Budget Law and the Polo's Parliamentary «ambushes» (during the debate and vote of confidence in February 1995 and during the attempt to pass a no-confidence motion in October 1995). News regarding institutional conflicts (generally the polemics between the Polo and President Scalfaro) and the election victories are also very important.

Finally, turning our attention to the conditional volatility (after having taken into account the effects of all the explanatory variables), this was unarguably higher in the period of the Dini government than during that of Berlusconi and the reasons would appear to be attributable to the hyper-sensitivity of the markets and the extremely high level of political fighting which distinguished the period. The peaks can be observed in the final phases of the approval of the mini-budget between the end of February and the «Black Friday» of 17 March 1995, probably as a result of the Polo's vacillating stance in a Parliament in which the government could muster only the narrowest of majorities.

BIBLIOGRAPHY

[1] AGMON T. - FINDLAY C., «Domestic Political Risk», *Financial Analysts Journal*, November-December, 1982, pp. 74-7.

[2] ALLVINE F.C. - O'NEILL D.E., «Stock market returns and the presidential election cycle. Implications for market efficiency», *Financial Analysts Journal*, September-October 1980, pp. 49-56.

[3] BAILLIE R.T. - McMAHON P., *The Foreign Exchange Market*, Cambridge (MA), Cambridge University Press, 1989.

[4] BOLLERSLEV T., «Generalized Autoregressive Heteroskedasticity», *Journal of Econometrics*, vol. 31, 1986.

[5] — —, «A Conditionally Heteroskedastic Time Series Model for Speculative Prices and Rates of Return», *Review of Economics and Statistics*, vol. 69, 1987.

[6] BOMHOFF E.J. - KORTEWEG P., «Exchange Rate Variability and Monetary Policy Under Rational Expectations. Some Euro-American Experience 1973-1979», *Journal of Monetary Economics*, vol. 11, 1983.

[7] BRANSON W.H., «Macroeconomic Determinants of Real Exchange Risk», in HERRING R.J. (ed.), *Managing Foreign Exchange Risk*, Cambridge, Cambridge University Press, 1983.

[8] BUITER W.H. - MARSTON R.C., *International Policy Coordination*, Cambridge (MA), Cambridge University Press, 1985.

[9] CHIOFI G. - TIVEGNA M., *Una banca dati per lo studio del tasso di cambio lira-DM, mark 1.00*, Università di Roma «Tor Vergata», 1996.

[10] CIFARELLI G., «Market efficiency, exchange rates and news. Model specification and econometric identification», *Financial Analysts Journal*, September-October 1980, pp. 49-56.

[11] — —, «Sulle determinanti degli errori di previsione a termine nel mercato dei cambi», *Quaderni del Dipartimento di Economia Politica*, n. 99, 1990.

[12] COPELAND L.S., «The Pound Sterling/US Dollar Exchange Rate and the News», *Economic Letters*, vol. 15, 1984.

[13] — —, *Exchange Rates and International Finance*, 2nd edn., Addison-Wesley, 1994.

[14] CORNELL B., «Money Supply Announcements, Interest Rates: Another View», *Journal of International Money and Finance*, n. 56, 1983.

[15] DAVIDSON J., «Econometric Modelling of the Sterling Effective Exchange Rate», *Review of Economic Studies*, vol. 211, 1985.

[16] DERAVI M.K. - GREGOROWICZ P. - HEGJI C.E., «Balance of Trade Announcements and Movements in Exchange Rates», *Southern Economic Journal*, n. 55, 1988, pp. 279-87.

[17] DIAMONTE R.L. - LIEW J.M. - STEVENS R.L., «Political Risk in Emerging and Developed Markets», *Financial Analysts Journal*, May-June 1996, pp. 71-6.

[18] DOUKAS S. - LIFELAND D., «Exchange Rates and the Role of the Trade Balance Account», *Managerial Finance*, n. 20, 1994, pp. 67-78.

[19] EDERINGTON L. - LEE S., «How Markets Process Information: News Releases and Volatility», *Journal of Finance*, n. 43, 1993, pp. 1161-91.

[20] EDWARDS S., «Exchange Rates, Market Efficiency and New Information», *Economic Letters*, vol. 9, 1982.

[21] — —, «Floating Exchange Rates, Expectations and New Information», *Journal of Monetary Economics*, 1983.

[22] — —, «Exchange Rates and News: a Multicurrency Approach», *Journal of International Money and Finance*, vol. 3, 1983.

[23] ENGEL C. - FRANKEL J.A., «Why Interest Rates React to Monetary Announcements: an Explanation from the Foreign Exchange Market», *Journal of Monetary Economics*, vol. 13, 1984.

[24] ENGLE R.E., «Autoregressive Conditional Heteroskedasticity with Estimates of the Variance of UK Inflation», *Econometria*, 1982, pp. 987-1008.

[25] ERB C.B. - HARVEY C.R. - VISKANTA T.E., «The Influence of Political, Economic and Financial Risk on Expected Fixed-Income Returns», *Journal of Fixed Income*, 1986, pp. 7-30.

[26] FRENKEL J., «Flexible Exchange Rates, Prices and the Role of News: Lessons from the 1970's», *Journal of Political Economy*, n. 89, 1981, pp. 665-705.

[27] FIORENTINI R., «Exchange Rates and News: the Case of the Italian Lira», *Quaderno n. 32 del Dipartimento di Scienze Economiche Marco Fanno*, Università di Padova, 1994.

[28] FLOOD R.P. - ROSE A.K., «Fixing Exchange Rates: a Virtual Quest for Fundamentals», *NBER, Working Paper*, n. 163, 1993.

[29] GOLDBERGER A.S., *Econometric Theory*, New York, John Wiley & Sons Inc., 1964.

[30] HALLWOOD P.C. - MACDONALD R., *International Money and Finance*, 2nd edn., Oxford, Blackwell, 1994.

[31] HARDOUVELIS G., «Econometric News, Exchange Rates and Interest Rates», *Journal of International Money and Finance*, n. 7, 1988, pp. 25-35.

[32] HOBBS G.R. - RILEY W.B., «Profiting from a Presidential Election», *Financial Analysts Journal*, March-April, 1984, pp. 46-52.

[33] HOGAN, K. - MELVIN M. - ROBERTS D., «Trade Balance News and the Exchange Rate: Is There a Political Signal?», *Journal of International Money and Finance*, supplement, vol. 10, 1991, pp. 90-99.

[34] IRWIN D., «Trade Deficit Announcements, Interventions and the Dollar», *Economic Letters*, n. 31, 1989, pp. 257-62.

[35] ITO T. - ROLEY V.V., «News from the US and Japan. Which Moves the Yen/Dollar Exchange Rate?», *Journal of Monetary Economics*, n. 19, 1987, pp. 255-77.

[36] MACDONALD R., «Some Tests of Rational Expectations Hypothesis in the Foreign Exchange Market», *Scottish Journal of Political Economy*, vol. 30, 1983.

[37] — —, «Tests of Efficiency and the Impact of New in Three Foreign Exchange Markets», *Bulletin of Economic Research*, n. 35, 1983.

[38] MACDONALD R. - TORRANCE T.S., «Some Survey Based Tests of Uncovered Interest Parity», in MACDONALD R. - TAYLOR M.P. (eds.), *Exchange Rates and Open Economy Macroeconomics*, Oxford, Blackwell, 1989.

[39] MACDONALD R. - MILBOURNE R., «Recent Developments in Monetary Theory», in GREENAWAY D. - BLEANEY M. - STEWART I. (eds.), *Ecompanion to Contemporary Economic Thought*, London, Routledge, 1991.

[40] MILLS T.C., *The Econometric Modelling of Financial Time Series*, Cambridge, Cambridge University Press, 1993.

[41] PAGAN A.R., «Econometric Issues in the Analysis of Regression With Generated Regressors», *International Economic Review*, vol. 25, 1984.

[42] PENTECOST E.J., *Exchange Rate Dynamics. A Modern Analysis of Exchange Rate: Theory and Evidence*, Cambridge, Cambridge University Press, 1993.

[43] SPADA I., *Le news e la volatilità del mercato dei cambi*, tesi di laurea, Roma, Università «Tor Vergata», 1994-95.

[44] SVENSSON L.E.O., «Recent Research on Exchange Rate Target Zones: an Interpretation», *Journal of Economic Perspectives*, 1992.

[45] TIVEGNA M., «News politiche ed economiche nelle fluttuazioni della lira. L'esperienza recente: 28 marzo 1994-29 dicembre 1995», *CEIS Working Paper*, n. 9, 1996.

[46] — —, *Analisi infragiornaliera del cambio lira-marco in periodi di particolare turbolenza tra il gennaio 1995 ed il febbraio 1996*, mimeo, 1996.

[47] URICH T.J. - WATCHEL P., «Market Responses to Weekly Money Supply announcements in the 1970's», *Journal of Finance*, vol. 36, 1981.

[48] WHITE H., «A Heteroskedasticity-Consistent Covariance Matrix Estimator and a Direct Test for IIeteroskedasticity», *Econometria*, vol. 48, 1980.

Size and Regional Aspects of Banking Efficiency: the Italian Puzzle

Adriano Giannola - Claudio Ricci - Gennaro Scarfiglieri*

Università di Napoli-Federico II   IMI Sigeco Sim, Roma   University of York, York

1. - Introduction

Over the last decade there have been many developments in the study of efficiency and of economies of scale in the banking sector. In Europe this subject is particularly delicate because it is linked with the evaluation of the appropriateness of the recent EU regulation of credit markets which aims to increase competition and market efficiency by limiting the power of intervention of central banks. In recent years the regulation has caused two main effects: at market level, banks have been involved in mergers and acquisitions that have increased their average size and at firm level, banks have seen their profits reduced as a result of increased competition. In this sense the measurement of efficiency and of

---

* Adriano Giannola is Professor of Banking and Economics, Claudio Ricci is Financial Analyst and Gennaro Scarfiglieri is Ph. D. Student.

The authors are grateful to P. Simmons (University of York) and L. Zanchi (University of Leeds) and to those who participated in seminars held at the Università di Napoli-Federico II, at the Università del Molise and the University of Leeds for helpful comments on an earlier draft of the paper. Usual disclaimers apply. They wish to thank Dr. Giacchetti of ABI for the provision of the data set. The views expressed here are those of the authors and do not necessarily represent those of the IMI Sigeco Sin.

N.B. the numbers in square brackets refer to the Bibliography at the end of the paper.

economies of scale plays a key role in the evaluation of central bank policies.

As far as we know there are only a few studies that have examined these issues in relation to the Italian case, with results often contradicting each other[1]. In fact, an important, and unsatisfactory, characteristic of this literature is the fact that the results change with the specification of the model, even when the specifications are very similar to each other. Moreover, while the differences in the specifications are mainly concerned with the differences in the approach to bank production, several aspects that seem at first sight to be exclusively of an accounting nature remain unconsidered. In fact these aspects are extremely important conceptually when correctly defining the structure of bank costs, independently from the chosen approach.

In our opinion, framing these problems correctly produces, on one hand, conclusions that are both divergent and more significant than the traditional ones, and, on the other, at least for the Italian case, improves the robustness and the reliability of the econometric results.

In order to respond to this problem, however partially, we present here the first results of a study of efficiency measurement that is based on a more correct and complete specification of banking costs.

The aim of this paper is to show how the measurement of efficiency and of economies of scale depends crucially on a correct interpretation of accounting data used in the estimation. In fact we claim that previous studies have generally neglected important sources of the fund provision of banks in a way which induces significant biases in the results. These sourdes are: 1) the provision funds that appear on the liabilities side of the balance sheet and that represent a source of loanable funds on which the bank does not pay any explicit interest (e.g. provisions for pension li-

---

[1] These include CARDANI A.M. - CASTAGNA M. - GALEOTTI M. [3], FAVERO C.A. - PAPI L. [7], GIANNOLA A. - LOPES A. [9], LOPES A. - RICCIOLIO C. [16], OLIVEI G. [19], RESTI A. [20] and VANDER VENNET R. [22].

abilities). These provisions are normally used by banks in their lending activity so that a shadow cost for their use must be added to the total cost. 2) the free financial capital, i.e., the difference between financial capital and the sum of tangible assets, intangible assets and shares in associated and related companies owned by the bank. If this difference is positive, it means that the bank is using shareholders' wealth in its operating activity. Therefore, a shadow cost must be added to the total cost for the foregone revenue. We will prove how the bias introduced by the neglect of these inputs is both quantitative and qualitative. Moreover, we propose a solution to the long debated matter of the treatment of interbank loans.

We use a new and extensive data set, that, to the best of our knowledge, is the largest ever used for a cross section analysis of the Italian banking sector[2]. By comparing the results obtained with and without the consideration of these additional inputs, we show that the traditional way of defining the cost incurred by banks when purchasing funds dramatically affects the estimation of efficiency and of economies of scale. In particular, we find that the general level of inefficiency is about 8%, with smaller banks being more inefficient than larger banks. In comparison with a model which ignores the additional inputs, the inefficiency must be increased, on average, by 12%, with significant changes in its size and regional distribution. Similarly we find strong evidence that banks experience economies of scale along the whole range of production as opposed to the traditional result of economies of scale found only at the lowest level of activity.

The paper is organised as follows: in Section 2 we present the methodological issues which form the basis of this paper; in Section 3 we will give a descriptive analysis of the nature of the bias; in Section 4 we will comment on the results of the econometric estimation; finally we state the conclusions of the paper.

---

[2] Data refer to 637 Italian banks in 1994. It must be recalled that Italian banks are about 1100 and that the funds processed by these 637 banks account for more than 85% of total funds processed by the entire Italian banking sector in 1994.

2. - Methodological Issues

There are two main issues when dealing with banking efficiency measurement: the choice of the estimation technique and the representation of the production process.

In the neoclassical theory, a firm is efficient if, given input prices, it produces the output at the minimum cost. The estimation of the efficiency can be pursued through the implementation of two alternative techniques: a non-parametric one, known as Data Envelopment Analysis (DEA), and a parametric one, known as stochastic frontier[3]. By solving a linear programming problem for each available observation, DEA derives a non-parametric non-stochastic production frontier in the input-output space. The efficiency is measured through the distance between the single observation and the production frontier. With the stochastic frontier technique a parametric cost frontier is estimated through econometric methods and the residuals are split into the two components that are attributable to stochastic disturbance and cost inefficiency. The strengths and weaknesses of each technique emerge immediately from this brief description (parametric vs. non-parametric and stochastic vs. non-stochastic). In what follows we will use the stochastic frontier technique, bearing in mind that our contribution could equally well be applied to the non-parametric approach.

A more complete description of the technique we use can be made as follows: suppose we represent the technology of a multi-product firm through a cost frontier $C = C(y, w)$, where y is the output vector and w is the vector of input prices. By definition, the cost frontier is the locus of the minimum costs at which an output vector, $[y_1, ..., w_m] \in Y$, can be produced, given the vector of prices of inputs $[y_1, ..., w_m] \in W$. In this sense, the distance of an observation from the corresponding point on the frontier can be interpreted as a measure of the inefficiency of the firms. However, there are two kinds of reasons why a firm is not on the frontier: first, the

---

[3] For a survey on the two techniques see LEWIN A.Y. - LOVELL C.A.K. [14]. For a comparison between the results obtained with the two techniques see FERRIER G.D. - LOVELL C.A.K. [8] and RESTI A. [20] for the Italian case.

firm may not be able to use the productive factors in the best way; second, there are random effects, beyond the control of the firm, that remove it from the frontier. Therefore, the equation to be estimated is usually of this kind:

$$(1) \qquad C = C\,(y,\,w)\,\exp\,(e) = C\,(y,\,w)\,\exp\,(v + u)$$

where the random variable e is the sum of two components, v and u.

The component v, which is assumed to be symmetric, with zero mean, will capture all the random effects that are outside the control of the firm while u, which has an asymmetric distribution with a non-zero mean, is a measure of the proper inefficiency. The terms v and u are assumed to be independently distributed as, respectively, a normal random variable and a half normal random variable, so as to assign decreasing probabilities to increasing values of inefficiency[4]. In analytical terms:

$$(2) \qquad u \sim |N\,(0,\,\sigma_u^2)| \quad \text{and} \quad v \sim N\,(0,\,\sigma_v^2)$$

If we express a firm's efficiency as the ratio between minimum cost (corrected for the stochastic disturbance) and observed cost, the inefficiency indicator is given by:

$$(3) \quad INEFF = 1 - [C\,(y,\,w)\,\exp\,(v)/C\,(y,\,w)\,\exp\,(v + u)] = 1 - \exp\,(-u)$$

The value of u can be obtained by applying on the maximum likelihood estimates the so-called Jondrow estimator[5], that gives the mean of u conditional on the information available in e, for each observation.

The other main issue of banking efficiency measurement concerns the definition of the production process. According to Humphrey [11] we can make a distinction between the production approach and the intermediation approach to bank behavi-

---

[4] For an introduction to alternative ways in which the error terms can be defined see GREENE W.H. [10].
[5] See JONDROW J. *et* AL. [12].

our. Following the so-called production approach, we can think
of banks as just producing services related to loan and deposit
accounts, using labour, capital and materials as inputs. In this
case the number of deposit accounts and loans outstanding is
the correct measure of multi-product bank output, and operating costs of the production are the measure to be used for total
cost[6]. Following the so-called intermediation approach, banks are
collectors of funds which are then intermediated into loans and
other assets. In this case the monetary volume of deposit accounts and loans is the correct measure of bank output, while
total cost must be considered as the sum of operating costs and
interest costs[7]. The problem of the nature of deposits as input
or output of the banking production has been debated at length
in the literature and a clear solution has not yet been found[8]. In
what follows we use the intermediation approach hypothesis and
consider labour, physical capital and funds as inputs of a productive process in which deposits and loans are outputs. In fact,
the criticisms of Kolari and Zardkoohi [13], that show how the
exclusion of cost of deposits can lead to overestimated economies of scale, and of Berger and Humphrey [2] that show the
bias in efficiency estimation introduced by the exclusion of deposits as output, seem to be too weighty to be ignored.

The main contribution this paper makes is to show how the
measurement of efficiency and of economies of scale depends crucially on a correct interpretation of accounting data used in the
construction of the proxies. In fact we claim that previous studies have generally neglected important sources of banks' fund collection so as to induce significant biases in the results.

The first of these sources is represented by the provision funds

---

[6] A variant of this approach is the so-called value added approach. In fact, according to BERGER A.N. - HUMPHREY D.B. [2] outputs are «those activities which
have large expenditures on labor and physical capital». However, as recognized by
the same authors, deposits possess also input characteristics and their cost must
be added to total cost.

[7] A variant of this approach is the so-called asset approach, in which only items
of the assets side are viewed as outputs. As we will see this approach is subject
to powerful criticisms.

[8] See COLWELL R.J. - DAVIS E.P. [5] and WYKOFF F.C. [23] for an extensive discussion of the two positions.

that appear on the liabilities side of the balance sheet. For example the provisions for pensions and similar obligations[9] represent a debt contracted at a rate that is lower than the market level so that the difference from the opportunity cost must be added to the total cost. In other words these funds are used by banks in their production activity so that a shadow cost for their use must be, on one side, added to the total cost as cost for the collection of funds and, on the other side, subtracted as lower labour cost. By omitting this additional input we are underestimating banks' fund collection cost and overestimating labour cost; moreover, if this input is not used to the same extent by all banks, we are also introducing a qualitative bias[10]. The same remarks apply to the provisions for contingencies[11].

Two more sources of funds that have usually been ignored by previous studies are subordinated debts[12] and funds of third parties administered by a bank[13]. Although these last two sources constitute a small faction of the overall collection of funds they nevertheless contribute to the creation of the bias[14], as we will see in the next section.

A third source of fund collection, which has in general been neglected by previous studies[15], is free financial capital, by which

---

[9] In the Italian case there are two different items that are entered in these provisions. On one side there are the provisions for pensions that are paid by the central government; on the other side, depending on agreements that are negotiated by the single bank with the unions, workers can have integrative pensions paid directly by the bank. If in a bank this agreement does exist the cost of labour and the cost for the collection of funds must be accordingly revised.

[10] The only papers we know that have explicitly taken into consideration this effect are GIANNOLA A. - LOPES A. [9] and LOPES A. - RICCIOLO C. [16]. However both of them do not reduce labour cost accordingly so as to end up with an overestimated price of labour.

[11] However these provisions must not be confused with the provisions for the general banking risk that is instead part of the bank financial capital.

[12] These are peculiar debentures that have a priority that is higher than that of shares but the lowest priority of all the other creditors.

[13] This can happen, for example, if a bank receives funds to be administered as a consequence of a legal sentence.

[14] The interest cost for the use of these two sources is in the income statement.

[15] The few exceptions are FAVERO C.A. - PAPI L. [7], GIANNOLA A. - LOPES A. [9], LOPES A. - RICCIOLIO C. [16] and McALLISTER P.H. - McMANUS S. [17]. However, as we will clarify later, each of these papers is subject to criticisms and deficiencies in the treatment of free financial capital.

TABLE 1

A TYPICAL BANK BALANCE SHEET

Assets	Liabilities
Cash	Loans from other banks
Loans to other banks	Debts towards non-financial institutions
Bonds	Provisions for pensions
Loans to non-financial institutions	Other provisions
Other assets	Other liabilities
Shares in associated and related companies	Subordinated debts
Tangible and intangible assets	Financial capital

TABLE 2

THE REARRANGEMENT OF A BANK BALANCE SHEET

Assets	Liabilities
Treasury	Debts towards non-financial institutions
Loans to non-financial institutions	Provisions for pensions
Other net assets	Other provisions
	Free financial capital
Operating assets	Tied up financial capital
Non-operating assets	Invested financial capital

we mean the difference between financial capital and the sum of tangible assets, intangible assets and shares in associated and related companies owned by the bank. In order to clarify the point consider the typical bank balance sheet and our rearrangement of it, depicted, respectively, in Tables 1 and 2.

Figuratively, a bank's financial capital can be split into three parts: 1) financial capital invested in non-operating assets (e.g. goodwill and shares in associated and related companies); 2) tied up financial capital, that is used to finance a bank's physical capital, i.e., invested in operating assets, and 3) free financial capital that is a source of funds collection, for which a shadow cost must be added to the total cost[16]. In the literature very few papers have dealt with this issue. McAllister and McManus, in a suggestive attempt to consider risk management as a typical bank output, take into account the opportunity cost of financial capital, regarding it as a shield for bank creditors. Similarly, Giannola - Lopes [9] and Lopes - Ricciolio [16] take into account only the opportunity cost of financial capital without distinguishing between tied up, invested and free financial capital. Favero - Papi [7] consider between the inputs a measure of financial capital available for investment that seems to coincide with our definition of free financial capital, even though it lacks an explicit definition. However, while attributing the similarities between their results and those of McAllister and McManus to the common consideration of financial capital as a production input, Favero - Papi [7] fail to investigate the reasons why their peculiar results are linked to the treatment of financial capital. In the next section we will provide the explanation of this link.

Another extensively debated question in both the intermediation approach and the asset approach is the consideration of interbank loans and of investment in securities and bonds as bank output. Loans from and to other banks are usually used by banks to address the problem of temporary mismatches between collected and invested funds. In fact, under the assumption of the absence of arbitrage opportunities on the interbank loan market, an activity consisting of borrowing from banks and lending to other banks does not represent any production activity[17]. Similarly, «securities must be excluded from the definition of output since in capital markets exhibiting low information costs banks add only negligible, if any, value to these assets»[18]. Moreover, the use of end of year data for activities that are very variable through time intro-

---

[16] For an interesting discussion on the belief of no opportunity cost associated with equity see LODERER C. [15].

[17] These considerations would not hold any more if we were dealing with banks specialized in arbitrage activities, like CPR in France or houses specialized in derivatives in the UK.

[18] See VANDER VENNET R. [22].

duces stronger distortion[19]. On the grounds of these remarks we suggest incorporating the net balance of interbank loans and the bonds held by banks in an item called treasury. The fact that for a bank this item is positive, as well as the balance of the corresponding interests, is a signal that throughout the year this bank has kept some funds under this heading to deal with temporary mismatches between collected and invested funds. If treasury is negative, as well as the balance of the corresponding interest, the bank is using it as a source of fund collection and therefore the interest paid must be added to total cost[20].

3. - The Nature of the Bias

In this section we will first describe the data set we have used and then we will investigate the nature and the direction of the bias introduced when the additional inputs illustrated in the previous section are not considered[21].

The data set is made up of the financial statements of 637 Italian banks[22] in 1994, provided by the Associazione Bancaria Italiana (ABI)[23]. For each bank there are the balance sheet, the in-

---

[19] In the same vein solutions like the one proposed by FAVERO C.A. - PAPI L. [7] cannot be considered satisfactory. In fact, they consider the whole amount of loans to other banks as output but, at the same time, consider net funds borrowed by other banks as input. If we consider two banks with the same amount of net funds borrowed by other banks but with different amounts of funds lent to and borrowed from other banks and apply Favero - Papi procedure we are clearly introducing a significant bias in the measurement of their output.

[20] The treatment of treasury we propose could be interpreted as an application of the user cost approach to banking production. According to this approach the identification of input and output must be made on the basis of the net contribution of each item to total profit. Having ruled out the possibility that lending funds to other banks or investing in bonds represent value creation we regard these activities as strictly necessary to banking production. Whenever treasury is used as a means of collecting funds we accordingly increase the total cost.

[21] The next section will measure the magnitude of the bias.

[22] We refer to a bak's unconsolidated account because our focus is on traditional banking activities.

[23] This is the number we are left with after deleting those observations that had either missing data in the variables used in this study (109) or erroneous, suspicious or inconsistent financial statements (32). By «suspicious financial statements» we mean those that have produced input prices outside a range of three

come statement and other information such as the number of employees and the number of operating windows. The banks are divided into five groups, following the size classification of the
Banca d'Italia: major, large, average, small and minor. The Banca
d'Italia makes this classification through an index of the operating capacity of the bank, using the items of the balance sheet concerned with deposits, shareholders' wealth and administered funds
of third parties. The observations have been ordered using two criteria: first we have followed the size classification of the Banca
d'Italia; then, within each group, observations have been further
organised into subclasses representing the region in which the
bank is mainly located. Following the classification of the Istituto Centrale di Statistica (ISTAT) the four regions are defined as
north-western, north-eastern, central and southern. A summary of
the sample composition is reported in Table 3.

TABLE 3

SUMMARY OF THE SAMPLE COMPOSITION

	NW	NE	C	S	Total
Major	4		3	1	8
Large	4	4	2	1	11
Average	9	8	3	3	23
Small	18	16	14	43	91
Minor	96	209	69	130	504
Total	131	237	91	178	637

In order to show the nature and the direction of the bias introduced by the missing consideration of the additional inputs
described in the previous section we will first illustrate the elements of total cost and then the composition of the cost of purchased funds. The total cost is defined as the sum of labour cost,
physical capital cost and cost of purchased funds. The cost of la-

___

23 note continued
standard deviations around the average. No particular pattern could be found in
the deleted observations so that no bias should have been introduced by their de-
letion. For alternative procedures of data reliability enhancement see KOLARI J. -
ZARDKOOHI A. [13], RESTI A. [20] and VANDER VENNET R. [22].

TABLE 4

PERCENTAGE OF PURCHASED FUNDS OBTAINED THROUGH
DEPOSITS AND BONDS

	NW	NE	C	S	Total
Major	92.88		90.46	91.64	91.82
Large	95.20	91.95	94.85	94.79	93.92
Average	90.99	92.23	92.30	92.60	91.80
Small	91.99	87.96	89.90	88.38	89.62
Minor	88.91	88.86	89.32	88.01	88.71
Total	89.83	88.96	89.66	88.23	89.03

bour has been calculated as the sum of expenses on wages and salaries, social security contributions and changes in pension provisions, corrected for the opportunity cost of pension provisions. The cost of physical capital is obtained by summing the depreciation of assets to a shadow cost of use of capital, which we fixed as 8.5% of its value[24]. To this figure we have added the rent and leasing expenses for the capital borrowed from others as well as the expenses on electricity, telephone, stationery and advertisement. The cost for the collection of funds has been calculated as the sum of the interest paid by banks to obtain the various funds they use for their lending activities. These funds come from four different sources: deposits, bonds[25], free capital and minor sources[26]. The analysis of the relative importance of the three categories of cost reveals that, on average, labour cost accounts for 21%, physical capital cost accounts for 17% and fund collection accounts for 62%. The weight of the different funds relative to the whole amount of collected funds is displayed in Tables 4, 5 and 6.

In Table 4 we report the incidence of the sources traditional-

---

[24] We use this figure, which is the official interbank loan rate for 1994, because it can be interpreted as a measure of opportunity cost. We will use this figure in all the calculations involving a foregone revenue.

[25] For example, certificates of deposit.

[26] In the category of minor sources we have included subordinated debts, funds of third parties administered by the bank, provisions for pensions, provisions for contingencies and treasury for those banks that use it as a source of fund collection.

TABLE 5

PERCENTAGE OF PURCHASED FUNDS OBTAINED THROUGH
FREE FINANCIAL CAPITAL

	NW	NE	C	S	Total
Major	3.23		2.44	−1.00	2.41
Large	2.20	4.30	0.01	−4.53	1.96
Average	5.65	5.31	4.49	1.99	4.90
Small	5.08	7.96	6.03	8.43	7.31
Minor	9.62	9.57	8.77	9.79	9.53
Total	8.25	9.23	7.81	9.79	8.82

TABLE 6

PERCENTAGE OF PURCHASED FUNDS OBTAINED THROUGH
MINOR SOURCES

	NW	NE	C	S	Total
Major	3.89		7.10	9.37	5.78
Large	2.60	3.74	5.14	9.74	4.12
Average	3.36	2.46	3.21	5.40	3.29
Small	2.92	4.08	4.08	3.19	3.43
Minor	1.46	1.57	1.91	2.20	1.76
Total	1.92	1.80	2.53	2.58	2.15

ly considered, ie. deposits and bonds. It is immediately apparent that there is a substantial part (about 11%) of the funds that is not covered by these sources. This means that traditionally there has been an underestimation of the inefficiency. The underestimation is not homogeneous through size and regional classes because smaller banks make use of alternative sources of funds more than bigger banks, and the same is true for southern banks as opposed to the banks of other regions. Tables 5 and 6 report, respectively, the percentages of funds collected through free financial capital and minor sources. The use of free financial capital has an increasing importance as bank size decreases: in the case of minor banks it covers up to 10% of the need for funds[27]. Similarly, north-

---

[27] If the percentage of funds collected through free financial capital is negative it means that operating assets are being financed through deposits and/or bonds and/or minor sources.

eastern and southern banks seem to rely more on this source than the banks of other regions. Examination of Table 6 reveals that bigger banks use minor sources as an alternative to free financial capital while southern banks, irrespective of their size, use these sources more than those of any other region.

On the grounds of these remarks it immediately emerges that the traditional definition of cost of the purchased funds has several shortcomings: 1) it underestimates the overall inefficiency of the system; 2) it introduces a bias in favour of the efficiency of southern banks; 3) it introduces a bias in favour of the efficiency of smaller banks and 4) it tends to underestimate the economies of scale of bigger banks.

4. - Econometric Analysis

In order to measure the bias introduced by the absence of free financial capital and minor sources we have estimated four models: the first one does not consider either of the two inputs and acts as a benchmark model; the second considers the use of minor sources; the third considers the use of free financial capital and the fourth considers both inputs. In these models total cost (*TC*) is built as described in the previous section; the outputs are deposits (*Y1*) and loans to non-financial institutions (*Y2*). Input prices are constructed as follows: the price of labour (*W1*) is the ratio between labour cost and number of employees; the price of physical capital (*W2*) is the ratio between physical capital cost and the sum of deposits and issued bonds[28], the price for the collection of funds (*W3*) is given by the ratio between the interest expenses on deposits and bonds and the sum of deposits and bonds[29]. Following the tradition of the efficiency estimation in the bank-

---

[28] This procedure, based on the assumption of a constant ratio between physical capital and collected funds, is useful in order to bypass the difficult problem of the measurement of the capital stock. It was first introduced by MESTER L.J. [18].

[29] The reason why we have considered only bonds and deposits when constructing this index is that the remaining part of the collected funds is mainly evaluated at the shadow rate of 8.50%.

ing industry, the functional form we will use is the translog[30], that is a quadratic approximation to an arbitrary cost function that satisfies some regularity conditions[31]. In the case of a multiproduct firm, producing m outputs by using n inputs, the translog cost function is:

$$(4) \quad \ln TC = \alpha_0 + \sum_{i=1}^{m} \alpha_i \ln y_i + \frac{1}{2} \sum_{i=1}^{m} \sum_{j=1}^{m} \alpha_{ij} \ln y_i + \sum_{i=1}^{n} \beta_i \ln w_i +$$

$$+ \frac{1}{2} \sum_{i=1}^{n} \sum_{j=1}^{n} \beta_{ij} \ln w_i + \sum_{i=1}^{m} \sum_{j=1}^{n} \delta_{ij} \ln y_i \ln w_j$$

The regularity conditions described earlier require that the following restrictions for the symmetry of the cross-product and cross-price derivatives hold:

$$(5) \qquad \qquad \alpha_{ij} = \alpha_{ji} \quad \forall i, j$$

$$\beta_{ij} = \beta_{ji} \quad \forall i, j$$

The restrictions for the homogeneity of degree one in input prices are:

$$(6) \qquad \qquad \sum_{i=1}^{n} \beta_i = 1$$

$$\sum_{i=1}^{n} \beta_{ij} = 0 \quad \forall j$$

$$\sum_{j=1}^{n} \delta_{ij} = 0 \quad \forall i$$

---

[30] This function was first proposed by CHRISTENSEN L.R. *et* AL. [4].

[31] In order to satisfy the regularity conditions the cost function must be non-negative, linearly homogenous and concave in the prices of the inputs. On the reasons why it represents an approximation to an arbitrary cost function, on the details of the regularity conditions and on the proofs of the formulas of this paragraph, see DIEWERT W.E. [6], where there is a comprehensive survey of the topic.

In a multiproduct firm overall economies of scale can be analysed through the relationship between a proportionate change of all the outputs and the corresponding change of the total cost. If the proportion of the change of outputs is bigger than that of the cost, we have economies of scale.

The degree of multiproduct scale economies is given by the index:

$$(7) \qquad ESCA = \sum_{i=1}^{n} y_i \, MC_i \; = \sum_{i=1}^{n} \eta_i$$

where MC_i and η_i are, respectively, the marginal cost and the cost elasticity of the i-th output[32]. In the case of the translog cost function we can write *ESCA* as:

$$(8) \qquad ESCA = \sum_{i=1}^{m} \left[\alpha_i + \sum_{j=1}^{m} \alpha_{ij} \ln y_j + \sum_{k=1}^{n} \delta_{ik} \ln w_k \right]$$

There will be increasing, constant or decreasing returns to scale depending on *ESCA*, respectively, less, equal or greater than one.

The cost function we have estimated is:

$$(9) \qquad \ln TC = \alpha_0 + \sum_{i=1}^{2} \alpha_i \ln y_i + \frac{1}{2} \sum_{i=1}^{2} \sum_{j=1}^{2} \alpha_{ij} \ln y_i \ln y_j + \sum_{i=1}^{3} \beta_i \ln w_i +$$

$$+ \frac{1}{2} \sum_{i=1}^{3} \sum_{j=1}^{3} \beta_{ij} \ln w_i \ln w_j + \sum_{i=1}^{2} \sum_{j=1}^{3} \delta_{ij} \ln y_i \ln w_j$$

This function has first been estimated using *OLS* to test for the general significance of the model obtaining results that are satisfactory overall: the test for autocorrelation and misspecifi-

---

[32] BAUMOL W.J. - PANZAR J.C. - WILLIG R.D. [1].

cation of the functional form have been passed, the adjusted *R*-squared and the *F*-statistic of the general significance are extremely high and most of the coefficients are significantly different from zero[33].

We have also checked for the restrictions of homogeneity in input prices that hold only if the level of significance is set at 90%. In addition we have implemented a test of the normality of regression residuals: the fact that it is rejected is reassuring because, if our hypotheses on the distribution of the disturbances of the cost frontier hold, the skewness of *OLS* residuals is not zero. The cost function has then been estimated by ML and, by applying the Jondrow estimator, we have obtained the inefficiency indicators. Tables 7, 8, 9 and 10 summarize the distribution of inefficiency under four different hypotheses: in Table 7 there are the results for the benchmark model, ie. the case in which neither the free financial capital nor minor sources are considered (model I); Table 8 represents the case in which minor sources are considered (model II); Table 9 represents the case in which free financial capital is considered (model III) and Table 10 represents the case with both the additional inputs (model IV). Table 11 reports the percentage change in the inefficiency indicator between models I and IV.

TABLE 7

INEFFICIENCY DISTRIBUTION IN MODEL I

	NW	NE	C	S	Total
Major	6.51		5.69	3.75	5.86
Large	6.99	6.47	7.35	13.77	7.48
Average	5.89	6.36	5.90	8.35	6.38
Small	6.34	5.92	6.90	7.74	7.02
Minor	6.63	6.17	8.00	8.43	7.09
Total	6.55	6.16	7.67	8.27	7.05

---

[33] Unless otherwise specified, the significance level is intended at 95%.

TABLE 8

INEFFICIENCY DISTRIBUTION IN MODEL II

	NW	NE	C	S	Total
Major	6.37		5.96	4.27	5.95
Large	6.90	6.65	7.95	15.33	7.77
Average	6.05	6.44	6.09	9.10	6.59
Small	6.56	6.24	7.58	8.33	7.50
Minor	6.83	6.38	8.41	8.92	7.40
Total	6.73	6.37	8.12	8.79	7.37

TABLE 9

INEFFICIENCY DISTRIBUTION IN MODEL III

	NW	NE	C	S	Total
Major	8		6.56	3.70	6.75
Large	7.37	7.56	7.02	11.37	7.74
Average	6.43	6.91	6.23	8.01	6.78
Small	6.49	6.77	7.12	8.73	7.69
Minor	7.45	6.77	8.68	9.61	7.89
Total	7.25	6.79	8.25	9.35	7.81

TABLE 10

INEFFICIENCY DISTRIBUTION IN MODEL IV

	NW	NE	C	S	Total
Major	7.35		6.76	4.19	6.74
Large	7.15	7.62	7.46	12.51	7.87
Average	6.49	6.86	6.33	8.54	6.87
Small	6.60	6.98	7.68	9.20	8.06
Minor	7.54	6.88	8.93	9.92	8.07
Total	7.31	6.90	8.55	9.70	8.01

TABLE 11

PERCENTAGE OF THE OVERALL CHANGE
IN THE INEFFICIENCY INDICATOR

	NW	NE	C	S	Total
Major	12		18.74	11.12	14.50
Large	1.33	16.71	0.75	−10.87	4.07
Average	9.38	6.34	6.67	1.41	6.64
Small	3.31	16.81	9.80	17.03	13.45
Minor	13.44	10.14	10.08	15.15	12.25
Total	11.43	10.53	9.97	15.09	12.11

From the examination of the tables it emerges that efficiency increases with the size of banks[34] and that there is a clear difference in favour of northern banks when compared to the rest of Italy.

The analysis of Table 11 gives rise to some further remarks. It appears that a correct specification of the fund collection cost increases the inefficiency indicator by 12% and that this increase is not homogeneous, neither in the classes of size nor in those of region. The banks that are in the highest and in the lowest range of the productive scale seem to suffer more from this correction, and similarly southern banks are clearly above the average increase when compared with the banks of other regions. Moreover, in some cases the change is such that a starting advantage in terms of efficiency is completely offset by the new specification of the model. This is the case, for example, with large north-eastern banks when compared with large north-western and central banks: the category that initially had the best performance becomes, after the correction, that with the worst. As expected, these remarks are strictly linked with the percentage of collected funds covered by deposits and bonds: in fact the correlation coefficient between the increases in inefficiency and the percentage of funds collected through alternative sources is 0.74.

When examining economies of scale all these remarks acquire an even stronger significance. In Tables 12 and 13 we report the values of the *ESCA* indicator, calculated in the previous four models, for the five size classes and for the whlole sample[35]. The crucial point emerging from these tables[36] is that while through a type I model we would have understood that economies of scale are experienced only by smaller banks[37] with a type IV model banks experience economies of scale along the whole productive scale.

---

[34] The opposite result has been found by CARDANI A.M. - CASTAGNA M. - GALEOTTI M. [3], GIANNOLA A. - LOPES A. [9], LOPES A. - RICCIOLIO C. [16] and RESTI A. [20], while a very similar one has been found by FAVERO C.A. - PAPI C. [7].

[35] In Table 12 *ESCA* is calculated with input prices that change among classes while in Table 13 with constant input prices.

[36] In Table 12 all but one *ESCA* values are different from 1 while in table 13 all of the indicators are different from 1, at 99% significance level.

[37] In fact CARDANI A.M. - CASTAGNA M. - GALEOTTI M. [3], GIANNOLA A. - LOPES A. [9]; LOPES A. - RICCIOLIO C. [16], RESTI A. [20] and VANDER VENNET R. [22] all find this result, while SCARFIGLIERI G. [21], by applying a model specification very similar to that used in this paper on 1993 data, finds identical results.

TABLE 12

DISTRIBUTION OF *ESCA* WITH VARIABLE INPUT PRICES

	Major	Large	Average	Small	Minor	Sample
Model I	1.0067	1.0035	0.9958	0.9832	0.9768	0.9792
Model II	1.0123	1.0087	1.0000	0.9857	0.9775	0.9805
Model III	0.9776	0.9803	0.9768	0.9758	0.9776	0.9774
Model IV	0.9802	0.9826	0.9782	0.9759	0.9762	0.9764

TABLE 13

DISTRIBUTION OF *ESCA* WITH INPUT PRICES HELD CONSTANT

	Major	Large	Average	Small	Minor	Sample
Model I	1.0035	0.9986	0.9944	0.9842	0.9768	0.9792
Model II	1.0098	1.0039	0.9988	0.9865	0.9776	0.9805
Model III	0.9745	0.9747	0.9754	0.9767	0.9776	0.9773
Model IV	0.9777	0.9771	0.9771	0.9766	0.9762	0.9764

This last result, that is not very intuitive, can be explained in the following way. Consider two firms, 1 and 2, producing, respectively, the output vectors y and y', such that:

$$(10) \qquad\qquad y' = 2\,y$$

If we set:

$$(11) \qquad\qquad C^v(y') = C^d(y') + E_1$$

$$(12) \qquad\qquad C^v(y) = C^d(y) + E_2$$

where $C^v(.)$ is the true cost of producing a given output vector, $C^d(.)$ is the distorted measure of the cost and E_i is a measure of the bias. If we write ratio between the true costs of the two firms as:

$$(13) \qquad\qquad \frac{C^v(\mathbf{y}')}{C^v(\mathbf{y})} = \frac{C^d(\mathbf{y}') + E_2}{C^d(\mathbf{y}) + E_1}$$

the previous result becomes immediately clear. In fact, by examining *(13)* it appears that, provided that E_1 is sufficiently greater than E_2, a ratio between distorted costs which indicates decreasing returns to scale is perfectly compatible with a situation in which the ratio between the true costs suggests increasing returns to scale.

5. - Conclusions

This paper examines productive efficiency and economies of scale of the Italian banking system. This has been done through a new, more complete, specification of the variables involved in the estimation. In the definition of fund collection sources we have introduced the notions of free financial capital and opportunity cost of provisions. The effect of these additional inputs appears to be powerful. In fact the results that we find are considerably different from those of other papers. Our results invert the established view of bigger banks being more inefficient than smaller ones, and in addition they show that banks experience economies of scale along the whole range of production and not just at the lower levels.

BIBLIOGRAPHY

[1] BAUMOL W.J. - PANZAR J.C. - WILLIG R.D., *Contestable Markets and the Theory of the Industry Structure*, New York, Hancourt Brace Jovanovich Inc., 1982.

[2] BERGER A.N. - HUMPHREY D.B., «Measurement and Efficiency Issues in Commercial Banking», in GRILICHES Z. (ed.), *Output Measurement in the Service Sector*, Chicago, University of Chicago Press, 1992.

[3] CARDANI A.M. - CASTAGNA M. - GALEOTTI M., «La misurazione dell'efficienza economica: un'applicazione al settore bancario italiano», *Ricerche Economiche*, vol. XLV, n. 1, 1991, pp. 57-77.

[4] CHRISTENSEN L.R. - JORGENSEN D.W. - LAU L.J., «Trascendental Logarithmic Production Frontiers», *Review of Economics and Statistics*, n. 55, 1973, pp. 28-45.

[5] COLWELL R.J. - DAVIS E.P., «Output Productivity and Externalities: the Case of Banking», *Bank of England*, Working Paper Series, n. 3, 1992.

[6] DIEWERT W.E., «Applications of Duality Theory» in INTRILIGATOR M.D. - KENDRICK D.A. (ed.), *Frontiers of Quantitative Economics*, Amsterdam, North Holland Publishing, 1974.

[7] FAVERO C.A. - PAPI L., «Technical Efficiency and Scale Efficiency in the Italian Banking Sector: a non-Parametric Approach», *Applied Economics*, n. 27, 1995, pp. 385-95.

[8] FERRIER G.D. - LOVELL C.A.K., «Measuring Cost Efficiency in Banking: Econometric and Linear Programming Evidence», *Journal of Econometrics*, n. 46, 1990, pp. 229-45.

[9] GIANNOLA A. - LOPES A., «Vigilanza, efficienza e mercato. Sviluppo e squilibri del sistema creditizio italiano», *Rivista Italiana degli Economisti*, n. 1, 1996, pp. 25-54.

[10] GREENE W.H., *Limdep 6.0*, New York, Econometric Software Inc., 1992.

[11] HUMPHREY D.B., «Costs and Scale Economies in Bank Intermediation», in ASPINWALL R.C. - EISENBEIS R. (eds.)., *Handbook of Banking Strategy*, New York, Wiley, 1985, pp. 745-83.

[12] JONDROW J. - LOVELL C.A.K. - MATEROV I. - SCHMIDT P., «On the Estimation of Technical Inefficiency in the Stochastic Frontier Production Function Model», *Journal of Econometrics*, n. 19, 1982, pp. 233-8.

[13] KOLARI J. - ZARDKOOHI A., *Bank Costs, Structure and Performance*, Lexington, (D.C.), Heath and Company, 1987.

[14] LEWIN A.Y. - LOVELL C.A.K., «Frontier Analysis: Parametric and Nonparametric Approaches», *Journal of Econometrics*, n. 46, 1990, pp. 1-5.

[15] LODERER C., *Tutti-frutti for financial managers*, mimeo, Universitat Bern, 1996.

[16] LOPES A. - RICCIOLIO C., «La misurazione dell'efficienza nell'industria bancaria italiana», Università degli Studi di Salerno, *Quaderni del Dipartimento di Scienze Economiche*, n. 12, 1994.

[17] McALLISTER P.H. - McMANUS D., «Resolving the Scale Efficiency Puzzle in Banking», *Journal of Banking and Finance*, n. 17, 1993, pp. 389-405.

[18] MESTER L.J., «A Multiproduct Cost Study of Savings and Loans», *Journal of Finance*, n. 42, 1987, pp. 423-45.

[19] OLIVEI G., «Efficienza tecnica ed economie di scala nel settore bancario italia: un approccio non parametrico», *Quaderni del Centro Baffi di Economia Monetaria e Finanziaria*, n. 67, 1992.

[20] Resti A., «L'efficienza delle banche italiane: risultati dell'applicazione comparata di tecniche econometriche e matematiche», Ufficio Studi Banca Commerciale Italiana, *Collana Ricerche*, January 1996.

[21] Scarfiglieri G., «Size and Efficiency in the Production Structure of the Italian Banking System», Università degli Studi di Napoli-Federico II, *Quaderni del Dipartimento di Teoria dell'Economia Pubblica*, forthcoming, 1997.

[22] Vander Vennett R., *Cost Characteristics of Credit Institutions in the EC, 20th Annual Meeting, European Finance Association*, vol. I, 1993.

[23] Wykoff F.S., «Comment» in Griliches Z. (ed.), *Output Measurement in the Service Sector*, Chicago (IL), University of Chicago Press, 1992.

A Non-Parametric Analysis of the Italian Banking System's Efficiency

Sergio Destefanis*

Università di Salerno

1. - Introduction

Many of the numerous works on technical efficiency analysis using production frontier calculations[1] have of late devoted much attention to non-parametric methods. These methods require a very limited number of hypotheses as regards the production process, as a producer's technical efficiency is assessed on the basis of production sets constructed by applying linear programming techniques without assuming the existence of a functional relation between input and output.

A distinction is usually made between those non-parametric methods which can be directly traced to the fundamental contribution of Farrell [12] (commonly grouped under the name of *Data Envelopment Analysis* or *DEA*) and those based on the *Free Disposal Hull* (*FDH*) approach which was first proposed by Deprins, Simar and Tulkens ([8]). This paper applies an extension of this latter method, which takes account of the existence of input and output slacks when calculating producers' technical efficiency, to the analysis of a

* The author, Researcher in Economic Statistics, is very grateful to Antonio Pavone for having generously made available his software for the non-parametric calculation of efficiency measurements. Obviously, the author bears sole responsibility for any errors or omissions.

N.B. the numbers in square brackets refer to the Bibliography at the end of the paper.

[1] Probably the most recent and complete reference on this is that of FRIED H.O. *et* AL. ([14]).

cross-section of 728 Italian banks belonging to different institutional categories (limited companies, credit societies, rural banks and credit co-operatives - SpA, banche popolari, casse rurali and casse di credito cooperativo respectively). Section 2 considers the main characteristics of the *FDH* approach and the nature of the extension (named corrected *FDH*, or *FDH-C*) used here. Section 3 contains a brief overview of the theoretical approaches to the analysis of the production process in banks, dwelling in particular on the definition of outputs and inputs. Section 4 briefly presents the data used while Section 5 illustrates the main results obtained, emphasising the territorial differences in technical efficiency, as well as any significance for efficiency of firm's size and of an environmental risk index. Section 6 presents some concluding considerations.

2. - Production Efficiency and *FDH* Approaches

The notion of efficiency of a production unit has been extensively dealt with in economic theory following the re-interpretation of the production function as a frontier of the set of production possibilities[2]. This set is defined by all the combinations of input and output which the producer can physically realise.

Consider for example Graph 1 which represents the usual production function $y = f(x)$:

GRAPH 1

PRODUCTION FUNCTION WITH A SINGLE INPUT
AND A SINGLE OUTPUT

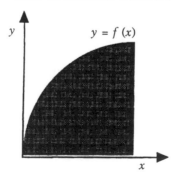

---

[2] See KOOPMANS T.C. [16], [17], DEBREU G. [7].

Each point of the production possibility set, characterised by an input-output pair, can be used to represent a production unit. The production function allows one to associate to each input quantity x the maximum possible amount of output y, so as to delimit the set of observations for the input-output pairs which characterise each production unit. It is in this sense that one speaks of the production function as a frontier and that the gap between a production unit and this frontier can be considered as a measure of its technical efficiency. More specifically, Koopmans ([16], [17]) proposes the following definition of technical efficiency; a unit engaged in the production of an output vector y by the use of an input vector x is technically efficient when the increase in an output necessarily implies either the reduction of another output or the increase of at least one input, and when the reduction of an input necessarily implies either the increase of another input or the reduction of at least one output. Hence a production unit is technically inefficient if it can obtain a given output vector after having reduced at least one input, or if it can increase at least one output using a given input vector.

In effect, we speak of: 1) input-oriented technical efficiency i.e., for a given level of output, the relation between the input corresponding to this output on the production function and the input actually used; 2) output-oriented technical efficiency i.e., for a given level of input, the relation between the output actually achieved and the output corresponding to this input on the production function.

Both parametric and non-parametric approaches are used in literature to derive a production frontier from data. In the former case, the frontiers of the production set are identified *a priori* with a production function, for example the Cobb-Douglas or the translog production function. If this function is estimated by maximum likelihood procedures, the difference between the production units observed and the values predicted by the production function can be broken down into two components: one purely random and one which represents the technical inefficiency of the units themselves[3].

---

[3] Indeed, if one uses the so-called stochastic parametric models, a given observation can be found above the production function as a result of purely random factors (which have nothing to do with the efficiency measurement). For an up-to-date overview of these methods, see FRIED H.O. *et* AL. [14]

Non-parametric approaches specify *a priori* not a given function, but rather some formal properties of the technology used (for example proportionality, convexity and free input and output disposal). Here again, the measure of efficiency shall be obtained with reference to the frontier of the production set. Starting from the work of Farrell [12] various linear programming methods have been developed to identify this frontier. Most of the procedures go under the name of *Data Envelopment Analysis (DEA)*[4]. Nonetheless, this paper will concern itself with a particular type of non-parametric approach known as the *Free Disposal Hull (FDH)*[5], based solely on the hypothesis of free input and output disposal. More specifically, for a given set of production units Y_0, the reference set $Y (Y_0)$ is characterised in terms of an observation i by the following postulate:

$$(x^i, y^i) \text{ observed}, (x^i + a, y^i - b) \in Y (Y_0) \ a, b \geq 0$$

where a and b are respectively input and output disposal vectors. In other words, as a result of the possibility to dispose of input and output free of charge, the reference set includes all the production units which use larger or equal inputs and which produce lesser or equal outputs than i. The reference set can be indifferently a production set, a set of input requirements (for given outputs) or a set of outputs possibilities (for given input).

Take for example Graph 2 which considers a production set characterised by an input (x) and an output (y). Each input-output pair represents a production unit. Starting from the observation K, one defines every observation to the right and/or below it (e.g., with a greater input and the same output, as in A; or with lesser output and the same input, as in B; or yet again with a greater input and lesser output, as in C) as dominated by K. As regards G, it is dominated not by K, as it uses more input but al-

---

[4] See CHARNES A. - COOPER W.W. and RHODES E. [6] and subsequently BANKER R.D. *et* AL. [3].
[5] A useful introduction to this method of analysis can be found in DEPRINS D. - SIMAR L. and TULKENS H. [8] and also in TULKENS H. [23], [24].

GRAPH 2

EFFICIENT AND INEFFICIENT PRODUCTION
UNITS IN THE *FDH* APPROACH

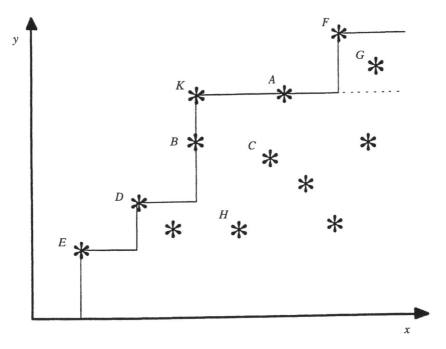

so produces more output, but by *F*. On the other hand, *D* and *E* are not dominated by *K* and *F* as they produce less output but use even less input. Similarly, *F*, is not dominated by any other observation, as it uses more input but also produces more output. In fact, *K, D, E* and *F* are not dominated by any production unit belonging to the reference set.

The *FDH* approach makes this comparison for each observation, and the observations dominated by other production units are considered inefficient. On the other hand, those units not dominated by any other observation are considered efficient producers, and make up the frontier of the reference set. In order to measure the technical efficiency of the production units the Debreu-Farrell measure[6], either output- or input-oriented, is adopt-

---

[6] See DEBREU G. [7] and FARRELL M.J. [12].

ed. In the former case, the technical inefficiency (or, as it is commonly called, the efficiency score) equals the complement to unity of the maximum expansion of output in line with the use of a given input. A technically efficient producer (and hence on the reference frontier) cannot implement such an expansion of output, obtaining a efficiency score of one. As regards the input-oriented Debreu-Farrell measure, it is given by the complement to unity of the maximum reduction of input which allows one to maintain the production of a given output. In the case of a production unit, such as H, simultaneously dominated by two units on the reference frontier (D and K), to this unit is ascribed the efficiency score from the more dominant efficient observation (in the case in question K for output and D for input).

This type of analysis can be extended to the case of n dimensions in input and output. In this case, equiproportional expansions (of all outputs) or contractions (of all inputs) are considered in order to characterise production units situated on the production frontier and the complement to unity of the maximum equiproportional reduction of all the inputs which allows production of a given output vector to be maintained is taken as the measure of technical inefficiency. A technically efficient producer cannot implement such an equiproportional reduction of all outputs, obtaining an efficiency score of one. Similar considerations apply when the Debreu-Farrell measure (DF) is calculated as the complement to unity of the maximum equiproportional expansion of all outputs consistent with the use of a given input vector.

It is fundamental to note that in *FDH* an inefficient producer is necessarily dominated by at least one other specific producer (who really exists). This differentiates *FDH* from *DEA*, as the latter maintains that inefficient producers are dominated by virtual observations built as linear combinations of sets of efficient producers. The possibility, in *FDH*, to highlight some production units which actually exist, and to carry out direct comparisons between these and the units which they dominate, can be considered one of the greater merits of this approach.

Furthermore, the absence of any sort of assumption on the

convexity of the production technology means that the frontiers obtained by *FDH* have greater probability of «being close to» the data than those obtained by *DEA*, when the reference set is characterised (at least locally) by the existence of non-convexity. Also as the frontier of the reference set consists of units which actually exist (rather than of a convex envelope), *FDH* is less sensitive to the presence in the reference set of anomalous (or wrongly measured) values than *DEA*. In fact, unlike with *DEA*, only the portion of the frontier corresponding to the anomalous value can be influenced by the latter's presence in *FDH*.

It is nonetheless important to emphasise how the definition of the reference frontier in *FDH* implies that a production unit can belong to it without dominating any other observation. Such a production unit (for example, *E*, in Graph 2) would be deemed efficient only by virtue of its location in an area of the reference set in which there are no other observations with which it can be compared. Following Tulkens's suggestion, such observations are defined efficient by default.

Furthermore, in *FDH* the efficient subsets coincide with the dominant observations. This drastically reduces the coincidence between efficient subsets and isoquants, and thus increases, for the same reason, the probability of discrepancies between Koopmans's definition and the DF measure of technical efficiency. In effect, a DF equal to one is a necessary but not sufficient condition for technical efficiency as defined by Koopmans. Intuitively, it is clear that the stepped profile of the *FDH* frontier is particularly suited to favour the existence of slacks, as is shown in the case with two inputs and one output depicted in Graph 3.

Graph 3 represents the set of input requirements for a unit with a technology comprising two inputs and one output. It can be easily ascertained that unit *A* is efficient even on the basis of Koopmans's definition. On the other hand, the input vectors of units *B*, *C* and *D* cannot be radially contracted allowing them to continue to produce the same output vector and nonetheless these units do not meet the criteria of technical efficiency definition provided by Koopmans. In fact, the quantity of input x_2 used by *C*

GRAPH 3

MEASUREMENT OF EFFICIENCY IN THE PRESENCE OF SLACKS

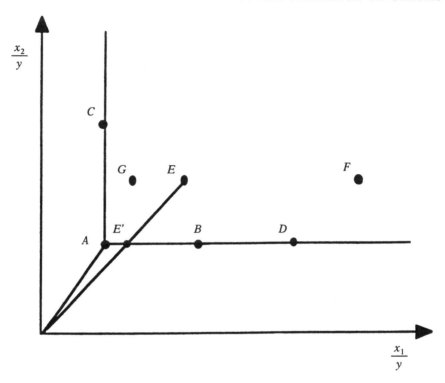

can be reduced without engendering any contraction in output. In other words, the input vector of unit C is characterised by the presence of slack in input x_2. The particular form postulated for the isoquant (which depends from its calculation using *FDH*) implies that the latter is equivalent only in part to a production subset which is efficient à la Koopmans. Given that DF requires only that an efficient vector lies on an isoquant, it follows that it cannot be a sufficient condition for Koopmans's criterion to be satisfied. Similar considerations apply with regard to the input x_1 used by B and D, as well as more generally, to the relations between the output-oriented DF measure and the definition of the same concept by Koopmans.

This example shows how it is easy in *FDH* to attribute the same DF result to production units with considerably different situations in respect of Koopmans's definition. It would there-fore appear worthwhile to propose a measure of technical effi-ciency which takes account of the influence of slacks when as-sessing the efficiency of production units. The intuition which lies at the basis of the extension of *FDH* used here[7] is that slacks can be assessed in terms of radial contractions of input (or ra-dial expansions of output) calculating a measure for the devia-tion of the input (or output) vector of an inefficient producer vis-à-vis the input (or output) vector of the respective dominant ob-servation.

The analytical instrument used to measure this is the cosine of the angle formed by the input (or output) vector of the respec-tive dominant observation and a virtual input (or output) vector obtained by radially contracting inputs (or radially expanding out-puts) of a given observation until they reach the frontier of the reference set. Let us look at Graph 3 again. If we take observa-tions A and E into consideration, the input vector of the latter will be contracted first to reach E', and subsequently the cosine of the angle formed by A and E' will be considered as a measure of slack. The same procedure allows us also to evaluate the slack which characterises an observation on the reference set (such as for ex-ample C). In this case the measure of slack will be simply the co-sine of the angle formed by A and C.

The measure of technical efficiency corrected for the pres-ence of slacks, denoted DF-C, will be given for each production unit by the product of the radial DF measure for the cosine de-fined above, denoted $cos\ (\omega)$. In order to understand the reasons for the use of the cosine function, consider the formula of the coefficient of the correlation ρ between the two vectors x^A and x^B:

$$\rho = \frac{x^{A'}\ x^B}{[[x^A]]\ [[x^B]]}$$

[7] A more detailed presentation of this proposal is to be found in Destefanis S. - Pavone A. ([9]).

where $[[x^i]]$ denotes the Euclidean norm of the vector x^i. But the scalar product of the two vectors x^A and x^B can be defined as:

$$x^{A'} x^B = [[x^A]] \; [[x^B]] \; cos \; (\omega)$$

It follows that: $\rho = cos \; (\omega)$

The core of this proposal can therefore be summarised as follows. The more the composition of the virtual vector resembles that of the vector of the dominant observation, the closer the cosine to unity and the smaller the difference between the corrected and the original measure. In other words, the correction is a monotonically positive function of the amount of slack (whose size is given by the lack of correlation with the dominant vector). The greater the slack, the greater the correction applied to the radial efficiency measure for the respective producer.

It should be noted that in the field considered here, the function $cos \; (\omega)$ can never take zero or negative values. In fact, the function $cos \; (\omega)$ of any two observations takes the value zero only if at least two outputs or inputs alternately take zero value at each of the points of observation (the angle between the two points of observation therefore becomes a right angle). In this case however, it is impossible for one of the observations to dominate the other in the sense of the *FDH* approach. On the other hand, negative values of $cos \; (\omega)$ imply that at least one output or input for one of the points of observation takes a value of less than zero. But this is excluded by the production theory's standard hypothesis of non-negativity of quantities. Furthermore, a conseguence of the equivalence between cosine and the coefficient of correlation between the two vectors is that the correction proposed can be adopted whatever the number involved (greater than one)[8] of outputs and inputs. Also, it is easy to understand in the light of this very equivalence that the correction is not influenced by changes in the output and input measurement units.

---

[8] It is barely necessary to recall that in the presence of only one input and one output, the problem of the existence of slacks is resolved in an elementary manner by using non-radial efficiency measures.

Destefanis and Pavone [9] considered in detail the results of the application of *FDH* and *FDH-C* to the same data (local Italian hospitals for 1988, 1990 and 1991). These results show consistent and systematic differences in the efficiency scores assigned to the dominated observations which lead to quite significant alterations in the efficiency rankings obtained with the traditional *FDH* approach and suggest that *FDH-C* has an actual practical significance as regards ranking of the observations. This paper will therefore use this algorithm to measure the technical efficiency of a cross-section of Italian banks.

3. - The Definition of Input and Output in Banks

The seemingly unending amount of literature which has been dedicated to the production process in banks testifies to their central position in the economic system. We do not intend here to furnish an overview, however cursory, of these contributions which are numerous and concern themselves with various analytical fields. It would however appear appropriate to focus our attention on an aspect of this literature which perhaps more than any other concerns the analysis of technical efficiency, namely the definition of the inputs used and the outputs obtained within the ambit of this process. In this respect, it is useful to rely on a classification proposed in Berger and Humprey [4] who claim there are two main schools of thought in this respect: the asset approach and the value added approach.

The asset approach, which substantially coincides with the more traditional intermediation approach, emphasises the bank's role as a financial broker which transfers savings from units with a surplus to those with a deficit. Hence, the company's product consists of the assets of the bank, first and foremost the loans issued to the units with a deficit, while the deposits granted to the company by the units with a surplus, together with the other elements of the bank's liabilities, are the raw materials of the production process and should be included in the inputs along with labour and capital.

In more specifically taxonomical terms, this approach holds that the following should be considered as banks' outputs: the loan portfolio, which includes all the customer loans; the securities portfolio, which includes shares, bonds and shareholdings; the interbank market loans. As regards inputs, we can consider as raw materials customer deposits, Banca d'Italia funding, loans obtained on the interbank market. The other inputs are capital, consisting of premises and equipment, the so-called free capital, namely the equity funds net of fixed assets, and labour, represented by the number of hours worked.

The principal characteristic of this approach is naturally the inclusion of deposits and other liability elements among the inputs. Now, even if this would seem to capture some fundamental elements which characterise the bank's production process, there are nonetheless strong theoretical perplexities in this respect, particularly as regards the inclusion of customer deposits among the inputs. It would, in effect, appear difficult to exclude the latter from the outputs, when their management generates a significant part of many banks' operating profit. Moreover, it is difficult to see how a bank's customers would be prepared to pay a price (in the form of bank commission) on something which is not part of a bank's product.

In the value added approach, which draws to a considerable extent on the fundamental elements of the so-called production approach, these perplexities are taken to their extreme logical consequences and customer deposits are included among banks' outputs. According to this approach, banks provide services to customers on both asset and liability sides (loans, deposits, bank and credit cards, etc.) using basically labour and capital as inputs. More specifically, the value added approach holds that if an asset or liability item absorbs a significant amount of labour and capital resources then it is included among the outputs. Otherwise, it should be included among the inputs or among the non-essential outputs. Hence the outputs include current accounts, savings accounts, commercial credit, loans and other banking services such as foreign exchange intermediation, tax collection and securities broking and placement activities. Among the inputs, on the other hand, we include Banca d'Italia funding and large-sum certificates of deposit as their acquisition requires no significant use of labour and capital. Finally, the non-essential outputs are assets which do not entail significant use of labour and capital such as for example portfolio Treasury notes.

Table 1 summarises the input and output variables considered in some recent non-parametric analyses of banks' production efficiency.

Table 1 clearly shows how both the approaches illustrated above are represented among these studies. Drake and Weyman-Jones [10] and Elyasiani and Mehdian [11] espouse essentially the asset approach, while Aly *et* AL. [1], [2], Ferrier and Lovell [3], Fried *et* AL. [15], Tulkens [25] and Resti [21] can be substantially classified as embracing the value added approach[9]. In fact, it cannot be stated that there currently exists a consensus in literature on which of the two schools of thought is preferable *a priori*. Rather, as Resti noted ([21], p. 275), it is the aims of the empirical investigation and the concrete availability of data which determine the choice of the paradigm to be used.

As will become clearer below, in this case the characteristics of the database available advise the adoption of the value added approach. In any case, a couple of concluding considerations can be made which are valid for both approaches. Firstly, in both of them the banks' production process is characterised not only by a number of inputs, but also by a number of outputs which are heterogeneous to each other, thus making it difficult to obtain a single scalar output index. As a result, the analysis of production efficiency for these institutions is considerably improved by the application of non-parametric techniques such as *FDH-C* which make it comparatively simple to take into account multi-input, multi-output production technologies. Secondly, as is shown by the study by Fried *et* AL. [15], it is extremely important in principle to include some index of the quality and range of banking products offered by the various institutions as outputs. In the absence of such,

---

[9] It should be noted that some of these authors - FERRIER G.D. - LOVELL C.A.K. [13]; FRIED N.O. *et* AL. ([15]), TULKENS H. [25], use as output data the numbers of bank transactions (number of current accounts, loans, etc.) and not their respective asset value, thus being closer to the traditional production approach.

TABLE 1

NON-PARAMETRIC ANALYSIS OF EFFICIENCY:
PROCEDURES AND VARIABLES

Authors	Procedure used	Output variables	Input variables
ALY *et* AL. [1] [2]	DEA	- loans - deposits	- number of employees - fixed assets - free capital
FERRIER-LOVELL [13]	DEA	- no. demand deposits - no. time deposits - no. loans - no. instalment loans - no. commercial loans	- number of employees - fixed assets - expenditure for materials
DRAKE-WEYMAN-JONES [10]	DEA	- mortgage loans - other assets - excess liquidity	- no. of employees - capital at book values - retail deposits - wholesale deposits - no. of branches

ELYASIANI-MEHDIAN [11]	DEA	- no. of commercial
		  loans
		- no. of mortgage
		  loans
		- other loans
		- portfolio securities
			- no. of employess
			- fixed assets
			- demand deposits
			- time deposits

TULKENS [25]	FDH	- no. of current
		  account
		  operations
		- no. of ATM operations
		- no. of foreign currency
		  operations
		- no. of brokerage
		  operations
		- no. of loans issued
		- no. of new accounts
		  opened
		- no. of credit cards
		  issued
		- other operations
			- hours worked
			- no of branches
			- no. of ATMs

FRIED *et* AL. [15]	FDH	- no. of loans - loan range index - loan interest rates - no. of deposits - deposit range index - deposit interest rates	- no. of employees - other operating costs

RESTI [21]	DEA	- loans
		- funds raised from
		  customers
		- net interbank loans
			- no. of employess
			- no. of branches
			- net interbank funds
			- large-sum
			  certificates of deposit

the efficiency gaps measured by empirical analysis could in fact derive from the differing characteristics of the output offered by the banks surveyed. Should it not be possible to have such indexes, it would therefore be advisable to avoid comparing banks belonging to different institutional categories and which therefore in all likelihood have a different composition of output.

4. - An Application for Banks. The Data

The data used in this paper refers to a sample of 728 Italian banks and is taken from the 1994 Rating data archive. The variables available for the afore-indicated sample are: total assets, total customer loans, total customer deposits, total securities funds raised (certificates of deposit and bonds), net interbank relations, equity, free capital, number of employees, number of branches, interest margin, labour costs, operating income, total bad loans. The banks taken into consideration were 505 rural banks (casse rurali) and credit co-operatives (casse di credito cooperativo) and 223 limited banks, credit societies and savings banks (SpA, banche popolari and casse di risparmio respectively) giving a total of 728 banks distributed throughout Italy. We eliminated from the original sample of 763 commercial banks 20 banks which stated they had zero employees, 2 banks which stated they had no branches, 4 banks which declared that funds raised from securities (certificates of deposit and bonds) amounted to zero and 9 banks with negative free capital, as the algorithm used for *FDH-C* can function only with positive variables. It is in any case reasonable to assume that these exclusions have not only not significantly diminished the informational content of the cross-section, but that they have also allowed the elimination of some potentially anomalous observations.

Some shortcomings can be noted if the variables available are compared with those listed in the previous section, above all as regards the asset approach. The Rating sample does not include data on Banca d'Italia funding. Furthermore, it is impossible to separate the portfolio securities from the total assets or to separate the total of securities funding raised into that raised from bonds and that from certificates of deposit (which are much more brokerable funds than bonds). These shortcomings in the data will also negatively influence the possibility of specifying the elements of a production set under the value added approach, but will be less serious if the securities portfolio management does not require a significant use of labour and capital and this asset item can therefore be considered as an unimportant output[10]. It should be noted in any case that the lack of data on the number of bank transactions (number of current accounts, loans, etc.) prevents the use of the value added approach in its form which is closest to the traditional production approach.

As is the case for most of the studies considered in Table 1, the Rating sample contains no data regarding the number of hours worked and as a result the labour input has to be measured by the number of employees. Furthermore, no measurements are available for banking services, such as foreign exchange intermediation, tax-collection, and securities broking and placement activities. As this absence also makes it impossible to construct appropriate indexes for the quality and range of banking products, it would appear advisable to compare only banks which belong to the same institutional category. In this case, considerations regarding the size of the sample counsel subdividing the sample into rural banks and credit co-operatives on the one hand, and limited banks, credit societies and savings banks on the other.

As Table 1 also shows, literature usually employs two types of variables to measure fixed capital: the book value of premises and equipment and the number of branches. We believe it appropriate to use the latter variable here as it is crucial for banks which aim at financial intermediation via a decentralised structure. On the other hand, it is impossible to separate the book value of premises and equipment from that of long-term investments in the Rating databank, and in any case the book value of fixed capital can be subject to errors of measurement deriving from the differing balance-

---

[10] For an analysis in favour of this hypothesis, at least for portfolio Treasury notes, see ONADO M. ([20], Chapter 10).

sheet criteria adopted (particularly relevant for comparisons between limited banks, credit societies and savings banks).

Finally, the Rating sample includes data only on net interbank flows, and not on the relative gross flows. Given that net interbank flows have a negative value in a hundred or so cases, to obtain a sample without negative values one would have to significantly reduce the cross-section by number. Moreover, in this case the conceptual requisites for believing that the observations to be excluded are potentially anomalous do not exist. In view of the lack of emphasis on this variable in literature – only Resti [21] includes net interbank flows in the analysis – it would appear opportune to maintain the cross-section of 728 banks in the empirical analysis, and disregard the net interbank flows when specifying the production sets.

In conclusion, it appears possible to state that the Rating database includes variables which enable it to be used for the empirical specification of an appreciably complete version of the value added approach. In effect, conditional on the assumption that the management of portfolio securities does not entail significant use of labour and capital, this database includes the more significant outputs for the value added approach (namely deposits and loans). As regards the possibility of adopting the asset approach, it should be noted that the reliability of the efficiency measurements based on this approach could be considerably reduced by the lack of a sufficient breakdown of the asset and liability items.

5. - An Application for Banks. The Empirical Analysis[11]

After some brief introductory comments, this section will illustrate the main results obtained by applying *FDH-C* to banks of the Rating sample. According to the value added approach, the outputs will include the total of customer loans and customer deposits. No account is taken of the rest of the assets, which, in ad-

---

[11] The efficiency measurements based on *FDH-C* were obtained by the software developed and kindly made available by Antonio Pavone. The Kruskal-Wallis and Tobit analyses were made using the Systat and Limdep software respectively.

dition to the capital, include portfolio securities that, as already noted, should not be essential outputs as understood by the value added approach. The inputs include not only the number of employees and branches but also the free capital. In effect, this variable, although it explicitly figures only once in the inputs presented in Table 1, is part of a company's funds and is traditionally considered a factor of some importance in respect of a bank's capacity to grant loans. On the other hand, it has already been used with good results in the parametric efficiency analysis of Locatelli and Prosperetti [18]. Finally, it should be borne in mind that it is not possible to include Banca d'Italia funding among the inputs, nor separate the funds raised from bonds and from certificates of deposit (which are much better brokerable funds than bonds). It would appear appropriate however to examine the possibility that the production set contains also the total funds raised by securities as an input. We will therefore have: the following production set according to the value added approach: 1) output: total loans and deposits; 2) input: number of employees, number of branches, free capital, total securities funds raised.

Table 2 shows some descriptive statistics for these variables which highlight the strong structural differences for the two big categories of institutions considered here.

Recall that the impossibility of building suitable indexes for the quality and range of banking products advised against comparing banks belonging to different institutional categories (on the one hand rural banks and credit co-operatives and on the other limited companies, credit societies and savings banks). These considerations are corroborated by the strong structural differences shown in Table 2. Hence, our efficiency analysis will reflect solely the outcome of the comparisons within the two main institutional categories, henceforth referred to as CRC and SPA respectively.

Table 3 shows the main results of the analysis which deals with input-oriented efficiency measuremet only. As can be seen, two different versions of the production set have been taken into consideration. In addition to employees and branches, account has also been taken respectively of free capital, and of this variable together with the total of securities funds raised. The criteria

TABLE 2

DESCRIPTIVE INPUT AND OUTPUT VARIABLE STATISTICS

SPA no. = 223		CRC no. = 505	
Loans			
Lower quartile:......................	255.345	Lower quartile:	21.646
Median:	689.522	Median:...............................	46.170
Upper quartile:	1.825.502	Upper quartile:....................	85.809
Customer deposits			
Lower quartile:......................	333.874	Lower quartile:	37.107
Median:	867.094	Median:...............................	69.844
Upper quartile:	2.036.705	Upper quartile:....................	129.063
No. of employees			
Lower quartile:......................	145	Lower quartile:	11
Median:	401	Median:...............................	23
Upper quartile:	954	Upper quartile:....................	46
No. of branches			
Lower quartile:......................	13	Lower quartile:	2
Median:	31	Median:...............................	3
Upper quartile:	68	Upper quartile:....................	5
Free capital			
Lower quartile:......................	35.728	Lower quartile:	4.932
Median:	88.879	Median:...............................	9.913
Upper quartile:	215.643	Upper quartile:....................	18.746
Funds raised from securities and certificates of deposit			
Lower quartile:......................	117.074	Lower quartile:	11.662
Median:	291.125	Median:...............................	22.943
Upper quartile:	768.662	Upper quartile:....................	47.745

adopted for comparing the different results are the average efficiency score of the dominated units and the number of dominant and efficient by default units obtained according to the type and number of inputs included in the production set. The higher the average efficiency score of the dominated units and the higher the number of dominant units, the greater the role played by the type and number of inputs included in the production set in explaining the production performance of the units considered, while a

TABLE 3

PRINCIPAL RESULTS OF THE *FDH-C* ANALYSIS

CRC (505 observations)

Output: Loans, deposits
Input: Employees, branches, free capital
Number of dominant observations: 157
Number of observations efficient by default: 80
Average efficiency for the dominated observations: 0.888
Sum of slacks for dominated observations:

For output (*s*)		For input (*s*)	
Expansion in %		Reduction in %	
Loans	22	Employees	6
Deposits	15	Branches	23
		Free capital	18

Output: Loans, deposits
Input: Employees, branches, free capital, securities funds raised
Number of dominant observations: 158
Number of observations efficient by default: 155
Average efficiency for the dominated observations: 0.878
Sum of slacks for dominated observations:

For output (*s*)		For input (*s*)	
Expansion in %		Reduction in %	
Loans	17	Employees	7
Deposits	20	Branches	23
		Free capital	18
		Sec. funds raised	26

SPA (223 observations)

Output: Loans, deposits
Input: Employees, branches, free capital
Number of dominant observations: 50
Number of observations efficient by default: 92
Average efficiency for the dominated observations: 0.877
Sum of slacks for dominated observations:

For output (*s*)		For input (*s*)	
Expansion in %		Reduction in %	
Loans	21	Employees	5
Deposits	16	Branches	19
		Free capital	37

Output: Loans, deposits
Input: Employees, branches, free capital, securities funds raised
Number of dominant observations: 31
Number of observations efficient by default: 144
Average efficiency for the dominated observations: 0.884
Sum of slacks for dominated observations:

For output (*s*)		For input (*s*)	
Expansion in %		Reduction in %	
Loans	18	Employees	5
Deposits	19	Branches	17
		Free capital	46
		Sec. funds raised	19

higher level of units which are efficient by default indicates that the inclusion of a given type and number of inputs only increases the non-comparability of the observations.

Consideration of these criteria leads to the result that for both the CRCs and the SPAs, the production sets which would appear to best account for the production performance of the units considered is that which takes employees, branches and free capital as inputs. In effect, the use of the securities funds raised together with free capital engenders no positive effects as the average efficiency score of the dominated units and the number of dominant units show only a slight increase or even decrease, while there is a significant increase in the number of units which are efficient by default. Furthermore, in both cases, the average efficiency scores are very similar. Finally, note that the results using the value added approach would appear to indicate that the slacks' input structure is heavily weighted towards the capital inputs. More specifically, slack would appear to be particularly pronounced in the CRCs as regards the number of branches. This result indicates that the proliferation of new branches after 1990 resulted in overbranching rather than overmanning for these banks (Resti [21], p. 295).

To analyse the characteristics of the efficiency scores in more detail, it would appear appropriate to focus on the production sets in which the inputs consist of employees, branches and free capital. To this end, a non-parametric analysis of the variance for the efficiency scores was first carried out, using the Kruskal-Wallis procedure (robust vis-à-vis the non-normality of the residuals) to examine the territorial distribution of the scores by macroregion and region. The existence of systematic patterns in the efficiency scores was then assessed using the Tobit analysis. A model with a limited dependent variable (such as Tobit) was used for the econometric analysis of the efficiency scores because, by definition, the efficiency score has a range of variation of between zero and one; ignoring these constraints on the variability of the efficiency scores could lead to distorted and inconsistent estimates. An attempt was also made here to link the distribution of the efficiency scores to two variables: the size of the company (measured by L(Att), the logarithm of the value of assets) and the riskiness of the environment (measured by the bad loans/total loans ratio, (SOFF%). Significance on the part of the former variable should indicate the existence of scale effects while the latter variable should capture the effect of the «quality» of the environment in which the bank operates.

One *a priori* consideration regarding the results is that the analysis of the territorial differences in efficiency is more informational in nature for the CRCs as they tend not to have branches outside their «home» region. In fact, the Kruskal-Wallis analysis, shown in Tables 4 and 5, indicates the existence of systematic elements in the territorial distribution of the efficiency scores solely for the CRCs. This indication in corroborated by the Tobit analysis of the relative patterns, which is shown in Tables 6 and 7. For the CRCs, the regions of mainland southern Italy are on average less efficient, while the SPAs would appear to have no significant territorial pattern. Note that to avoid the so-called multicollinearity trap, it was necessary to subsume a macroregion or region in the constant, which in the estimates shown here was always the median macroregion or region. Hence, the coefficients of the territorial dummies represent the gap of the coefficient of a given macroregion or region vis-à-vis that of the median macroregion or region.

There were significant differences between the CRCs and SPAs also as regards the role of the size of the bank and the riskiness of the environment. In the case of the SPAs, neither of the variables gave rise to any significant effects, while for the CRCs there is evidence of (albeit rather weak) scale effects and SOFF% has a negative coefficient and reduces the significance of the dummies (of a negative sign) for southern Italy. This type of evidence is compatible with the existence of a direct relation between problems of «quality» of the environment of southern Italy and the level of inefficiency of southern Italian CRCs[12]. Naturally, this point and the significance of the size variable both require further analytical investigation.

---

[12] There are *a priori* reasons for believing that the co-operative structure and the more informal procedures employed in lending decisions make the CRCs more sensitive to the environment in which they operate. See on this matter CANNARI L. - SIGNORINI L.F. [5].

TABLE 4

EFFICIENCY SCORES DF-C, FOR DOMINATED OBSERVATIONS
CRC (505 OBSERVATIONS)
ANALYSIS OF THE KRUSKAL-WALLIS VARIANCE*

North-West	N = 79	Emilia Romagna	N = 41
North-East	N = 257	Tuscany	N = 39
Centre	N = 80	Umbria	N = 4
South (mainland)	N = 69	Marche	N = 20
Sicily-Sardinia	N = 20	Lazio	N = 15
Piedmont	N = 12	Abruzzo	N = 13
Valle d'Aosta	N = 3	Molise	N = 3
Lombardy	N = 62	Campania	N = 22
Liguria	N = 2	Puglia	N = 15
Trentino-Alto Adige	N = 138	Basilicata	N = 5
Veneto	N = 56	Calabria	N = 11
Friuli-Venezia Giulia	N = 22	Sicily	N = 20

* Groups: North-West, North-East, Centre, South mainland, Islands.
K-W statistic = 9.29, *P*-value = 0.05 ~ χ^2 (4)
Groups: Piedmont, Valle d'Aosta, Lombardy, Liguria, Trentino-Alto Adige, Veneto, Friuli Venezia Giulia, Emilia Romagna, Tuscany, Umbria, Marche, Lazio, Abruzzo, Molise, Campania, Puglia, Basilicata, Calabria, Sicily.
K-W statistic = 24.54, *P*-value = 0.14 ~ χ^2 (18)

TABLE 5

EFFICIENCY SCORES DF-C, FOR DOMINATED OBSERVATIONS
SPA (223 OBSERVATIONS)
ANALYSIS OF THE KRUSKAL-WALLIS VARIANCE*

North-West	N = 57	Tuscany	N = 17
North-East	N = 59	Umbria	N = 8
Centre	N = 50	Marche	N = 7
South (mainland)	N = 40	Lazio	N = 15
Sicily-Sardinia	N = 17	Abruzzo	N = 8
Piedmont	N = 16	Molise	N = 1
Lombardy	N = 36	Campania	N = 11
Liguria	N = 5	Puglia	N = 14
Trentino-Alto Adige	N = 7	Basilicata	N = 3
Veneto	N = 15	Calabria	N = 6
Friuli-Venezia Giulia	N = 9	Sicily	N = 15
Emilia Romagna	N = 28	Sardinia	N = 2

* Groups: North-West, North-East, Centre, South mainland, Islands.
K-W statistic = 5.56, *P*-value = 0.25 ~ χ^2 (4)
Groups: Piedmont, Valle d'Aosta, Lombardy, Liguria, Trentino-Alto Adige, Veneto, Friuli Venezia Giulia, Emilia Romagna, Tuscany, Umbria, Marche, Lazio, Abruzzo, Molise, Campania, Puglia, Basilicata, Calabria, Sicily.
K-W statistic = 21.98, *P*-value = 0.23 ~ χ^2 (18)

TABLE 6

A TOBIT ANALYSIS OF THE EFFICIENCY PATTERNS
CRC (505 observations)

Dependent variable = efficiency score from model
Output: Loans, deposits
Input : Employees, branches, free capital

Variable	Coefficient	t-ratio	Variable	Coefficient	t-ratio
Log-likelihood = −79.02198			*Log-likelihood = −73.46187*		
Constant	1.0175	46.690	Constant	0.89962	7.289
North-West	0.59803E-02	0.196	North-East	−0.33342E-02	−0.133
North-East	0.75418E-02	0.308	Centre	0.87418E-02	0.285
South (mainland)	−0.64328E-01	−2.109	South (mainland)	−0.19898E-01	−0.582
Islands	0.29877E-01	−0.640	Islands	0.45041E-01	0.858
			L(Att)	0.12381E-01	1.211
			SOFF%	−0.71875E-02	−3.164
Log-likelihood = −68.85028			*Log-likelihood = −62.55388*		
Constant	1.0009	35.119	Constant	0.74043	5.586
PIE	−0.10975E-01	−0.183	PIE	−0.50021E-01	−0.748
VDA	0.71383	0.095	VDA	0.71164	0.095
LOM	0.13927E-01	0.377	LOM	−0.13266E-01	−0.279
TAA	0.47720E-01	1.459	TAA	0.21520E-01	0.478
VEN	−0.20986E-01	−0.566	VEN	−0.42532E-01	−0.896
FVG	0.24441E-01	0.499	FVG	0.38412E-02	0.067
LIG	0.71383	0.078	LIG	0.72862	0.080
TUS	0.15239E-01	0.370	EMR	−0.36042E-01	−0.718
UMB	0.12074E-01	0.125	TUS	−0.57859E-02	−0.114
MAR	0.14637E-01	0.292	UMB	−0.12084E-01	−0.120
LAZ	−0.79469E-02	−0.145	LAZ	0.24392E-02	0.039
ABR	0.50398E-01	0.904	ABR	0.84764E-01	1.313
MOL	−0.63531E-01	−0.606	MOL	−0.35582E-01	−0.327
CAM	−0.32475E-01	−0.685	CAM	0.53300E-03	0.009
PUG	−0.74071E-01	−1.393	PUG	−0.70844E-01	−1.158
BAS	−0.35821E-02	−0.042	BAS	0.29380E-01	0.324
CAL	−0.14898	−2.550	CAL	−0.10657	−1.579
SIC	−0.15186E-01	−0.308	SIC	−0.35600E-01	0.578
			L(Att)	0.25846E-01	2.403
			SOFF%	−0.62337E-02	−2.580

TABLE 7

A TOBIT ANALYSIS OF THE EFFICIENCY PATTERNS
SPA (223 observations)
Dependent variable = efficiency score from model
Output: Loans, deposits
Input : Employees, branches, free capital

Variable	Coefficient	t-ratio	Variable	Coefficient	t-ratio
Log-likelihood = –54.82719			*Log-likelihood = –54.78033*		
Constant	1.0413	19.596	Constant	1.0761	7.144
North-West	0.91493E-01	1.503	North-West	0.86818E-01	1.241
North-East	–0.44481E-03	–0.008	North-East	–0.59700E-02	–0.089
Centre	–0.78135E-02	–0.131	Centre	–0.10786E-01	–0.171
South (mainland)	–0.40617E-01	0.653	South (mainland)	–0.37665E-01	0.595
			L(Att)	–0.18132E-02	–0.182
			SOFF%	–0.93476E-03	–0.240
Log-likelihood = –46.26945			*Log-likelihood = –46.20192*		
Constant	1.0573	26.093	Constant	0.74043	5.586
PIE	0.46554E-01	0.685	PIE	0.46392E-01	0.684
VDA	0.90991E-01	1.636	VDA	0.93786E-01	1.671
LOM	–0.10058	–1.241	LOM	–0.10199	–1.258
TAA	–0.12326E-01	–0.189	TAA	–0.11214E-01	–0.172
VEN	–0.31966E-01	–0.417	VEN	–0.34352E-01	–0.447
FVG	–0.60821E-02	–0.062	FVG	–0.54148E-02	–0.055
LIG	0.85261E-01	1.210	LIG	0.84252E-01	1.170
TUS	0.19417E-01	0.226	TUS	0.16453E-01	0.191
UMB	–0.13232	–1.667	UMB	–0.13326	–1.676
MAR	–0.49006E-01	–0.775	MAR	–0.52256E-01	–0.785
LAZ	–0.97845E-01	–1.277	LAZ	–0.99663E-01	–1.240
ABR	0.69404	0.051	ABR	0.68589	0.050
MOL	0.73782E-01	–0.938	MOL	0.66510E-01	0.813
CAM	–0.44624E-01	–0.687	CAM	–0.49633E-01	–0.726
PUG	0.41229E-01	0.318	PUG	0.38501E-01	0.295
BAS	0.12236	1.098	BAS	0.11474	0.972
CAL	–0.42254E-01	–0.655	CAL	–0.49931E-01	–0.671
SIC	0.69404	–0.072	SIC	0.69620	0.072
			L(Att)	–0.36140E-02	–0.357
			SOFF%	0.40044E-03	0.578

6. - Concluding Considerations

This paper has concerned itself with analysing the technical efficiency of a cross-section of 728 Italian banks belonging to different institutional categories (limited companies, credit societies, rural banks and credit co-operatives) using data for 1994 and applying an extension of the non-parametric *FDH* method to take account of input and output slacks. Like the traditional *FDH* approach, this procedure makes no assumptions regarding the functional form of the production technology used by the banks and enables one to allow for the typical multiproduct nature of the banking sector's output.

The main results of the analysis, in which the production set was developed starting from the so-called value added approach, can be summarised as follows. As regards the number of efficient units and the average efficiency score for both the CRCs and the SPAs, the production set whose inputs are employees, branches and free capital would appear to provide the better account of the production performance of the units considered, while the inclusion of securities funds raised among the inputs would not appear to make any significant difference. Another interesting result is that the input structure of the slacks is, in the value added approach, heavily weighted towards capital inputs, showing that the proliferation of branches after 1990 has engendered a significant overbranching in the banking sector.

Moreover, econometric analysis of the determination of the efficiency scores shows that the territorial efficiency patterns differ significantly according to whether CRCs or SPAs are being considered. An attempt was also made to relate the distribution of the efficiency scores to two variables: the size of the bank and the riskiness of the environment (measured by the ratio between bad loans and total loans). These variables are significant only for CRCs, and in this case they diminish the significance of the dummies (of negative sign) for southern Italy. This type of evidence is compatible with the existence of a direct relation between environmental problems in southern Italy and the level of inefficiency of southern Italian CRCs, but in any case requires additional analytical investigation.

BIBLIOGRAPHY

[1] ALY H.Y. - GRABOWSKI R. - PASURKA C. - RANGAN N., «The Technical Efficiency of US Banks», *Economic Letters*, n. 28, 1988, pp. 169-75.

[2] — — — — — — — — — — — — — —, «Technical, Scale and Allocative Efficiencies in US Banking: an Empirical Investigation», *Review of Economic and Statistics*, vol. 27, pp. 211-8.

[3] BANKER R.D. - CHARNES A. - COOPER W.W. - SWARTS J. - THOMAS D.A., «An Introduction to Data Envelopment Analysis with Some of its Models and Their Uses», *Research on Governmental and Nonprofit Accounting*, vol. 5, 1989, pp. 125-63.

[4] BERGER A.N. - HUMPREY D.B., «Measurement and Efficiency Issues in Commercial Banking», FED Finance and Economics, *Discussion Series*, n. 151, 1990.

[5] CANNARI L. - SIGNORINI L.F., *Rischiosità e razionamento: un'analisi dell'efficienza allocativa delle banche di credito cooperative*, Roma, Banca d'Italia, mimeo, 1995.

[6] CHARNES A. - COOPER W.W. - RHODES E., «Measuring the Efficiency of Decision-Making Units», *European Journal of Operational Research*, vol. 2, 1978, pp. 429-44.

[7] DEBREU G., «The Coefficient of Resource Utilisation», *Econometrica*, vol. 19, 1951, pp. 273-92.

[8] DEPRINS D. - SIMAR L. - TULKENS H., «Measuring Labour Efficiency in Post Offices» in MARCHAND M. - PESTIEAU P. - TULKENS H. (eds.), *The Performance of Public Enterprises: Concepts and Measurement*, Amsterdam, North Holland, 1984, pp. 243-67.

[9] DESTEFANIS S. - PAVONE A., «L'analisi dell'efficienza nell'ambito dell'approccio FDH. Un'estensione e un'applicazione per gli ospedali di zona», *Quaderni di Ricerca*, n. 3, Roma, ISTAT, 1996.

[10] DRAKE L. - WEYMAN-JONES T.G., «Technical and Scale Efficiency in UK Building Societies», *Applied Financial Economics*, vol. 2, 1992, pp. 1-9.

[11] ELYASIANI E. - MEHDIAN S., «Productive Efficiency Performance of Minority and Nonminority-Owned Banks: A Nonparametric Approach», *Journal of Banking and Finance*, vol. 16, 1992, pp. 933-48.

[12] FARRELL M.J., «The Measurement of Productive Efficiency», *Journal of the Royal Statistical Society*, Series A, General, vol. 120, 1957, pp. 253-81.

[13] FERRIER G.D. - LOVELL C.A.K., «Measuring Cost-Efficiency in Banking», *Journal of Econometrics*, vol. 46, 1990, pp. 229-45.

[14] FRIED H.O. - LOVELL C.A.K. - SCHMIDT S. (eds), *The Measurement of Productive Efficiency: Techniques and Applications*, London, Oxford University Press, 1993.

[15] FRIED H.O. - LOVELL C.A.K. - VANDEN ECKAUT P., «Evaluating the Performance of US Credit Unions», *Journal of Banking and Finance*, vol. 17, 1993, pp. 251-65.

[16] KOOPMANS T.C., «An Analysis of Production as an Efficient Combination of Activities», in KOOPMANS T.C. (ed.), *Activity Analysis of Production and Allocation*, Chapter 3, New York, Wiley, 1951.

[17] — —, *Three Essays on the State of Economic Science*, New York, McGraw Hill, 1957.

[18] LOCATELLI R. - PROSPERETTI L. (eds.), *La produttività nelle aziende di credito - analisi su dati di bilancio*, Milano, Sole 24 Ore, 1987.

[19] LOVELL C.A.K., «Production Frontiers and Productive Efficiency», in FRIED H.O. - LOVELL C.A.K. - SCHMIDT S. (eds.), *The Measurement of Productive Efficiency: Techniques and Applications*, London Oxford University Press, 1993.

[20] ONADO M., *Economia dei sistemi finanziari*, Bologna, il Mulino, 1992.

[21] RESTI A., «Il dibattito su efficienza delle banche e economie di scala: il contributo della Data Envelopment Analysis ed un'applicazione a dati italiani», *Politica Economica*, vol. 10, 1994, pp. 269-311.

[22] THIRY B. - TULKENS H., «Allowing for Technical Inefficiency in Parametric Estimation of Production Functions for Urban Transit Firms», *Journal of Productivity Analysis*, vol. 3, 1992, pp. 45-65.

[23] TULKENS H., «La performance productive d'un service public. Définition, méthodes de mesure et application à la Régie des Postes en Belgique», *L'Actualité Economique, Revue d'Analyse Economique*, Montreal, vol. 62, 1986; pp. 306-35.

[24] — —, «Non-Parametric Efficiency Analyses in Four Service Activities: Retail Banking, Municipalities, Courts and Urban Transit», Louvain-la-Neuve, Université Catholique de Louvain, *Discussion Paper*, n. 9050, 1990.

[25] — —, «On FDH Efficiency Analyses: Some Methodological Issues and Applications to Retail Banking, Municipalities, Courts and Urban Transit», *Journal of Productivity Analysis*, vol. 4, 1993, pp. 179-210.

Challenges to Competitive Banking: a Theoretical Perspective

Arnoud W.A. Boot* - Anjolein Schmeits**

Abstract

The increasingly competitive environment poses challenges to bankers. This chapter emphasizes relationship banking as a prime source of the banks' comparative advantage. The proliferation of transaction-oriented banking (trading and financial market activities) does, however, seriously challenge relationship banking. We identify two key dimensions. First, competition from financial markets destabilizes (traditional) durable relationships. We argue that, contrary to what many believe, banks may optimally respond by increasing relationship-specific investments. Second, transaction-oriented activities increasingly become an integral part of banking institutions. In the context of the Barings debâcle we illustrate how transaction-oriented banking may undermine the banks' competitive edge in relationship banking.

---

* Professor of Finance, Faculty of Economics and Econometrics, Department of Financial Management, University of Amsterdam, Roetersstraat 11, 1018 WB Amsterdam, the Netherlands.

** Doctoral candidate, Faculty of Economics, Department of Finance and CentER, Tilburg University, PO Box 90153, 5000 LE Tilburg, The Netherlands.

Acknowledgements: We thank Franco Bruni, Piet Duffhues, Marius Jonkhart, David Lewellen, Bert Scholtens, Stewart Myers, Anjan Thakor and Raghu Rajan for their helpful comments.

1. - Introduction

In recent years, banks have been confronted with ever-increasing competition from non-banking financial institutions and the financial markets. Mutual funds, like Fidelity and Merrill Lynch, compete fiercefully for the banks' core deposit base. Commercial paper, medium term notes and other financial market innovations challenge the banks' traditional lending products. The last 25 years have shown a spectacular proliferation of new financial instruments. Examples of such financial innovations are plentiful: zero-coupon bonds, Collateralized Mortgage Obligations, Eurodollars, warrants, callable bonds, and all kinds of derivatives (from plain-vanilla interest-rate swaps to collars and caps). Many of these product innovations may have been infeasible were it not for contemporaneous advances in financial market microstructure and trading practices. The ongoing revolution in information technology has improved information dissemination and enhanced overall market liquidity. Consequently, the business of banking is changing rapidly. 'Traditional' relationship banking is under siege. The proliferation of financial innovations, advances in securitization and underwriting push funding to the financial markets. Does this tilt the comparative competitive advantage to the transaction-oriented financial markets?

The challenge for bankers is to draw the right conclusions. Fads need to be distinguished from long term trends. While banks - on average - have been quite profitable in the last few years, their real competitive strength has been questioned. In particular, many suggest that the banks' traditional comparative advantage in relationship banking has been diluted by transaction-oriented finance available in the financial markets. This begs the question: what is the future of relationship-based bank lending? And will banks continue (?) to lose market share to the financial markets? We will evaluate the future of relationship-oriented funding. Our basic message is that the fundamentals of banking have not changed. For many of the modern 'funding vehicles' bankers' traditional skills are indispensable. In many other cases, bank loans may continue to be the optimal instruments. The threat to banks may, therefore, come from bankers themselves. They may falsely interpret modern banking (and their own future!) as transaction- rather than relationship-oriented. As the *Economist* puts it in the context of the experience of securities firms:

> Perhaps the worst feature of the 1980s - which has subsequently returned to haunt the securities firms - was the abandonment by most of them of the old relationships with their customers. [. . .] 'The aim was to do a deal, any deal' remembers one manager who prefers not to be named (*ECONOMIST*, 15 April 1995, special section: 'A Survey of Wall Street', p. 13).

Our evaluation however would be incomplete without considering the internal organization of banks. More specifically, the relationship/transaction dimension also shows up *within* banks. Banks traditionally focused on relationship-based activities, but increasingly combine transaction- and relationship-based activities. Modern universal banks for example engage in bank lending (often relationship-based) but also in proprietary trading (purely transaction-oriented). These mixtures of activities become more and more common; conglomeration seems the current trend. Also here transaction-oriented activities pose a serious challenge. Some focus on a possible clash of cultures: dynamic (transaction-oriented) traders against traditional (relationship-oriented) bankers. We will emphasize potentially severe free-rider problems in conglomerate banks. Combining banking activities may reduce transparency and, therefore, reduce the effectiveness of market discipline. The absence of market discipline may result in free-rider problems between divisions, since each division does not fully internalize the consequences of its own actions. In the context of the Barings debâcle, we will argue that safer relationship-oriented activities may effectively underwrite risky transaction-oriented activities. As a consequence transaction-oriented activities may face an artificially low cost of funds and could free-ride on relationship-oriented activities. Relationship banking may have suffered.

The overall focus on the distinction between relationship and transaction orientation seems very instructive for evaluating current practices in banking. We will argue that banks' recent strategic choices may have undermined rather than strengthened their competitiveness. In particular, banks may have neglected relationship finance and relationship-oriented activities in general. Consequently, relationship banking may have suffered as a self-fulfilling prophecy.

The organization of the study is as follows. In Section 2 we analyze the economics of banking, and seek to identify the comparative economic advantages of banks in the funding of corporations. Our analysis identifies relationship-oriented banking as a characteristic of value enhancing financial intermediation. Section 3 discusses the future of relationship banking and particularly the desired responses of banks. The internal organization - the potential free-riding of transaction-oriented banking on relationship banking - discussed in Section 4, and we draw conclusions in Section 5.

2. - The Economics of Banking

2.1 *Traditional versus Modern Banking*

Traditional commercial banks hold nonmarketable or illiquid assets that are funded largely with deposits. There is typically little uncertainty about the value of these deposits which are often withdrawable on demand. The liquidity of bank liabilities stands in sharp contrast to that of their assets, reflecting the banks' *raison d'être*. By liquifying claims, banks facilitate the funding of projects that might otherwise be unfeasible.

The banks' assets are illiquid largely because of their information sensitivity. In originating and pricing loans, banks develop proprietary information. Subsequent monitoring of borrowers yields additional private information. The proprietary information inhibits the marketability of these loans. The access to information is the key to understanding the comparative advantage of banks. In many of their activities banks exploit their information and the related network of contacts. This relationship-oriented banking is a characteristic of value enhancing financial intermediation. The relationship and network orientation does not only apply to traditional commercial lending but also to many areas of modern banking.

One might be tempted to interpret modern banking as trading-oriented, or rather transaction-oriented. So does an investment bank - generally considered a prime example of modern banking - facilitate a firm's access to public capital markets. The investment bank's role could be interpreted as that of a broker; that is matching buyers and sellers for the firms' securities. In this interpretation investment banks just facilitate transactions, which would confirm the transaction orientation of modern banking. The investment banks' added value would then be confined to their networks, that is their ability to economize on search or matching costs. As a characterization of modern banking however, this would describe their economic role too narrowly. Investment banks do more. They - almost without exception - *underwrite* those public issues, that is absorb credit and/or placement risk. This brings an investment bank's role much closer to that of a commercial bank engaged in lending; the processing and absorption of risk is a typical intermediation function similar to that encountered in traditional bank lending.

In lending, a bank manages and absorbs risk (for example credit and liquidity risks) by issuing claims on its total assets with different characteristics from those encountered in its loan portfolio. In financial intermediation theory this is referred to as *qualitative asset transformation* (see Greenbaum and Thakor (1995)). Underwriting by an investment bank can be interpreted analogically; risk is (temporarily) absorbed and is channelled through to the claim holders of the investment bank. The role of investment banks is therefore more than just purely brokerage. Underwriting requires information acquisition about the borrower which is supported by a relationship orientation. Thus, characterizing financial market funding as transaction-oriented and bank lending as relationship-oriented is too extreme.

2.2 Are Bank Loans Special?

The previous comments in the Introduction may leave the impression that public capital market financing is a, potentially superior, substitute for bank lending. This, however, is unwarranted. Bank lending has distinctive comparative advantages. In particular, it may support enduring close relationships between debtor and financier that may mitigate information asymmetries. This has several components. A borrower might be prepared to reveal proprietary information to its bank, while it would have never disseminated this information to the financial markets (Bhattacharya and Chiesa (1995)). A bank might also be more receptive to information because of its role as enduring and dominant lender. This amounts to observing that a bank might have better incentives to invest in information acquisition. While costly, the substantial stake that it has in the funding of the borrower, and its, hopefully, enduring relationship - with the possibility of information reusability over time - increase the value of information.[1]

The bank-borrower relationship is also less rigid than those normally encountered in the financial market. The general observation is that a better information flow facilitates more informative decisions. This is in line with the important ongoing discussion in economic theory on rules versus discretion, where

---

[1] Diamond [1984] introduces intermediaries as delegated monitors. See Chan, Greenbaum and Thakor [1986] for a discussion on information reusability, and James [1987] and Lummer and McConnell [1989] for empirical evidence. And see also the recent 'stories' provided by Berlin [1996] supporting the special role of banks.

discretion allows for decision making based on more subtle - potentially non-contractible - information.[2] Two dimensions can be identified. One dimension is related to the nature of the bank-borrower relationship. In many ways, it is a mutual commitment based on trust and respect. This allows for *implicit* - unenforceable - long-term contracting. An optimal information flow is crucial for sustaining these 'contracts'. Information asymmetries in the financial market, and the non-contractibility of various pieces of information would rule out long-term alternative capital market funding sources as well as *explicit* long-term commitments by banks. Therefore, both bank and borrower realize the added value of their relationship, and will seek to foster their relationship.[3]

The other dimension is related to the structure of the explicit contracts that banks can write. Bank loans are generally easier to renegotiate than bond issues or other public capital market funding vehicles. The renegotiation allows for a qualitative use of flexibility. Sometimes this is a mixed blessing because banks may suffer from a soft-budget constraint (the borrowers may realize that they can renegotiate *ex post*, which could give them perverse *ex ante* incentives). In reality, bank loans, therefore, often have *priority*. With priority a bank may strengthen its bargaining position and thus become tougher.[4] The bank could then credibly intervene in the decision process of the borrower when it believes that its long-term interests are in danger. For example, the bank might believe that the firm's strategy is flawed, or a restructuring is long overdue. Could the bank push for the restructuring? If the bank has no priority, the borrower may choose to ignore the bank's wishes. This is because the bor-

---

[2] See for example Simon [1936] and Boot, Greenbaum and Thakor [1993].

[3] Mayer [1988] and Hellwig [1991] discuss the commitment nature of bank funding. Boot, Thakor and Udell [1991] address the *credibility* of commitments. Schmeits [1996] formally considers the impact of discretion (flexibility) in bank loan contracts on investment efficiency.

[4] See Dewatripont and Maskin [1995] on the issue of soft-budget constraints. Berglöf and Von Thadden [1993], Diamond [1993] and Gorton and Kalin [1993] address the priority structure.

rower realizes that the bank cannot enforce its demands. The bank could threaten to call the loan, but the borrower - anticipating the dreadful consequences not only for himself but also for the bank - realizes that the bank would never carry out such a threat. However, when the bank has priority, the prioritised claim may insulate the bank from these dreadful consequences. It could now *credibly* threaten to call the loan, and enforce its wishes upon the borrower. This then identifies an important advantage of bank financing: *timely intervention*.[5]

These observations highlight the complementarity of bank lending and capital market funding. Prioritised bank debt facilitates timely intervention. This feature of bank lending is valuable to the firm's bondholders as well. They might find it optimal to grant bank debt priority over their own claims, and in doing so, delegate the timely intervention activity to the bank.[6] Consequently, the borrower may reduce its total funding cost by accessing both the bank-credit market and the financial market.

The overall conclusion is that bank lending potentially facilitates more informative decisions based on a better exchange of information. While not universally valuable this suggests a benefit of relationship banking.[7]

2.3 Securitisation: A Threat to Bank Lending?

Securitisation is an example of a financial innovation - or an innovation in funding technology - that suggests a potential

---

[5] One could ask whether bond holders could be given priority and allocated the task of timely intervention. Note that bond holders are subject to more severe information asymmetries and are generally more dispersed (that is have smaller stakes). Both characteristics make them ill-suited for an 'early intervention task'.

[6] The bond holders will obviously ask to be compensated for their subordinated status.This is - ignoring the timely intervention effect - 'a wash'. In other words, the priority (seniority) or subordination features can be priced out. That is, as much as senior debt may *appear* cheaper (it is less risky), junior, or subordinated debt, will appear more expensive.

[7] See for example Petersen and Rajan [1994] and Houston and James [1995] for empirical evidence.

gain of (transaction-oriented) markets at the expense of bank lending. Is this true? Let's first evaluate the economics of securisation.[8]

Securitisation is a process whereby assets are removed from a bank's balance sheet. Asset-backed securities rather than deposits would then fund dedicated pools of bank-originated assets. Securitisation is an example of the unbundling of financial services. More specifically, banks would no longer fund those assets, instead the investors buying the asset-backed securities would provide funding. As we will emphasize, securitisation does not signal the demise of banks, even if it becomes an economically important innovation (and thus substantially reduces the banks' on-balance sheet assets). To see this point, one needs to analyze the traditional lending function in some detail.

The lending function can be decomposed into four more primal activities: origination, funding, servicing and risk processing. Origination subsumes screening prospective borrowers and designing and pricing financial contracts. Funding relates to the provision of financial resources. Servicing involves the collection and remission of payments as well as the monitoring of credits. Risk processing alludes to hedging, diversification and absorption of credit, interest rate, liquidity and exchange-rate risk. Securitisation decomposes the funding activity; banks would no longer fund securitised assets.

The economics of securitisation dictates that the originating bank *credit enhances* the issue. Credit enhancement is typically achieved through the provision of excess collateral or with a letter of credit. Effectively this means that the originating bank continues to bear the consequences (losses) if the securitised assets do not perform. The credit enhancement reduces the riskiness of the asset-backed claims from the investors' perspective, but more importantly it addresses conflicts of interest rooted in

---

[8] Gorton and Pennachi [1995] provide an economic rationale for bank loan sales and securitisation. See also Boot and Greenbaum [1995].

the originating bank's proprietary information. With private information in possession of the originating bank, the market requires assurance that the bank will not exaggerate the quality of the assets it seeks to sell. As with a warranty in product markets, credit enhancement discourages misrepresentation by requiring the originator to absorb a portion of the losses owing to default. Similarly, credit enhancement signals the market that the originator will perform a thorough credit evaluation and an undiminished monitoring effort. Credit enhancement, therefore, reduces the information sensitivity of securitised claims by enhancing their marketability.

Securitisation could lead to a *reconfiguration* of banking. But even with widespread securitisation the incremental value of banks would largely be preserved.[9] They would originate and service assets, while also processing the attendant risk in order to sustain these activities. Banks would, therefore, continue to screen and monitor borrowers, design and price financial claims, and provide risk management services.

How important will securitisation become? We can only give a very tentative answer. So far, securitisation barely exists in Europe. In the US securitisation has spread rapidly in the last decade but almost exclusively for car loans, mortgages and credit-card receivables. The standardisation and modest size of these credits allows diversification of idiosyncratic risks upon pooling. Private information distortions - as discussed above in the context of credit enhancement - are thought to be less severe for these standardised credits. What does this imply for the larger, more customised and heterogeneous commercial loans? These tend to be more information sensitive. Their quality is, therefore, more dependent on the rigour of initial screening and subsequent monitoring. Hence, the pooling of commercial loans

---

[9] See also Boyd and Gertler [1994]. They argue that banks have not lost importance. Their argument is that a substitution from on-balance sheet to off-balance sheet banking may have (falsely) suggested a shrinking role for banks. As in the description of securitisation in the text, much of the banks' value added in the primal activities would be preserved.

does less to dissipate their information sensitivity, attenuating the benefits of securitisation.

These considerations, however, do not preclude the securitisation of business credits. They merely elevate the cost. For example, with more information-sensitive assets, the originating bank may need to retain a larger portion of the credit risk; credit enhancement becomes more important. If the information sensitivity is too severe, credit enhancement, short of total recourse may not overcome the private-information problem. Thus, the potential advantages of securitisation largely would be lost, and traditional bank lending would continue to dominate. However, for an increasing array of moderately information-sensitive assets, securitisation might become the preferred intermediation technology. As our discussion of the economics of securisation suggests, banks even then continue to be indispensable for most of the primal activities that were previously combined together in bank lending. More importantly, the comparative advantage of banks rooted in proprietary information about their clientele would be preserved.

3. - Relationship Banking: the Strategic Challenge

Many believe that a competitive environment may threaten relationships. Borrowers might be tempted to switch to other banks, or to the financial market. When parties anticipate a shorter expected 'life span' of their relationships they may respond by reducing their relationship-specific investments. More specifically, anticipated shorter relationships inhibit the reusability of information, and thus diminish the value of information. Banks may then find it less worthwhile to acquire (costly) proprietary information, and relationships suffer. Paradoxically, shorter or weaker relationships actually become a self-fulfilling prophecy.

These arguments highlight the negative spiral that may undermine relationship banking. An important observation is that this negative spiral might be self-inflicted. While competitive banking challenges relationships, the bankers' response - cutting back on information acquisition - may actually damage relationship banking most.

Relationships facilitate a continuous flow of information between debtor and creditor which may guarantee a smooth access to funding. These relationships may give banks a comparative advantage. But also borrowers need to invest in relationships; relationship banking after all is a mutual commitment. Borrowers, however, face an equal challenge: how to benefit from competitive pricing without jeopardizing the benefits of relationships (see Rajan [1992])? This is the *relationship puzzle*.

The *relationship puzzle* has no obvious solution. Relationships may foster the exchange of information, but may simultaneously give lenders an information monopoly and undermine competitive pricing. Transaction-oriented finance, however, may give little incentive to acquire information but is potentially subjected to more competition. There might be no winners in this process; for example, transaction-oriented finance may not be feasible where relationship-oriented finance retreats. More specifically, markets for transaction-oriented finance may fail when problems of asymmetric information are insurmountable. This argument is used by some to highlight the virtues of (relationship-oriented) bank-dominated systems (for example, Germany and Japan) *vis-à-vis* market-oriented systems.[10]

As discussed in Section 2, bank lending, securitisation of loans and underwriting of public capital market issues may all benefit from a relationship orientation. The distinction between relationship-oriented finance and transaction-oriented finance, or between bank-dominated systems and market-oriented systems, may, therefore, be less well defined than it appears. What might be true is that a bank-dominated system invites oli-

---

[10] A fascinating academic literature is emerging on the design of financial systems. See Allen [1993], Allen and Gale [1995] and Boot and Thakor [1996a]. One objective of this literature is to evaluate the pros and cons of bank-dominated and financial market-dominated systems.

gopolistic behaviour such that competition is contained (and relationships preserved) while a market-dominated system surpresses competition less.

A less competitive financial system may thus *preserve* relationships more. Competition threatens relationships, but it may simultaneously elevate the importance of relationships as a distinct competitive edge. This is the *relationship paradox*. A relationship orientation can alleviate competitive pressures. Thus, a more competitive environment should encourage banks to become client-driven, and customise services. Since a relationship orientation may earn banks a substantial added-value, banks would then isolate themselves from pure price competition.[11]

4. - Internal Organisation and Relationship Banking

4.1 *A Need for Transparency*

Banks have increasingly become (somewhat) opaque institutions. Some degree of opaqueness is an unavoidable consequence of the business of banking, and reflects the banks' *raison d'être*. Relationship-oriented finance goes hand in hand with proprietary information. Opaqueness of bank loan portfolios is therefore unavoidable. More transparency at this level would be a mixed blessing. Banks would find it easier to fund themselves ('the market could then better assess the quality of a bank's loan portfolio'), but a widespread availability of (proprietary) infor-

---

[11] Boot and Thakor [1996b] develop this intuition further. They show that competition may indeed induce banks to divert resources to relationship-specific activities. In their model banks choose between 'passive' transaction lending and more intensive relationship lending. Transaction lending competes head-on with funding in the financial market. Competition from the financial market (as well as inter-bank competition) will lead to more resource-intensive relationship lending, and reduce transaction lending. The *absolute* level of relationship lending is, however, non-monotonically increasing in the level of competition; too much competition will ultimately shrink total bank capacity, and also constrain relationship lending.

mation - if at all possible - would diminish the banks' competitive edge. For our discussion here, it is important to note that the very nature of loan portfolios causes opaqueness, rather than *deliberate* policies of banks. Much of the banks' opaqueness, however, seems to be 'self-inflicted', and thus deliberate.

Banks like to *combine* many different activities. This distinguishes banks from many of their competitors, for example, non-banking financial institutions like mutual funds and finance companies (see Merton [1993]). The latter often choose to specialise and, therefore, are much more transparent. Banks generally choose to diversify their activities. Although few would readily deny that some degree of diversification is necessary, banks seem to engage in a very broad variety of activities. The question that arises is what is the optimal conglomeration of bank activities?

This question is of particular importance because self-inflicted opaqueness may come to haunt banks in a more competitive environment. Outsiders - including the banks' financiers - may not be able to assess the performance of banks sufficiently. More importantly, opaqueness gives outsiders very little control over the bank. Bank managers, therefore, may have excessive discretion. This may elevate a bank's cost of funds. As a result, bank lending would be disadvantaged and securitisation and/or financial market funding would benefit. Securitisation - for example - could be interpreted as a mechanism that seeks to enhance accountability and transparency by giving the market a direct claim to a specific group of assets.[12]

Banks have so far done little to mitigate opaqueness. The European experience is that opaqueness has grown, witness the consolidation and despecialisation of banking in many countries. Even until quite recently, the opaqueness meant that bankers themselves did not really know the profitability of many of their activities. Cross-subsidies were the rule, and internal

---

[12] Dewatripont and Tirole [1995] discuss the benefits of securitsation in the context of these transparency arguments.

cost accounting was rudimentary. However, some improvements have been made. Banks now have a better understanding of the costs and benefits of different lines of their businesses. Some of the implicit or explicit cross-subsidies are now recognized. While cross-subsidies may sometimes be an optimal competitive response, often they will not be sustainable in a competitive environment.

Banks face a challenge in that they may need to become more transparent. This is in apparent conflict with the current trends in banking. Banks increasingly combine transaction- and relationship-based activities. Trading activities within banks have grown enormously and seem sometimes to be in conflict with the 'traditional' relationship-oriented activities. These developments have broadened the activities of banks and may have reduced transparency. An interesting example is proprietary trading, an activity that has gained importance, and - on paper - seems to have contributed significantly to the profitability of banks in recent years.

4.2 Proprietary Trading and Free-Riding

A noteworthy example of a banking institution where proprietary trading gained importance rapidly was the Barings Bank, a British bank with a long tradition in corporate banking. Some interpret the Barings debâcle as a meltdown caused by a clash of cultures: agressive and ambitious traders versus traditional and conservative bankers. For them, better internal controls and external supervision aimed at aligning incentives seem obvious remedies. We believe that the economics of banking dictate a much more fundamental analysis, one that transcends the specifics of Barings and calls into question the banks' strategic choices in general.

Our analysis will highlight that in the absence of market discipline banks may only arbitrarily allocate capital to their different activities and charge a cost per unit of capital that is even

more arbitrary. This line of argument implies that the proprietary trading activity is free-riding on the bank at large. This - as
we will show - may have three consequences: (i) proprietary
trading appears more profitable than it really is, (ii) a proprietary trading unit does not sufficiently internalise risks, and (iii)
other - mainly relationship-oriented - activities of banks face an
unfairly high cost of funds. The implications are twofold. First,
proprietary traders may operate with little market discipline.
Consequently, the only corrective mechanisms are internal controls and external supervision. Second, banks may become less
competitive in their relationship-oriented activities. Thus, proprietary trading would undermine the banks' real competitive
edge. We now turn to a more detailed analysis of the trading
activity.

It is important to realize that much of modern (investment)
banking is relationship-oriented. Proprietary trading is one of
the few activities that is not. The trading involves arbitrage
between different markets and/or different financial products.
Arbitrage does strictly speaking not involve risk. However, on an
intra-day basis, traders do not cover (all) their positions, and
thus accept considerable risk. This is a type of speculation.
Banks also speculate on an inter-day basis; this is 'real' speculation. They may use their 'vision' and try to benefit from anticipated developments in interest rates, exchange rates, and so on.

Banks' trading activities have been a considerable source of
earnings in the last few years. But has it been as profitable as
some believe? The trading activity involves substantial risks,
thus establishing the fair risk-adjusted cost of funds is important. This cost is, given the specific nature of the trading activities, substantially different from the cost of funds of the bank as
a whole. Banks try to resolve this by allocating (costly) capital to
the trading unit. Thus, the trading unit's funding cost is artificially grossed-up by adding the cost of its 'capital at risk'. This
internal capital allocation process is not only arbitrary but may
also be flawed.

The presumption in these internal capital allocations is generally that capital has one price. A bank's cost of capital might be set for example at 15 per cent. Some believe that capital is twice as expensive as (risk-free) financial market debt financing. Whatever the presumption, capital does *not* have one price. Standard capital structure theory tells us that the per unit cost of capital depends on the risks that this capital is exposed to. More risk generally implies a higher cost of capital. The per unit cost of capital will, therefore, also go up when leverage goes up. These arguments are obviously a direct consequence of the crucial link between risk *and* return. Two important implications now follow. First, the per unit cost of capital *will not* be the same for all of the bank's activities. The level of risk *and* the risk characteristics will determine the unit cost of capital for each of the activities. Applying a bank's cost of capital to its proprietary trading unit is, therefore, wrong. Given the generally well diversified, and thus low risks, found in the bank at large, the (non-diversifiable) risks taken in the trading unit dictate a much higher cost of capital.

The second implication is more general: banks should not choose to engage in certain activities solely because they have the capital. The critical observation is that 'putting capital to use' elevates the per unit cost of capital. Therefore, engaging in proprietary trading to exploit the bank's capital and reputation will elevate the cost of this capital, and as a consequence increase the cost of funds for the bank at large. Banks that consider themselves 'overcapitalized' and decide to put this capital to use may thus not create value at all. This argument may also explain why banks consider capital (prohibitively?) expensive. If potential investors anticipate that banks will put their capital to use at all cost, they will gross-up their required return accordingly. Banks then can issue equity only at discount prices.[13] These beliefs and

---

[13] One could counter that much of the banking literature has focused on equity holders' incentives to engage in excessively risky activities. Note that these moral hazard incentives depend on the possibility of shifting risk to debt holders (or the deposit insurer) without compensating them. The debt holders then effectively subsidse risky activities. While these incentives might be relevant for poorly capitalised institutions (for

anticipations create a perverse equilibrium. Given the bankers state of mind - fixed priced, expensive capital that needs to be put to use as quickly as possible - the market responds rationally by charging a high price for capital. And given these anticipations by the market, the bankers' beliefs are justified and confirmed in equilibrium. Banks however bear the burden and may benefit, therefore, from prudently using their capitalization.[14]

The arguments above explain why proprietary trading has been granted an artificially low cost of capital, at the expense of a (potentially) prohibitively high cost of capital for the bank as a whole. This is the free-riding we alluded to earlier. With these (artificial) cross-subsidies proprietary trading appears more profitable than it really is. And, more importantly, other - mainly relationship-oriented activities - are implicitly taxed. Banks then may mistakenly conclude that relationship banking activities are not profitable. Since these may account for much of the banks' true value-added, bankers themselves need to reassess the desirability of proprietary trading as an *integral part* of their businesses.[15]

5 - Conclusion

This chapter highlights *the* major challenges facing 'modern' banks: how to identify and protect their true comparative advantages. We believe that relationship banking offers distinct benefits, and see it as the banks' *raison d'être*. However, relationship banking has suffered from the proliferation of transaction-oriented banking along two dimensions.

---

example the US Savings and Loans in the 1980s), they are much less compelling for adequately capitalised institutions.

[14] Another compelling argument is that banks' credit ratings have become increasingly important due to the proliferation of off-balance sheet banking. The viability of banks in their off-balance sheet activities (for example writing guarantees as in underwriting and securitisation) necessitates sufficient capitalisation and high credit ratings (see Boot and Greenbaum [1995]).

[15] See Boot and Schmeits [1996] for an in depth analysis of the costs and benefits of conglomeration.

One is the external dimension. Financial markets have gained market share. Banks find it more difficult to hold on to their clientele. Borrowers might be tempted to switch to other financiers, and traditional relationships suffer. We have argued that the optimal response might be to invest more in relationships. Banks then may isolate themselves from pure price competition.

The second dimension is an internal one. Transaction-oriented banking has also become more important *within* banks. Banks tend to broaden their activities; transaction banking (like proprietary trading) coexists with relationship banking. In the context of the Barings debâcle, we have argued that relationship lending activities may implicitly subsidise transaction-oriented activities. Consequently, also along this dimension relationship banking may suffer.

Future research should be directed at further developing the basic themes of this chapter. While we may have provided some important insights in the functioning of banking institutions and their optimal competitive responses, the financial sector largely remains a black box.

BIBLIOGRAPHY

ALLEN, F. 'Stock Markets and Resource Allocation', in *Capital Markets and Financial Intermediation*, C. Mayer and X. Vives (eds), Cambridge University Press, 1993.

ALLEN, F. and GALE, D. 'A Welfare Comparison of the German and U.S. Financial Systems', European Economic Review 39, 1995, 179-209.

BERGLÖF, E. and VON THADDEN E.L. ,'Short-Term versus Long-Term Interests: Capital Structure with Multiple Investors', *Quarterly Journal of Economics* 109, 1994, 1055-84.

BERLIN, M. 'For Better and for Worse: Three Lending Relationships', *Business Review Federal Reserve Bank of Philadelphia*, December, 1995, 3-12.

BHATTACHARAYA, S. and CHIESA, G. 'Proprietary Information, Financial Intermediation, and Research Incentives, *Journal of Financial Intermediation* 4, 1995, pp. 328-57.

BOOT, A.W.A., THAKOR, A.V. and UDELL, G. 'Credible Commitments, Contract Enforcement Problems and Banks: Intermediation as Credibility Assurance', *Jornal of Banking and Finance* 15, 1991, 605-32.

BOOT, A.W.A., GREENBAUM, S.I. and THAKOR, A.V. 'Reputation and Discretion in Financial Contracting', *American Economic Review* 83, 1993, 1165-83.

BOOT, A.W.A. and GREENBAUM, S.I. 'The Future of Banking: What Should Corporate America Expect?, *Business Week Executive Briefing*, 1995, Vol. 8.

BOOT, A.W.A. and SCHMEITS, A. 'Market Discipline in Conglomerate Banks: Is an Internal Allocation of Cost of Capital Necessary as Incentive Device?', working paper, December, 1996.

BOOT, A.W.A. and THAKOR, A.V. 'Financial System Architecture', *Review of Financial Studies*, 1996a.

BOOT, A.W. A. and THAKOR, A.V. 'Can Relationship Banking Survive Competition?', working paper, June, 1996b.

BOYD, J.H. and GERTLER, M. 'Are Banks Dead, or Are the Reports Greatly Exaggerated?', Federal Reserve Bank of Minneapolis, working paper, 1994.

CHAN, Y., GREENBAUM, S.I. and THAKOR, A.V. 'Information Reusability, Competition and Bank Asset Quality', *Journal of Banking and Finance* 10, 1986, 255-76.

DEWATRIPONT, M. and MASKIN, E. 'Credit and Efficiency in Centralized and Decentralized Economies', *Review of Economic Studies* 62, 1995, 541-55.

DEWATRIPONT, M. and TIROLE, J. *The Prudential Regulation of Banks*, MIT Press, Cambridge, Massachussetts.

DIAMOND, D. 'Financial Intermediation and Delegated Monitoring', *Review of Economic Studies* 51, 1984, 393-414.

DIAMOND, D. 'Seniority and Maturity of Debt Contracts', *Journal of Financial Economics* 33, 1993, 341-68.

GORTON, G. and KAHN, J. 'The Design of Bank Loan Contracts, Collateral, and Renegotiation', NBER working paper 4273, 1993.

GORTON, G. and PENNACCHI, G. 'Banks and Loan Sales: Marketing Non-marketable Assets', *Journal of Monetary Economics* 35, 1995, 389-411.

GREENBAUM, S.I. and THAKOR, A.V. *Contemporary Financial Intermediation*, Dryden Press, 1995.

HELLWIG, M. 'Banking, Financial Intermediation and Corporate Finance', in *European Financial Integration*, GIOVANNI, A. and MAYER, C. (eds), Cambridge University Press, 1991.

HOUSTON, J. and JAMES, C. 'Bank Information Monopolies and the Mix of Private and Public Debt Claims', working paper, March, 1995.

JAMES, C. 'Some Evidence on the Uniqueness of Bank Loans', *Journal of Financial Economics* 19, 1987, 217-35.

LUMMER, S. and McConnell, J. 'Further Evidence of the Bank Lending Process and the Reaction of the Capital Market to Bank Loan Agreements', *Journal of Financial Economics* 25, 1989, 99-122.

MAYER, C. 'New Issues in Corporate Finance', *European Economic Review* 32, 1988, 1167-83.

MERTON, R.C. 'Operation and Regulation in Financial Intermediation: A Functional Perspective', in *Operation and Regulation of Financial Markets*, P. Englund, (ed.), Economic Council, 1993.

PETERSEN, M. and RAJAN, R. 'The Benefits of Lending Relationships: Evidence from Small Business Data', *Journal of Finance* 47, 1994, 1367-400.

RAJAN, R. 'Insiders and Outsiders: The Choice Between Informed and Arm's Length Debt', *Journal of Finance* 47, 1992, 1367-400.

SCHMEITS, A. 'Flexibility and Discretion in Contract Design', working paper, August, 1996.

SIMON, H.C. 'Rules versus Authorities in Monetary Policy', *Journal of Political Economy* 44, 1936, 1-30.

Notes on the Contributors

Michele Bagella is Full Professor of Monetary Economics and Director of the Department of Economics at the University of Rome Tor Vergata.

Mario Baldassarri is Full Professor of Economic Policy at the University of Rome La Sapienza.

Emilio Barone is Bank Executive at Sanpaolo IMI, Rome and Professor of Economics, Security Market, Luiss Guido Carli University, Rome.

Leonardo Becchetti is Associate Professor of Economics at the University of Rome Tor Vergata.

Arnoud W.A. Boot is Professor of Finance, Faculty of Economics and Econometrics at the University of Amsterdam.

Antonio Braghò is responsible for on-line channels at Sanpaolo IMI, Rome.

Andrea Caggese is a Ph.D. student at the London School of Economics.

Giorgio Calcagnini is Associate Professor of Economics at the University of Urbino.

Gabriella Chiesa is Full Professor of Economics at the University of Bologna.

Luca G. Deidda is at the School of Oriental and African Studies, University of London.

Sergio Destefanis is Associate Professor of Economic Policy at the University of Salerno.

Francesco Drudi is an economist at the World Bank.

Andrea Generale is an economist at the Bank of Italy, Rome.

Adriano Giannola is Full Professor of Money and Banking at the University of Napoli Federico II and President of the Banco di Napoli Foundation.

Pier Luigi Gilibert is Director of the Credit Risk Department at the European Investment Bank, Luxembourg.

Giovanni Majnoni is an economist at the World Bank.

Luigi Paganetto is Full Professor of International Economics and Dean of the Faculty of Economics, University of Rome Tor Vergata.

David Paton is Senior Lecturer of Industrial Economics at Nottingham Trent University.

Claudio Ricci works for Sanpaolo IMI Sigeco Sim, Rome.

Enrico Saltari is Full Professor of Economics at the University of Urbino.

Gennaro Scarfiglierii is employed at the Central Direction-Strategy, Planning and Control, Poste Italiane, SpA, Rome.

Anjolein Schmeits is a doctoral candidate, Faculty of Economics at Tilburg University, the Netherlands.

Massimo Tivegna is Full Professor of Economic Policy at the University of Teramo.

Leighton Vaughan Williams is Director of the Betting Research Unit and lecturer at Nottingham Trent University.

Clas Wihlborg is Professor of Finance at the Copenhagen Business School.

Index